Mason's Forensic Medicine fo

Mason's Forensic Medicine for Lawyers

Sixth Edition

Helen Whitwell
Emeritus Forensic Pathologist on the Home Office Register

Katy Thorne
Barrister, Doughty Street Chambers

Alexander Kolar
Forensic Pathologist on the Home Office Register

Paul Harvey
Barrister, Doughty Street Chambers, and Lawyer, Registry of the European Court of Human Rights

Bloomsbury Professional

Bloomsbury Professional Limited, Maxwelton House, 41–43 Boltro Road, Haywards Heath, West Sussex, RH16 1BJ

© Bloomsbury Professional 2015

Bloomsbury Professional is an imprint of Bloomsbury Publishing Plc

A CIP Catalogue record for this book is available from the British Library.

ISBN 978 1 78043 476 6

Typeset by Phoenix Photosetting, Chatham, Kent
Printed and bound in Great Britain by CPI Group (UK) Ltd, Croydon, CR0 4YY

Contributors

Chapter 2
With Dr Simon Stockill (Medical Director and Director of Primary Care at NHS Leeds West Clinical Commissioning Group)
and Heather Kolar (Clinical Negligence Solicitor, Switalskis Solicitors)

Chapter 5
With Sara Williams (Barrister, Doughty Street Chambers)

Chapter 15
With Dr Bernadette Butler (Sexual Offences Examiner, The Havens, Kings College Hospital NHS Foundation Trust)
and Dr Anna Riddell (Clinical Director for Children's Health at Barts Health NHS Trust)

Chapter 16
With Dr Catherine Adams (Consultant in Forensic Odontology, UKDVI & Powys Teaching Health Board)

Chapter 17
With Simon Elliott (Consultant Forensic Toxicologist, Managing Director at ROAR Forensics)

Chapter 18
With Professor Ian Wall (Forensic Physician, Academic Dean, Faculty of Forensic and Legal Medicine)

Chapter 19
With Kate O'Raghallaigh (Barrister, Doughty Street Chambers)

Foreword

This book is essential reading and an invaluable tool for all practitioners and expert witnesses engaged in the field of forensic medicine. It provides the clearest exposition of so many areas of forensic pathology that hitherto have been so very often buried beneath pages and pages of indecipherable jargon. For the busy practitioner the information is readily accessible, the glossary of terms and simple diagrams instantly informative, which makes it an ideal courtroom companion. For me it is a 'must have' book.

David Hislop QC

Preface to the Sixth Edition

Mason's Forensic Medicine for Lawyers has a distinguished and important history, and this new edition aims to reach those high standards. Professor Ken Mason produced the very first edition in 1978. Sharon Cowan and Dr Bill Hunt, with his own inimitable style, continued the work for the fifth edition. This edition builds on previous editions, to allow for the needs of both undergraduate and lawyer, and will be of particular importance to those in practice in medico-legal work. It will also be of use to medical practitioners who are witnesses in court proceedings, whether as experts or as to fact.

We have completely revised the book to cover advances in the medico-legal world and to refocus the work to be of interest to a wider audience too. We have been greatly assisted by outstanding experts in clinical forensic medicine, odontology and toxicology as well as law.

We have been hugely aided by electronic transmissions – at various times, the team has been scattered far and wide across the globe, from New Zealand to Strasbourg, Wales to Scotland and the River Avon to London!

We are grateful for the help given by Bloomsbury Professional, including Kiran Goss and Peter Smith, and by Sharon Lilly, my expert PA. We are also particularly grateful to Bernard Knight for permission to reproduce images from his book, *Lawyers' Guide to Forensic Medicine*. Last but not least, thanks to all our family and friends.

Helen L. Whitwell
September 2015

Preface to the First Edition

In my inaugural address to the University,[1] I defined forensic medicine as medicine applied to the protection and assistance of individuals in relation to the community. This concept was based on the forum as being a public place in which those responsible to the public in many spheres argued and defended their views rather than being limited to the criminal court.

It seemed to me that forensic medicine should be taught to medical students in this wide spirit whereas, paradoxically, it was the law students who, in having to decipher and understand the reports of their expert medical witnesses, needed the greater exposure to the details of pathology despite the fact that they had no medical background. I could find no textbook extant which would satisfy their particular needs; what follows is an attempt to fill the gap. One of the main difficulties has been to find the right pitch of knowledge and the book has, in the process of writing, settled into an outline of the LLB course in forensic medicine presently given at Edinburgh University. It is, however, hoped that it will still be found useful by practising advocates, solicitors, procurators fiscal and coroners.

I recently read a review which stated that the day of the single-author textbook has gone, and it is certain that multiple authorship ensures that each facet of the work is covered by an expert practising in that sphere: the single author attempting a wide range must lose a sense of immediacy.

In an effort to compensate for this, I have shown drafts of the majority of chapters to persons particularly well qualified to criticise and advise. Helpful criticism does not, however, necessarily mean approval and, lest naming one's reviewers might be taken as implying their shared responsibility for, and satisfaction with, the end result, I intend to express my thanks anonymously to the many members of the forensic fraternity, the academic staff of the Faculties of Medicine and of Law in Edinburgh University, the NHS officials, the government and local authority officers and others who have responded so kindly to my calls for help; my gratitude loses no sincerity in its generality.

Three special personal acknowledgements are, however, called for. Professor Keith Simpson and Mr Alistair R Brownlie have been good enough to read the whole manuscript from the point of view of the forensic pathologist and of the lawyer respectively. They have given invaluable advice although, again, it should be stressed that their participation does not necessarily imply agreement with the views expressed. Mr Charles N Stoddart has reviewed the text with particular reference to the legal technicalities. In doing so, he has not only improved the book's acceptability to lawyers but has also offered many helpful criticisms; he has my sincere thanks for undertaking a most time-consuming task.

---

1 *Ambitions for a Motley Coat* (1974), Inaugural Address no. 56, University of Edinburgh.

I owe my secretarial assistant, Mrs Gladys Hamilton, a debt of gratitude for unstinting cooperation and much encouragement. A number of temporary assistants have had a hand in the typing but the great bulk of this has been undertaken by Miss Iris Falconer with great skill and good heart.

Finally, I have to thank my wife for letting it happen. At a time in our lives which was, for several reasons, difficult, she spent many lonely hours of televiewing without complaint; I hope this book is worthy of her memory.

Edinburgh
1978   JKM

Contents

Table of Statutes

Table of Statutory Instruments

Table of Cases

Chapter 1

Introduction to human anatomy and physiology

Medicine: an introduction to terms

1.1   This textbook intends to give the legal practitioner a better understanding of the expert evidence provided by healthcare workers in both the civil and criminal courts and in consultation. The medical report that is useful to all interested parties cannot be written without technical terms and concepts, and lawyers may well need an explanation of the phraseology that the medical witness uses. The initial part of the introduction may appear unduly elementary to some, but could be useful, if only as a source of aides-memoire, to others.

Systems of the body

1.2   The systems of the body relate to parts of the body whose functions are integrated, irrespective of their relative position in the body. These 'systems' are referred to frequently in medical reports and most are dealt with in greater detail in this chapter. In summary, the medical witness may refer to:

- The *nervous* system, comprising the brain and spinal cord (central nervous system) and the peripheral nerves.

- The *musculoskeletal* system, comprising the bones, tendons and muscles.

- The *cardiovascular* system, comprising of the heart and blood vessels.

- The *respiratory* system, running from the nose to the lungs and including the diaphragm and chest muscles.[1]

- The *gastro-intestinal* system, comprising not only the gut from mouth to anus but also those organs whose function is to control the processing of food, i.e. the salivary glands, the liver and the pancreas.

- The *genito-urinary* system, comprising, although quite distinct functionally, the genital and urinary systems, and they are commonly combined because of their close anatomical association. The genital system includes the ovaries, uterus, vagina and vulva in the female, and the testes, ducts and penis in the male. The main components of the urinary system are the kidneys, the ureters, the bladder and the urethra, and the prostate gland in the male.

---

1   The close working association of the heart and lungs leads to the frequent use of the term 'cardio-respiratory system'.

- The *lympho-reticular* system, which is responsible for functions primarily related to defence against infection. The main solid organs are the spleen, the thymus gland and the numerous lymph nodes, including specialised nodes such as the tonsils.

- The *endocrine* system, comprising those glands that control body function by secretion of hormones into the bloodstream. The most important, from the forensic aspect, are the pituitary, the adrenal and the thyroid glands.

All of these systems are interlinked. For example, all require a functioning cardiovascular system and the blood within, while the musculoskeletal system, in particular, is reliant on the proper functioning of the nervous system. Medical specialities are based on these systems.

Anatomical matters

Planes

1.3   The medical expert will describe the relative position of an injury or lesion in relation to the human body in the 'anatomical position' – that is, the body standing erect, with the palms of the hands facing forward (see Figure 1.1). The front part of the body is the *anterior* aspect, and the rear part of the body is the *posterior* aspect. The inner part of the body is the *medial* aspect, and the outer part of the body is the *lateral* aspect.

The body can be divided into various planes separating (broadly) the body into two equal divisions. The *sagittal* plane is a vertical division along the midline of the body separating the left and right halves. The *coronal* plane is a vertical division

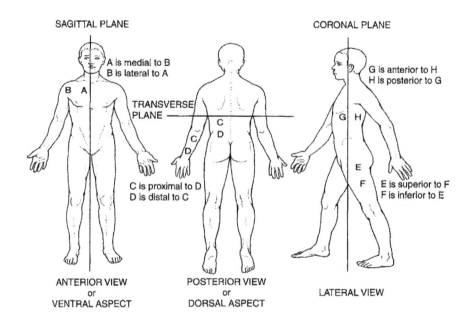

Figure 1.1 The planes of the body and some of the terms used for anatomical reference.

2

separating the anterior and posterior aspects of the body through the side of the body. The *transverse* plane is a horizontal division separating the top and the bottom of body, broadly, through the mid part of the chest.

Relationships

1.4   Marks can be described relative to these planes, landmarks of the body or other marks. The descriptors are typically anterior, posterior, medial, lateral, superior, inferior, proximal and distal.

Utilising Figure 1.1, if point A is on the same side of the body as point B and is nearer the midline, then A is *medial* to B and B is *lateral* to A.

Anatomically, proximal and distal are used, in particular, in relation to limbs due to their greater flexibility of position. A proximal mark will be closer to the commencement of the limb (the superior end in the anatomical position) than a distal mark. For example, on Figure 1.1, point C is *proximal* to D and D is *distal* to C.

Proximal and distal are also used 'functionally' as well as 'anatomically'. For example, anatomically the small intestine lies distal to the transverse colon, but it is functionally proximal to it.

The forearm has two additional reference marks related to the bones of the forearm. The ulnar border is on the medial aspect of the forearm in the anatomical position, whereas the radial border is on the lateral aspect of the forearm in the anatomical position. This is demonstrated on Figure 1.1.

Anatomical confusion

1.5   Two areas of anatomy cause some confusion between the medical and lay use: limbs and digits.

The first area relates to the common lay designation of the arm as the upper limb and the leg as the lower limb. Anatomical speaking, the upper limb is separated into the arm (between shoulder and elbow) and forearm (between elbow and wrist) and the lower limb is separated into thigh (between hip and knee) and leg (between knee and ankle). As can be appreciated, the term 'upper arm' could mean the lay term for the anatomical arm, or the medical term for the upper part of the anatomical arm.

The second area relates to the naming or numbering of digits of the hand and feet. The digits of the hand are named and not numbered. These are thumb, index, middle, ring and little fingers respectively. The digits of the feet are numbered from 1st to 5th from medial to lateral aspects. The 1st digit is commonly known as the great toe but the consequential renumbering of the digits (i.e. the correct 2nd toe as the 1st toe) that occasionally occurs is erroneous.

Anatomical divisions and susceptibility

1.6   At its simplest, the body is divided into the head, the limbs and the torso. The interior of the head is the cranial cavity, while the torso consists of the thoracic, abdominal and pelvic cavities. The structural protection of these cavities differs markedly.

Cranial cavity

1.7   The rigid skull surrounds the cranial cavity, which contains the brain. This affords a high degree of protection, as it can 'absorb', to some extent, force. However, once it is fully developed, and component skull bones are fused, the skull also inhibits expansion of the cranial contents, in particular the brain, which results in an inherent weakness.

Thoracic cavity

1.8   The thoracic cavity (or thorax) houses principally the heart and the lungs. Unlike the skull, a functional principle of the thorax is elasticity and freedom of movement. The chest wall consists of a mobile combination of ribs and muscles, which is variably protective.

Abdominal (or peritoneal) cavity

1.9   The abdominal cavity lacks a bony structure, except the lumbar spine posteriorly. Its contents are, therefore, susceptible to injury both by penetrating and by blunt forces.

The major contents lie within an internal covering envelope known as the peritoneum, which forms a cavity. These major contents include the stomach, a significant proportion of the intestines, the liver and the spleen. These structures are relatively loosely connected to each other and to the peritoneal lining by ligaments, and have considerable mobility as a result.

Those structures lying behind the peritoneum, including the kidneys, are described as retroperitoneal (in effect, behind the peritoneum). These are supported principally by adipose tissue (fat) and, as a result, are more rigidly fixed and, in general, better protected.

Pelvic cavity

1.10   The pelvic cavity adjoins, and is in direct continuation with, the lower part of the abdominal cavity. It is bounded by the two pelvic bones (hips), and contains the urinary bladder and, in the female, the uterus and ovaries and, in the male, the prostate.

Anatomical factors affecting propensity to injury

1.11   The ability of the various organs to move has great importance in relation to injury. A mobile object can, to some extent, slide away from direct violence, whilst a fixed organ is more susceptible to crushing, resulting in tearing of the organ and blood vessels leading to laceration and bruising. This is covered in Chapter 7.

No organ is totally mobile, and each organ is attached to a relatively rigid structure. These more mobile organs are particularly susceptible to shearing forces or indirect injury. An example of this is addressed in Chapter 10, relating to tearing of the aorta (the major blood vessel), due to the mobile heart and mobile initial part of the aorta being pulled away from the descending aorta, which is firmly attached to the spinal column.

Unsurprisingly, the size of an organ will influence the likelihood of its being directly affected. The liver is very large as compared to the kidney.

Another important factor is the difference in density between adjacent structures. This is most extreme where air, fluid and solid structures are adjacent, and these structures are vulnerable to damage from internal vibration and other stresses. This is particularly important in blast injury and is covered in Chapter 13.

The elasticity of the organ is another major determinant in this type of trauma, while the physical condition of an individual organ at the time of stress may affect its response (e.g. a diseased spleen is more likely to rupture than a normal organ).

Cellular structures

1.12   The solid portions of the body are composed of myriad cells held together by ground substance. The cells are organised so as to form either epithelium or connective tissue.

Epithelium

1.13   The epithelium comprises of cells that either line (or cloak) the organ's surface (including the internal aspects of an organ) and also some that form the structure of solid organs. The cell may have a 'specialised' function – for example, to secrete a substance, such as within the gastro-intestinal system, or to waft particles away, such as dust, within the respiratory system, whose cells are frequently ciliated (hairy projections). Malignant overgrowth of an epithelial cell is known as carcinoma.

The skin is a complex epithelium with many functions as a result. Its primary function is to retain the body fluids. Destruction of the skin by burning leads to a massive loss of fluid, resulting in dehydration and surgical shock. This concept of shock is discussed later in relation to the cardiovascular system.

Connective tissue

1.14   The connective tissue comprises of cells that connect not only the various epithelia but also parts of the body to each other. It includes fat, muscle, fibrous tissue (including tendons) and bones. A network of blood vessels permeates the connective tissues. Malignant overgrowth of the connective tissue is known as sarcoma.

The connective tissues are particularly important in the healing of wounds. When the continuity of part of the body, such as the skin, is interrupted, bleeding takes place. This is partly stemmed by contraction of the cut ends of the vessels, the pressure exerted by the lost blood within the tissues, and the natural (haemostatic) clotting systems. Wandering tissue-repair cells enter the area, and new blood vessels penetrate it over time. This provokes the appearance of young fibrous connective tissue cells. The vessels then age, and the tissues become tough and bloodless (scarring). The recognition of these stages is the basis of 'ageing' of wounds.

Blood

1.15   Blood is a specialised form of connective tissue consisting of cells and fluid. The fluid is known as the plasma, and it carries soluble foodstuffs, electrolytes, waste products and messenger substances (hormones). Hormones provide the body's system of communication between organs. The blood cells are described as being either red (erythrocytes) or white (leucocytes). The red cells' function is the carriage of oxygen. The white cells are, in general, concerned with the defence of the body against infection. 'Sarcomatous' overgrowth of the white cells results in leukaemia, which is classified according to the precise type of cell involved. Platelets, concerned with blood coagulation, also circulate in the plasma.

Nuclei and DNA

1.16   All cells, except platelets and red blood cells, have a nucleus and cytoplasm (a water-rich substance surrounding the nucleus). The platelets and red blood cells have no nucleus. The nucleus controls cell reproduction and contain 23 pairs of chromosomes which, in turn, consist of 'genes'. One of each of the pairs of genes is provided by each parent (i.e. mother and father). Normal cell division and tissue growth result from mitosis, in which each chromosome reproduces itself. The two 'new' cells therefore contain the same chromosomes as their progenitor.

The exception lies in the sex cells or gametes (spermatozoa in the male, or ova in the female), which divide by a process of meiosis and contain only 23 single chromosomes. The fusion of two gametes thus results in a zygote (the earliest stage of an embryo) with the normal nuclear configuration.

The genes contain the deoxyribonucleic acid (DNA) which determines the unique constitution of each individual (or of each pair of identical twins). One pair of chromosomes dictates the sex of the subject. These sex chromosomes are designated X and Y. The presence of a Y chromosome in the pair indicates maleness.

Cardiovascular system

1.17   The fundamental requirement of tissues is the supply of oxygen and other nutrients. The respiratory system collects the oxygen (and disposes of waster gases and products), and the cardiovascular system distributes it around the body.

Red blood cells

1.18   The red blood cells carry the oxygen by binding the oxygen molecule to haemoglobin (a combination of iron and protein), which it subsequently relinquishes in the target organs. The maximum exchange between the haemoglobin and the

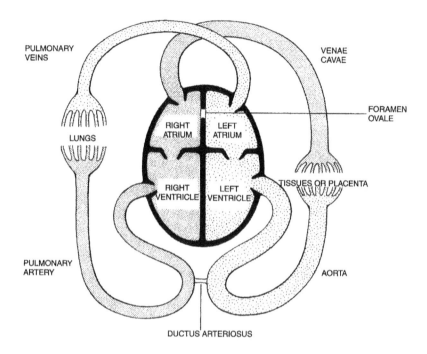

Figure 1.2 Diagrammatic illustration of the cardiovascular system. The foetal connections used to bypass the lungs are shown in white.

tissues (both the lung and target organ) is when blood passes through vessels that are approximately the same diameter as the individual red blood cells, which are the capillaries.

There are around five million red blood cells (or erythrocytes) for every cubic millimetre of blood.

Red blood cells and capillaries

1.19　　The narrowest vessels are the capillaries, and these allow the transfer of gases, water and electrolytes (salts).

The capillaries are very sensitive to oxygen deficiency or hypoxia. Significant hypoxia affects the capillary's permeability (i.e. the capillary's ability to allow the passage of gases, water and electrolytes), and the abnormal capillary permeability that results is mainly responsible for the condition of physiological shock. Shock, in medical terms, is not a matter of mental distress, but a profound biochemical disturbance, triggered by alterations of the distribution of body water, especially blood volume, caused by the hypoxia.

Physiological shock is a condition of medico-legal importance, as it occurs commonly as a result of trauma. Anything that reduces the blood pressure, such as haemorrhage or fluid loss (due to burning), can precipitate the self-perpetuating condition. Low blood pressure causes capillary damage. The capillary damage allows fluid to escape into the tissues inappropriately. The localised fluid loss, in turn, reduces the blood pressure further.

Blood pressure

1.20   Blood pressure is a measure of the maintenance of the pumping function of the heart as well as the peripheral resistance of the vasculature (i.e. the internal resistance to the passage of blood within the systemic circulation and, in turn, how hard the heart has to pump to overcome it), and the measurement commonly encountered in medical reports is a measure of the pressure within the arteries.

The pressure is described in two phases:

(1)   The systolic pressure: a measure of the maximum pressure achieved as a result of the heartbeat.

(2)   The diastolic pressure: a measure of the residual pressure maintained while the heart is refilling.

In general, it is the diastolic pressure that reflects most accurately the level of strain upon the system.

Heart

1.21   The heart is a complex muscular structure comprising of two conjoined pumps, notionally the left- and right-sided systems. The left side receives oxygenated blood from the lungs and pushes it towards the target organs. The right side receives deoxygenated blood from the target organs and pushes it towards the lungs.

The heart consists of specialised muscle tissue, the myocardium, and is enclosed in a fibrous sac, the pericardium.

The pumping musculature/chambers are the ventricles. They are connected proximally to the atria. The atria are separated from the ventricles by non-return valves (on the left, the mitral valve and, on the right, the tricuspid valve). The atria essentially are large collection chambers for the blood to fill. The non-return valves, which separate the ventricles from the arteries, are called, on the left, the aortic valve and, on the right, the pulmonary valve.

The size and weight of the heart are dictated largely by the condition of the ventricles, which, in turn, depends mainly upon the peripheral resistance to the flow of blood. A ventricle that is coping with increased resistance will grow in bulk or hypertrophy; one that is failing to do so will dilate.

Natural disease of the heart and blood vessels accounts for some 80% of the sudden deaths reported to the coroner or procurator fiscal. It provides a major preoccupation for the autopsy pathologist and is discussed in detail in Chapter 6.

Arteries and veins

1.22   The blood passes from the ventricles to the tissues through arteries. The main artery of the body is the aorta, which branches into vessels of descending

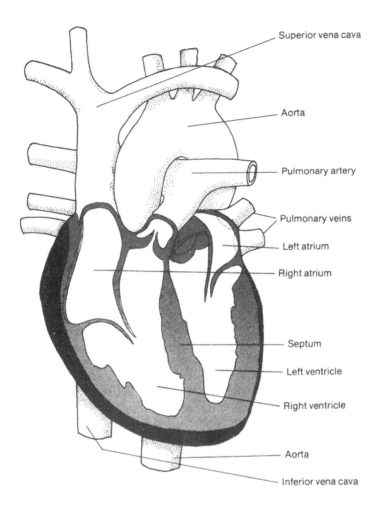

Superior vena cava

Aorta

Pulmonary artery

Pulmonary veins

Left atrium

Right atrium

Septum

Left ventricle

Right ventricle

Aorta

Inferior vena cava

Figure 1.3 Heart. (From: *Lawyers' Guide to Forensic Medicine*, Knight, B., 1998, Cavendish Publishing Ltd, reproduced by permission of Taylor & Francis Books UK.)

calibre until the capillaries are reached. The capillaries then coalesce into tributaries or veins, which ultimately form two main rivers – the superior vena cava, coming from the upper part of the body, and the inferior vena cava from the lower – which return the blood from the systemic circulation to the right atrium.

All blood vessels have three coats: the intima, media and adventitia. The intima, a normally thin inner lining, is subject to the degenerative change of atheroma (furring of the coronary arteries – covered in Chapter 6). The media is a muscular intermediate coat. The adventitia is a loose outer covering responsible for the supply of nutrients to the vessel itself and for its stability in the body.

As the arteries steadily decrease in size, pressure must be maintained within them to ensure adequate blood flow; the arteries therefore have thick muscular walls. The veins, by contrast, receive blood fed by tributaries resembling a river. The walls are thus thin, and darker, purple deoxygenated blood can often be seen through them.

Pulmonary circulation

1.23   The blood returning in the venae cavae is de-oxygenated and requires re-oxygenation via the lungs. In order to do this, the blood passes from the right atrium to the right ventricle into the pulmonary artery. The pulmonary arteries again divide until capillaries are formed within the lungs.

These capillaries surround the smallest air pockets in the lungs, the alveoli. The partial pressure of oxygen in the alveolar air is higher than that in the blood; thus, oxygen passes into the blood. The oxygenated blood returns via the pulmonary veins to the left atrium, thus completing the pulmonary circulation.

Pulmonary capillaries are similarly sensitive to changes in blood volume and oxygen content as the systemic circulation (i.e. the circulation derived from the left side of the heart supplying the target organs). As a result, fluid loss from them results in pulmonary oedema, or 'fluid on the lungs'. This becomes self-perpetuating and thus progressively worse.

Vascular injury

1.24   Injury to any vascular structure is, unsurprisingly, associated with bleeding as a complication. The severity of this bleeding is dependent on three factors:

(1)   The size of the vessel. In general, the larger the vessel damaged, the more dangerous to life the injury.

(2)   The type of vessel. Damage to a high-pressure artery is more dangerous than damage to a low-pressure vein of comparable size.

(3)   Secondary effects. These include effects that result from oxygen deprivation in specific organs, but also those due to occupation of space by escaped blood. For example, haemorrhage into the fixed skull cavity will be more deleterious than the same amount of bleeding into the abdomen.

Coagulation

1.25   Mechanisms intended to control or stem bleeding within the body are known as haemostatic mechanism or haemostasis. This mechanism is reliant on a number of inter-related factors: the properties of blood and the ability of the vessels to contract.

The properties of blood relate to 'coagulation factors' and platelets.

Coagulation factors, mainly designated by a Roman numeral (i.e. Factors I–XIII), are protein substances circulating in the plasma that form part of a complicated chain reaction activated in the presence of calcium. The result of this reaction is to form thrombin. The thrombin, in turn, reacts with the circulating protein, fibrinogen, to form fibrin, which acts as the scaffolding of a clot. Deficiency or absence of any factor can break the chain and cause what are collectively known as bleeding diatheses (or tendencies). Abnormalities of Factor I (fibrinogen), Factor II (prothrombin), Factor VII (proconvertin) and Factor IX (Christmas Factor) are the most important. Deficiency of Factor VIII results in the hereditary disease haemophilia, and lack of Factor IX is responsible for haemophilia B or Christmas disease. The coagulation factors are synthesised in the liver: severe liver disease therefore predisposes to the bleeding condition commonly encountered in many alcoholics. A system of blood factors, comparable to that involved in coagulation, exists in order to prevent the blood clotting in the normal circulation.

The platelets, firstly, release substances that activate the coagulation mechanism and, secondly, aggregate to form 'plugs' at the site of injury to a vessel and thus consolidate the fibrin clot. Excessive bleeding is, therefore, likely if platelets are absent – as happens in disease, bone marrow abnormalities or structural abnormalities.

To some extent, vessels can contract to stem the bleeding, interacting with the coagulation system above. The ability of a vessel to contract is dependent on the health of the vessel and its size.

Bleeding diatheses and medico-legal issues

1.26 Bleeding diatheses are of medico-legal importance. The response to injury will be abnormal: trivial wounds may result in severe haemorrhage or excessive bruising. This may influence their interpretation as to the time of infliction and the forces involved. Normally the condition can be treated by replacement of the deficient substance. A failure to identify or appreciate the abnormal state prior to a surgical or dental operation raises the issue of negligent practice. Historically, replacement therapy was associated with the introduction of blood-borne viruses (such as human immunodeficiency virus (HIV), hepatitis B and C) and prion disease (such as variant Creutzfeldt-Jakob Disease, vCJD) into recipients. Measures introduced over decades have prevented their transmission.

Inappropriate coagulation

1.27 Inappropriate coagulation within the body is another major cause of disease and a consequence of trauma. Blood coagulation and haemostasis occur normally only at the site of injury. Intravascular coagulation occurs either locally in a diseased vessel or as a generalised condition resulting from severe shock.

A thrombus forms within the vessel. If this breaks off, it becomes an embolus.

Emboli can involve both the arterial and the venous blood systems. If forming in the arterial system, they will lodge in the tissues; in the venous system, they lodge in the lungs and cause pulmonary thrombo-embolism. The major significance of these abnormal states is discussed in Chapter 6.

Haematological system

1.28 As has already been described, the blood consists of two major components: the cellular component, and the plasma in which the cells float. If the blood is clotted, the resulting altered fluid component is known as serum.

Serum and plasma

1.29   Serum is technically easier for the laboratory to process, and it is common to speak of 'serum concentrations', but the substances measured will have been circulating similarly in the plasma.

The plasma is responsible for the transport of carbon dioxide and of the products of ingestion and metabolism of fat, proteins and carbohydrates. It contains many of the mineral salts on which the biochemical balance of the body depends and also the hormones. The clotting factors, described previously, are also present in the plasma, which, normally, constitutes approximately 60% of the blood volume; a relative fall in this proportion leads to a viscous blood and local tissue hypoxia owing to stagnation.

Cellular components

1.30   The cells of the blood are divided into the red series (erythrocytes) and the white series (leucocytes) with a platelet component.

Erythrocytes

1.31   The oxygen-transporting function of the red blood cells has been described. A relative lack of red cells constitutes anaemia, which may result from either haemorrhage, from an inability to form haemoglobin (usually due to a lack of iron, its inorganic component) or from an inappropriate destruction of the haemoglobin.

Forensically, two situations relating to this are particularly important:

(1)   Some poisonous substances convert the haemoglobin into forms that are less capable or incapable of accepting oxygen. The most important of these substances is carbon monoxide.

(2)   Inherited abnormalities of haemoglobin occur and are known as haemoglobinopathies. The best known is sickle cell anaemia. These abnormalities may be structural (e.g. sickle cell anaemia) or qualitative (e.g. thalassaemia which forms the persistence of a fetal type of haemoglobin in the adult).

These conditions are of some importance forensically. Sufferers may be hypersensitive to low blood oxygen tensions arising from any cause, such as anaesthesia, air travel, or conditions of severe oxygen demand (including any physiologically stressful situation, such as a struggle and restraint). They also have a strong ethnic distribution, such as sickle cell anaemia in the Afro-Caribbean population.

Leucocytes

1.32   The leucocytes are basically of two types: the polymorphonuclears and the mononuclears. The polymorphonuclear cells constitute the body's tactical defence against acute infection. The mononuclear cells are more akin to a strategic force which comes into action more slowly but whose influence persists for some time. They are particularly responsible for the formation of antibodies and for the ability of the body to recognise a foreign intruder. Human immunodeficiency virus targets this component.

Bone marrow

1.33   Blood cells are formed in the bone marrow, which is found in the centre of virtually all bones of the body. Bone marrow comprises cellular components (i.e. the blood cell-forming component) and fatty elements. The extent of the fatty elements increases proportionally with age. Poison or ionising radiation that affects the bone marrow will, in turn, affect the blood cells.

Spleen and the lympho-reticular system

1.34   The spleen, bone marrow and lymphatic system of the ducts and glands form the lympho-reticular system.

The spleen lies in the left upper abdomen and is covered by the lower portions of the ribcage. It is an organ that is not absolutely essential to a normal life, and its main medico-legal significance lies in the ease with which it is ruptured, particularly in the context of vehicular accidents. Deliberate rupture of the spleen was once a vogue as a method of murder in malarial-induced fragility but, in the western world, it is also prone to traumatic rupture in glandular fever.

A major function of the spleen is the removal of aged blood cells and, equally importantly, the preservation and recycling of the important components of the cells. In the absence of a spleen, other organs adapt and undertake parts of its function, resulting in essentially only an increased risk to infection that can be reduced with appropriate antibiotic prophylaxis.

The lymphatic system is also responsible for the circulation of the extracellular fluid (lymph), which bathes the cells of the body. The lymphatic and cardiovascular systems are united where the main lymph duct empties itself into the larger veins of the upper thorax. Malignant cells are thus readily disseminated in the lymph and set up secondary deposits (metastases).

Respiratory system

1.35   Oxygen is a requirement of all tissues and, without it, cells die. The most sensitive cells of the brain will die if deprived of oxygen for some five minutes or less, although this is variable depending on other factors. It is the function of the respiratory system to trap the oxygen, to transfer it to the haemoglobin, and to remove the main product of internal combustion, carbon dioxide, which circulates dissolved in the blood plasma.

Anatomy

1.36   The respiratory system involves all the structures along which air is passed, from the nose or mouth to the airspaces of the lungs (the alveoli). Air is passed to the lungs from the nose or mouth. The initial stages involve passage along the pharynx (structures at the back of the oral and nasal cavities), through the larynx (the area around the Adam's Apple) to the trachea (windpipe). The larynx is protected by three bones or cartilages: the hyoid, thyroid (Adam's Apple) and cricoids. These structures are of importance in the diagnosis of pressure to the neck (see Chapter 11). The trachea splits into a left and a right main bronchus which, in turn, divide into lobar bronchi, one to each major lobe of the lungs.

The right lung has three lobes, and the left has only two. The right lung is therefore slightly larger than the left lung. The left lung must make way for the heart, which lies in the left thorax. The bronchi (cartilage airways) split into bronchioles (cartilage-free airways), which end in the air sacs, and alveoli, which are surrounded by the pulmonary capillaries. The lungs are contained within two layers of a fibrous envelope, the pleura. It serves two purposes: firstly, it maintains a negative pressure (i.e. pressure within the chest cavity being lower than environment) between the two layers, keeping the lungs in a position of expansion; and, secondly, it reduces the friction between the lungs and the chest wall. The formation of pleural adhesions is a frequent result of pulmonary disease.

Respiration

1.37   Respiration is facilitated by air being drawn into the lungs by the muscles of respiration (that is, the chest muscles and diaphragm).

The movement of air downwards is created by negative pressure. The physical act of respiration is directed by both the autonomic (involuntary) and voluntary nervous systems (see **1.46** below). Normally, an individual does not consciously think about breathing, but can control their breathing if desired. Overall, the autonomic innervation has overarching control. It is very difficult (if not impossible) to die from holding one's breath, and an irrespirable medium, such as water or a poisonous gas, will be inhaled despite conscious resistance.

Expiration requires no muscular effort. In respiratory failure, positive pressure breathing must be applied, such as by a ventilator or by mouth-to-mouth resuscitation.

The process of respiration is one of equilibrating the tensions of the various gases in the air and body fluids. In keeping with most physical systems, substances will move from areas of high pressure (or concentration) to areas of low pressure/concentration. Towards the end of respiratory effort, the oxygen tension (or, in effect, concentration) is high in the alveolar space and low in the pulmonary capillary blood. Oxygen passes into the plasma and forms oxyhaemoglobin in the red blood cells. Similar processes apply once the oxygenated haemoglobin arrives at its target organs. High oxygen tension in the capillary peripheral blood corresponds to low oxygen tension in the tissue fluids, resulting in oxyhaemoglobin releasing oxygen to the tissues.

The removal of carbon dioxide utilises the same pressure of movement from high pressure to low pressure.

Protective mechanisms

1.38   The epithelial cells forming the lining of the air passages bear numerous fine hair-like structures, known as cilia. These propel inhaled small dust particles back up the air passages and are the first line of defence. Smoking tobacco, or any other substance, and some forms of atmospheric pollution, will damage or paralyse the cilia, so that inhaled particles are not removed, with consequent danger of infection.

Exposure of the lungs to large quantities of dust can lead to disease, such as pneumoconiosis or asbestos-related diseases. These are often industrial in origin.

There are also protective cells (alveolar macrophages) in the lower parts of the respiratory tract, the lungs.

Consequences of injury and debility

1.39   Physical injury to the lungs remains a common event. For example, the lungs are vulnerable to penetration by foreign objects (such as a bullet or blade) or the ends of broken ribs.

In relation to penetration, a number of consequences may be encountered:

• The negative pressure in the pleural space may be lost and the lung can collapse. This results in inefficient blood oxygenation, but the immobile lung is very vulnerable to infection.

• Haemorrhage and its severity is dependent on the size of the vessels and structures involved.

Blunt injury to the lungs and rest of the respiratory tract is commonly caused by crushing injury, such as in vehicular accidents or falls from a height.

The lungs are vulnerable to blast injury or shock waves due to the large number of gas/fluid interfaces. This results in haemorrhage, laceration and destruction of the walls of the alveolar spaces. This is covered in Chapter 13.

Another major medico-legal issue involving the lungs is the development of pneumonia following prolonged bed-rest and hospitalisation. Irrespective of cause, with prolonged hospitalisation and immobility, the lungs are less efficiently expanded and consequent oedema and congestion arise, predisposing to infection, particularly with increasing age and other conditions. Other factors, such as intubation (insertion of tube into the airways to facilitate air entry), and merely being hospitalised and exposed to infective agents as a result, play a role.

Nervous system

1.40   Anatomically, the nervous system is divided into the central nervous system (CNS) and the peripheral nervous system, which involves all the nerves that extend from the CNS to the remainder of the body.

Central and peripheral nervous systems

1.41   The central nervous system (CNS) comprises of the brain and spinal cord. It has a core running from the head to the 'tail', with nerve fibres carrying information and commands in both directions.

The spinal cord forms the lower part of the CNS. The spinal cord is subsequently divided into 'segments', broadly related to the vertebrae of the spinal column.

Immediately above the spinal cord lies the hindbrain, consisting of the medulla and pons, where many centres organising the vital functions of the body (e.g. respiration) are situated.

Next there is a narrow midbrain and, above this, the forebrain of which the central core is the thalamus and hypothalamus, where the instinctive or animal processes are organised.

Two major, bilaterally symmetrical, masses are connected to the centre core; these are the cerebellum, which overlies and is part of the hindbrain, and the cerebrum (covered by the cerebral cortex), which forms the major part of the forebrain. These areas are concerned with the more complicated functions of the body.

The cerebellum essentially coordinates movements and posture. Anatomically, the cerebrum is divided into four lobes. The frontal lobes are concerned mainly with personality but also, posteriorly, with the initiation of muscle movements. The parietal lobes are associated with sensation. The occipital lobes are concerned with vision. The temporal lobes are mainly associated with speech, hearing and equilibrium.

1.42   In essence, special areas within each lobe are related to special areas of the body and, as a result, the consequences of a head injury or a cerebrovascular event (a 'stroke') can have reasonably predictable consequences.

The highly developed cerebral cortex acts, in many ways, as a controller of the instinctive thalamus. Thus, some drugs, in particular alcohol, which appear to be stimulatory in nature are, in fact, depressants; the most highly developed parts of the brain are most easily affected and this leads to diminished cognitive control of activity.

Passing through the outer aspects of each vertebrae are an efferent (outgoing) and afferent (incoming) nerve root. The efferent root is related to action (i.e. motor function) whilst the afferent root is related to receiving information (i.e. sensory).

The motor and sensory nerve pathways pass respectively downwards and upwards in the spinal cord between the brain and the nerve roots appropriate for the area of the body that they supply.

Emerging from the brain are a series of nerves known as the cranial nerves (analogous in form to the peripheral nerves) that are involved in nervous control of the special senses (e.g. auditory, visual, olfactory and taste); facial and oral cavity musculature/sensation; and, importantly, the vagus nerve. With the exception of the optic nerve (cranial nerve II), this forms part of the peripheral nervous system.

Injury

1.43   Damage to the spinal cord will result in functional abnormality in a regional distribution (i.e. the region supplied by nerve roots below the point of damage). For example, severance of the spinal cord at the neck will result in paralysis of all four limbs (quadriplegia), whereas severance in the thoracic region leads only to paralysis of the lower limbs (paraplegia).

Division of the nerve root will show a segmental distribution, either anaesthetic (sensory) or paralytic (motor). Damage to a peripheral nerve will cause similar changes, either in a group of muscles (or wide area of skin) or in an individual muscle, depending on the size of the nerve affected.

Response to injury

1.44　　Some regrowth and recovery of function is possible in the peripheral nerves following injury. By contrast, there is no true regeneration in the CNS, bar some clinical recovery of function, which may appear as the pressure effects of haemorrhage, oedema and others reduce.

This consequence applies not only to the nerve fibres but also to the neurons or nerve cells from which ultimate nervous function is derived. A child is born with the maximum number of brain cells that it will possess, and the decreasing mental capacity of senility is, to some extent, a measure of how these degenerate during life.

Reflexes

1.45　　In the event of damage to the spinal cord, some function can be retained through spinal reflexes, which operate without the direct control of the brain. These include the uncontrolled emptying of the bladder when it is full. Similar reflex reaction may be seen in the limbs when the brain itself is dead, and this must be distinguished from conscious movement that would, if present, be evidence of residual cerebral activity.

Autonomic nervous system

1.46　　The autonomic nervous system runs alongside the conscious control and, as its name implies, is automatic and involuntary. It is responsible for all those activities that are subconscious, such as the beating of the heart, the production of sweat and the movement of the bowel.

It is separated into two groups: sympathetic and parasympathetic groups, which are antagonistic to each other. For example, the sympathetic system will quicken the heartbeat, while the parasympathetic system through the vagus nerve (an important component of the parasympathetic system) will slow it.

This system (and, in particular, the vagus nerve) is at the heart of the important pathological concept of reflex cardiac arrest. The concept is that a sudden 'unnatural' stimulation of the sympathetic system leads to reflex compensatory action of the parasympathetic nervous system, which slows the heart with the potential to cease its function. This is covered in Chapter 12, but reflex cardiac arrest as a means of causing death is suggested as a mechanism in certain categories of death, often where the precise mechanism is unclear.

Meninges and the skull

1.47　　The coverings of the brain and spinal cord are of particular forensic importance. From outwards in, after skin and soft tissues, the skull covers the brain and the spinal cord is covered by the vertebral column. These rigid structures protect the nervous structure from direct violence to some extent, but have obvious disadvantages. There is no room for expansion or displacement of the contained organs and, if fractured, the broken bones themselves can potentially lacerate the brain or spinal cord.

Within its bony coverings, the CNS is surrounded by a tough membrane, which is known as the dura (mater). Large blood vessels flow between the bone and the dura. Numerous small veins drain into the dural sinuses. Head injury can therefore result in either extradural or subdural haemorrhage.

Subsequent to the dura mater is the arachnoid mater, a thin membrane lying directly under the dura and upon the brain surface.

This subarachnoid space contains the cerebrospinal fluid, the main function of which is to give some leeway for expansion and to act as a water cushion for the brain. Also in close approximation are the main arteries supplying the brain, which pass from the neck to supply the brain substance. Rupture of these vessels, due to injury or natural disease, results in subarachnoid haemorrhage.

The thin pia mater so closely adheres the brain that there is, effectively, no subpial space. Any haemorrhage occurring in this area is of (superficial) intracerebral type.

Gastro-intestinal system

1.48   The function of the gastro-intestinal system is to accept food, digest it, store it and circulate it to the tissues in a form that provides a ready source of energy, and excrete unused residues.

Overview

1.49   The alimentary canal starts at the mouth and leads into the straight 'tube' of the oesophagus, which traverses the length of the thorax. The oesophagus opens into the stomach which, in turn, empties into the duodenum or first part of the small intestine. The jejunum and ileum form the second and third parts of the small intestine, which are about 6 metres (20 feet) in length and closely coiled within the abdomen. The large intestine consists of: the caecum and its attached vermiform appendix; the ascending, transverse, descending and sigmoid colon; and the rectum, which opens to the exterior at the anus. The word 'bowel' is used interchangeably with the intestine, such that the large bowel corresponds to the large intestine.

The peritoneum lines the abdominal cavity and surrounds the walls of the cavity and the organs of the abdominal cavity, including the intestines. The envelope of peritoneum that is attached to the posterior abdominal wall, and from which the small intestine is suspended, is known as the mesentery, and the major blood vessels that supply the intestine lie within this. Tissues that lie behind the posterior part of the peritoneum are said to be retroperitoneal in position.

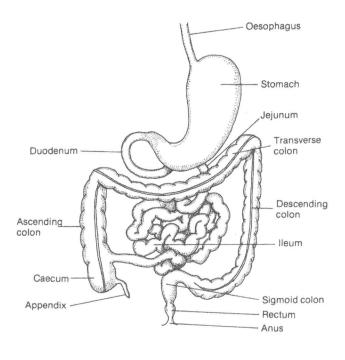

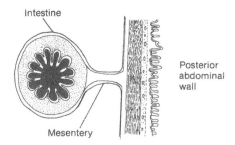

Figure 1.4 Gastro-intestinal tract. (From: *Lawyers' Guide to Forensic Medicine*, Knight, B., 1998, Cavendish Publishing Ltd, reproduced by permission of Taylor & Francis Books UK.)

Hepato-biliary system (liver, gallbladder and pancreas)

1.50   Constituents of food absorbed from the bowel are passed to the liver, where they are processed and stored. The liver is the largest organ in the body and occupies the upper right quadrant in the abdomen.

It has numerous functions including: the metabolism of carbohydrates, fats and proteins; the storage of a readily available source of energy (glycogen); the processing of waste material derived from breakdown of body tissue; the preparation of many of the substances essential for blood clotting; and the formation of bile, which is stored in the gallbladder and passed into the intestine where it assists in digestion. It also plays a significant part in the metabolism of alcohol.

Failure to secrete bile, or to excrete it into the bowel, shows itself as jaundice.

Enzymes produced from the pancreas are also essential to digestion. The pancreas lies in the posterior part of the abdomen and empties its secretion into the duodenum.

Medico-legal consequences

1.51 In relation to drug toxicity, drugs may be given orally and can result in localised irritation and injury. Many drugs are detoxified in the liver and can result in direct damage.

The function of the liver may also be impaired by hepatitis (an infection or inflammation of the liver). Autopsy personnel are at particular risk to blood-borne viral hepatitides, hepatitis B and C.

Alcohol has particular vulnerability on the gastro-intestinal system, and this is highlighted in Chapter 17.

Trauma to the stomach and intestines may have serious consequences. Rupture of any component allows entry of its contents into the abdominal cavity. Those contents are irritants (e.g. stomach acidity) and heavily contaminated by bacteria (particularly the large bowel), which predisposes to infection of the abdominal cavity (peritonitis) and, subsequently, septic shock.

The bowel is relatively resistant to blunt (non-penetrating) trauma, but both the intestine and its mesentery can be ruptured when massive force is applied from outside over a limited area, compressing them against the bony spine.

The sheer bulk of the liver increases its susceptibility to penetrating injury, but it is at its most vulnerable in crushing accidents or in conditions that set up severe vibrations in the body, such as falls from a height. The pancreas, on the other hand, is well protected and is only occasionally injured.

Urinary system

1.52 The urinary system's role is to remove soluble waste products circulating in the plasma of the blood and excrete them in the urine.

This system is demonstrated in Figure 1.5 and consists of a pair of kidneys, placed retroperitoneally (i.e. behind the peritoneal or abdominal cavity) in the abdomen (with their upper portions covered by the lower ribs). From the kidneys pass a pair of tubes, the ureters. Each ureter drains into the bladder, a muscular reservoir whose outflow is protected by a sphincter (a ring-shaped muscle that, in constriction, prevents escape).

Urine which is stored in the bladder is passed to the outside of the body through a single pipe, the urethra. The urethra in the female is comparatively short; whereas, in the male, it is long and passes through the prostate gland and the penis.

The opening of the female urethra lies close to the bacterially contaminated anus, and thus ascending cystitis (bladder infection) is common in women.

By contrast, men, with increasing age, are subject to prostatic hypertrophy, which leads to stasis of the urine in the bladder and, again, infection.

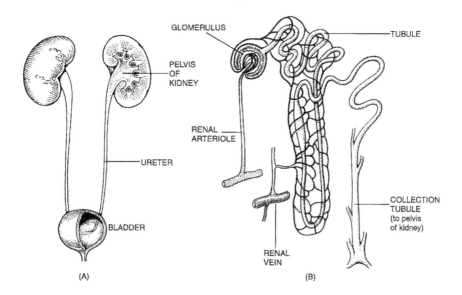

Figure 1.5 The anatomy of the urinary system. (A) Macroscopic structure.
(B) Microscopic appearance of a nephron.

Kidneys

1.53   The kidneys play a major part in the regulation of the body's biochemical status. This is achieved through the functional unit known as a nephron comprising of a glomerulus and tubules.

A glomerulus is essentially a collection of blood capillaries enclosed in a capsule. The elimination of waste products arises primarily by pressure filtration (i.e. movement from high to low concentration) through these capillaries. The wall of the capillary acts as a semi-permeable membrane, allowing the passage of water and small dissolved particles but retaining large molecular-size particles, such as proteins.

Filtration pressure results in what is effectively a protein-free blood plasma within the capsular space of the glomeruli. This contains not only waste products but also materials that are of value or even essential to the body, notably glucose and sodium.

The glucose, sodium and water are reabsorbed in the proximal tubules, while complex reactions designed to regulate the degree of acidity of the blood take place in the distal tubules.

The distal tubules run into collecting tubules which act as tributaries to the ureters. The importance of clearly distinguishing between the glomeruli and the tubules is that the function of the tubules is active and requires the use of energy. They are, therefore, very dependent on an effective blood supply and, since the vessels to the tubules have already supplied the needs of the glomeruli, conditions at tubular level are prone to the development of an 'energy crisis'; any condition that interferes with the free delivery of oxygen to the tissues will affect the renal tubules with particular severity.

Any disease of the kidneys can have a general effect on the cardiovascular system, most commonly hypertension (or increased blood pressure), and any cardiovascular disease can in turn affect the kidneys.

Glomerulonephritis

1.54   The body has the capability to recognise foreign materials within its substance and, save in exceptional circumstances, defend itself against invasion. The defence mechanism is referred to as an immune reaction, and the foreign substance that precipitates it is known as an antigen. The immune reaction may be of two types:

(1)   Humoral: this involves the formation of circulating antibodies which react specifically with antigens.

(2)   Cellular: this involves migrant cells seeking and either destroying or eliminating the intruder. This is the principal mechanism responsible for the rejection of transplanted tissues.

A major result of antigenic challenge is to stimulate the body's powers of recollection. Thus, the first intrusion or contact causes comparatively gradual recognition followed by a reaction. The pattern of the foreign substance is remembered, the templates of antibody production are retained, and a second attack can be met by the immediate mobilisation of reserves. Repeated stimuli result in increasing immunity. Normally, this system is entirely to the body's advantage. It forms the basis, for example, of vaccination against various infectious diseases.

1.55   Occasionally, the body may recognise a wholly appropriate part of the body (i.e. self) as being non-self or foreign. This, in turn, will elicit the body mounting an inflammatory response against the appropriate part of the body. This seems to arise for two broad reasons. The first mechanism is incompletely understood but the body reacts against its own tissues without any stimulus from outside. This constitutes auto-immune disease. The second mechanism relates to the fact that an individual antigen may be common to substances of dissimilar nature. Having recognised an antigen, the body will react to it similarly, irrespective of mode of presentation. Such a direct error of identification may occasionally result in severe disease of the glomeruli.

Immune complexes are formed when a foreign antigen stimulates and combines with an antibody. In relation to streptococcus infection (a common, bacterial cause of sore throats), the immune complexes that are formed may become deposited on the glomerular capillary walls and establish a secondary reaction. The subsequent damage to the capillary walls and the efforts of the glomeruli to remove the deposited material result in a glomerulonephritis. This is a diffuse condition in which all of the glomeruli are equally at risk. Fortunately, in most cases the glomeruli return to normal, and clinical recovery is the rule. Occasionally, however, the disease progresses and, after a variable time, the kidneys cease to function, requiring replacement by machine or transplant.

Similarly, the functional integrity of the glomerular filtration membrane may be compromised to a lesser extent and the protein is lost steadily into the urine. This is known as the nephrotic syndrome.

Acute renal failure

1.56   The development of acute renal failure is associated with physiological shock. Shock is a matter of inadequate oxygenation of the tissues. The condition may arise from blood loss, which, in turn, may be due either to bleeding or to destruction of the blood (haemolysis) within the body:

- Haemolysis may result from inherent enzyme deficiency diseases, auto-immune diseases, infection of the blood cells (such as in malaria) or, occasionally, from the inadvertent precipitation of an immune reaction, e.g. a mismatched blood transfusion.

- Reduction of the plasma component of the blood may follow burning, severe surgical trauma or unusual conditions such as crushing of the muscles or sub-atmospheric decompression.

Acute renal failure may accompany any of these conditions and, in the majority of cases, it is recoverable, provided that some mechanism can be substituted for the kidneys during a period of recuperation. This substitution treatment is known as haemodialysis, in which the blood is diverted to a man-made membrane simulating the glomerulus.

The passage of dissolved substances from the blood across this membrane can be controlled by altering their concentration in the 'bath' fluid, which takes the place of the filtrate in the glomerular capsule; in effect, an 'osmotic gradient' can be established for any constituent of the plasma.

Both the glomeruli and the tubules may be involved in inflammation resulting from infection ascending from the bladder.

Renal infection

1.57   Infection of the kidney (pyelonephritis) can be as damaging as primary glomerular disease. Infection is often ascending (i.e. originating from the bladder).

Bladder

1.58   The bladder is controlled by the autonomic nervous system, and the muscle is generally in a state of relaxation; distension results in reflex contraction and expulsion of urine. Autonomic urination is prevented by additional control of an external sphincter through the voluntary nervous system.

As the nerve supply to the bladder sphincter originates in the lower part of the spinal cord, any injuries of the cord will likely compromise the control of urination, and the bladder will revert to automatic action. Apart from the social inconvenience, ascending infection of the urinary tract is common.

Urethra

1.59   The different anatomy of the urethra in the male and female has a profound effect on the establishment of infection in the bladder.

In the female, it is not difficult for organisms on the skin of the external genitalia to pass in a retrograde fashion to the bladder, while the inherent laxity of the perineum predisposes to prolapse and inefficient emptying. Inflammation (cystitis) is, therefore, common in women.

The male urethra, by contrast, can protect the bladder from external invasion relatively well, but the prostate gland is subject to enlargement of either a benign or cancerous nature. Obstruction to the flow of urine due to prostatism is a common accompaniment of later middle age; the resultant 'back pressure' may have serious effects on the kidneys themselves, while the stagnation of urine induced is, as in the female, conducive to the establishment of infection. The process may be accelerated by the need to pass catheters into the distended organ.

Stagnation

1.60   Stagnation of urine leads to its prolonged contact with the inner wall of the bladder. Injurious substances that are excreted in the urine may selectively injure the bladder. Some hydrocarbons are active in the production of carcinoma, which may arise as a result of occupation.

Injury to the urinary system

1.61   The kidneys lie posteriorly in the body and are comparatively well protected by large muscle masses. The kidneys also lie in good shock-absorbing beds of fatty tissue. Laceration by direct trauma is, therefore, comparatively rare and the kidneys are not often injured in traumatic deaths that inflict severe damage to other solid organs. They can be injured by kicks to the flanks, and very severe internal injury may be present despite an absence of obvious external damage. However, the kidneys are vulnerable to sharp force injury.

The body can function perfectly well with a single normal kidney. However, this poses subsequent risks with age and as natural disease develops.

The ureters are well protected from external injury.

The bladder in both male and female is closely associated with the bones of the pelvis and is vulnerable to injury associated with fracture of the pelvis.

Reproductive system

Male

1.62   The male reproductive system consists of the twin testes, which usually descend into the scrotum just before birth.

The organs are formed of coiled tubules in which the spermatozoa (or male gametes) mature. A spermatozoon consists of a head, a neck and a tail. Some 400 to 500 million spermatozoa are shed with a normal ejaculation. The bulk of the seminal fluid is derived from the epididymis, one of which lies close to each testis; together they drain into the vas deferens. The vas deferens on each side opens into the urethra at the base of the bladder. Other small glands contribute to the total seminal ejaculate.

Female

1.63   The female reproductive organs consist, first, of two ovaries, which lie on each side of the pelvis.

Between the onset of menstruation and menopause, each ovary has a finite store of eggs or ova (the female gametes), which greatly exceeds the requirements for the maturation each month of, normally, a single egg.

The ovaries on each side are connected to the uterus by the Fallopian tubes, down which the ova pass. There is a potential space between the ovary and the receptor end of the tube; occasionally, ova are fertilised and yet do not reach the uterus, in which case an ectopic pregnancy is established.

The outlet of the uterus is a tightly closed canal surrounded by the cervix, which juts into the vagina.

The vagina opens through the vulva. In the virgin state, the vaginal opening is protected by the hymen, a sheet of fibrous tissue with, usually, a small opening which will permit the passage of normal secretions. This area is addressed further in Chapter 15.

The vulva consists, internally, of paired labia minora which join anteriorly and posteriorly as commissures (an anatomical join). The posterior commissure is known as the fourchette; this is likely to be damaged during forceful intercourse and during childbirth. The labia majora lie outermost; they are joined in front at the mons veneris but posteriorly merge into the tissues of the perineum.

Fertilisation and pregnancy

1.64   In normal circumstances, spermatozoa injected into the vagina migrate to the Fallopian tube where a single male gamete fertilises an ovum, thus forming a zygote. An unfertilised ovum will die in a couple of days, but a fertilised ovum passes to the uterus where it is implanted some six days after fertilisation. After about three months' development, a placenta forms, which is attached to the growing fetus by the umbilical cord. The fetus is surrounded by a fibrous sac known as the amnion and floats in amniotic fluid.

The birth process is started by contractions of the uterus and dilatation of the cervix, usually with rupture of the amnion. If the placenta becomes detached, the fetus will die and be expelled as a foreign body; the placenta itself will be similarly rejected should the fetus itself die. Unnatural dilatation of the cervical canal will cause the uterus to contract. Any of these situations can be simulated in order to procure abortion.

Endocrine system

1.65   The body contains a number of glands that discharge hormones into the bloodstream. These hormones have specific actions on various parts of the body; over-production or failure of the endocrine glands can result in disease or dysfunction of the target organs. There are seven different glands secreting at least 30 hormones, which are significantly inter-related through complex feedback loops.

Pituitary gland

1.66   At the head of the system is the pituitary gland, which lies in the base of the skull within the pituitary fossa.

The pituitary stimulates activity in many of the other glands but is itself sensitive to circulating hormones: once sufficient hormones are present in the blood, this mechanism inhibits further stimulation. In addition to its supervisory function over the other glands, the pituitary itself controls growth, the secretion of urine and the contraction of the uterus during childbirth.

Damage to the pituitary gland is, therefore, a serious condition. It is a common result of fracture of the base of the skull, and the gland may be damaged by the effects of localised haemorrhage after complicated childbirth.

Thyroid gland

1.67   The thyroid gland lies in the neck and is responsible, in part, for mental and physical growth in childhood and for the general rate of metabolism in adults.

Deficiency of thyroid hormone leads to cold and apathy, while an excess results in production of heat and hyper-excitability. The position of the thyroid renders it susceptible to bruising, which may be of some evidential value in cases of pressure to the neck.

Parathyroid gland

1.68   The four parathyroid glands are small and closely associated anatomically with the thyroid. They control the distribution of calcium between the bones and the body as a whole.

Adrenal gland

1.69   The adrenal glands lie superiorly against the kidneys. Their central part (or medulla) secretes adrenaline, which affects the tone of the blood vessels and also the heart rate; its action is similar to that of the sympathetic nervous system. Adrenaline is secreted in response to sudden stress and, in effect, brings the body to a 'fighting' state in response to alarm. When given therapeutically, it has profound effects on blood pressure and blood distribution.

The outer part or cortex of the adrenal glands secretes the corticosteroids which control the salt and water balance of the body (and, hence, the distribution of the muscle/fat tissues), exert an effect on the metabolism of carbohydrates, and influence the sex glands and the response of the body to infection or other conditions which result in inflammation.

Corticosteroids can be used to suppress the immune response. Abnormalities of secretion are important in the expression of secondary sex characteristics (i.e. those appearing at puberty); thus, an excess of virilising hormones in females leads to the adreno-genital syndrome, which may lead to misdiagnosis of sex at birth.

Pancreas

1.70   The pancreas secretes the hormone insulin, the absence of which causes diabetes mellitus, in which the storage of carbohydrate is inhibited and the blood contains excess amounts of sugar: hyperglycaemia. The converse situation, hypoglycaemia, results from an excess of insulin. This is a rare natural condition but is an obvious hazard of the treatment of diabetes. Hypoglycaemia can be fatal, and injection of insulin has been used as a method of homicide. This is covered briefly in Chapter 17.

Musculoskeletal system

1.71   The musculoskeletal system consists of the bony skeleton (see Figure 1.6) to which the muscle masses are attached, often through the medium of tendons.

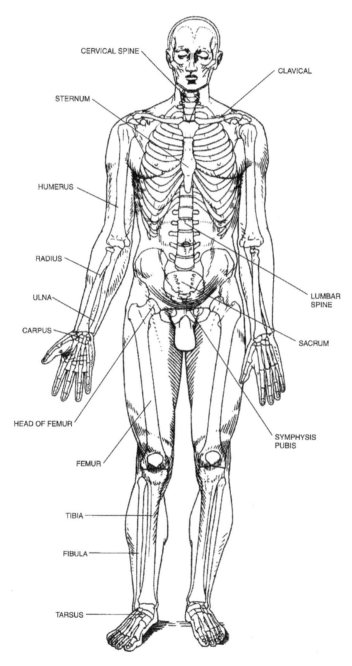

Figure 1.6 The major relationships of the human skeleton. (From an original diagram by Professor G J Romanes.)

Muscles

1.72 Those muscles which can be activated at will are known as voluntary muscles (or striated muscles, because of their striped or streaked appearance under the microscope).

Many organs (e.g. bladder and bowel) are equipped with muscle that is not under conscious control and is therefore known as involuntary (or, from its microscopic appearance, smooth) muscle.

Bone

1.73 Bones provide the supporting structure of the body, and are generally divided into two types based on their density: compact (or cortical) and cancellous. Compact bone is the dense outer covering around the central cancellous bone. The cancellous bone is the central core of a bone comprising trabeculated spicules of bone similar to a sponge, with thin strands of bone forming an irregular meshwork of bone and spaces. The spaces are the bone marrow (see paragraph **1.33** above).

Bones are also classified based on their shape:

- Long bones: these are the 'classic' bone, comprising a long shaft and expanded ends.

- Short bones: these bones are cuboidal in shape (for example, the bones of the wrist).

- Flat bones: these bones comprise two flat compact bones separated by cancellous bone (for example, many of the skull bones and plates of the pelvis).

- Sesamoid bones: these are small rounded bones found in tendons.

- Irregular bones: these are variably shaped bones that do not fit into the other classifications (for example, many of the bones of the facial skeleton).

In relation to the long bone, the shaft of the bone is known as the diaphysis. The ends are known as epiphysis. The end of the diaphysis adjacent to the epiphysis is the metaphysis and separates the diaphysis from the epiphysis.

Joints and cartilage

1.74 When bones articulate (form a joint) and mobilise with each other, these are known as joints. The surfaces of joints are covered by cartilage. Cartilage is also formed at bony junctions when some mobility is needed. The prime examples of this are the junctions between the breastbone and the ribs and between the two pelvic bones. Such a union is known as a symphysis.

Skull and spinal column

1.75 The skull is divided simply into the vault, which covers the brain, and the base, on which the brain rests.

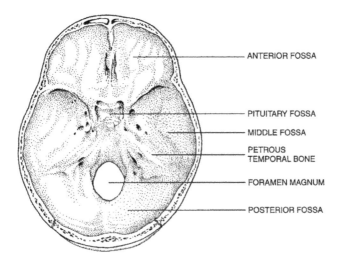

ANTERIOR FOSSA

PITUITARY FOSSA

MIDDLE FOSSA

PETROUS
TEMPORAL BONE

FORAMEN MAGNUM

POSTERIOR FOSSA

Figure 1.7 The inner surface of the base of the skull. The frontal lobes rest in the anterior fossae, the temporal lobes in the middle fossae and the cerebellum lies in the posterior fossae. The spinal cord passes through the foramen magnum. The weakest part of the base of the skull runs along the line of the petrous temporal bone through the multiple foramina and the pituitary fossa – recovery from fracture of the base can lead to permanent pituitary dysfunction.

The base is formed of three fossae or depressions: the anterior, middle and posterior fossae. The lobes of the brain are accommodated in these three depressions.

The skull rests on the spinal column, which is formed of a number of individual vertebrae. The uppermost is known as the atlas bone.

The atlas and six small vertebrae form the cervical spine. Below this are 12 thoracic vertebrae with which the ribs articulate posteriorly. Immediately below this are five large vertebrae lying in the small of the back, which form the lumbar spine, and below this are the fused vertebrae of the sacrum, which makes up the rear wall of the pelvic cavity. The tail of primates is represented by the small coccyx.

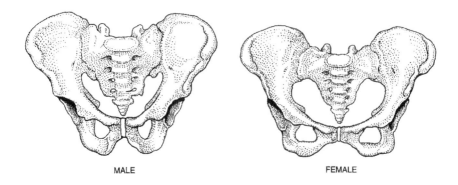

MALE

FEMALE

Figure 1.8 The pelvic bones of the male (left) and the female (right).

The sacrum joins the two pelvic bones posteriorly and, anteriorly, the pelves are united at the symphysis pubis, which allows for some expansion during childbirth but which is often split in severe accidents.

Chest

1.76   The chest wall is usually comprised of 12 pairs of ribs, numbered from superior to inferior. Posteriorly, they are attached to the vertebral column via a number of joints and, anteriorly, they are attached to the sternum (or breastplate) via a cartilaginous connection.

Limbs

1.77   The upper limb is comprised of a series of bones and joints.

The shoulder girdle is formed by the scapulae or shoulder blades posteriorly and the clavicles or collar bones anteriorly. The humerus articulates with these to form the shoulder joint.

At the elbow, the humerus forms a joint with the two bones of the forearm: the ulna (on the little finger side) and the radius (on the thumb side).

The bones of the wrist are collectively known as the carpus, those of the hand as the metacarpals, and those of the fingers as the phalanges. The knuckles refer to the metacarpophalangeal joints (between metacarpal and phalanges) or interphalangeal joints (between the phalanges themselves). Naming is similarly confused as to that of the fingers, and it is generally safer to name as the respective joint of the thumb to little finger respectively.

Similar structure exists in the lower limb.

The thigh bone or femur has its large circular head embedded in the acetabulum of the pelvis.

The neck of the femur, which effectively carries the weight of the torso, is a mechanically weak point, due to its angulation, and is of great forensic importance owing to the ease with which it can be accidentally broken, especially with increasing osteoporosis (brittle bone). A fracture of this area requires either prolonged bed rest or surgical insertion of a pin before the broken ends will reunite. Both these predispose to the development of pneumonia or embolism, and this is covered in Chapters 6 and 7.

The femur articulates at the knee joints with the large tibia, which lies medially in the lower leg, and with the slender fibula, which lies laterally.

The bones of the ankle are known as the tarsus and include two particularly large individual bones, the talus and the calcaneus. The foot contains the metatarsals and the toes (the phalanges).

Fractures

1.78   A fracture is a breach of the continuity of a bone, and the term will be used medically to cover all types and severity of such injuries.

Fractures may be described by a number of methods. The most straightforward relates to the relative location of the fracture.

Fractures may be simple or compound. A simple fracture is contained within the skin, but a compound fracture is open and the fracture end breaches the skin surface.

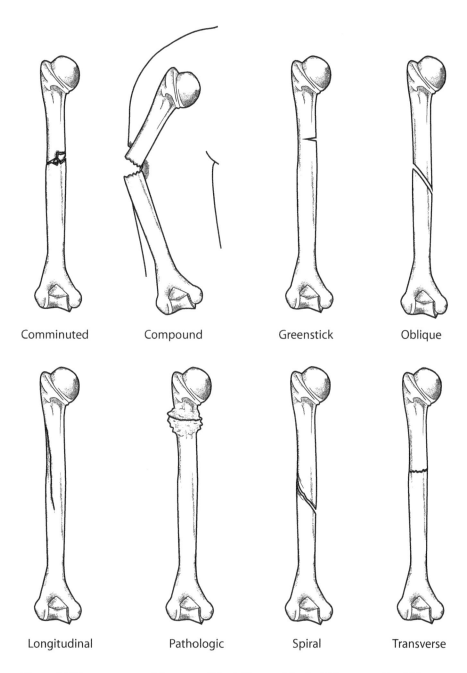

| Comminuted | Compound | Greenstick | Oblique |

| Longitudinal | Pathologic | Spiral | Transverse |

Figure 1.9 Fracture types. (Courtesy of Ruth Bowen, Medical Illustrator, Cardiff University.)

Fractures may be classified based on their type. This may, in turn, give some indication of the mechanism by which the fracture was caused. These include:

● Transverse fracture (a fracture that is perpendicular to the shaft of the bone) and is commonly encountered from direct trauma bending and snapping the bone. A greenstick fracture is a variant in young children, where the fracture is confined to the outer part of the bone due to the relative flexibility of the bone.

● Spiral fracture (a fracture that is twisted and spirals along the length of the shaft) and is commonly encountered from trauma resulting from twisting of the bone.

● Compression fracture (a fracture that compresses and reduces the volume of a bone, particularly the vertebrae).

● Comminuted fracture (a fracture that is multi-fragmented).

● Depressed fracture (a fracture that pushes the bone inwards) and is invariably associated with the skull.

● Compound fracture, where pieces of bone are exposed outside the body.

Fractures may also be classified according to the relative position on the bone. The most important, in this regard, is a metaphyseal fracture. This is a fracture where the metaphysis is sheared from the adjoining bone. Metaphyseal fractures have a high specificity or strong association for non-accidental injury in children, and this is covered in Chapter 14.

The condition of the bone may make it more vulnerable to fracture in response to lesser forces. In relation to the elderly, osteoporosis is a key example. Osteogenesis imperfecta (an inherited bone condition) and rickets (a consequence of vitamin D deficiency) are important examples in children. Fractures may also be encountered in the context of collagen disorders, such as Ehlers-Danlos disease.

Skin

1.79   The skin is an organ in its own right, having a number of vital functions including sensation, thermoregulation, water resistance and synthesis of structures, such as vitamin D. With loss of integrity of the skin, potentially fatal complications, especially with burns, can result.

Skin is broadly composed of two layers:

(1)   Epidermis. The epidermis is the outer layer and performs predominately the barrier function. It is formed of an epithelial layer, known as a stratified squamous epithelium.

The epidermis is further sub-divided into a number of layers. The epidermis has no blood vessels, and its requirements are supplied from the dermis.

(2)   Dermis. The dermis is the inner layer and houses the skin appendages, such as hair follicles and sweat glands. It is made up of connective tissues and supports the overlying epidermis.

The epidermis and dermis are separated by a thin fibrous membrane known as a basement membrane.

The effects of various types of injuries to the skin are considered in subsequent chapters; see, for instance, Chapters 7 (wounding), 8 (firearms) and 13 (burns).

Chapter 2

An introduction to clinical medicine and clinical investigation

With Simon Stockill and Heather Kolar

2.1   The first chapter provided an overview of the structural basis of the human body and how it is affected by disease. This chapter provides an overview on how clinical medicine interacts with that 'structural basis' and how clinical medicine is practised, particularly within the United Kingdom.

Regulation

2.2   The General Medical Council (GMC) is the statutory body in the United Kingdom for regulating doctors and ensuring good medical practice. The GMC has historically had the authority to register all doctors and, in doing so, to provide assurance to the public that the doctor is properly qualified at the time of registration and is bound – at penalty of losing their registration – to abide by the duties of a doctor as set out in *Good Medical Practice*.[1] At its core, the guidance sets out, with almost poetic simplicity, the standards to which a doctor must adhere. While people may often refer to the doctors' Hippocratic Oath, this ancient (and somewhat outdated) ethical code has for many years been obsolete and the vast majority of doctors have never sworn any oath, instead being bound by GMC.

Since 2012, the powers of the GMC have increased and now include the legal requirement, in addition to registration, for doctors to obtain a five-year licence to practise, renewable only after satisfactory completion of annual appraisals of practice based on *Good Medical Practice* (the latest version being published in 2013). The precise format of these annual appraisals differs between different medical specialities, as devised in conjunction with academic professional bodies such as the medical royal colleges, but their purpose is the same: to give the public confidence that a licensed doctor is keeping up to date with advances in medical practice and undertakes their duties as set out by the GMC within the standards acceptable to their peers.

2.3   In addition to the regulatory function of the GMC, another central acronym of considerable importance for the practice of modern medicine is 'NICE'. Originally

---

1   See www.gmc-uk.org/guidance/good_medical_practice.asp.

set up in 1999 as the National Institute of Clinical Excellence, with a remit to provide national guidance and advice on healthcare treatments, its role was expanded into social care in 2013 to become the National Institute for Health and Care Excellence. Its three key roles are:

(1)   Producing evidence-based guidance and advice for health, public health and social care practitioners.

(2)   Developing quality standards and performance metrics for those providing and commissioning health, public health and social care services.

(3)   Providing a range of informational services for commissioners, practitioners and managers across the spectrum of health and social care.

The value of NICE is that it provides a framework to support decision-making which takes account of best available evidence (or expert opinion). It allows the practitioner a wider perspective than their own personal professional experience, however broad or deep, can afford. It is increasingly forming the basis for easily accessible support tools to improve clinical decision-making and reduce unwarranted clinical variation and to inform patients of the evidence and their expectations of care.

While many other professional, academic, scientific research and special interest groups issue guidelines and advice to doctors, increasingly NICE has primacy by virtue of its sheer size, scope and validity of its recommendations, but also because it is enshrined in the NHS constitution. This 'bill of rights and responsibilities' for users and staff of the NHS was launched in 2010, and it sets out that medicine should not be de-personalised, advocating that doctors should follow guidance to inform good practice, and that good practice can sometimes means varying what to do to meet an individual's needs or personal goals.

2.4   No discussion of regulatory bodies which impact on medical practice in England would be complete without mention of the Care Quality Commission (CQC), with different regulatory arrangements existing in the devolved health services of Scotland, Wales and Northern Ireland. Set up in 2004 by the amalgamation of various predecessors, CQC is the independent watchdog of health and care services; it states its role is to 'makes sure hospitals, care homes, dental and GP surgeries, and all other care services in England provide people with safe, effective, compassionate and high quality care, and encourages these services to make improvements'.[2] While not directly a regulator of individual medical practice (the role of the GMC), its teams of inspectors, which include doctors as well as lay people and various other professionals, have powers to force improvements in organisations which provide care and ultimately to shut down poor-quality providers.

2.5   Together, the GMC, NICE and CQC form an important context for a doctor's practice of medicine. However, there are signs that a cultural shift may be occurring in the NHS, not least championed by leaders from within the clinical professions, of pushing the focus onto individual and team-based continual quality improvement in partnership with patients rather than continual quality assurance, regulation and compliance with rules and regulations set by authorities.

2   See www.nhs.uk/nhsengland/thenhs/healthregulators/pages/carequalitycommission.aspx.

The clinical method

2.6   The clinical method used in a clinical consultation is generally regarded as consisting of a number of steps set out below:

(1)   Taking a history (to elicit symptoms).

(2)   Performing an examination (to elicit signs).

(3)   Undertaking any necessary investigations.

(4)   Making a diagnosis.

(5)   Agreeing and implementing a management or treatment plan.

(6)   Arranging appropriate follow-up.

2.7   The first stages of the consultation provide the 'data' on which to diagnose the condition, based on the hypothetico-deductive model of reasoning. The doctor takes the patient's presenting complaint and then embarks on setting up a series of hypotheses, combining a mixture of the most likely and the most serious first, looking for recognisable patterns of symptoms and then, by a process of elimination, attempts to rule our each hypothesis in turn until a working diagnosis is reached which can be tested using further investigations. While not all clinical settings are the same and adaptations clearly made, the principles remain the same.

All this must be undertaken in a 15-minute out-patient hospital clinic consultation, a 10-minute General Practitioner consultation, or as quickly as possible in the Emergency Department.

A doctor seeing a patient present with a problem for the first time (such as a General Practitioner or Emergency Department doctor) is often faced with a set of undifferentiated symptoms which need to be differentiated into their relative importance.

The General Practitioner will usually have the benefit of holding the patient's lifelong medical notes (often summarised into an easily accessible electronic form) containing a list of the patient's medications, recent investigation results and hospital correspondences. They may also know the patient well, including a knowledge of family and social circumstances. This allows them to undertake a truncated but focused version of the clinical method, as much is already known.

The Emergency Department doctor is likewise expected to focus on the main presenting problem and to recognise when a problem needs urgent medical intervention – for example, the severe headache representing a potentially serious intra-cranial haemorrhage, or 'brain haemorrhage', as opposed to the once-weekly migraines.

A junior hospital doctor admitting a patient for a routine surgical procedure already usually knows what the problem is and therefore has a different task, but is still reliant on the clinical method.

History

2.8   The first part of the clinical method is obtaining a history. This may or may not be from the patient, dependent on, for example, their age and general condition.

The history is usually taken and presented in the medical records in a relatively standardised format:

- Presenting Complaint (often abbreviated to PC). The reason why the patient has presented – for example, chest pain. In the medical records, this will often be summarised as a few words.

- History of Presenting Complaint (HPC). An overview of how the condition presented is obtained.

- Past Medical History (PMH). A summary of the patient's prior medical history is obtained and assessed for its relevance to the current condition.

- Family History (FH). This may be of relevance in the context of inheritable conditions, predispositions and concerns.

- Drug History, including drug allergies or sensitivities (often, but not always, abbreviated to DH).

- Social History (SH). This includes areas around smoking, alcohol consumption and drug misuse as well as, increasingly, the requirements of old age and disability.

Follow-up questioning – dependent on the particular presenting complaint, or other conditions which emerge during the history, such as those relating to childhood development and immunisations, pregnancy and childbirth issues, contraception use or sexual health history – may be required.

The history taking will invariably conclude with a 'systems review' (see Chapter 1), whereby common symptoms from the various clinical systems are put to the patient in an attempt to elicit any further information that may be of use in making a diagnosis.

2.9   One of the most common histories taken relates to pain. A common acronym present in the records will be SOCRATES, although others are utilised. This refers to:

- Site: The location of pain, such as the chest.

- Onset: How did the pain start?

- Character: This will include the nature of the pain, such as a sharp intermittent pain.

- Radiation: Does it radiate or move anywhere? For example, cardiac pain will often radiate to the left upper limb.

- Association: Are there any other associated symptoms?

- Timings: How long did it last and, if intermittent, timeframes?

- Exacerbating/relieving factors: Does anything improve or worsen the pain? For example, breathing will worsen pleuritic chest pain?

- Severity: How severe is the pain?

Special situations in history taking

2.10   Although the method of history taking is standard, a number of circumstances arise where other considerations are necessary:

- Children. Specific guidelines exist for when a child can expect the same rules of confidentiality as an adult and when a medical professional is or is not duty bound to make contact with a parent, guardian or social care professional. These guidelines are based on the primacy of the interests of the child.

- The patient who does not speak English as a first language, where the use of interpreters in medical consultations can be a minefield.

- People who cannot communicate in any spoken language.

- People who offer third-party or corroborating history.

Examination

2.11   The next stage of the clinical method is the examination. There is a general order to performing and recording the clinical examination, which starts by looking from the 'end of the bed' at the whole person, and then progresses by starting physical contact with the patient's hands, neck, head and the remaining systems.
Similar to the history, there is a traditional sequence to the examination of:

- Inspection.

- Palpation.

- Percussion (a technique of tapping on a finger overlying an organ, such as lung or liver, in order to assess the density of the underlying tissue).

- Auscultation (the listening, usually aided with a stethoscope, to various noises made by liquid or gas passing through a tube, such as breath sounds in the airways, bowel sounds in the intestine, or a cardiac murmur caused by turbulent flow through a diseased heart valve).

- Movement (the ability of a joint to move in the way it should or of the nervous system to control such movements, e.g. analysis of gait).

Not all elements will be required in the examination of a single part of the body or system. Some very specific examinations exist for certain systems, such as hearing and balance, for vision and eye movements, or for joints involved in locomotion. Similar to the history, it is rare to complete a full examination, and the examination is invariably targeted. Many conditions have specific clinical examination tests that can be undertaken in more detail, depending on the general findings or symptoms in the history.

2.12   The following areas will be considered in the examination:

(1)   General observations. For example, level of consciousness, alertness and orientation in time, place and person and any obvious distress; pallor or jaundice, cyanosis (blueness of lips due to low oxygen levels) or clubbing (an

abnormality of finger nails seen in certain chronic illnesses); body temperature; lymph node swelling.

(2)   Cardio-respiratory system. Pulse, blood pressure, respiratory rate, peripheral oxygen saturation, audible respiratory noises (wheeze, stridor).

(3)   Abdominal system. This includes an assessment of organs such as the liver, spleen and kidneys, as well as the digestive tract and the abdominal aorta (the large main blood vessel carrying blood to the lower half of the body).

(4)   Genito-urinary system. This includes, in the female, a gynaecological examination and breast examination and, in the male, a genital examination as indicated.

(5)   Endocrine system. Both general and specific signs of hormone-related illnesses are assessed.

(6)   Central nervous system. This will involve testing the cranial nerves, such as smell, vision, eye movements and certain facial movements, as well as general function of the central nervous system.

(7)   Peripheral nervous system. This will include testing of the limbs for muscle tone, power, coordination, sensation and reflexes.

(8)   Musculoskeletal system. This will include assessing individual joints as well as overall functions such as gait.

Investigation

2.13   The use of specialist investigations is usually for one of four specific purposes:

(1)   Ruling out a serious illness.

(2)   Confirmation of a suspected illness.

(3)   Monitoring of treatment response, safety or recovery.

(4)   Screening.

Some examples of clinical investigations are set out below.

Haematology

2.14   These tests assess either the number, shape and size of cells or their constituents circulating in blood. These matters are overviewed in Chapter 1, but include the number of different types of white blood cells indicating an infection, or haemoglobin indicating an anaemia, or platelet and coagulation tests for bleeding disorders.

Clinical biochemistry and molecular pathology

2.15   This speciality assesses the concentration of chemical compounds in various body fluids, most commonly blood serum, plasma or urine. Common tests include

39

measuring electrolytes (sodium, potassium) and various compounds which indicate the health of the heart, kidney, liver, bone, thyroid, ovaries, and parts of the brain. Certain medically prescribed drugs also require close monitoring.

Microbiology (bacteriology, virology, mycology)

2.16   This specialism involves identification of the organisms (and how to treat them).

Immunology

2.17   This overlaps with molecular pathology and involves the specific measurement of substances, such as antibodies associated with the body's response to disease or those conditions caused by the immune system attacking the body itself (for example, rheumatoid arthritis). Immunology is discussed in Chapter 1.

Histopathology (including cytology)

2.18   The pathological specialities encompass a wide array of diagnostic and laboratory medicine specialities principally involving the identification of disease in tissue and cell samples. Cytology is a sub-speciality whereby the diagnosis is made on the structure of the cells, whereas histopathology involves more reliance on the structure of the tissue and cells. Obvious distinction can be made when considering diagnosis of breast cancer. A 'core' of tissue can be obtained whereby the diagnosis can be made on the tissue and cellular changes, whereas an 'aspirate' of tissue can be obtained whereby the cellular architecture is lost, but abnormalities of the cell structure allow a diagnosis.

Forensic pathologists form only a small part of the pathological workforce. The forensic pathologist's area of expertise is in conducting autopsy examination and the interpretation of injuries, natural disease and other associated matters arising from that. The interpretation of injuries in the living is also part of their established role.

Radiology

2.19   Radiology is the use of various imaging techniques to visualise the anatomy of parts or systems of the body. The number of radiological methods is increasing, and methods used with each technique are varyingly complex. The main techniques are set out in Box 1.

Box 1: Radiological techniques

Name of technique	Method
Projection or plain (film) radiography (or X-ray)	Involves passing X-rays (a form of ionising radiation) through a body before striking a film plate. The X-rays are varyingly absorbed by the body (e.g. they are well-absorbed by bone), so the extent of X-rays striking the film plate is variable, producing (after processing) an outline of the absorption.

Name of technique	Method
Computerised Tomography (CT) (also known as computerised axial tomography or CAT scans)	Involves X-rays but a single scan will involve many hundreds of X-ray emissions. The absorption profile of these emissions is interpreted by computer to produce three-dimensional images.
Magnetic Resonance Imaging (MRI scans)	Involves similar principles to computation as CT scanning, but is reliant on the creating of magnetic fields to produce the contrast for the image. MRIs are better for soft tissue conditions than CT scans.
Ultrasound scanning	Relies on ultrasonic sound waves being transmitted into the body, and the relative timing and intensity of the wave reflection against structures allow an image to be constructed. Three-dimensional modelling with ultrasounds is possible.
Nuclear Medicine (radionucleotide) scans Positron Emission Tomography (PET scans)	Often combined with CT or MRI scans. Used to assess either function or structural abnormalities of the body. Nuclear medicine tests differ from most other imaging modalities, in that diagnostic tests primarily show the physiological function of the system being investigated, as opposed to traditional anatomical imaging such as CT or MRI. Usually involve an injection or ingestion of radioactive substance into the body and then a scan to see how the substance has built up in the body.

Diagnosis, treatment and follow-up

2.20   The main aim of the clinical consultation is to arrive at a diagnosis or, at least, a number of working differential diagnoses which can then guide a treatment or management plan.

In agreeing a management plan (whether that involves issuing a prescription, giving advice or referral to further health services), it is generally now regarded as good practice to see the patient as a partner in that process. This involves setting treatment goals that are personalised to the patient and also agreeing a plan of how to achieve them.

After most medical interventions, whether a straightforward consultation with a GP or a complex surgical procedure, it is usual for follow-up arrangements to be made. These clearly will vary depending on the nature of the risk that is being mitigated by seeing the patient again and checking on progress or otherwise. It is not unusual in primary care settings, such as general practice or emergency rooms, for patients to be discharged (that is, the episode of care having effectively been completed) but with a 'safety net' follow-up being offered such as 'come back if you're no better in a week'. A key element of the diagnosis should always be keeping an open mind and being willing to continually review the evidence.

Medical records

2.21   As an area of medical training (at all levels), the importance of the medical record often receives less attention than it warrants. The key is understanding the purpose of the record. The medical record's primary purpose is to provide a method of communicating (usually between medical professionals) or an aide-memoire about a patient's condition to guide their safe and effective treatment and facilitate continuity of care.

Medical records can be in a number of formats but most commonly consist of either electronic notes or handwritten notes.

2.22   For a non-medically qualified lawyer, a set of medical records can seem daunting. General Practitioner's records these days are, in general, electronic, but there may be a need to review a patient's old Lloyd George records (that is, those handwritten records on small cards which were kept in a brown card docket). Lloyd George records are, in general, very sparsely written but give background information. Modern electronic GP records will usually hold a summary of complaints, an up-to-date drug history, as well as often having the correspondence scanned in. These are, in general, very readable and simply set out, making identification of the various parts of the examination easy. It is always apparent who has seen the patient and when.

2.23   The following should be obtainable from electronic records:

- The person completing the record.

- The date and time of the consultation with the entry recorded.

- Prescriptions issued.

- Further details, such as whether and when follow-up appointments were booked and tests ordered. Referrals made can also usually be seen from the record. It may be that further technical searches of the records are needed, to identify such details or more specific questions asked when asking for copies of medical records, as these details may not be immediately apparent.

- It is also usually possible to investigate whether a note has been amended, by whom and when. (It should be noted that this was key in the investigation of Dr Shipman.)

2.24   Hospital records are less straightforward. These are, in general, still handwritten, making the first challenge the interpretation of the author's handwriting. Invariably, records are also not signed by, or readily attributable to, a specific clinician. They will be separated into clinical records and nursing records, as well as therapy records produced separately. It may also be that some records are held electronically, so do not necessarily make their way into the hard copy bundle. Operation notes are a frequent contender here, but also High Dependency Unit records. To obtain a complete picture of the patient's condition at a specific time, it is necessary to consider the clinical records, nursing records as well as investigation results, which are all collated separately.

Disclosure of medical records

Patient's own medical records

2.25   The process of obtaining a copy of a client's medical records is reasonably straightforward. The Data Protection Act 1998 means that everyone has a right to apply for access to health information held about them. The health institution can levy a fee for making the records available, but this is capped at £50 for providing a full copy set of records held. The capped fee for electronic records is £10. A request for disclosure should be met within 40 days but, while institutions are encouraged to deal with requests within 21 days, often the process can take much longer. Some institutions start to count the 40 days from receipt of the disclosure fee, so the process can be sped up by sending this with the request; while, if the records are required urgently for some reason, a quick telephone call to the Trust's legal team can often work wonders to help move matters along. A signed and dated form of authority from the patient must be sent to the institution, but the form can request the disclosure to be made direct to a third party.

Deceased person's medical records

2.26   The process is more complex when trying to obtain disclosure of a deceased's medical records. Here, disclosure can be obtained direct by next of kin, a Personal Representative or executor under the Access to Health Records Act 1990. There is no restriction on the fee for disclosure that can be levied, which can rise into hundreds of pounds. The application will normally need to be made to NHS England, to whom all records are passed for storage following a death. However, it is worth checking with the last treating institution first, as some are quicker than others at passing records on to NHS England for storage.

Disclosure of medical records can often be obtained via the coroner or, in criminal proceedings, through the police, but this may not be the comprehensive set of hospital and GP records that would be obtained by a legal practitioner in, for example, a clinical negligence investigation. It is normally restricted to either the GP or hospital records, depending upon the circumstances of death. Practitioners should ensure that all relevant records are disclosed.

Medical records of a third party

2.27   Frequently, the medical records of a complainant or witness may be disclosable. For example, this may be due to mental health issues, record of inconsistent history or the record of the examination. In criminal proceedings, there are protocols for such third party material, and the police should normally obtain and provide the records. In any event, consent is needed from the patient. In some cases, public interest immunity claims from disclosure may be made (see Chapter 20).

Medical records may be censored by an institution, to remove details about third parties from a set of records prior to disclosure. This usually extends to nothing more than blanking out names or other such details with a black marker.

Consideration should also be given as to whether all relevant papers have been disclosed by an institution. Often, details of investigations conducted – Serious

Untoward Incident Reports (SUIRs) or Serious Incident reports (SIs) as they are also known – do not appear within a person's medical records, but they hold relevant data and should be requested and obtained. A copy of Trust protocols can also be relevant and, while not part of a person's medical records, are important when considering the care provided. These are often provided upon request, but applications for them – as other information that may be of interest – can also be obtained under the Freedom of Information Act 2000.

Simple rules for written medical records

2.28   The following simple rules apply for written medical records (whether electronic or handwritten):

(1)   Contemporary. The doctor should write notes at (or as near as practical to) the time of the consultation, to aid recollection. They should be chronological, and an entry in a medical record should state the date and time. If notes are added later, this should be made clear, often including the reason for the delay.

(2)   Identifiable and authenticated. The individual writing the note should be clear with their name, designation and signature.

(3)   Legible, both in terms of handwriting and also grammar and spelling.

(4)   Comprehensive and accurate. The record needs to be as comprehensive as possible in the time available and recording as many salient points as possible:

    (a)   Who is recording the note? Who was present at the consultation? When was the consultation and, if different, when was the record made?

    (b)   The significant and relevant details of the history.

    (c)   The significant and relevant details of the examination.

    (d)   Any investigations considered or requested.

    (e)   A working diagnosis.

    (f)   The management plan.

    (g)   The follow-up plans / safety net arrangements.

(5)   Alterations. Like all statements and records, alterations are common but, where present, they should be dated, timed and signed. It is best practice to ensure that the original version can still be reviewed.

(6)   Honest, factual and consistent. It should be non-judgemental about people but making clear the clinical judgements made about the evidence within the process of applying the clinical method. It also worth remembering that a doctor's recording of what has been said may be very different from a patient's recollection.

(7)   Written in black ink, as this is more readable on photocopies.

Medical shorthand

2.29 It is also useful to be aware of medical shorthand commonly used, all of which is self-explanatory, but can at first confuse. For example, PMH (past medical history) and PC (presenting complaint) have been discussed above. The health care worker will record the length of time in hours, days, weeks as 1/24, 1/7 or 1/52 respectively.

Procedures are also recorded in shorthand; for example, most people will recognise shorthand used in general language, such as MRI (magnetic resonance imaging) and US (ultrasound scan) discussed above, but others are less well known, such as EUA (examination under anaesthetic).

An important concept is the presence of $^\circ$ ('o' in superscript) before a symptom or sign. This refers to an absence of that sign or symptom. For example, $^\circ$SOB would indicate no shortness of breath.

2.30 A basic medical dictionary is always helpful to assist a non-medic in their review, explaining frequently used shorthand as well as identifying parts of the body and giving an overview of procedures. A copy of the British National Formulary (BNF) is also handy; updated normally twice a year, it lists drugs available upon prescription, their use, indications, cautions (warnings), contra-indications (when they should not be used) and dosage. An out-of-date copy can usually be picked up very cheaply and is usually acceptable in helping the non-medic in their review of a patient's drug history.

A non-exhaustive list of common medical abbreviations can be found at the end of the chapter.

Medical career structures

2.31 Qualification as a medical doctor takes place after training at one of the various medical schools in the UK or elsewhere. This may last for four, five or six years depending on the type of degree and previous qualifications of the medical student. Many medical students enter straight from school, while others have undergraduate degrees in a variety of subjects. Medical students are frequently found on the ward and make entry into the medical records. They are often termed 'student doctors' as well as medical students.

After qualification and internships, doctors undertake 'specialist' training in a number of specialities and sub-specialities. These are broadly separated into hospital-based and non-hospital-based specialities.

The non-hospital-based speciality is the archetypal 'general practitioner' or 'family medicine' specialist.

The hospital-based specialities are broadly separated into three fields: medical specialities, surgical specialities and the miscellaneous/ancillary specialities.

The miscellaneous specialities include pathology and radiology.

The medical, surgical and ancillary specialities are subdivided further into system-based specialities, such as neurology and neurosurgery respectively; and further sub-divisions into increasingly complex areas arise.

Forensic medicine

2.32   Forensic medicine is a broad and, to some extent, ill-defined speciality.

The establishment of the Faculty of Forensic and Legal Medicine within the Royal College of Physicians, which includes forensic and allied legal medicine, has led to an improved structure. This includes the work of police surgeons (care of detainees) as well as forensic psychiatry. Legal medicine incorporates medically qualified coroners and medico-legal advisers for medical defence unions.

The structure of forensic pathology in the United Kingdom is varied, although training is the same based on the Royal College of Pathologists' model through the speciality training model discussed below. In Scotland and Northern Ireland, the forensic pathologists are based in university departments or State Pathologist Departments. In England and Wales, the forensic pathologist is registered by the Home Office and their name is held on a list with other pathologists 'who have sufficient training and experience to act on behalf of coroners and police in suspicious death and homicide cases'.[3] They are widely known as 'Home Office Pathologists', although this name is not approved by the Home Office. They may work within the NHS, within a university department or be self-employed. Standards for forensic pathology are covered in Chapter 3.

Medical hierarchy

2.33   Similar to other professional specialities, there is a hierarchy in medicine based on experience and qualification:

Name	Experience
Foundation Doctor *Foundation and registrars are known as Junior Doctors*	This is a newly qualified doctor, and the period of employment lasts for two years. During the course of the first year, the doctor has only provisional registration (FY1 or F1) with the General Medical Council, prior to obtaining full registration for the second year (FY2 or F2). The F1s, F2s (and formerly SHOs) do the bulk of the 'ground work' in hospital medicine. They were previously known as Pre-Registration House Office (PRHO), and Senior House Officer (SHO) after registration.
Speciality Registrars (StR) *Foundation and registrars are known as Junior Doctors*	On completion of the foundation stage, the doctor will enter Speciality Training towards a final speciality. These are training positions for the doctor's intended final career specialisation. A number following the StR indicates the year of their training and thus their experience. They were previously known as Specialist Registrars (SPR). Doctors intending to become General Practitioners (post Foundation years) will undertake General Practitioner Training and are known typically as GP Registrars or GP speciality trainees.

3   See www.gov.uk/forensic-pathology-role-within-the-home-office.

Name	Experience
Consultant	A doctor who has competed their training programme and, in effect, can act independently / without supervision from another consultant within the NHS. On completion of their training, a Certificate of Completion of Training (CCT) is obtained. At this stage, the doctor is entitled to be appointed to consultant positions.
Speciality or staff grade doctors	These are non-training grade doctors that are not in consultant positions.
General Practitioner	A fully qualified General Practitioner will have completed their training and obtained their CCT.

Glossary

A non-exhaustive list of abbreviations

+ to +++	Increasing extent of symptoms. For example, SOB +++ would indicate marked increase in shortness of breath.
ADL	Activities of Daily Living. E.g. going to the toilet.
AF	Atrial Fibrillation. A common cardiac arrhythmia.
AFB	Acid Fast Bacillus. Its importance is in its relation to a diagnosis of tuberculosis.
AIDS	Acquired Immunodeficiency Syndrome.
ARDS	Adult Respiratory Distress Syndrome. A very severe, and often terminal, lung inflammation.
ARVC	Arrhythmogenic Right Ventricular Cardiomyopathy. An inherited cardiac condition.
ASD	Atrial Septal Defect. A hole between the left and right atrium.
ATN	Acute tubular necrosis. A common cause of acute kidney injury, particularly in the context of shock.
AV	Atrioventricular.
AVM	Arteriovenous malformation. An abnormal connection between arteries and veins that bypasses the capillary system. Important in neuropathology as a potential cause of death.
AXR	Abdominal plain film X-ray.
Ba	Barium, particularly used in radiology as a contrast medium.
bd	Twice daily (usually associated with medication), from *bis die*.
BKA	Below knee amputation.
BNF	British National Formulary.
Bpm	Beats per minute.
Ca	Carcinoma or Calcium.
CABG	Coronary artery bypass graft. An operation whereby the coronary artery blood flow to the heart muscle is replaced or bypassed by novel vessels.
CBD	Common Bile Duct.

CCF	Congestive Cardiac Failure.
CHB	Complete Heart Block.
CHD	Coronary Heart Disease or Congenital Heart Disease.
CI	Contraindications.
CNS	Central Nervous System.
COAD or COPD	Chronic Obstructive Airways or Pulmonary Disease. The combination of emphysema and bronchitis usually caused by smoking.
CPR	Cardiopulmonary Resuscitation.
CRF	Chronic Renal Failure.
CRP	C-reactive Protein. A protein produced by the liver that is a marker of a systemic inflammatory process.
CSF	Cerebrospinal Fluid.
CT	Computerised Tomography.
CVP	Central Venous Pressure. A measure of the blood pressure near the right atrium and an indicator of general function of the heart.
CVS	Cardiovascular System.
CXR	Chest X-ray.
D and V	Diarrhoea and Vomiting.
DCM	Dilated Cardiomyopathy. An cardiac condition associated with dilatation of the heart chambers.
DIC	Disseminated Intravascular Coagulation. A common terminal condition of inappropriate usage of clotting factors resulting in bleeding.
DM	Diabetes Mellitus.
DU	Duodenal Ulcer.
DVT	Deep Vein Thrombosis. Clotting in the deeper veins, especially of the leg.
ECG	Electrocardiogram. A graphical representation of the electrical signals of the heart.
ECHO	Echocardiogram. A radiological imaging scan of the cardiac function.
EEG	Electroencephalogram. A graphical representation of the electrical signals of the brain.
ENT	Ear, Nose and Throat.
FB	Foreign Body.
FBC	Full blood count.
FROM	Free Range of Movements.
GA	General Anaesthetic.
GB	Gallbladder.
GCS	Glasgow Coma Scale.
GI	Gastrointestinal.
GU	Genito-urinary.
Hb	Haemoglobin.
HAV, HBV etc	Hepatitis x virus.

HIV	Human Immunodeficiency Virus.
HOCM/HCM	Hypertrophic Obstructive Cardiomyopathy. An inherited cardiac condition.
HRT	Hormone Replacement Therapy.
Ib	In the same place, from *ibidem*.
ICP	Intra-cranial pressure.
IDA	Iron Deficiency Anaemia.
IDDM	Insulin Dependent Diabetes Mellitus.
IHD	Ischaemic Heart Disease.
IM	Intramuscular (often relating to injection).
INR	International Normalised Ratio. This relates invariably to warfarin usage and the degree of clotting in comparison to normal.
IVC	Inferior Vena Cava.
IV	Intravenous.
IVDA	Intravenous Drug Abuse.
JVP	Jugular Venous Pressure.
LBBB	Left Bundle Branch Block. A type of heart block.
LFT	Liver Function Test.
LIF	Left Iliac Fossa. A region of the abdomen.
LP	Lumbar Puncture. A method of obtaining CSF samples.
LRTI	Lower Respiratory Tract Infection.
LUQ	Left Upper Quadrant.
LVF	Left Ventricular Failure.
LVH	Left Ventricular Hypertrophy (expansion of the heart muscle).
MI or AMI	Myocardial Infarction.
mmHg	Millimetres of mercury. Relevant to pressure measurement.
MR	Modified Release.
NAD	No apparent disease.
NBM	Nil by mouth.
NG	Nasogastric (tube).
NIDDM	Non-Insulin Dependent Diabetes Mellitus.
NR	Normal Range.
NSAID	Non-Steroidal Anti-Inflammatory Drug (e.g. aspirin and ibuprofen).
OCP	Oral Contraceptive Pill.
OD	Overdose. Alternatively, once daily, from *omni die*.
PE	Pulmonary Embolism. A consequence of a DVT detaching and lodging in the pulmonary vasculature.
PEA	Pulseless Electrical Activity. A cardiac arrest associated with a functional electrical heart rhythm but no mechanical cardiac activity.
PR	*Per rectum* or by rectum.
PV	*Per vaginam* or by vagina.
RBBB	Right Bundle Branch Block. A type of heart block.

RA	Rheumatoid Arthritis.
RBC	Red Blood Cell.
RIF	Right Iliac Fossa. A region of the abdomen.
RUQ	Right Upper Quadrant.
RVF	Right Ventricular Failure.
RVH	Right Ventricular Hypertrophy (expansion of the heart muscle).
Rx	Treatment.
SC	Subcutaneous.
SE	Side Effects.
SL	Sublingual (below the tongue).
SOB	Shortness of Breath.
SOBOE	Shortness of Breath on Exercise.
SR	Slow Release,
STAT	Immediately, from *statim*.
STD or STI	Sexually Transmitted Disease or Infection.
SVC	Superior Vena Cava.
SXR	Skull X-ray.
TB	Tuberculosis.
TIA	Transient Ischaemic Attack, also known as a mini-stroke.
TOP	Termination of Pregnancy.
UC	Ulcerative Colitis. An inflammatory bowel condition.
U&E	Urea and Electrolytes (a blood test).
URTI	Upper Respiratory Tract Infection.
UTI	Urinary Tract Infection.
VF	Ventricular Fibrillation. Irregular heart rhythm associated with cardiac arrest.
VSD	Ventricular Septal Defect. A hole between the left and right ventricles.
WBC	White Blood Cell.
WCC	White Cell Count (a blood test).
ZN	Ziehl Neelsen Stain. Its importance is in its relation to a diagnosis of tuberculosis.

Chapter 3

The autopsy procedure

3.1   A number of terms are used to describe the process of examining a dead body after death, and they are used somewhat interchangeably. These include autopsy, necroscopy and post-mortem examination. The precise nature of the autopsy examination is heavily dependent on jurisdiction and the precise objective of the examination.

In general, autopsy examinations are separated into two groups: 'consented/ clinical/academic' and 'legal/forensic' autopsies. In the former, the consent is obtained from the next of kin; whereas, in the latter, the consent is, in essence, obtained from the state. The medico-legal systems relating to the investigation of death are described in Chapter 5.

Irrespective of the nature of the post-mortem examination, the basic structure is similar to all medical consultations: history, examination and ancillary investigations. In addition, particularly within the medico-legal setting, interpretation and conclusions will need to be set out within the written report.

Medico-legal autopsy

3.2   For the forensic autopsy in a suspicious death, the course of the post-mortem examination includes:

- Identification of natural disease, injuries and other features (such as those to assist with identification and timing of death).

- Retention of material for toxicological analysis and other speciality investigations (such as neuropathological examination of the brain).

- Interpretation of the combined effects of the conditions detected.

- Establishing the cause of death (and provide appropriate opinion).

Timing of a post-mortem examination

3.3   The timing of any post-mortem examination is dependent on a number of factors. It is rarely, if indeed at all, essential to work 'through the night' as was done in the past. It has been appreciated that tired personnel become inefficient personnel. If there has been a scene examination, the current practice would be, following the scene examination, which in some cases may take place over many hours or even days, for the body to be then transported back to the relevant mortuary and a post-mortem examination done the following day. The transport of the body in a suspicious case would be undertaken from the scene under supervision of the police, with transfer in an appropriate vehicle back to the mortuary.

Prior to the post-mortem examination

3.4   The pathologist's role in any post-mortem examination, whether that be a medico-legal autopsy or otherwise, needs to take into account a number of features. These include the following.

Health and safety issues, including whether or not the mortuary is equipped to a standard to allow proper investigation of the death. If there are serious concerns about this then the coroner and other relevant authorities should be notified. Circumstances where this may arise include: cases of known infectious diseases; suspected infectious diseases including high-risk cases, such as those individuals with a history of drug use; and other potential hazards, for example cyanide poisoning. This may necessitate removal to a properly equipped mortuary. Guidelines for appropriate mortuaries, particularly in suspicious cases, are provided by the Forensic Science Regulator.

There may be circumstances where the pathologist feels that further expertise is required either as a replacement for his/her own or as an additional aid. These include specialist neuropathological and paediatric post-mortem examinations. The latter is covered in Chapter 14.

As indicated above (see **3.1**), it is essential that the correct consent has been obtained and documented. This usually takes place verbally but can arise by fax, email or hard copy. It is essential that the pathologist does not undertake any examination without confidence that the relevant consent procedures are in place.

Persons present at the post-mortem examination

3.5   Persons present will vary depending on the circumstances. With a hospital-consented post-mortem examination, there is the pathologist together with an anatomical pathology technician (or mortuary technician). In addition, attending clinicians who may have been involved in the care of the patient should be encouraged to attend.

With a medico-legal autopsy, in addition to the mortuary technician, there will be a number of police personnel, including scene of crime officers who are responsible for collecting and documenting the various samples taken, as well as photographic personnel. In practice, this usually involves two or three additional personnel. The Senior Investigating Officer, together with other officers, may also be present, either within the mortuary or observing from a gallery. On rare occasions, a pathologist who is acting for the defence may be present at the initial post-mortem in order to facilitate the examination as well as the potential earlier release of the body to the relatives. In practical terms, however, this is an infrequent event, as availability of pathologists is limited.

It should be appreciated that the pathologist is part of a team in case of a suspicious death. For example, in terms of collecting samples and specimens, this is done in conjunction with the scene of crime officers.

The post-mortem examination

Identification of the body

3.6   This is of extreme importance. In a suspicious death where the pathologist has been to the scene, identification is usually on a continuity basis. Not infrequently the identity of an individual may not be known at the scene. In cases where the body has been brought separately to the mortuary from either a deceased's home or other place, continuity should have been undertaken by either the police officers or the undertakers transporting the body, and the body bag should be appropriately labelled. Despite advances in documentation, including video recording, mistakes in identification still may occur.

History and circumstances

3.7   There may be extensive documentation of a history in a particular case, including hospital records as well as radiological findings. In other cases, the history may be minimal or absent, simply indicating the place where the body has been found. Contemporaneous notes of information given at this time are essential for the purposes of the pathologist's report.

Initial examination

3.8   At a suspicious death, the body will have been placed on the mortuary dissection table with any clothing and other items that may be present. Removal of clothing and retention of any property is undertaken at this stage with the aid of the scene of crime officers and the anatomical mortuary technician. Items of clothing are usually bagged individually. Any marks of importance on clothing should be noted and photographed prior to removal – for example, gunshot residue, blood, grease marks, foreign material such as glass, bullets and indeed any other items. Any medication or other substances should likewise be documented. It may be necessary to cut clothing to avoid interference with bloodstains or other marks.

External examination of the body

3.9   This is the examination of the body for evidence of natural disease and injury. In its early part, it will include establishing demographic features, such as the height and weight of the deceased, as well as the presence of tattoos or other marks such as old scars. The height should be measured accurately as, if the body is in rigor and the feet flexed, this can add centimetres if not undertaken from the top of the head to the heel. Other features to note are hair, including length and colour. If the deceased is unidentified, careful note should be made of all potentially identifying features. Age should also be estimated and, in this, it is important to keep wide parameters.

3.10   External features or markers of natural disease should be noted. The presence of nicotine or tar staining of the fingers will suggest smoking and the multitude of diseases that are associated with it. Other features such as clubbing of the fingers (or 'drumstick' enlargement of the ends of the fingers and fingernails) can be a sign of a variety of malignancies and other serious conditions. A wide variety of natural disease processes will have features and signs that can be identified externally.

The major area of forensic pathology is the identification of injuries and other signs of an unnatural death. These areas are covered in the appropriate subsequent chapters.

Internal examination

3.11   In a suspicious case or forensic case, it is essential that the pathologist does the dissection him or herself. In routine hospital cases and non-suspicious cases, the anatomical mortuary technicians will often undertake varying degrees of dissection depending on the local practice. This can lead to problems if a 'routine' case turns out subsequently to be suspicious, as it can be very difficult to identify subtle forms of injury. Also, in this situation, it is unlikely that photographs will have been taken and hence documentation will be extremely limited. In a suspicious or forensic case, any dissection undertaken by the anatomical mortuary technician will be at the direction of the pathologist and under his or her responsibility.

3.12   This dissection commences with a vertical cut along the central part of the body to expose the chest and abdominal regions. A v-shaped incision is made from the base of the neck to behind the ears, to facilitate appropriate examination of the neck. An incision of the scalp along the posterior vertex behind the ears is made, to facilitate entry to the skull. If the incisions for the scalp and neck are joined, the tissues of the face can be dissected from the bone to examine both soft tissues and bone. The deeper tissues of the back and the limbs can be directly examined by similar incisions. The bones of the skull are removed typically by an electric saw to expose the brain, whereas shears are used to remove the front of the ribcage. The organs themselves can be removed by a variety of techniques to produce a varied number of 'blocks' of organs to be examined.

3.13   Of particular importance in the forensic case is examination of the neck structures, which is best done *in situ* (whilst the neck structures are still within the body). In a 'routine' post-mortem examination, these may have been removed by the technician with varying degrees of artefactual damage (that is, damage caused by the post-mortem procedure).

3.14   The organs are subsequently removed, either as individual organs or in groups or blocks. This allows organs to be examined in continuity with each other. The major organs are removed, weighed and sliced so that the internal appearance can be appreciated (see **3.17** below). The heart and brain are more complex to dissect. Retention of the whole brain, following appropriate fixation in formalin, is usually essential in head injury cases. Likewise, the heart may be retained in cases of sudden death.

3.15   Special dissection of various areas may also be undertaken after consideration. These should be done taking into account the history – for example, examination for bruising to the hands in a case of assault.

Samples retained

Samples for toxicology

3.16   These most commonly include blood and urine. A detailed description is given in Chapter 17. Common toxicological tests include the testing for presence of alcohol and drugs of abuse. Samples from the liver, lung, hair, stomach contents and the brain may also be taken.

Histology

3.17   Small samples of tissues are retained for histological examination. This is a process whereby tissues are preserved in formalin, which solidifies the tissue. The tissue is then put into paraffin wax, and extremely thin sections are cut, placed on glass and stained with a variety of chemicals. These are then viewed with a microscope to assess the state of natural disease or injury.

3.18   Similarly, if whole organs are to be retained for examination, they should also be placed into formalin to fix. Tissue processing into slides takes place after the organ is fixed, usually for several days or longer.
  Other samples may be taken, including the following:

- Samples for microbiology: lung swab and/or CSF (cerebrospinal fluid), in case of infection.

- Samples in cases of sudden unexpected death in infancy (which are covered in Chapter 14).

3.19   All three UK jurisdictions require that any material obtained in the course of criminal investigation and which may be relevant to the investigation should be retained until the end of criminal proceedings and completion of any appeals procedure. Due to various 'controversies' pertaining to organ retention during the 1990s and early 2000s, strict guidelines were put in place, including now the statutory regime set out in the Human Tissue Act 2004 and Human Tissue (Scotland) Act 2006, which contain appropriate exceptions for the criminal justice process. In the criminal justice context, it is essential that material be retained, including those cases where there may potentially be legal proceedings. This is because examination, for example, of the brain in detail, including histology, may reveal damage or disease which has a direct bearing on the case. This includes areas of importance such as the issue of causation. This may raise issues with the relatives, necessitating sensitive handling and explanation. Full documentation with regard to the chain of evidence is also necessary.

The report

3.20   Production of a report is essential in any post-mortem examination and, in particular, those suspicious deaths where court proceedings subsequently take place. Pathologists vary as to their documentation. Some dictate at the time of the examination. In this instance, it is essential that tapes or electronic files are retained. This is easier with electronic data, as both the original and any subsequent amendments can easily be seen. With a hand-held dictaphone the tape/cassette should be retained. Other pathologists produce handwritten notes including, at times, diagrams. The latter are generally an aide-memoire for the pathologist rather than detailed accurate diagrams/plans, which are more appropriate for presentation to a jury.

The report should cover all the essential facts, including the date and time of death of the individual as well as all the parameters noted in the external and internal examinations. Samples retained should be documented.

Of particular importance are the conclusions at the end of the report, which are intended to clarify, for legal personnel as well as others, the main findings in the case relating to death. For example, in a stabbing case, details of the fatal wound or wounds would be noted, together with any additional injuries of significance. The presence of defensive injuries would also be highlighted. Natural disease and any findings relating to toxicology would be commented on. The report in a suspicious case with potential court proceedings would need to meet the requirements of Part 33 of the Criminal Procedure Rules. In England and Wales, a critical conclusions check is undertaken by another suitably qualified forensic pathologist, which, in this jurisdiction, refers to a pathologist who is on the Home Office Register. This is a 'quality control' mechanism in particular to confirm that the conclusions drawn are justifiable from the available information.

3.21   For England and Wales, reports will also need to conform to the timetable set out in the Crime and Disorder Act 1998 (Service of Prosecution Evidence) Regulations 2005. It should be noted, however, that, in many cases, from the pathologist's point of view, this timetable is optimistic at best and unrealistic in many circumstances. This is not infrequently due to the requirements for detailed neuropathological examination. In such a case, the brain will need to be fixed for a few weeks, and various sections and additional tests will be undertaken, a process which can approach at best two to three months in length. Complex toxicology, likewise, may also take some time. In these instances, a production of a stage report may be appropriate.

In non-criminal cases or 'routine' coronial cases, there may be a standard pro forma form which may be used. This has advantages, in that all areas indicated on the form will be covered. However, there is usually not room for detailed description of any injuries as well as any necessary comments.

Standards for medico-legal post-mortem examinations

3.22   In England and Wales and in Northern Ireland, the Home Office has responsibility for forensic pathology. In addition, the General Medical Council is responsible for maintaining the medical register with the principles that govern this register.

3.23   Many jurisdictions have produced codes of practice in medico-legal post-mortem examinations. In the UK, the major code of practice for forensic pathology in England and Wales and in Northern Ireland is a joint document produced by the Home Office, the Forensic Science Regulator, the Department of Justice and the Royal College of Pathologists. This document is specifically for forensic pathologists in the above jurisdictions. The code of practice is consistent with the Recommendation R (99)3 of the Committee of Ministers of the Council of Europe (on the harmonisation of medico-legal autopsy rules) which was adopted in February 1999. The guidelines refer to cases where there is a likelihood of serious criminal charges. These include murder, manslaughter, infanticide, serious assault and serious offences involving road traffic collisions. Other jurisdictions, in particular the United States, Canada, Australia and New Zealand, have also produced documents relating to practice of forensic pathology and/or medico-legal autopsies.

3.24   The medico-legal autopsy should be distinguished to some extent from the clinical autopsy, the incidence of which has declined markedly over the last few decades owing, in the main, to consent from the next of kin as well as medical personnel less often requesting an examination. In most medico-legal jurisdictions, consent for an autopsy is not required from the relatives, although recent changes in the law, in particular in New Zealand and Australia, have given relatives the right to object. The rules are typically produced on an individual case basis.

The 'routine autopsy'

3.25   The 'routine autopsy' examination is a colloquialism for a legal post-mortem examination conducted where the police have not taken an active interest. In essence, the death is not treated as suspicious. The vast majority of post-mortem examinations conducted in the United Kingdom (and elsewhere) are of this type. The death may still have been as a result of a criminal act, and deaths associated with road traffic collisions are an important example of this. The greatest difference between the 'routine autopsy' and the 'forensic autopsy' in England and Wales is that the majority of 'routine autopsies' are conducted by general histopathologists without speciality training in forensic pathology. It should be noted that the percentage of 'routine' coronial post-mortem examinations is considerably higher in England and Wales than in other similar jurisdictions, such as Canada, Northern Ireland, Australia and New Zealand. Detailed review of circumstances as well as medical history can contribute to a reduction in the post-mortem rate. The development of a 'medical examiner system' is currently under way, albeit slowly.

3.26   Photography, toxicology and tissue sampling are variable, with no retention in many cases. In other jurisdictions, a specially trained forensic pathologist will conduct these examinations. There is a professional document produced by the Royal College of Pathologists regarding standards in post-mortem examinations that appear not to be suspicious. However, the standards of these post-mortems is variable. This is highlighted in the study on the coroner's autopsy conducted by the National Confidential Enquiry into Patient Outcome and Death (see the summary and conclusions at page 4 of the report, available at www.ncepod.org.uk/2006.htm).

Autopsy radiology

3.27 Radiology has always been an important adjunct to autopsy pathology. The key examples are in the post-mortem examination of ballistic and child deaths. A wide array of techniques, from conventional (plain film) radiology to Computed Tomography (CT and MRI) scanning, are utilised.

As well as providing useful information to the forensic pathologist at the time of the post-mortem examination, they also provide an additional record for review at a later date. There is considerable interest in the potential role of radiological investigation as a replacement for the routine coronial autopsy. This area is in its infancy in the United Kingdom but, in due course, it may be that radiological investigation could replace conventional routine coronial autopsy as a first-line modality technique. However, it will not replace all routine coronial autopsies and there are significant cost implications.

Scene examination

3.28 Examination of the scene by the forensic pathologist remains an activity expected of the forensic pathologist, although, more recently, the importance of such examinations has reduced. The advent of essentially instantaneous photography has meant that appreciation of the scene environment can be made without necessarily visiting the scene. Detailed photographic recording of the scene is essential, usually by videoing as well as still photography. The expansion of the role of other crime scene experts has correctly removed some historic functions of forensic pathologists. The increasing importance of DNA evidence, and the resultant prospect of DNA contamination by excess unnecessary personnel, has also reduced the number of scene examinations undertaken.

The scene examination may be important in respect of obtaining temperature measurements for the assessment of time of death. However, with the inherent problems in this area, it has limited value (see further Chapter 4). Subtle forms of homicide, such as suffocation and external pressure to the neck, may also benefit from scene attendance by the pathologist. Intimate samples (swabs of the genitalia) may be necessary at the scene, depending on the circumstances.

Subsequent scene reconstruction may aid, for example, in differentiating a fall from an assault. Scene reconstruction may also be valuable in road traffic cases.

The second autopsy

3.29 The 'second autopsy' is an autopsy examination undertaken invariably at the request of solicitors acting on behalf of an alleged offender (or, in England and Wales, for the coroner) to facilitate release of the body of a victim of homicide where no charges have been brought against any offender.

The process may take one of two forms: a formal physical examination; or a paper review of the original autopsy material, including photographs.

The former, which includes examination of the body, has the advantage that the second pathologist can at least confirm to the court that he has examined the body, which seems to hold greater sway with courts than the latter approach. In spite of that, viewpoint examination is often hampered by decomposition, which can obscure the injuries to such an extent that the original post-mortem photographs are the superior means of examination. From the author's perspective, additional injury of significance is rarely identified externally, albeit the occasional additional stab wound may be appreciated in stabbing deaths where the number of wounds is high. Internally the major organs are usually too decomposed to make additional comment. The most frequent additional finding (or correction) is of incorrect numbering of injuries associated with sequentially numbered structures (for example, ribs). In the majority of second autopsies, no additional useful finding are identified, although the interpretation of the findings between pathologists may differ.

The original pathologist should be invited to attend, and it is beneficial for the original pathologist to do so. However, given the diaries of most forensic pathologists and the disparate locations of mortuaries, attendance cannot be guaranteed.

On occasion, a second pathologist may consider additional special dissection in addition to that undertaken at the initial examination (for example, to further identify deep bruising).

3.30 Each individual pathologist will have their own wish list of material required for a second post-mortem examination. This will usually include a case summary (often the police's MG/5 documentation) and a set of the post-mortem photographs. The attendance of an officer with some understanding of the case is imperative to assist the pathologist.

Unfortunately, there remains a misapprehension amongst some police officers that the pathologist conducting a second post-mortem examination is not an independent witness to the court but rather a witness for solicitors, and this can lead to difficulties. However, in the majority of cases, the police are helpful to the second pathologist.

3.31 The attendance of solicitors at the second post-mortem is variable and up to personal choice. From the author's experience, the most useful aspect is that the solicitor becomes aware of the extent of the injuries: that they are, in effect, as bad as suggested by the police.

3.32 The timetable for production of the second pathologist's report is variable. In some cases, the report can be produced relatively rapidly with the original pathologist's draft post-examination but, in the majority of cases, the final report of the original pathologist and the ancillary investigations will need to be reviewed. Supplemental reports may be necessary at various stages of the legal proceedings.

Exhumations

3.33 By definition, an exhumation is the retrieval of a previously buried body in order for a further examination to be undertaken. A previous post-mortem examination may have taken place or, alternatively, no such examination may have been undertaken. In addition, features such as embalming may be present. Legal consent for exhumation is complex and varies with jurisdiction: in England and Wales and in Northern Ireland, ministerial or ecclesiastical authorisation is required, depending on the place of burial; in Scotland, a sheriff's warrant is required. It is essential that this consent is obtained and that the assistance of the cemetery authorities is obtained in terms of identifying the relevant location. The presence and assistance of a funeral director is also desirable. Whilst, traditionally, such examinations have taken place at dawn, in the author's experience this can attract unjustifiable publicity, and it may be easier for the exhumation to take place during normal working hours. There is no legal requirement for such a timing.

3.34   In some cases of exhumation, the issue of poisoning may arise. In these cases, it is essential to ask the opinion of a toxicologist with regard to sampling, which may include surrounding soil as well as other coffin contents. The attendance of a toxicologist may be advisable in cases of suspected poisoning.

As with all procedures, it is essential that detailed photographic recording is undertaken, at all stages from prior to retrieval of the coffin to its removal to the mortuary for further examination.

In most exhumation cases, radiology is essential for exclusion (or otherwise) of bony or other trauma. This may reveal old or recent fractures.

3.35   There is considerable variability in the state of a body, depending on the burial environment. The body may be surprisingly well preserved and provide much information; whilst, in other circumstances, disintegration may be almost complete.

Further reading material

General textbooks

- Saukko, P. & Knight, B. *Knight's Forensic Pathology* (2004, 3rd Edition)

Professional working documents

- 'Good medical practice'. London. General Medical Council. 2006

- 'Standards for coroner's pathologists in post-mortem examinations that appear not to be suspicious'. The Royal College of Pathologists. Feb 2014

- Brinkmann, B., Mangin, P. 'Recommendation R (99)3. The harmonisation of medico-legal autopsy rules and its explanatory memorandum' *Forensic Science International* (Special Issue) 2000; 111(issues 1–3): 5–29

- 'Code of Practice and performance standards for Forensic Pathology in England, Wales and Northern Ireland'. Home Office, the Forensic Science Regulator, Department of Justice and the Royal College of Pathologists. 2012

- 'RCR/RCPath – Statement on standards for medico-legal post-mortem cross section imaging in adults'. The Royal College of Pathologists. 2012

Articles in journals

- Aghayev, E., Christe, A., Sonnenschein, M., Kyen, K., Jackowski, C., Thali, M.J., Dirnhofer, R, Vock, P. 'Post mortem imaging of blunt chest trauma using CT and MRI; comparison with autopsy' *Journal of thoracic imaging*; 23(1): 20-7. 2008

- Basso, C., Burke, M., Fornes, P., Gallagher, P.J., De Gouveia, R.H., Sheppard, M., Thiene, G., Vand Der Wal, A. 'Guidelines for autopsy investigation of sudden cardiac death' *Association for European cardiovascular pathology virchows archiv*; 452(1): 11-8. 2008

- Biggs, M.J., Brown, L.J., Furness, P.N. 'Online survey of current autopsy practice' *Journal of clinical pathology*; 62(6): 525–9. 2009

- Bolliger, S.A., Thali, M.J., Ross, S., Buck, U., Naether, S., Vock, P. 'Virtual autopsy using imaging; bridging radiological and forensic sciences. A review of the virtopsy and similar projects' *European radiology*; 18(2): 273–82. 2008

- Hudson, M.L., Allan, C.A., Bedford, K.R., Buckleton, J.S. Stuart, K. 'The impact of Maori cultural values on forensic science practice in New Zealand' *Journal of Forensic Sciences*; 53(2): 380–3. 2008

- Lynch, M.J., Woodford, N.W. 'Objections to medico-legal autopsy – recent developments in case law' *Journal of Law and Medicine*; 14(4): 463–8. 2007

- Melinek, J., MD, Thomas, L.C., MD, Oliver, W.R., MD, MS, MPA, Schumunk, G.A., MD, Weedn, V.W., MD, JD and the National Association of Medical Examiners Ad Hoc Committee on Medical Examiner Independence. *National Association of Medical Examiners Position Paper: Medical Examiner, Coroner and Forensic Pathologist Independence*

- Molina, D.K., Dimaio, V.J. 'The sensitivity of computed tomography (CT) scans in detecting trauma; are CT scans reliable enough for courtroom testimony?' *Journal of trauma – injury infection and critical care*; 65(5): 1206–7. 2008

- Pollanen, M.S. 'Deciding the cause of death after autopsy – revisited' *Journal of Clinical Forensic Medicine* 12(2005); 113–121

- Ruder, T.D., Hatch, G.M., Thali, M.J., Fischer, N. 'One small scan for radiology, one giant leap for forensic medicine – post mortem imaging replaces forensic autopsy in a case of traumatic aortic laceration' *Legal Medicine*; 13(1): 41–3. 2011

- Rutty, G.N., Morgan, B., O'Donnell, C., Lefth, P.M., Thali, M. 'Forensic institutes across the world place CT or MRI scanners or both into their mortuaries' *Journal of trauma – injury, infection and critical care*; 65(2): 493–4. 2008

- Weber, M.A., Ashworth, M.T., Risdon, R.A., Hartsley, J.C., Malone, M., Sebire, N.J. 'The role of post mortem investigation in determining the cause of death in sudden unexpected death in infancy' *Archives of disease in childhood*; 93(12): 1048–53. 2008

Chapter 4

Medical aspects of death

4.1 For the purpose of this chapter, death essentially relates to the irreversible failure of the cardiovascular system.

Without a functioning heart and competent vasculature, the transport of oxygen (and other nutrients) to target organs is stopped resulting in tissue death. Heart function is autonomous. It cannot be deliberately sped up or slowed down by thought, unlike the motor control of our limbs, for example. This is ultimately controlled by the brainstem. An intact cardiovascular system can continue to be active after respiration has discontinued and/or replaced by a machine; but, in normal circumstances, the state of the cardiovascular system provides the most useful distinction between life and death.

The irrecoverable death of the brain, which may be delayed for some minutes following cessation of the circulation, is another measure considered. However, this is complicated by the concept of 'brain-stem death' in relation to artificial survival. This is considered in paragraph **9.30** onwards.

Ultimately, the medical doctor (or appropriate medical ancillary practitioner), in pronouncing life extinct, will assess not only the cessation of the cardiovascular system, but also the cessation of respiratory and cerebral functioning. Each health care system has its own protocols. Cessation of respiratory function may include no respiratory effort for more than a minute, and cessation of cerebral function may include unreactive dilated pupils and no response to a painful stimulus.

Despite protocols, there are exceptionally rare modern prophetical stories of individuals 'waking up' after being declared dead.

The main function of the doctor called to an unexplained death is to decide that death has taken place and to pronounce life extinct; other considerations must be secondary.

This decision may be difficult in the event of grossly diminished cardiac output – as may occur in hypothermia or in drug-induced central nervous system depression. This is even more complex when the two are combined, which is a relatively common occurrence. The scene of an unexplained death (and equally in a more acute medical setting for paramedics) is rarely an ideal environment for medical assessment.

- Death essentially relates to the irreversible failure of the cardiovascular system.

The early post-mortem changes

4.2 In the immediate period after death, typically the first few days, the body will undergo several characteristic changes that occur irrespective of the bodily or environmental conditions. However, it is worth noting that the timeframe and extent of these initial post-mortem changes can be affected by the local environment or the individual themselves.

The classical early changes are rigor mortis, hypostasis and the cooling of the body.

Rigor mortis

4.3   Rigor mortis is the most-recognised post-mortem phenomenon and is the source of the colloquialism 'stiff' in reference to the dead body. It is the result of a complex enzymatic process.

As the enzymatic processes of the body fail, so too does the elimination of waste products and, biochemically, this is associated with changes to the actomyosin (a protein filament combination) involved in musculature contracture; clinically, the resultant stiffening of the muscle fibres presents as a fixation of the joints, which can be broken down only by force.

The detailed biochemistry behind rigor mortis falls outside the scope of this text. Simply keeping the muscle fibres in their 'flaccid' rest state requires energy and, at this stage, the actin and myosin are separate. In life, the energy is acquired predominately from aerobic (oxygen) derived means, with a lesser component from anaerobic means (stores of energy in the form of glycogen).

After death, aerobic means are terminated, but the glycogen stores allow the energy within to be utilised to maintain the separate 'flaccid' state. In the initial post-mortem period the body is 'flaccid'. As the stores of glycogen reduce and, in turn, adenosine triphosphate (the substance responsible for intracellular transfer of energy) reduces, the actin and myosin combine to form 'rigid' actomyosin. The stiffening of the muscles commences when the level of this substance is reduced to 85% of the normal, but the process is not appreciated clinically until levels are significantly more reduced. With increasing post-mortem interval, decomposition damages the structure of the muscle cells and the muscle once again is flaccid.

The onset of rigor mortis is ultimately a chemical reaction and thus can be influenced by 'external' conditions.

4.4   In warm and hot environments, the chemical reaction is encouraged and thus rigor mortis appears more rapidly and (also due to more rapid autolysis) disappears more rapidly. In very cold environments, the onset of rigor mortis can be stopped and only begins to appear once the body has been brought into a warm environment. Situations where the quantities of glycogen prior to death are reduced, such as following vigorous exercise, may result in a more rapid onset of rigor mortis.

All muscle fibres are uniformly affected, but stiffening will be demonstrable earliest in those bundles of smallest mass.

The bundles with the smallest mass are typically around the face and the finger joints. The larger muscle groups, such as those of the lower limbs, only become apparent towards the end of the onset of rigor. Typically, the early stages in a temperate environment are noticeable after an hour or so to the facial region, but rigor mortis is typically noticeable in the limbs after three to six hours and is usually fully established throughout the body in eight to 18 hours. Clearly, these timeframes are very variable; but, in general, they may be accelerated in the summer and retarded in the winter.

The ability to appreciate rigor mortis is dependent on the muscle bulk. Children and emaciated adults with more limited muscle bulk may not develop appreciable rigor mortis at all.

4.5   The muscles will remain in rigor until the processes of degeneration and putrefaction cause secondary laxity.

Rigor will disappear in much the same anatomical order as it became established but, again, the process is variable. The body is generally free of rigor some two to three days after death, but it may persist for a longer period.

Rigor mortis may be 'broken' whilst established by applying reasonably pressure to the joint (for example, extending or flexing it). Once rigor is broken, it will not re-establish.

Not all 'stiffening' of the body is due to rigor mortis. The invariable examples relate to cold/frozen body and the heat-altered body. Most individuals will have encountered these features, either on removing meat from a freezer or the toughness of over-cooked meat.

Cadaveric spasm (or rigidity) is the instantaneous development of rigor-like stiffening after death. Cadaveric spasm is an extremely rare occurrence, and is said to involve deaths arising in 'high emotional tension' and will often involve the hands, which may be found grasping some object. The mechanism is not understood but is more complex than the enzymatic mechanisms involving typical rigor mortis.

- Rigor mortis, or the stiffening of the body after death, is as the result of complex enzymatic chemical reaction.

- It will typically appear within a few hours after death before being lost by decomposition over a few days.

- As with any chemical reaction, its onset and disappearance can be affected by 'external factors', the most common being temperature.

- Not all stiffening after death is due to rigor mortis, and instantaneous rigidity after death is encountered.

Hypostasis

4.6   Hypostasis is the pooling of blood after death to discolour the skin.

During life, blood is moved around by the body by the force generated by the contractions of the heart. After death, the only force acting on the contents of the vasculature is gravity. Under the effect of gravity combined with reduction in the muscular tone of the vessels, the blood pools in a gravitational distribution and becomes evident on the skin, contrasting with the paler bloodless superior areas. This is known as hypostasis.

Coarser, very dark spots of haemorrhage may arise in areas of intense hypostasis, and their frequency increases as the post-mortem interval progresses.

Areas of pallor are also encountered in the hypostasis as sustained pressure prevents pooling of the blood, and it is common to find that generalised lividity of the back is notably absent from the buttocks and shoulder blades which take the main weight of the recumbent body.

Similar changes are also evident in the internal organs, most noticeably the lungs, where they have been mistaken in the past for bleeding and pneumonia.

A body that is vertical after death (for example, following hanging) will have hypostasis predominant in the distal parts of the lower limbs and, to a lesser extent, in the upper limbs.

In the young, very old, anaemic and those who have suffered significant blood loss prior to death, hypostasis may be unappreciable or even absent. The difficulty in appreciating it increases with darker skin colouration.

The timing of its appearance shows significant variance in the published literature, confirming its uselessness as an indicator of time of death.

In general, it is usually first appreciated around 30 minutes to two hours after death, although it may appear more rapidly. It is suggested that hypostasis can occur in life if an individual is suffering from significant cardiac failure reducing the efficiency of cardiac contractions. There is no significant supportive evidence. Hypostasis is generally at its maximum after 6 to 12 hours.

4.7   In the initial period, the hypostasis is 'mobile' before becoming 'fixed'.

In the early period, the blood remains 'mobile' or unfixed, and changing the body position will allow a new pattern of hypostasis to develop, although remnants of the original hypostasis will often remain, especially if the time since death is more prolonged.

As the post-mortem interval increases, the viscosity of the blood increases and the hypostasis becomes 'fixed', and changing the position of the body will not change the positioning on the body. This probably represents hypostasis' main forensic significance, in establishing the position of the body after death and, particularly, in demonstrating that it has been moved. The onset of fixation of hypostasis is exceptionally variable, but typically arises after around 24 hours.

The colour of hypostasis is typically a reddish to reddish-blue hue, but the colour is variable and affected by a number of factors. No reliance should be placed on the blueness of the hypostasis as an indicator of the mode of death. Hypostasis may be relatively bright red in colour, and this is a common occurrence in bodies that have died or been stored in cold environments (e.g. a mortuary refrigerator); this is because, in cold environments, re-oxygenation of the haemoglobin arises passively. The most well-known change in colouration of hypostasis is poisoning by carbon monoxide, where a cherry-pink colour is usually obvious in a good light. The change is often most striking when the musculature is observed later in the course of the post-mortem examination. Chemicals and drugs which convert the haemoglobin of the blood into methaemoglobin will produce hypostasis of a dark-brown hue; the same result follows poisoning by some aromatic hydrocarbons.

Problem areas: differentiation of hypostasis and bruising, and hypostasis and so-called asphyxial signs

4.8   Two areas that warrant further consideration are the differentiation between hypostasis and bruising, and hypostasis and so-called asphyxial signs. The first of these, bruising, is a relatively simple matter. Apart from the fact that bruises are commonly localised, they are, by definition, the result of bleeding into the tissues as opposed to stagnation of blood in the vessels. Incision into the skin can easily differentiate between the two, the exception being the coarse haemorrhages that arise in intense hypostasis (discussed above) which arise due to extravasation of blood out of the vasculature. The appearance beneath the skin on incision is similar to superficial areas of bruising. In such cases, the surrounding intense hypostasis and their coarse characteristic bruising assist in their recognition.

The latter area, again, is usually straightforward; but, under certain circumstances, distinguishing asphyxial changes from hypostasis can be difficult (see further **11.31**).

- Hypostasis is the pooling of blood under the effects of gravity after death. This is most prominent over the skin surface but is encountered in the internal organs.

- The colour of hypostasis is typically a reddish to reddish-blue hue, but the colour is variable and affected by a number of factors.

- In the initial period, the hypostasis is 'mobile' before becoming 'fixed'.

- Hypostasis can give an indication of the body position after death.

- It has no use in formal time of death calculation.

Body cooling

4.9   The human body in life is maintained at a temperature in the order of 37°C, although there are variances between individuals, time of the day, physical activity, illness etc.

After death, the means by which the temperature is maintained cease (although not necessarily immediately) and the body cools. It is on this principle that time of death estimation using body temperatures is based, and this area is further discussed below.

Time of death in the early post-mortem period

4.10   Time of death 'calculations' have adopted a mythical accuracy amongst the general public, media and even some courts. In reality, the results of the estimation of the post-mortem time interval have very limited use in the courts.

It may have some use in the early investigative period – for example to assist with targeting of a period of time to review for CCTV footage.

The number of potential methods suggested to estimate the post-mortem interval is vast – which is, in effect, a testament to the inherent inaccuracy and unreliability in all methodologies.

Body cooling

4.11   The classic method of estimating time of death involves the utilisation of the body's cooling.

Theoretically, this temperature falls according to a sigmoid curve, and this is demonstrated in Figure 4.1. In reality, although the body cools, it does *not* cool like an experimental cylinder to which the laws of physics can be applied without reservation. A large number of variables are involved which, in terms of practicality, reduce the accuracy of estimates substantially.

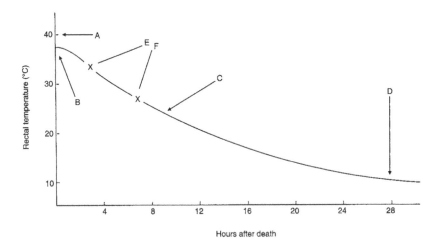

Figure 4.1 The uncertainties in the post-mortem body temperature.
A = The deceased's temperature in life.
B = The isothermic stage, greatly dependent upon the body's insulation.
C = The rate of fall which is influenced by the environmental conditions.
D = The room temperature.
In the event, two readings taken at E and F and extrapolated to 37°C will give as accurate a result as is likely to be obtained.

Some of the factors that can influence the rate of cooling include:

(1)   **The body temperature at the time of death**. Conditions that tend to raise the temperature at the time of death – for example, infection or cerebral haemorrhage – will result in an artificially short estimate of the post-mortem interval based on temperature recordings; hypothermic states will produce the opposite effect.

(2)   **Clothing**. The rate of fall in body temperature of a reasonably clothed body is approximately two-thirds that of a naked one.

(3)   **Body insulation**. A fat body is better insulated against heat loss compared with a lean one, while those with a large surface area in relation to the body weight will cool faster than those of more massive physique; thus, children and the aged will always cool faster than well-nourished adults.

(4)   **Convection currents**. A body will cool faster in moving air than one in a closed environment. The effect may be considerable.

(5)   The **environmental temperature** is a variable that will always affect the rate of cooling, but the time taken for the body to reach either a high or a low ambient temperature is the same, because the rate of fall will be correspondingly slow or fast.

(6)   The **isothermic** or **plateau** stage. These factors will not only influence the rate of cooling but will also dictate the length of time taken for the body to *start* to cool (point B in Figure 4.1). The shorter the actual time since death, the greater the mathematical significance of this unknown variable.

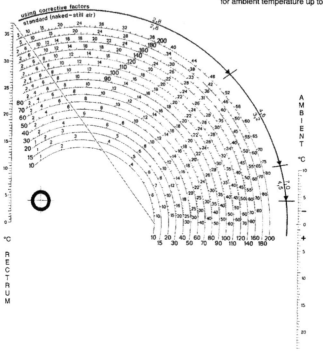

TEMPERATURE TIME OF DEATH

RELATING NOMOGRAM

for ambient temperature up to 23 °C

PERMISSIBLE VARIATION OF 95 % (±h)

The nomogram expresses the death-time (t) by:

$$\frac{^T rectum - {^T} ambient}{37.2 - {^T} ambient} = 1.25 \exp(B \times t) - .25 \exp(5 \times B \times t); B = -1,2815 (kg^{-.625}) + .0284$$

The nomogram is related to the chosen standard i.e. naked body extended lying in still air. Cooling conditions differing from the chosen standard may be proportionally adjusted by corrective factors of the real body weight, giving the corrected body weight by which the death-time is to be read off. Factors above 1.0 may correct thermal isolation conditions and factors below 1.0 may correct conditions accelerating the heat loss of a body.

HOW TO READ OFF THE TIME OF DEATH
1. Connect the points of the scales by a straight line according to the rectal and the ambient temperature. It crosses the diagonal of the nomogram at a special point. 2. Draw a second straight line going through the center of the circle, below left of nomogram, and the intersection of the first line and the diagonal. The second line crosses the semi-circles which represent the real or the corrected body weights. At the intersection of the semi-circle of the body weight the time of death can be read off. The second line touches a segment of the outermost semi-circle. Here the permissible variation of 95% can be seen.
Example: Rectal temperature 26.4°C; ambient temperature 12°C; body weight 90 kg. Result: Time of death 16 ± 2.8h.
Statement: The death occurred within 13.2 and 18.8 (13 and 19) hours before the time of measurement (with a reliability of 95%).
Note: Use the evaluated mean ambient temperature of the period in question (e.g. contact the weather station).
Recommendation: If the values of the mean ambient temperature and/or the body weight (see 'corrective factors') are called in question, repeat the procedure with other values which might be possible. The possibly wider range of death-time can be seen in this way.

REQUIREMENTS FOR USING THE METHOD
–   no strong radiation (e.g. sun, heater, cooling system)
–   no strong fever or general hypothermia
–   no uncertain severe changes of the cooling conditions during the period between the time of death and examination (e.g. the place of death must be the same as where the body was found).

EMPIRIC CORRECTIVE FACTORS OF THE BODY WEIGHT FOR BODIES OF AVERAGE WEIGHT (REFERENCE: 70 KG)

dry clothing/covering	in air	Corrective Factor	wet through clothing/covering wet body surface	in air	in water
		0.35	naked		flowing
		0.5	naked		still
		0.7	naked	moving	
		0.7	1-2 thin layers	moving	
naked	moving	0.75			
1-2 thin layers	moving	0.9	2 or more thicker	moving	
naked	still	1.0			
1-2 thin layers	still	1.1	2 thicker layers	still	
2-3 thin layers		1.2	more than 2 thicker	still	
1-2 thicker layers	moving or	1.2	layers		
3-4 thin layers	still	1.3			
more thin/thicker	without	1.4			
layers	influence	...			
thick bedspread		1.8			
		...			
+ clothing combined		2.4			
		2.8			

Note: For the selection of corrective factor (c.f.) of any case, only the clothing or covering of the lower trunk is relevant! Insulating bases (e.g. thick foam upholstered base) slow down the cooling even of naked bodies up to c.f. of 1.3; bases which accelerate the cooling (e.g. concrete base of a cellar) require c.f. round .75 for naked bodies or reduce c.f. for clothing by 0.1 to 0.2 units.

Provided the corrective factor chosen is 1.4 or above the following table should be consulted if the real body weight differs greatly from the reference of 70 kg since there is a

DEPENDENCE OF THE CORRECTIVE FACTORS OF THE BODY WEIGHT UNDER STRONGER INSULATION CONDITIONS

real body weight [kg]

4	6	8	10	20	30	40	50	60	70	80	90	100	110	120	130	140	150
									1.3								
1.6	1.6	1.6	1.6	1.5					1.4					1.3	1.2	1.2	1.2
2.1	2.1	2.0	2.0	1.9	1.8				1.6				1.4	1.4	1.4	1.3	1.3
2.7	2.7	2.6	2.5	2.3	2.2	2.1	2.0		1.8			1.6	1.6	1.6	1.5	1.4	1.4
3.5	3.4	3.3	3.2	2.8	2.6	2.4	2.3		2.0		1.8	1.8	1.7	1.6	1.6	1.5	1.5
4.5	4.3	4.1	3.9	3.4	3.0	2.8	2.6	2.4	2.2	2.1	2.0	1.9	1.8	1.7	1.7	1.6	1.6
5.7	5.3	5.0	4.8	4.0	3.5	3.2	2.9	2.7	2.4	2.3	2.2	2.1	1.9	1.9	1.8	1.7	1.6
7.1	6.6	6.2	5.8	4.7	4.0	3.6	3.2	2.9	2.6	2.5	2.3	2.2	2.1	2.0	1.9	1.8	1.7
8.8	8.1	7.5	7.0	5.5	4.6	3.9	3.5	3.2	2.8	2.7	2.5	2.3	2.2	2.0	1.9	1.8	1.7

Example: Real body weight 20 kg. Chosen corrective factor (reference 70 kg) 1.6. Use a corrective factor of 1.9 resulting in a corrected body weight of 38 (40) kg.

REFERENCES: MARSHALL T K, HOARE F E (1962): Estimating the time of the death. J Forensic Sci 7: 56-81; 189-210; 211-221. HENSSGE C (1988): Death time estimation in case work, I. The rectal temperature time of death nomogram. Forensic Sci Int 38: 209-236. HENSSGE C (1992): Rectal temperature time of death nomogram: Dependence of corrective factors on the body weight under stronger thermic insulation conditions. Forensic Sci Intern 54: 51-66. ALBRECHT A et al (1990): On the application of the rectal temperature time of death nomogram at the scene of death. (German, summary in English). Z Rechtsmed 103: 257-278.

Figure 4.2 Henssge's time of death nomogram (by kind permission of the author).

4.12   The most well-recognised method of utilising body temperatures is the work of Henssge. The nomogram based on his formula was the mainstay of estimation, only being recently replaced with various widely available electronic 'apps'. The nomogram is reproduced in Figure 4.2 (but caution should be employed, as general printing and photocopying results in slight alterations that can have a significant effect on the estimate).

Henssge's formula takes into account the body weight as well as introducing empirical 'corrective factors' such as clothing, location of body and air movement. The nomogram results in a value which is the estimate of post-mortem interval with a 95% confidence interval that the death arose within 2.8 hours (at its most accurate) of it.

In reality, what is provided is a post-mortem interval range varying from 5.6 hours to 14 hours in which 95% of deaths would have arisen. In essence 5% (or 1 in 20) of deaths would have occurred outside the predicted timeframe.

A major problem with body temperatures is the means by which measurement is taken. The usual means of obtaining the core temperature is by positioning a mercury thermometer in the rectum. As can be imagined, this results in the prospect of causing localised damage, and the poorly lit and constrained scene is not an ideal location for such an examination.

The precise correlation or reliability of other sites, such as tympanic and nasal measurements, is not fully known.

As such, given the limited usefulness of post-mortem interval estimates, core temperature measurement should not be routinely undertaken.

Gastric emptying

4.13   Gastric emptying has also been suggested as a method to estimate the time of death.

The principle of the use of gastric contents and their emptying was that the contents spent a predictable time in the stomach and underwent uniform changes under the action of gastric acids. This has been disproved, and these methods have no use in the estimation of post-mortem interval. This does not mean that gastric contents in themselves are without use, as specialist analysis can be undertaken to identify the precise contents of the 'last meal', which can assist in providing confirmation that the death was proximate to that meal.

Vitreous humour

4.14   The vitreous humour is the gel-like liquid that is present within the eye globe; as well as being useful for toxicological examination, it is suggested as a means to estimate the post-mortem interval.

The basis is that contents of the globe are more protected and, as a result, the post-mortem changes are more predictable/uniform. In reality, the majority of mechanisms relate to the leaching out of potassium from within to the outside of the cells secondary to decomposition. It is the increase in potassium level that is the marker of the post-mortem interval. A wide variety of extremely complex 'formulae' are available, giving varied estimates and thus suggesting at this point that they are of limited value to the court.

Entomology

4.15   Entomology can be used, to some extent, to provide an estimate of post-mortem interval. Entomology is the study of insects, and the forensic use of entomological sciences is well-established. The scope of entomology falls outside this textbook, but the basis is that the unprotected body will be invaded by a variety of species of flies and other insects. Different species will invade at different points after death and, in due course, they will lay eggs that go through various stages of development upon the body. This course is relatively predictable, although subject to modification, particularly environmental temperature, and thus a prediction of the post-mortem interval can be made, albeit usually in terms of months, seasons and years. Mycology, the study of fungal growth, may also be utilised.

Rule of thumb

4.16 The rule of thumb approach suggested by Knight (see Further reading material) provides a rapid 'spot check' on the post-mortem interval. In a way, this is a very useful method of providing rapid information to investigators, but it is of no value to the courts and relies on the presence or absence of rigor mortis and generalised warmth to the body:

- < 3 hours: body warm and flaccid.

- 3 to 8 hours: body warm and stiff.

- 8 to 36 hours: body cold and stiff.

- > 36 hours: body cold and flaccid.

- Time of death 'calculations' have very limited accuracy, and so the results of the estimation of the post-mortem time interval have limited use in the courts.

- The most well-recognised method of utilising body temperatures is through the work of Henssge and his nomogram. This still has large errors.

- Other methods are suggested, but they invariably have their own (larger) errors.

- A 'rule of thumb' approach is described.

Changes associated with increasing post-mortem interval

4.17 Beyond three days or so, decomposition becomes increasingly pronounced. Decomposition may undergo different forms dependent on local environments, and several forms may occur within the same body.

The characteristic decomposition change is putrefaction, although adipocere formation and mummification are also encountered.

Putrefaction

4.18 Putrefaction is liquefactive decomposition and is associated with prominent discolouration and changes to the body. The process of putrefaction begins with death but only becomes manifest after a few days; in its simplest form, it is a bacteria-driven process that results in the liquefaction of soft tissues. The bacteria that progress decomposition are in fact commensal to the body, the gut flora.

It is first encountered as discolouration of the lower right part of the abdominal skin before spreading around the body. Putrefaction is first seen in the front right lower portion of the abdominal skin (right iliac fossa) as a red-green discolouration, due to decomposition of the haemoglobin in the tissues surrounding the bacteria-rich caecum. As the decomposition progresses, the red-green discolouration will spread across the body, disfiguring it, especially as the underlying soft tissues become increasingly liquid-like. Before the changes become extreme, the decomposition can spread preferentially along the intricate network of the superficial veins, especially those close to the abdomen, which become swollen and stained. This is known as 'marbling', as it is supposed to resemble to some extent a marbled mosaic, but in reality it has a more arborescent appearance.

Internally, the organs begin to decompose and liquefy. The pancreas, due to its heavy content of enzymes designed to digest 'foodstuff' and loss of protective mechanisms, is usually first affected. However, with increasing time, all organs decompose, although those with a fibrous structure are able to resist initially.

Gas production

4.19   Gas production resulting in bloating is common, as well as blistering of the skin.

Gas is produced by the bacteria and this results in gas in the soft tissues and cavities causing a distended and bloated appearance to the already discoloured body. At this stage, 'purging' of decomposed fluids from the orifices is seen, due to increased internal pressure caused by the gases. The appearances may closely simulate those of ante-mortem haemorrhage and must be interpreted with caution.

Due to the loss of normal integrity of the skin, the skin will start to lift and peel, resulting in skin slippage; or gas and liquid may form in the lifted skin, resulting in blistering of the skin.

Timeframes

4.20   There is no precise putrefaction timeframe; this is because, again, many variables – particularly the condition of the body before death, the temperature and humidity of the environment and the relative sterility of the area – are involved.

Thus, bodies of those who have died while suffering an acute infection or of those subjected to open injury will decompose faster than the norm; and particularly rapid changes occur in dead bodies in warm environments, either from natural environmental heat or induced by local heating.

The surrounding environment will have a consequence on the rate of decomposition. Putrefaction of the body is normally delayed in water, unless this is heavily contaminated by sewage. In ordinary circumstances, an immersed body will tend to float after a week to 10 days, but this will be greatly modified by clothing and water temperature; in deep cold water, a body may not surface for some three weeks or, indeed, may never do so. There is a similar retardation of putrefaction in coffins, in which bursting of the body, an almost invariable accompaniment of putrefaction in the open, is an uncommon finding.

Resistive organs

4.21   Due to relative resistance to putrefaction of some organs and changes, important findings may still be evident in a significantly decomposed body.

Muscular and particularly fibrous tissues are resistant, and certain organs – for example, the uterus and the prostate gland – may be recognisable for a considerable time; this is of obvious importance in identification. Vascular walls tend to resist decomposition, and evidence of coronary insufficiency can often be discovered when the general appearances would suggest that a search would be unlikely to be rewarding; this will be particularly so if calcification has occurred. Genuine areas of haemorrhage, such as intracranially, may persist and be recognisable for some time.

On extremely rare occasions, a body may appear to have resisted decomposition to an unusual degree. This is typically a natural phenomenon in the closed environment of the coffin. An association between body preservation and poisoning by metallic compounds is part of the folklore of forensic medicine and of no diagnostic value. If it does occur, it probably relates to pre-mortem dehydration pushing towards mummification rather than putrefaction.

Adipocere

4.22   Adipocere (adi-po-cere) is the post-mortem formation of an initially greasy-waxy (but later chalky-brittle) substance that results from the hydrolysis of fats.

It typically arises in moist environments and is prevalent in bodies recovered from water or in bodies buried in wet ground. However, it is encountered in non-moist environments, and it is postulated that the body contains sufficient water within it to allow adipocere formation.

The presence of adipocere almost invariably means that the body has been dead for some months or years, although it can be encountered after three or so weeks, to some minor extent. An important feature of adipocerous formation is its ability to retain recognisable characteristics, both of the individual and also any injuries.

Mummification

4.23   Mummification is the desiccation or drying out of tissues.

In the presence of drying conditions and the absence of bacterial contamination, the tissues may become desiccated rather than putrefied. The skin adopts a dry leathery orangey-brown appearance and the internal organs have a leathery dried quality. Ultimately, the mummified tissues may be reduced to powder but, in the meantime, the general appearance of the body may be remarkably preserved. The bodies of young infants, which are relatively sterile internally, tend to mummify more readily.

The development of dark horizontal linear bands on the whites of the eyes is a form of desiccation known as 'tache noire'.

Skeletisation

4.24   Skeletisation is the complete loss of soft tissues. Ultimately, all the soft tissues of the body will decompose, the tendons and other highly fibrous tissues being most resistant, resulting in the skeletonised remains. The time for complete skeletisation is extremely variable and depends not only on the natural processes of decomposition but also upon predators from the insect and animal worlds, and from fungi and other moulds. Probably the main determinants are environmental temperature and the degree of exposure to carnivorous animals and fly larvae.

Although the time can be much shorter, it is probably fair to estimate a skeleton with which are associated remnants of fibrous tissue as having been dead for approximately one to two years; but, from this point, estimates of the interval since death can be assessed in brackets only of years or even decades.

The environment is all-important – bones many hundreds of years old have been discovered well preserved, particularly in dry caves. Numerous scientific techniques, including some of considerable sophistication (such as the analysis of radioactive carbon), have been introduced for the dating of skeletons but are beyond the scope of this book.

- Putrefaction is liquefactive decomposition and is associated with prominent discolouration and changes to the body.

- Gas production resulting in bloating is common, as well as blistering of the skin.

- Internal changes mirror the external appearances.

- Some organs, such as prostate and uterus, resist putrefaction.

- Adipocere is the post-mortem formation of an initially greasy-waxy (but later chalky-brittle) substance that results from the hydrolysis of fats.

- Mummification is the desiccation or drying out of tissues.

- Skeletisation is the complete loss of soft tissues.

Difficult areas: post-mortem artefacts and injuries

4.25   The post-mortem changes have been euphemistically called 'the great pretenders' for their ability to mimic injuries and other changes. Artefacts may arise at all stages of the death, including in the immediate peri-mortem period; for example, injuries resulting from resuscitation are not uncommon.

As previously discussed, hypostasis may mimic bruising or the changes associated with pressure to the neck.

Injuries may also be encountered from post-mortem animal activity of various degrees of severity. Carnivorous animals, such as rodents and foxes, as well as marine animals, such as fish, may cause a variety of injuries and remove significant quantities of soft tissues, often to the bone.

Accidental dismemberment is encountered and the larger carnivorous animal may remove limbs, per se, to an alternative location. Animal injuries in the main are relatively characteristic and easy to distinguish from alternative causes.

Injuries from some insects resemble small abrasions.

Injuries secondary to resuscitation efforts are a common occurrence and, as a result, are commonly encountered. External cardiac massage is associated with causing traumatic injuries to the torso, both to the skin surface and the deeper structures. Injuries to the bony skeleton represent the most commonly encountered consequent injury, with the sternum and front parts of the ribs being more commonly injured. Fractures of the outer aspects of the rib cage are far less common but encountered.

Fractures of the rear of the rib cage are not encountered. Internally, a vast array of injuries are described.

Consideration of resuscitation injuries is well-reviewed in the forensic pathology literature, particularly as resuscitation is often utilised as an explanation for the presence of inflicted injuries, especially in children. Further reading material is listed at the end of this chapter, but discussion with the appropriate pathologist is recommended.

A body may be injured by malfeasance or accidental trauma after death. Perimortem injuries, in particular relating to abrasion and bruising, are discussed in Chapter 7. Similarly, post-mortem application of heat will produce burning similar to that encountered in the close pre-mortem period.

Further reading material

General textbooks

● Saukko, P. & Knight, B. *Knights' Forensic Pathology* (2004, 3rd Edition)

● Mason, J.K. & Purdue, B.N. *The Pathology of Trauma* (2000, 3rd Edition)

● Spitz, W.U. *Spitz and Fisher's Medicolegal Investigation of Death* (2006, 4th Edition)

● Shkrum, M.J. & Ramsay, D.A. *Forensic Pathology of Trauma* (2007)

● Payne-James, J., Jones, R., Karch, S.B. & Manlove, J. *Simpson's Forensic Medicine* (2011, 13th Edition)

● Henssge, C., Knight, B.E., Krompecher, T., Madea, B., Nokes, L. *The Estimation of the Time Since Death in the Early Postmortem Period* (2002, 2nd Edition, Arnold)

Articles in update textbooks

● Benecke, M. 'Arthropods and Corpses' in Tsokos, M., editor. *Forensic Pathology Reviews*. Volume Two. Humana Press; 2005. 207–240

● Darok, M. 'Injuries Resulting From Resuscitation Procedures' in Tsokos, M., editor. *Forensic Pathology Reviews*. Volume One. Humana Press; 2004. 293–303

● Leadbeatter, S. 'Resuscitation Injuries' in Rutty, G.N., editor. *Essentials of Autopsy Practice*, Volume 1. London: Springer; 2001. 43–62

● Swift, B. 'The Timing of Death' in Rutty, G.N., editor. *Essentials of Autopsy Practice, Current Methods and Trends*. London: Springer; 2006. 189–214

● Tsokos, M. 'Postmortem Changes and Artifacts Occurring During the Early Postmortem Interval' in Tsokos, M., editor. *Forensic Pathology Reviews*. Volume Three. Humana Press; 2005. 183–237

Articles in journals

- Krompecher, T. 'Experimental evaluation of rigor mortis. V. Effect of various temperatures on the evolution of rigor mortis' *Forensic Sci. Int.* 17:19–26, 1981

- Biddinger, P.W. 'Postmortem wound dehiscence. A report of three cases' *Am. J. Forensic Med. Pathol.* 8:120–122, 1987

Chapter 5

Coroners' courts and fatal accident inquiries

With Sara Williams

Introduction

5.1   Within the United Kingdom's three legal jurisdictions, there are distinct systems responsible for investigating deaths. In England and Wales and in Northern Ireland, the principal mechanism is the coroners system. In Scotland, the equivalent mechanisms are investigations by the relevant procurator fiscal and fatal accident inquiries. The relevant law and principal features of the different mechanisms, as well as the differences between coroners in England and Wales and Northern Ireland, are set out below.

England and Wales

Overview of the coroners system

5.2   The Coroners and Justice Act 2009 (the '2009 Act') was implemented on 25 July 2013. The 2009 Act supersedes entirely the previous coroners' regime which was in place before its implementation.

From the date of enactment – 25 July 2013 – the law and rules under the Act apply to all coroner inquiries, investigations and inquests, even those which were started before that date.

The newly created post of Chief Coroner is the national head of the coroner system and is appointed by the Lord Chief Justice from candidates from the High Court or circuit benches. He or she is an independent judicial officer and has the power to conduct or take over inquests. The Chief Coroner makes an annual report to the Lord Chief Justice, based on reports of all inquests, and controls the issue of 'reports on action to prevent future deaths'. The Chief Coroner is also responsible for the training and guidance issued to coroners and approving coroner appointments, as well as generally managing the inquest system. The Office of the Chief Coroner can be contacted via the judiciary.gov.uk website, via email (chiefcoronersoffice@ judiciary.gsi.gov.uk) or at their offices at the Royal Courts of Justice.

The Ministry of Justice maintains annual national statistics[1] on all deaths which are reported to all coroners.

---

1   Ministry of Justice, 'Coroners statistics 2013', 15 May 2014, which comprises all returned (as required in law) coroners and burials statistics: www.gov.uk/government/collections/coroners-and-burials-statistics. Updates are hosted on the same site.

Under the Chief Coroner, the Lord Chief Justice may appoint any number of Deputy Chief Coroners, although at the time of writing no such appointments have been made. England and Wales is divided into coroner areas for which the relevant local authority may appoint one senior coroner and one or more area coroners. Those posts are assisted by assistant coroners. There is now a requirement for all coroners to satisfy the legally qualified judicial appointment condition (qualified barrister or solicitor with at least five years' experience). The Chief Coroner has created a specialist pool of coroners who will conduct investigations and inquests into deaths of service personnel on active service.

Duty, purpose and scope of the coroners' inquest

Informing the authorities of a death

5.3   There is a duty under section 16 of the Births and Deaths Registration Act 1953 for certain persons (such as relatives present at the death, other persons present at the death, and occupiers of the house where the death occurred, if they were aware of the death) to inform the Registrar of Births and Deaths of the details of the death, within five days. Often, that person would be the medical practitioner who attended during the last illness, who has a duty to sign and provide to the Registrar a certificate giving the cause of death.

The Registrar and/or the medical practitioner will inform the coroner of the death if there appears to be a requirement for an inquest, such as where the cause of death is unknown, or where the GP had not seen their patient for the preceding 14 days.

Purpose and scope of inquests

5.4   The purpose of an inquest is to establish the facts and explanation of a death which may be due to an unnatural cause. The inquest enquires into only the following: the identity of the deceased; how, when and where the deceased came by his or her death; and any required Registration Act details.

Coroners' courts use an inquisitorial system as opposed to an adversarial one, and the inquest process cannot be concerned in establishing civil or criminal liability for the death, although it may investigate possible breaches by agents of the state (e.g. police, prisons or hospitals) of Article 2 of the European Convention on Human Rights, the right to life. Where employees of the state may bear responsibility for loss of life (whether by their actions or omissions), the right to life in Article 2 ECHR may be engaged.

A coroner *must* appoint a jury for deaths in which the coroner has reason to suspect that the death: (i) occurred in state detention where it was violent, unnatural or the cause is unknown; (ii) may be the responsibility of a police officer; or (iii) is the result of an notifiable accident, poisoning or disease.[2]

A coroner *may* appoint a jury for a death if the coroner 'thinks that there is sufficient reason for doing so'.[3]

---

2   Coroners and Justice Act 2009, s 7(2).
3   Section 7(3).

5.5 The 2009 Act has changed the nature and scope of the law governing inquests. It is supplemented by three sets of Regulations:

- the Coroners Allowances, Fees and Expenses Regulations 2013;

- the Coroners (Investigations) Regulations 2013; and

- the Coroners (Inquests) Rules 2013;

and by Guidance provided by the Chief Coroner.

The role of the coroner

5.6 The role of a coroner is to determine whether an inquest is necessary or required by statute, and to decide if a post-mortem is necessary and appoint a suitably qualified practitioner (such as a pathologist). They must adjourn any inquest until criminal proceedings are complete in cases of homicide, death caused by a road traffic violation, or assisted suicide, or where requested to do so by the Director of Public Prosecutions. The coroner must then conduct the inquest and ensure that the formalities are observed; they should take notes of evidence, examine witnesses, and conduct a full and proper inquiry while controlling the scope of the inquiry. In a case involving a jury, the coroner must fairly summarise the evidence and direct the jury as to law and possible conclusions.

As a public authority, the coroner is also obliged to act in a way which is compatible with the European Convention on Human Rights, including the right under Article 6 to a fair trial in any criminal proceedings that might follow the inquest. A Memorandum of Understanding between the Coroners' Society and the Health and Safety Executive seeks to limit the potential for prejudice to any such proceedings.[4] For more information about coroners and their roles and duties, see the Coroners' Society and the judiciary websites and practitioner texts.[5]

Investigations

5.7 Section 1 of the 2009 Act sets out the duty to hold a coroner's 'investigation' into a death if they have reason to suspect that:

- the deceased died a violent or unnatural death;

- the cause of death is unknown; or

- the deceased died in custody or otherwise in state detention.

The threshold is not high, and the High Court must order a fresh inquest if it finds that a coroner wrongly decided not to call a jury. 'State detention' is a well-defined concept and is defined as those 'compulsorily detained by a public authority within

---

4 See www.hse.gov.uk/aboutus/howwework/framework/mou/mou-coroners.pdf.
5 See eg www.coronersociety.org.ukwww.gov.uk/after-a-death/when-a-death-is-reported-to-a-coronerwww.judiciary.gov.uk/related-offices-and-bodies/office-chief-coroner.

the meaning of section 6 of the Human Rights Act 1998'.[6] (For further information, see e.g. Clayton and Tomlinson 'The Law on Human Rights' or Harris, O'Boyle, and Warbrick 'Law of the European Convention on Human Rights'.)

Section 5(2) requires, in deaths which engage Article 2 ECHR, that 'how' a death occurred is to be read as including 'in what circumstances the deceased came by his or her death'.[7]

The detail of the different stages of the investigation is set out in the Coroners (Investigations) Regulations 2013. The coroner may conduct preliminary enquiries (for example, a post-mortem examination or other investigation) to see if section 1 is triggered. The inquest will form the end part of some investigations. The inquest has thus become a subset of an investigation. The coroner will no longer be obliged to open an inquest at an early stage to allow for the release of bodies for burial or cremation.

Once a coroner has decided that the duty to investigate has arisen, he or she must attempt to identify the deceased's personal representatives or next of kin and inform them of the decision (Regulation 6). Section 47 of the 2009 Act increases the list of 'interested person[s]' in rule 20 of the Coroners Rules 1984 ('the 1984 Rules') and notably includes the Independent Police Complaints Commission (IPCC) where the death is the subject of an IPCC investigation.

Regulation 26 provides that a coroner must notify the Chief Coroner in cases where the investigation has lasted more than a year from the date when the death was reported to the coroner. The coroner must also inform the Chief Coroner when the investigation has been completed or discontinued and provide reasons for the delay.

Post-mortems

5.8   The rules and regulations covering post-mortem examinations are detailed in sections 14 and 15 of the 2009 Act and Regulations 8 to 14 of the Coroners (Investigations) Regulations 2013.

The 2009 Act does not define 'post-mortem examination'. This is intended to allow other forms of examination as an alternative to an invasive dissecting autopsy. The alternatives envisaged are the use of non-invasive methods such as CT and/or MRI scanning, upon which the Chief Coroner issued guidance to coroners in 2013. The term 'post-mortem' is wide enough to include the examination or testing of organs and tissue fluids which may be requested after an initial autopsy has been carried out.

Section 15 of the 2009 Act removes the restriction on where a post-mortem examination takes place. These will no longer need to be in the coroner's area or neighbouring area. When the body is removed to another area, the coroner must keep possession and control of it (paragraph 4 of Schedule 2). Regulation 8 requires that post-mortems should take place as soon as reasonably practicable.

The coroner will appoint the pathologist or other medical practitioner but, if the person died in hospital, the family may ask for the pathologist to be unconnected

---

6   CJA 2009, s 48(2).
7   This section uses the familiar words of the House of Lords in *R (Middleton) v West Somerset Coroner and Another* [2004] UKHL 10 at para 36.

to that hospital. In some areas, particularly London, coroners tend to use forensic pathologists on the Home Office list or register, but that is not the case countrywide. If an offence of homicide is suspected, the coroner must consult the chief officer of police in charge of the inquiry.

The Home Office register of forensic pathologists is a list of forensic pathologists who meet the criteria for registration, as detailed in 'The Process and Criteria for Recommendation for Admission to the Home Secretary's Register of Forensic Pathologists'. Following some controversy about bad practice, pathologists on the Home Office register are now governed by Suitability Rules and a Code of Practice, which govern how complaints about misconduct of pathologists on the register should be made and dealt with.

5.9   There are a number of persons who must be notified of the time, date and place of the post-mortem and are entitled to be represented by a medical practitioner, or to attend themselves if they are a medical practitioner.

The persons to be notified are:

- the next of kin or the personal representative of the deceased, or any other interested person who has notified the coroner in advance of his or her desire to be represented at the post-mortem examination;

- the deceased's regular medical practitioner, if he or she has notified the coroner of his or her desire to be represented at the post-mortem examination;

- if the deceased died in hospital, that hospital;

- if the death of the deceased may have been caused by an accident or disease which must be reported to an enforcing authority, that enforcing authority or the appropriate inspector or representative of that authority;

- if the death may have been caused by improper medical treatment by a medical practitioner, a representative of that practitioner;

- a Government department which has notified the coroner of its desire to be represented at the examination; and

- if the chief officer of police has notified the coroner of his or her desire to be represented at the examination, the chief officer of police.

Any other interested person with the consent of the coroner may also attend a post-mortem.

5.10   The pathologist will prepare a post-mortem report. If further reports are required (such as toxicology, histology or neuropathology), an interim report will be prepared for the coroner and a final report once all other medical investigations have been completed. Under rule 13 of the Coroners (Inquests) Rules 2013, the coroner must disclose any report to the interested persons. The report must not be disclosed to anyone else without the consent of the coroner.[8] For further information regarding

---

8   Coroners (Investigations) Regulations 2013, reg 16.

pathologists and the rules governing them, see the Home office website and the Royal College of Pathologists website.[9]

According to rule 20 of the Coroners (Investigations) Regulations 2013, a coroner must release the body for burial or cremation as soon as is reasonably practicable, and must inform the next of kin of any delay if longer than 28 days. However, they must not release the body until it is no longer needed for the investigation. Rule 22 provides the coroner with the power to direct exhumation of a body already buried. The post-mortem need not be invasive, and the Chief Coroner has issued guidance for the use of post-mortem imaging such as CT and MRI scans in ascertaining a cause of death.

5.11   After a post-mortem has been conducted, the coroner must discontinue the investigation where the cause of death is revealed and he or she thinks that it is not necessary to continue the investigation (2009 Act, s 4(1)). Section 4(2) provides that the investigation must continue if there is reason to suspect a violent or unnatural death or that the death was in custody or other state detention. Thus, if the post-mortem revealed a natural cause, the investigation would have to continue and proceed to inquest where the death was in custody or state detention. Both the deceased's family and defendants in any potential criminal proceedings should be permitted to conduct a second post-mortem (except when there are reasonable grounds for refusal).[10]

Following the scandal of the retention of organs of children by the Alder Hey Children's Hospital without consent, and the Kennedy Inquiry into heart surgery on children at the Bristol Royal Infirmary, the Human Tissue Act 2004 was passed to regulate the removal of tissue from a living or dead person. The provisions, which require the consent of the person or their next of kin for the removal or storage of any 'relevant material', do not apply to anything done for the purposes of the coroner.[11] Any material preserved or retained during the post-mortem examination which relates to the cause of death or identity of the deceased must be notified to the coroner, who must in due course notify the relatives of that material and specify for how long it is to be retained.[12]

Pre-hearing procedure and pre-inquest review hearings

5.12   Paragraphs 1 to 6 of Schedule 1 to the 2009 Act and Regulation 8 provide for the suspension of investigations and adjournment of inquests during criminal investigations or criminal proceedings connected with the death or pending inquiries under the Inquiries Act 2005.

Rule 13 of the Coroners (Inquests) Rules 2013 provides that the coroner must provide disclosure of documents to interested parties on request, unless there are legal prohibitions on disclosure, the consent of the author cannot reasonably be

---

9   See eg www.gov.uk/government/publications/suitability-rules-for-forensic-pathologists-2013www.gov.uk/government/publications/standards-for-forensic-pathology-in-england-wales-and-northern-irelandwww.gov.uk/government/uploads/system/uploads/attachment_data/file/354645/Current_Home_Office_Register.pdfwww.gov.uk/forensic-pathology-role-within-the-home-officewww.rpath.org.uk.

10   *R v South London Coroner ex p Ridley* [1985] 1 WLR 1347.

11   Human Tissue Act 2004, s 11.

12   Coroners (Investigations) Regulations 2013, reg 14.

obtained, the document relates to contemplated or commenced criminal proceedings, or the document is irrelevant.

Rule 6 formally recognises that pre-inquest review hearings (PIRs) are often held before the main inquest hearing. Where possible, coroners should set out in advance of the hearing, for all interested persons, an agenda in writing and, where appropriate, invite written submissions to be considered at the hearing. Such hearings are not a statutory requirement but have been accepted as a sensible method of administering the inquest process. New Rule 11 confirms that PIRs will now be held in public. They do not strictly form part of the inquest itself and, therefore, the purpose and form of the hearing are matters for the coroner. They often involve issues such as lists of witnesses, scope of the inquest, disclosure of documents to and by the coroner to interested parties,[13] and bundles of documents available to the coroner and the parties.[14]

A coroner must release the body for burial or cremation as soon as is reasonably practicable, and, if not possible within 28 days, must notify the next of kin. Coroners should normally withhold a body from a family if they are on notice that a potential defendant in criminal proceedings may require a second post-mortem.[15]

The coroner's officer

5.13   The coroner's officer is part of the staff of the coroner and has a number of duties, both investigative and administrative. Their duties include:

- Liaising with all parties, including the pathologist and the police (if the death is suspicious) and the press.

- Obtaining evidence, including statements from witnesses and medical reports.

- Arranging for removal and identification of the body.

- Tracing and liaising with the relatives of the deceased regarding the post mortem, funeral arrangements and the inquest.

- Arranging the inquest, including summonsing jurors, organising witnesses and arranging for payments.

They are often the person that any member of the public, whether bereaved or an interested party or a witness to a death, has as a point of contact with the coroner. The post is a non-statutory office and coroner's officers are often former or current police officers and they are responsible for investigating on behalf of the coroner. This normally involves taking written statements ('depositions') from witnesses, which are given to the coroner before the inquest. This tradition has inherent advantages including: experience and training in investigation techniques; experience in evaluating evidence and assisting bereaved families; and close working relationships with the investigating police force. However, it is controversial, as investigations into deaths in custody call for an inquiry which is completely independent from the police force.

13 Health and Safety at Work etc Act 1974, ss 28(3), (7). These subsections allow HSE to make disclosure beyond that envisaged by the Freedom of Information Act 2000.
14 See www.hse.gov.uk/enforce/enforcementguide/wrdeaths/coroner.htm#information.
15 *R v Bristol Coroner ex p Kerr* [1974] 2 All ER 719.

Other staff available to coroners, dependent on the area, are largely administrative and clerical.

Interested persons

5.14   There is no set definition of an 'interested person' under the 2009 Act; however, the Rules give some guidance. Rule 20(2) states that an interested person is entitled to be represented at the inquest, and the term 'interested persons' should include persons such as law enforcement agencies and professional disciplinary bodies who might have had no reason to be present or represented at the inquest, but whose public functions are engaged by facts and matters which are disclosed during the inquest.[16]

Rule 20 sets out entitlement to examine witnesses:

'(1) Without prejudice to any enactment with regard to the examination of witnesses at an inquest, any person who satisfies the coroner that he is within paragraph (2) shall be entitled to examine any witness at an inquest either in person or by an authorised person:

Provided that—

(a) the chief officer of police, unless interested otherwise than in that capacity, shall only be entitled to examine a witness by an authorised person;

(b) the coroner shall disallow any question which in his opinion is not relevant or is otherwise not a proper question.

(2) Each of the following persons shall have the rights conferred by paragraph (1)—

(a) a parent, child, spouse, civil partner, partner and any personal representative of the deceased;

(b) any beneficiary under a policy of insurance issued on the life of the deceased;

(c) the insurer who issued such a policy of insurance;

(d) any person whose act or omission or that of his agent or servant may in the opinion of the coroner have caused, or contributed to, the death of the deceased;

(e) any person appointed by a trade union to which the deceased at the time of his death belonged, if the death of the deceased may have been caused by an injury received in the course of his employment or by an industrial disease;

(f) an inspector appointed by, or a representative of, an enforcing authority, or any person appointed by a government department to attend the inquest;

(g) the chief officer of police;

(h) any other person who, in the opinion of the coroner, is a properly interested person.'

16 Matthews, *Jervis on Coroners*, p 415.

The hearing – main principles

5.15   Section 5 of the 2009 Act stipulates that the matters to be ascertained are confined to the identity of the deceased and to 'how, when and where' the deceased came by his or her death. By that section, the coroner and/or a jury are prohibited from expressing an opinion on any other matter. Section 10(2) says that 'a determination' (the answers to the section 5 questions) may not be framed in such a way as to appear to determine criminal or civil liability (this was formerly rule 42 of the Coroners Rules 1984).

Historically, the scope of 'how' the deceased came by his death was not defined and was interpreted in different ways. In *R v HM Coroner for North Humberside and Scunthorpe (ex parte Jamieson)* [1995] QB 1, the Court of Appeal held that the phrase 'how the deceased came by his death' was limited and was to be confined to the question of 'by what means' the deceased died. Cases not involving the duty under Article 2 ECHR to investigate are now often called a Jamieson inquest, or a domestic inquest.

5.16   In *R v HM Coroner for Inner London West District ex parte Dallaglio* [1994] 4 All ER 139 (the 'Marchioness' case), the Court of Appeal appeared to draw back from such a strict interpretation and instead encouraged considerable flexibility in the discretion of coroners as to the scope of the inquest. The court held that 'the inquiry is almost bound to stretch wider than strictly required for the purposes of a verdict. How much wider is pre-eminently a matter for the Coroner' (Simon Brown LJ at p 155).

Some of the principles of an inquest hearing are summarised by Lady Justice Hallett in *R (Sreedharan) v HM Coroner for the County of Greater Manchester and others* [2013] EWCA Civ 181:

> 'It is the duty of the Coroner as the public official responsible for the conduct of inquests, whether he is sitting with a jury or without, to ensure that the relevant facts are fully, fairly and fearlessly investigated. He must ensure that the relevant facts are exposed to public scrutiny. He fails in his duty if his investigation is 'superficial, slipshod or perfunctory'. But the responsibility is his. He must set the bounds of the inquiry and rule on the procedure to be followed (*R v North Humberside Coroner, ex p. Jamieson* [1995] QB 1).'

The scope of inquiry at an inquest can extend wider than is strictly required for the production of the verdict. The inquiry is not, therefore, restricted to the 'last link in the chain of causation' (*Dallaglio*, cited above).

5.17   An inquest is not a trial. It is an inquisitorial process designed to discover the truth. The limits on the questions that may be asked are that they must be relevant to the issues to be determined under section 5 and 'proper'. Coronial proceedings are not subject to the usual rules applicable to civil or criminal trials. An interested party may not, therefore, have the benefit of procedural safeguards which would apply to a trial, but will have the protection of section 10(2) of the Act which forbids a verdict from imputing civil or criminal liability.

The threshold of the legal test for evidential sufficiency in the coroners' courts is different from that of the criminal courts. The test in criminal cases for evidential sufficiency (that is, whether the evidence in a case is sufficient such that that evidence should be left to a jury who may safely decide an issue or issues upon it) is based on *R v Galbraith* [1981] 1 WLR 1039. However, more is needed in the context of leaving evidence to juries in the coroners' courts. In *R (Secretary of State for Justice) v HM Deputy Coroner for the Eastern District of West Yorkshire* [2012] EWHC 1634 (Admin), Haddon-Cave J ruled that coroners must apply a so-called '*Galbraith*-plus' test:[17]

> It is clear, therefore, that when coroners are deciding whether or not to leave a particular verdict to a jury, they should apply a dual test comprising both limbs [per the approach in Galbraith] or 'schools of thought', i.e. coroners should (a) ask the classic pure Galbraith question, "Is there evidence on which a jury properly directed could properly convict, etc.?" [...] *plus* (b) also ask the question, "Would it be *safe* for the jury to convict on the evidence before it?"' [emphasis added]

This analysis of '*Galbraith*-plus' as applicable to the sufficiency test in the coroners' courts is undoubtedly driven by human rights considerations. Specifically, it is driven by the imperative of Article 2 ECHR, which has been interpreted such that the right to life necessarily includes and protects the right to adequate investigation into risk to life and consequent death.

Article 2 or enhanced inquests

5.18   Article 2 inquests are based on the principle that the duty of the state to protect life and the prohibition on taking life pursuant to Article 2 ECHR (that is, right to life) would be ineffective if there was no effective procedure for investigating deaths and the background circumstances of deaths which occur in state settings. Therefore, the incorporation of Article 2 into domestic law brings with it the procedural obligation to carry out an effective investigation and to ensure, so far as possible, 'that the full facts are brought to light; that culpable and discreditable conduct is exposed; that suspicion of deliberate wrongdoing (if unjustified) is allayed; that dangerous practices and procedures are rectified; and that those who have lost their relative may at least have the satisfaction of knowing that lessons from his death may save the lives of others' (*R (Amin) v Secretary of State for the Home Department* [2004] 1 AC 653).

Where Article 2 is engaged, the Act specifies that, in considering 'how', 'when' and 'where' the deceased came by his death, the coroner or jury must decide not simply 'by what means' but 'by what means and in what circumstances' he met his death.[18] Under the old rules, this was established by the case of *R (Middleton) v West Somerset Coroner* [2004] 2 AC 182. Thus, Article 2 inquests have come to be known as 'Middleton' or 'enhanced' inquests.

There is now, in practice, little difference between the Jamieson and Middleton-type inquest as far as inquisitorial scope is concerned. The difference is likely to come only in the verdict and the findings (*R (Smith) v Oxfordshire Assistant Deputy Coroner* [2011] 1 AC 1).

---

17 Law sheet no. 2: *Galbraith* plus', published on 11 September 2013, at p 1, www.judiciary.gov.uk/Resources/JCO/Documents/coroners/law-sheets/law-sheets-no2-galbraith-plus.pdf.
18 CJA 2009, s 5(2).

5.19 Enhanced inquests generally involve the coroner sitting with a jury. Section 7 of the 2009 Act provides that the coroner *must* sit with a jury if the death:

- occurred in custody or 'in state detention' and was either violent or unnatural, or of an unknown cause;

- resulted from an act or omission of a police officer, or a member of a service police force; or

- was caused by a notifiable accident, poisoning or disease.

Deaths in state custody that appear to be due to a natural cause will not now have to sit with a jury at inquest, although the coroner will still have *discretion* to call a jury if they think that 'there is sufficient reason for doing so'. Interested parties will have the right to make submissions to the coroner on whether there should be a jury in these circumstances. Cases where death occurred during medical treatment in state detention are an ambiguous area (see *R v Poplar Coroner ex parte Thomas* [1993] QB 610; and *R v Birmingham Coroner ex parte Benton* [1997] 8 Med LR 362). Voluntary in-patients and sectioned patients in psychiatric hospitals have the right to Article 2 enhanced inquests (*Rabone v Pennine Care NHS Foundation Trust* [2012] UKSC 2, [2012] 2 AC 72).

In non-custody deaths, whether the enhanced form of inquest will be required will depend on the precise circumstances of the particular case. Only those inquests that are concerned with a possible breach of Article 2 by an agent of the state have this wider scope; other types of inquest can be more limited.

The hearing – procedure

5.20 The coroner must inform the next of kin or personal representative of the deceased, and any other interested persons who have made themselves known to the coroner, of the date and place of the hearing.

Witnesses will give evidence on oath or affirmation, and are examined firstly by the coroner, then may be examined by any interested party, and finally by the witness's representative if applicable (Coroners (Inquests) Rules 2013, rr 19–21). The protection against self-incrimination is preserved in Rule 22.

Written evidence (which includes admissions) may be given only after:

(a) the coroner has announced at the inquest the nature of the evidence, the name of the maker of the evidence and the right of interested parties to see the written evidence and object to it; and

(b) the coroner is satisfied that it is not possible for the maker of the evidence to give evidence within a reasonable time; or

(c) there is good and sufficient reason why the maker of the evidence should not attend the hearing; or

(d) it is unlikely to be disputed (rule 23).

However, any document made by a deceased which is relevant to the purposes of the inquest *must* be admitted. A witness may give evidence via video link or behind a screen if that would improve their evidence (Coroners (Inquests) Rules 2013, rr 17,

18). No person may address the coroner or the jury as to the facts of who the deceased was or how, when and where they came to their death (rule 27). Submissions must be limited to the law. In jury inquests, once the evidence is concluded the coroner sums up the case to the jury.

The conclusion

5.21   An inquest conclusion (formerly known as a 'verdict') must not be framed in such a way as to appear to determine any question of criminal liability on the part of a named party or civil liability. The conclusion is recorded on the 'inquisition' (the form which the jury complete) and includes the record of their decision as to the four questions: who, when, where and how.

The following are examples of the type of substantive conclusions that might be returned:

- Natural causes.

- Industrial disease.

- Alcohol or drug related.

- Suicide (and suicide while the balance of mind was disturbed).

- Accident/misadventure.

- Road traffic collision.

- Lawful killing.

- Unlawful killing.

- Open conclusion.

- Still birth.

- Neglect.

The conclusion is reached 'on the balance of probabilities', although the higher, criminal standard of proof (i.e. 'beyond reasonable doubt') is required to find 'unlawful killing' or 'suicide'. There is an evidential burden on the state to show that they were not responsible for injuries caused to prisoners while in detention and, once the evidential burden is met, the elements of unlawful killing must be proved beyond reasonable doubt.[19]

Narrative conclusions

5.22   In Article 2 inquests, narrative conclusions are required, as the coroner or jury must make a determination of the circumstances in which the deceased came by his death. Increasingly, as an alternative to the traditional 'short-form' conclusion,

---

19 *R (Cash) v HM Coroner for Northamptonshire* [2007] 4 All ER 903.

which is limited in nature, coroners are making use of 'narrative' conclusions in domestic inquests as well. A narrative is a factual account of the findings of the inquest and may or may not refer to the terms given above. The narrative may be answers to a set of questions posed by the coroner to him or herself or the jury and should culminate in an expression of the jury's conclusions on the 'main' or 'important' issues which are often used to indicate particular breaches of duties or failures to foresee risks.

Reports to prevent future deaths (PFDs)

5.23   A coroner is now under a statutory duty to prevent future deaths and will provide a prevention of future deaths (PFD) report (2009 Act, Sch 5, para 7). There is also a mandatory duty to respond to the PFD report and provide the coroner with a timetable for the proposed action to take place. The reports and responses must be sent to the Chief Coroner and interested parties, and they should be sent to a person who the coroner believes may have power to take action or who may find it useful.

The report should include anything revealed by the investigation which gives rise to a concern that circumstances creating a risk of other deaths will occur or will continue to exist in the future, and which the coroner believes should result in action to eliminate or reduce that risk.

Persons who receive a copy of the report have 56 days to provide a written response setting out what action has been or will be taken, or to provide an explanation as to why no action is proposed.

Challenging the coroner's decision

Section 13 applications

5.24   Section 13 of the Coroners Act 1988 (preserved by the 2009 Act) provides that the High Court may order an investigation under Part 1 of the 2009 Act to be held by the same or another coroner and/or quash the conclusion or finding of the original inquest if satisfied either:

● that the coroner has failed to hold, or decided wrongly not to hold, an inquest, or

● where an inquest or investigation has been held, that (whether because of fraud, rejection of evidence, irregularity of proceedings, insufficiency of inquiry, the discovery of new facts or evidence or otherwise) it is necessary or desirable in the interests of justice that an investigation or, as the case may be, another investigation be held.

An application to the High Court must be made or authorised by the Attorney-General, but there is no time limit to such an application.

In the case of *Attorney General v HM Coroner of South Yorkshire (West)* [2012] EWHC 3783 (Admin) (the 'Hillsborough' case), the court made a number of comments with regard to the interests of justice test under section 13, and when to seek a fresh inquiry. The court stated that:

> 'the emergence of fresh evidence which may reasonably lead to the conclusion that the substantial truth about how an individual met his death was not revealed at the first inquest, will normally make it both desirable and necessary in the interests of justice for a fresh inquest to be ordered.'[20]

This emphasis on 'the substantial truth', rather than merely the short-form verdict, appears to suggest that the possibility of a different narrative verdict or cause of death could require a new inquest, even if the short-form verdict might be the same.

Judicial review

5.25   The only other remedy of a coroner's decision is judicial review in the High Court. The grounds for seeking judicial review of a coroner's decision are the traditional grounds for judicial review (that is, illegality, including acting incompatibly with a person's Convention rights, irrationality and procedural impropriety). The funding of judicial review has become much more restricted in recent years, as the Government and Parliament have sought to reduce the legal aid budget by limiting both the amount of legal aid available and when judicial review claimants will be eligible for legal aid, although certain of these restrictions have been found to be unlawful by the courts. At the time of writing, funding is not available until permission to apply for judicial review has been given by the High Court.

Northern Ireland

5.26   The Coroners Service for Northern Ireland is based in Belfast. Since 2006, there has been in place a single Coroners Service, headed by a High Court Judge, with one Senior Coroner and three coroners. The coroners travel throughout Northern Ireland to conduct inquests.

Coroners in Northern Ireland operate under the Coroners Act (Northern Ireland) 1959 and the rules made thereunder. Coroners must be practising barristers or solicitors and are appointed by the Lord Chancellor.

5.27   There is a wide-ranging duty under section 7 of the 1959 Act imposed on a number of individuals to inform the coroner of the death:

> 'Every medical practitioner, registrar of deaths or funeral undertaker and every occupier of a house or mobile dwelling and every person in charge of any institution or premises in which a deceased person was residing, who has any reason to believe that the deceased person died, either directly or indirectly, as a result of violence or misadventure or by unfair means, or as a result of negligence or misconduct or malpractice on the part of others, or from any cause other than natural illness or disease for which he had been seen and treated by a medical practitioner within twenty-eight days prior to his death, or in such circumstances as may require investigation (including death as the result of the administration of an anaesthetic), shall immediately notify the coroner within whose district the body of the deceased person is of the facts and circumstances relating to the death.'

20 At para [10].

Doctors also have a duty in such circumstances to complete a death certificate; however, such a certificate can only be completed by a doctor who had seen and treated the deceased for the fatal illness within 28 days prior to death, knows of the death and knows it to be entirely natural. In all other circumstances, the coroner must be advised and no death certificate will be completed.

Inquests are inquisitorial in nature; there are no 'parties', as in other types of proceedings, and the coroner takes the lead in the investigation.

5.28   A key difference between the English and Northern Irish systems is in the obligation to hold an inquest. In England, an inquest will be held in all cases of unnatural deaths. In Northern Ireland, the coroner *may* hold such an inquest, under section 13 of the 1959 Act.

As in England, there is a rule against self-incrimination afforded to those giving evidence at the inquest. Until recently, the position in Northern Ireland was that the person suspected of causing the death could not be compelled to give evidence; however, this rule was amended in 2002 to ensure that all witnesses are now compellable.[21]

Another key difference is the obligation in Northern Ireland to make 'findings' in the form of a concise statement as to the cause of death.[22] In England, the verdict will be simplified, and merely read 'accident', 'misadventure' and so forth, whereas in Northern Ireland the findings will be fuller and more comprehensive.

Scotland

5.29   In Scotland the investigation of deaths has two stages: an initial investigation by the relevant local prosecutor, the procurator fiscal, and subsequently, where appropriate, the Scottish equivalent of the coroner's inquest, the fatal accident inquiry (FAI). FAIs were introduced by the Fatal Accidents Inquiry (Scotland) Act 1895 ('1895 Act'). The Fatal Accidents and Sudden Deaths Inquiry (Scotland) Act 1976 ('1976 Act') repealed and replaced both the 1895 Act and the 1905 Act of the same name. The 1976 Act made four major changes, in that it:

(a)   dispensed with the need for juries;

(b)   gave extensive powers to the Lord Advocate in managing inquiries;

(c)   widened the scope of the inquiry to include those deaths occurring whilst in legal custody or detention; and

(d)   extended the jurisdiction of inquiries to cover the offshore oil industry.

5.30   Section 1 of the 1976 Act provides that an FAI will commence where a death appears:

(a)   to have occurred from an accident whilst the deceased was an employee or otherwise engaged in his occupation (if self-employed, or an employer);

---

21 Coroners (Practice and Procedure) Rules (NI) 1963, Rule 9, as amended by SR 2002 No 37.
22 *R v HM Coroner for North Humberside and Scunthorpe ex p Jamieson* [1994] 3 WLR 82.

(b)   to have occurred whilst the deceased was in custody or otherwise in state detention; or

(c)   to be sudden, suspicious, unexplained, or where it is in the public interest to investigate.

There is no legal definition of 'accident'.

Investigations by the procurator fiscal

5.31   The Lord Advocate has overall responsibility in investigating deaths in Scotland, but in practice the task is undertaken by the local procurators fiscal (see Chapter 20). Around half of all reported deaths are investigated by the procurator fiscal to whom it has been reported. Any death which falls into one or more of the following categories needs to be reported to the procurator fiscal:

- deaths occurring by violent, suspicious or unexplained causes;

- deaths occurring through negligence or neglect on the part of an individual;

- suicide;

- deaths resulting from accidents;

- deaths arising out of the use of a vehicle;

- deaths resulting from drowning;

- death resulting by burning, scalding, or as a result of fire or explosion;

- deaths of children;

- deaths occurring at work;

- deaths related to the deceased's occupation, such as industrial disease or poisoning;

- deaths occurring as a result of an abortion or attempted abortion;

- deaths occurring from medical treatment, or the absence of such where it may have contributed to the death;

- deaths occurring by poisoning or suspected poisoning, including by prescription drugs;

- deaths occurring in prison or otherwise in legal custody;

- deaths of a person of unknown residence, who died other than in a house; and

- any death that is not deemed to have resulted through natural causes.

All suspicious deaths will be reported to the procurator fiscal, who will commence initial investigations. Where a death is sudden or unexplained, the police will also play a role in the investigation under the direction of the procurator fiscal.

Cases which attract significant public interest may be examined in the form of a different public inquiry, such as one under the Inquiries Act 2005 ('the 2005 Act'), although this is a matter for the Scottish Ministers and not the procurator fiscal. An example of such an Inquiry is the 2008 Inquiry into hepatitis C/HIV acquired infection from NHS treatments in Scotland with blood and blood products, headed by Lord Penrose.

The main role of the procurator fiscal is to examine whether the death came about as a result of criminality or negligence. If the procurator fiscal is satisfied that the death was due to natural causes, he will invite the GP or hospital doctor to issue a death certificate.

Deaths in hospital/under medical care

5.32   Where the deceased is under medical care at the time of death, the death will usually be reported to the procurator fiscal. Deaths arising out of the following categories fall to be investigated:

- deaths occurring unexpectedly;

- deaths which are clinically unexplained;

- deaths associated with a lack of medical care (including surgical, anaesthetic, nursing or other medical care);

- deaths attributed to a therapeutic or diagnostic hazard (such as X-rays);

- deaths due to anaesthetic complications; and

- deaths caused by the withdrawal of life support.

In the above circumstances, the doctor concerned with the care of the patient, or the doctor present at the time of death, has overall responsibility to inform the procurator fiscal of the death without delay. The procurator fiscal may require a written report into the death and this may be sought from the doctor or medical team responsible for the deceased's care. Following receipt of the report, the procurator fiscal will either take the decision that the death requires no further enquiry, or he will seek independent forensic reports. Often, this will involve instructing a doctor to carry out a post-mortem.

5.33   Where the death occurred whilst the deceased was under the care of medical professionals, the independent forensic pathologist will provide guidance to the procurator fiscal on the following issues:

- whether the patient was properly and sufficiently examined prior to the medical procedure;

- whether all due precautions were taken during the medical procedure, including during administration of anaesthetic or medication; and

- whether there were any factors which could have been discovered that indicated the procedure had a significant risk to life.

Post-mortems

5.34   Post-mortems are commonly carried out in cases where the death is thought to be suspicious. In order to so instruct, authority must be given by a sheriff, albeit such authority is rarely refused. A post-mortem will be ordered where:

- the procurator fiscal's inquiries cannot be completed unless the cause of death is fully established;

- there are suspicious circumstances;

- there are allegations of criminal conduct; or

- the death was associated with anaesthesia in connection with a surgical operation and the fact that all precautions were taken must be established.

The procurator fiscal may request one or two doctors to carry out the post-mortem. Where there are suspicious circumstances, or where criminal proceedings may arise from the findings, two doctors will usually be instructed to carry out the post-mortem. Where the death appears to have been caused as the result of a suicide, accident or non-suspicious natural death, one doctor is usually instructed. The procurator fiscal is responsible for deciding which medical experts to instruct as part of the investigation.

Certain investigations will always require a post-mortem. Inquiries into sudden infant death syndrome (SIDS, or 'cot death') is one such example; notwithstanding the views of the deceased's relatives, a post-mortem will be carried out unless there are clear and compelling reasons for not doing so.

Fatal accident inquiries

5.35   At the conclusion of the procurator fiscal's investigation, a fatal accident inquiry ('FAI') may be required to establish the exact circumstances of the death. Very few investigations result in an FAI; section 1(1)(b) of the 1976 Act provides that, where it appears to the Lord Advocate to be expedient in the public interest that an inquiry under the Act should be held into the circumstances of a death on the grounds, among others, that the death was sudden or unexplained or has occurred in circumstances such as to give rise to serious public concern, the procurator fiscal can apply to the sheriff to hold an FAI.

The FAI takes place before a sheriff in the Sheriff Court. Like the coroner's inquest, the proceedings are inquisitorial and are public, subject to reporting restrictions in relation to children under 17 years of age.

The object of the FAI is to reach various conclusions as to the circumstances surrounding the death; in particular, various determinations will be made (see below). The FAI cannot make any findings of fault or blame against individuals; it is essentially a fact-finding exercise. The civil rules of evidence and the civil standard of proof apply. Section 6 of the 1976 Act provides that the FAI should determine:

- when and where the death occurred;

- the cause of death;

- what, if anything, could have prevented the death;

- the defects in any system of work which contributed to the death (including accidents); and

- any other facts relevant to the death.

The procedure of the FAI is similar to that of a coroner's inquest. The procurator fiscal adduces evidence of the witnesses, who are then subject to cross-examination. Civil rules of evidence apply. The hearing is held in public, subject to any reporting restrictions for those under 17 years of age.

Following the FAI, a full report will be compiled setting out full details of the FAI, including a summary of the evidence, the submissions made by all parties, and forming a determination.

Reporting obligations

5.36 The procurator fiscal must report certain categories of death to the Crown Office. These categories are:

- where there are any suspicious circumstances;

- where there is a possibility of instigating criminal proceedings;

- where the death is believed to have been a result of suicide;

- where the death occurred in circumstances that are likely to be prejudicial to public health and safety, and those circumstances may be continued or repeated;

- where the death is due to a medical error; or

- where there had been a request by a person having an interest in the death that a public inquiry be held into the circumstances of the death.

Determinations

5.37 Section 6 of the 1976 Act provides for the sheriff to produce a determination, or verdict. In doing so, the sheriff will reach conclusions on five issues:

(a) time and place of the death;

(b) the cause of the death;

(c) any precautions which may have avoided the death;

(d) any defects in the system of working which may have avoided the death; and

(e) any other relevant considerations.

In contrast to the coroner, the sheriff is not obliged to come to a medical conclusion on the precise cause of death, once the possibility of criminal proceedings has been ruled out.

References

- Ministry of Justice Guide to Coroners and Inquests and Charter for coroner services: www.justice.gov.uk/downloads/burials-and-coroners/guide-charter-coroner.pdf

- The Coroners' Society of England and Wales: www.coronersociety.org.uk/

- Speeches by the Chief Coroner: www.judiciary.gov.uk/media/speeches/speakers/hhj-peter-thornton-qc

- Guidance from the Chief Coroner: www.judiciary.gov.uk/related-offices-and-bodies/office-chief-coroner/guidance-law-sheets/coroners-guidance/

- P. Matthews, *Jervis on Coroners*, 2014, Sweet & Maxwell

- L. Thomas et al, *Inquests, A Practitioner's Guide*, 2014, Legal Action Group

- Review of Fatal Accident Inquiry Legislation: The Report, www.scotland.gov.uk/Publications/2009/11/-2113726/4

- Inquests and Human Rights in Northern Ireland, John L Leckey LLM, Coroner for Greater Belfast (2005)

- Death and the Procurator Fiscal, Crown Office, November 1998

Chapter 6

Sudden natural death

6.1   Around 75–80% of cases coming to post-mortem examination in England and Wales are found to have died of natural causes. In Scotland, where deaths are certified without post-mortem examination, it is probable that the percentages remain the same. There is a variation between cities and also between cities and rural areas. This area of medicine is in the realms of public health, where mortality and morbidity in the varying regions throughout the United Kingdom are monitored.

Sudden death is defined as an unexpected death following rapidly from the onset of symptoms. The World Health Organisation's definition is 24 hours after the onset of symptoms, although many authors take this to be too long a period of time. In forensic practice, most sudden deaths occur within minutes or seconds.

The majority of deaths within this group, particularly so in the elderly population, are due to cardiovascular pathology. One of the issues in relation to concealment of homicide in this group of individuals is that toxicological examination is not routinely done in the vast majority of cases of death, whether or not they are sudden, in the United Kingdom. In other jurisdictions, toxicological analysis is routine. This, of course, raises the issue of a toxicological cause of death, both in those individuals who are relatively healthy prior to death and those in nursing homes or other care institutions. This was particularly pertinent in the case of Harold Shipman.

There are significant differences between deaths certified by a clinician and findings at post-mortem examination.

Coronary artery disease

6.2   Coronary heart disease is the commonest single cause of death in most industrialised countries, and the risk increases throughout life but is common from the age of 45 onwards. Medico-legal issues arise in terms of association with potential stress, whether that be physical or emotional, as well as issues for insurance companies in relation to life expectancy. Coronary artery disease is also known as 'ischaemic heart disease' or 'coronary atherosclerosis', and many pathologists use the terms rather loosely. Probably the best descriptive term is ischaemic heart disease, of which coronary atherosclerosis or coronary artery atheroma is the major cause. Other causes of heart disease will be covered later in this chapter.

Coronary artery atheroma

6.3   The anatomy of the heart has been covered in Chapter 1. In summary, the heart is supplied by three main coronary arteries, the left main stem of the coronary artery providing the anterior descending and circumflex coronary arteries with the anterior descending branch of the left and the right coronary artery. These supply the ventricles of the heart with blood/oxygen. When stenosis (narrowing) of these arteries occurs, blood supply will be reduced or may be completely obstructed, and a process known as myocardial infarction (localised tissue death of the heart muscle) will occur. The coronary arteries are prone in later life to developing coronary atherosclerosis where atheromatous material which comprises fat and connective tissue is laid down within the inner lining of the blood vessel. These so-called plaques are prone to ulcerate or attract the formation of a thrombus (blood clot) over the surface which may lead to sudden acute occlusion of the blood vessel. The plaques can also degenerate and rupture into the lumen (the inside space) of the blood vessel. In post-mortem pathology, approximately 30% of cases of death due to coronary artery atheroma show the presence of an acute thrombus in association with an atheromatous plaque. The remainder show narrowing or complete obstruction due to complex atheroma. The atheromatous plaques are also liable to calcify, and the blood vessels become rigid and tortuous in this situation.

It is likely that the immediate cause of death in ischaemic heart disease where no thrombus has been identified is that of an arrhythmia (irregular heart beat), usually ventricular fibrillation (an arrhythmia resulting from uncoordinated contractions of the ventricles), as the blood supply to the myocardium (heart muscle) becomes impaired. Myocardial infarction occurs when the muscle becomes deprived of oxygen. If an individual survives, tissue will remain. This renders the heart liable to further damage, including thinning of the heart muscle wall. In a post-mortem examination of an individual with ischaemic heart disease caused by coronary atheroma, the diagnosis in the absence of an occluding thrombosis or overt myocardial infarction is one of excluding other causes and establishing a degree of coronary artery atheroma sufficient to cause death. However, it should also be realised that, whilst coronary artery atheroma may be present, an individual may die of other causes totally unrelated to this (for example, gunshot wounds, a drug overdose or natural causes such as acute pneumonia). In the case of Harold Shipman, a number of cases had post-mortem examinations, but no toxicological analysis was done. Thus it was impossible to prove/disprove the actual cause of death – he used morphine. This was subsequently identified later in a number of victims following exhumation.

Post-mortem examination

6.4   Serial sectioning of the arteries should be undertaken. It is generally said that this should be at no more than 3mm intervals in order not to miss a plaque. The most common site of occlusion is in the anterior descending branch of the left coronary artery, followed by the right coronary artery usually at a more distal location than that in the anterior descending branch of the left coronary artery.

How much narrowing is necessary?

6.5   There is some debate as to the degree of narrowing sufficient to cause ischaemia/myocardial necrosis (individual cell death). It has been said that at least 80% of a blood vessel needs to be narrowed; however, to some extent this is variable and ischaemia is recognised to take place at lesser degrees of narrowing.

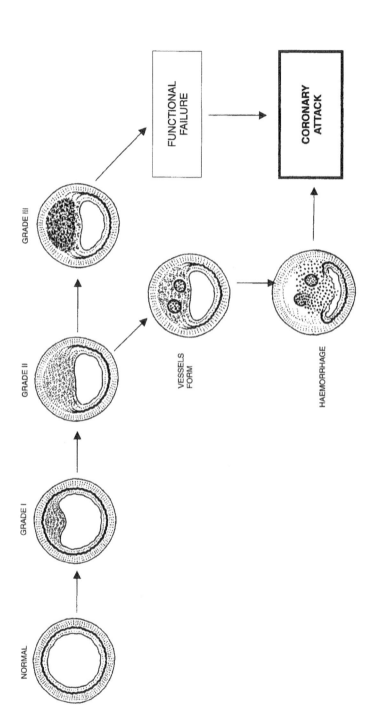

Figure 6.1 Development of a coronary attack. Atheroma forms, Grade II disease representing more than 50% restriction of the lumen. The plaque becomes vascularised and haemorrhage results in sudden occlusion. Alternatively, calcified arteries may not be able to dilate to satisfy an urgent need for increased blood supply. It should be noted that simple Grade II disease may lead to insufficiency if the muscle mass of the heart increases without an increase in vessels.

Other variables which are of significance are underlying fibrosis (scarring) of the heart, underlying ventricular hypertrophy (thickening of the heart muscle) or dilatation (dilatation of the heart chambers with thinning of the walls), as well as other heart disease.

Myocardial infarction

6.6   Myocardial infarction occurs when there is narrowing or occlusion of a coronary artery so that the blood supplying the myocardium is deprived of oxygen. The muscle becomes ischaemic (suffers lack of oxygen due to lack of blood flow). If there is survival, the early stages (after 18 hours or so) show mottling and haemorrhage within the heart muscle which subsequently after some weeks becomes scarred. Histological examination may be of importance in establishing the age of an area of myocardial infarction. Early changes show necrosis of the myocytes (heart muscle cells) with infiltration by acute inflammatory cells as the heart muscle is dead. Subsequent examination shows replacement by fibrous tissue (scar tissue 'similar' to a skin scar).

Role of stress – physical or otherwise

6.7   It is well recognised that physical and/or emotional stress may play a role in sudden death. The circumstances within the medico-legal setting where this may occur are during the course of a physical fracas where the deceased may have underlying heart disease. This stress can easily be related to physical injuries such as blows, punches or kicking or the emotional stress. It is likely that the systemic blood pressure is raised, contributing to a relative lack of oxygen arriving at the already compromised heart. In a number of these cases, the linkage between any act and death is temporal in nature. It is recognised that the so-called 'stress' of such an event may cause physiological changes for some while after the event, which is often known as 'post-exercise peril'.

- Ischaemic heart disease is the commonest cause of sudden death in the population, particularly in the older age group.

- Occlusion of a coronary artery with thrombus is seen in around a quarter to a third of cases.

- Frank myocardial infarction is seen in around 20% of cases.

- Stress, either physical or emotional, may play a role.

Other cardiac causes of sudden death

Hypertensive heart disease and systemic hypertension

6.8   Hypertension is defined as raised blood pressure. Blood pressure is determined by the measurements relating to the heart pumping blood around the body. When the blood is moving around the body, the strength of the heart moving the blood is measureable. If the blood pressure is raised, this puts additional strain on the heart.

There are two measurements for blood pressure, known as the systolic and the diastolic. An average normal reading would be 120mg of mercury systolic and 80mg diastolic. Typically, measurements take place using a sphygmomanometer, although there are newer methods for continual monitoring of the blood pressure over the day. Rises in blood pressure are associated with an increased incidence of stroke or heart attacks. Modern treatments have become much more effective at managing hypertension than in the past. The left ventricle becomes hypertrophic (increased in thickness). The hypertrophic ventricle may become dilated, particularly in the background of heart disease. The additional thickness of the myocardium increases the need for blood supply through the coronary arterial system. This leads to a predisposition to myocardial hypoxia as well as arrhythmias. The normal heart weight is around 400g, although it depends on the height and weight of the body. Hypertensive heart disease is often found when there is coronary artery atherosclerosis. The other organs, such as the kidney and brain, may show features of underlying hypertension.

- Hypertension is a relatively common condition, now reduced in incidence due to treatment.
- There is an increased risk of sudden death due to coronary artery disease as well as strokes.

Myocarditis

6.9   This is inflammation of the heart. This is usually viral in origin and it is a rare but well recognised cause of sudden death. Diagnosis will only be confirmed on histological examination, as the findings at post-mortem examination may be non-specific, with the myocardium appearing normal or showing some areas of pallor. It is not infrequently over-diagnosed.

Channelopathies

6.10   These are increasingly recognised to cause sudden death and various arrhythmias, as advances in molecular pathology occur. It is likely that a number of instances of sudden adult death syndrome are as a result of channelopathies where no other cause is found. The gene defects affect the function of the myocytes (muscle cells). The heart appears structurally normal. Channelopathies are caused by abnormalities in the genes which control the function of the myocytes of the heart. They are becoming increasingly recognised as a cause of death in younger adults alongside the cardiomyopathies.

Cardiomyopathies

6.11   These are a common cause of death particularly in the younger age group. Genetic screening in families is indicated in these cases. These include hypertrophic cardiomyopathy, dilated cardiomyopathy and arrythmogenic right ventricular hypertrophy. These conditions affect the myocardium, which becomes abnormal and enlarged. They are well recognised to cause sudden death. This may occur in the background of physical activity. Some countries have introduced screening for sportsmen.

Aortic aneurysm

6.12   Aortic aneurysm is a common cause of death in the older age group. It is due to systemic arteriosclerosis affecting the abdominal aorta. The wall of the aorta becomes weakened and a bulge-like structure forms on the wall of the aneurysm, which becomes stretched and thinner. This usually presents with either back or abdominal pain, rapidly progressing to systemic shock due to the significant blood loss present within the abdominal cavity, usually in the retroperitoneal space. Screening for aortic aneurysms has increased in recent years, leading to earlier interventional surgery.

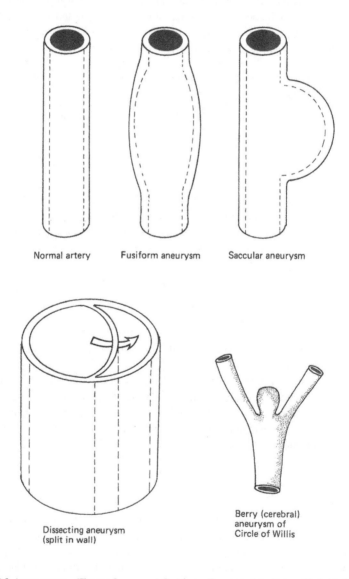

Figure 6.2 Aneurysms. (From: *Lawyers' Guide to Forensic Medicine*, Knight, B., 1998, Cavendish Publishing Ltd, reproduced by permission of Taylor & Francis Books UK.)

Dissecting aneurysm

6.13   In this condition, the wall of the aorta splits, with blood tracking within the wall. This usually occurs in the thoracic aorta, with rupture into the pericardial sac around the heart, or rupture into the abdominal cavity.

Valvular disease

6.14   Aortic stenosis (which is narrowing of the aortic valve leading to the aorta) is relatively common in the older age group. The valve may show calcification and/or be congenitally abnormal. As a result of the stenosis, the left ventricular myocardium hypertrophies with an increase in heart weight. The flow of blood to the myocardium from the coronary arteries is reduced, as there is reduced pressure caused by the narrowed valve. Sudden death is recognised to occur in these circumstances.

- Rare conditions causing sudden death include myocarditis, channelopathies and cardiomyopathies. The latter two need genetic investigation.

- Aneurysms (including aortic and thoracic) are usually associated with arteriosclerosis.

Non-cardiac causes of sudden death

Asthma

6.15   Asthma is a well-recognised and common cause of sudden death, particularly in the younger age group. Individuals who suffer from asthma may have attacks caused by a variety of substances such as house dust. The main and smaller airways become constricted and blocked by mucus plugs (thick mucus). The individual experiences severe difficulty in breathing, which may lead to status asthmaticus (an asthma attack that is not responsive to first-line treatment) necessitating urgent medical treatment.

Pneumonia

6.16   This is inflammation/infection of the lung, where a particular condition called consolidation occurs, with the alveoli spaces (air spaces) filled with fluid and inflammatory cells. Consolidation refers to the fact that the tissue is firm, being non-aerated (lacks air), and feels solid. The pneumonias can be classified further into lobar pneumonia (where a single lobe of the lung is involved in the process) and broncho-pneumonia (where infection spreads throughout the lungs, from the bronchi and bronchioles).

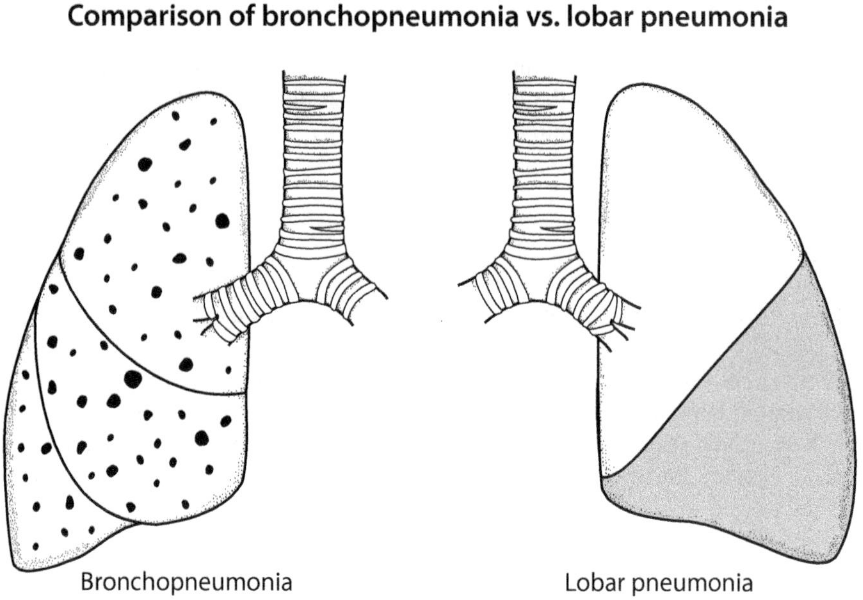

Comparison of bronchopneumonia vs. lobar pneumonia

Bronchopneumonia   Lobar pneumonia

Figure 6.3 Pneumonias. (Courtesy of Ruth Bowen, Medical Illustrator, Cardiff University.)

Lobar pneumonia

6.17   The incidence of this has decreased following antibiotic usage. It is still seen, however, in those with immunosuppression and neglect (for example, in alcoholics). It is commonest in the adult age group. The causative organism is the bacteria, streptococcus pneumoniae. Without antibiotic treatment, this can rapidly be fatal. Clinical features include a fever and pain on breathing. Various complications, including abscess formation, may occur. Pathologically, various stages can be identified, the earliest stage being one of acute congestion where the lung appears red (contains many blood cells) and contains frothy fluid, followed by late consolidation where the lung appears grey due to the presence of multiple dead and degenerating white cells.

Broncho-pneumonia

6.18   This occurs when bacteria colonise the bronchioles with extension into the alveoli leading to multiple areas of consolidation/infection. This can be caused by many bacteria. It is commonly seen in the very young age group, as well as the elderly, and where there is an underlying disease such as a stroke or malignant process. Some individuals are predisposed to broncho-pneumonia due to chronic bronchitis and other chronic lung disease. It is also known as the 'old man's friend' as it is not infrequently a terminal event in the elderly.

There are other less common causes of pneumonia by a variety of bacteria and other organisms. These include Legionnaire's Disease. This is known to occur following contamination of water in institutions, including hotels and hospitals. In addition, a number of viruses may also cause pneumonia. These include influenza, where death may occur extremely rapidly as a result of primary influenzal pneumonia.

Tuberculosis

6.19   This is a significant disease worldwide and it is increasingly recognised in the United Kingdom; there has been an increasing incidence particularly of drug-resistant tuberculosis. Tuberculosis is a condition which may affect many organs. It is categorised into primary pulmonary tuberculosis where the bacteria (tubercle bacillus) give rise to what is called a primary lesion in the lung which spreads to the lymph nodes adjacent to the lung. Primary tuberculosis normally heals, although infection may spread from such a primary lesion with abscess formation or pneumonia.

Re-infection tuberculosis

6.20   This occurs either as a reactivation of a dormant primary lesion or further infection. Large cavitating (large 'holes') lesions occur in the lung, and there is a risk of generalised lung infection as well as spreading via the blood to other organs. Widely disseminated tuberculosis is known as miliary tuberculosis, due to its appearance on X-rays of extensive numbers of small foci of infection resembling millet seeds.

Chronic bronchitis and emphysema

6.21   These are chronic lung conditions. Often, there may be a history of smoking or exposure to various industrial compounds. The bronchitis is characterised by thickened abnormal bronchi and bronchioles, with a tendency to chest infection. Emphysema is characterised by enlarged alveolar spaces which may also be known as bullae. Again, there is a tendency to additional chest infections.

Deep vein thrombosis and pulmonary embolus

6.22   In this condition, clotting of the blood occurs in the veins within the leg or thigh. It is most commonly seen in association with immobility such as following surgery, long-haul flights or an individual confined to bed. The situation where an individual is injured due to trauma, either following surgery or immobility, may be contentious in terms of proving a link between the trauma and the mode of death. With deep vein thrombosis, portions of the blood clot break off and enter into the circulation and are subsequently transported to the lungs. Large clots also known as thrombo-emboli block the major pulmonary arteries which supply the lungs, with subsequent acute heart failure. Smaller emboli may lodge deep within the lung tissue. Diagnosis of pulmonary emboli in life may be difficult and may only be identified at post-mortem examination. Preventative measures – for example, while in hospital and pre-surgery – with anticoagulant agents, such as low molecular weight heparins and/or compression stockings, may be indicated.

A genetic predisposition, Factor V Leiden thrombophilia, occurs in a percentage of the population, which causes abnormalities in blood clotting leading to an increased evidence of vulnerability of deep vein thrombosis. See also Chapter 10.

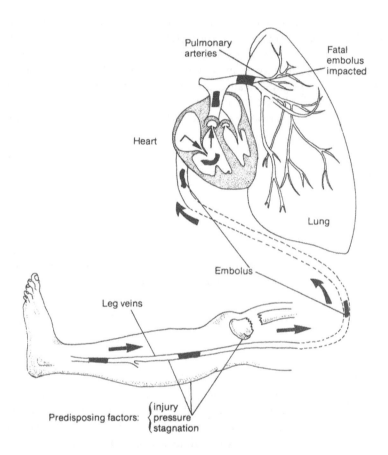

Figure 6.4 DVT/PE. (From: *Lawyers' Guide to Forensic Medicine*, Knight, B., 1998, Cavendish Publishing Ltd, reproduced by permission of Taylor & Francis Books UK.)

Epilepsy

6.23   Sudden unexpected death in epilepsy (SUDEP) is a diagnosis based on a history of epilepsy and exclusion of other causes. Epilepsy is characterised by sudden attacks of neurological dysfunction known as fits or seizures. It may occur due to a primary brain abnormality, or epileptic seizures may occur secondary to other conditions such as hypoglycaemia (low blood sugar). SUDEP is well recognised to occur in the younger age group, particularly in the background of alcohol intoxication, and toxicology often demonstrates sub-therapeutic (low levels) or negative levels of anti-convulsant medication.

It particularly occurs at night whilst asleep. The precise mode of death in these cases is unclear, although it is likely to be due to cardiac arrhythmia.

Status epilepticus is a condition of repeated seizures and should be differentiated from a SUDEP-type death. Status epilepticus is a medical emergency, with the necessity for hospital admission and therapeutic intervention to reduce the continual seizure activity.

- Asthma is a significant cause of death in the younger age group which requires urgent medical treatment.

- Lobar pneumonia is infection of a lobe of the lung usually caused by bacteria.

- Broncho-pneumonia involves both lungs. It is commonly seen in the elderly in association with an underlying disease such as a stroke.

- Other lung infections include viruses, Legionnaire's Disease and tuberculosis.

- Deep vein thrombosis and pulmonary embolism are of significance in the medico-legal setting linking trauma, surgery or immobility to the cause of death.

- Screening for Factor V Leiden thrombophilia increases vulnerability to blood clotting.

- SUDEP (sudden unexpected death in epilepsy) is associated with alcohol and low or absent levels of anti-convulsants.

- Differentiation from status epilepticus (which shows repeated seizures) should be made.

Subarachnoid haemorrhage

6.24   Spontaneous subarachnoid haemorrhage occurs most commonly in the middle age group. An aneurysm is a swelling of the blood vessels on the base of the brain on the Circle of Willis. This is covered in Chapter 9. Death typically occurs after sudden collapse. In a number of cases, a recent history of a severe headache may be elucidated.

Intracerebral haemorrhage

6.25   This is covered in Chapter 9. The main causes are those secondary to hypertension, but also amyloid and some cerebral tumours may cause bleeding. Rarely, an intracerebral haemorrhage with sudden death may be the presenting feature of a brain tumour.

Further reading material

General textbooks

- Payne-James, J., Jones, R., Karch, S.B., Manlove, J. *Simpsons Forensic Medicine* (2011, 13th Edition, Hodder Arnold)

- Sheppard, M. *Practical Cardiovascular Pathology* (2011, 2nd Edition)
- Sauko, P. & Knight, B. *Knight's Forensic Pathology* (2004, 3rd Edition, Arnold)

Articles in update textbooks

- Cunningham, K.S. & Pollanen, M.S. 'Sudden Death from Pulmonary Causes' in Turk, E.E. *Forensic Pathology Reviews*. Volume Six, 2011
- Gill, J.R. 'The Medicolegal Evaluation of Fatal Pulmonary Thromboembolism' in Tsokos, M. *Forensic Pathology Reviews*. Volume Two, 2005
- Madea, B. & Dettmeyer, R. 'Sudden Unexpected Death Related to Viral Myocarditis' in Tsokos, M. *Forensic Pathology Reviews*. Volume Two, 2005
- Morris, J.A., Harrison, L.M. & Lauder, R.M. 'Sudden Death from Infectious Disease' in Turk, E.E. *Forensic Pathology Reviews*. Volume Six, 2011
- Pomara, C. & Fineschi, V. 'A Forensic Pathological Approach to Sudden Cardiac Death' in Tsokos, M. *Forensic Pathology Reviews*. Volume One, 2004
- Tsokos, M. 'Asthma Deaths' in Tsokos, M. *Forensic Pathology Reviews*. Volume Four, 2006

Articles in journals

- Hesdorffer, D.C., Tomson, T., Benn, E., Sander, J.W., Nilsson, L., Langan, Y. *et al.* 'Combined analysis of risk factors for SUDEP' *Epilepsia* 2011; 52: 1150–9
- Lucena, J., Rico, A., Vazquez, R., Martin, R., Martinez, C., Salguero, M., Miguel, L. 'Pulmonary embolism and sudden-unexpected death: prospective study on 2477 forensic autopsies performed at the Institute of Legal Medicine in Seville' *Journal of Forensic and Legal Medicine* 16(4): 196–201, 2009 May
- Mobilia, F., Casali, M.B., Gallieni, M., Genovese, U.R. 'Lethal pulmonary thromboembolism: an autopsy-based study on a rare but legally relevant event' *Medicine, Science and the Law* 54(2): 78–83, 2014 Apr
- Neligan, A., Bell, G.S., Johnson, A.L., Goodridge, D.M., Shorvon, S.D., Sander, J.W. 'The long-term risk of premature mortality in people with epilepsy' *Brain* 2011; 134: 338–95
- Neligan, A., Bell, G.S., Sander, J.W. 'Sudden death in epilepsy' *BMJ* 2011: 343

Chapter 7

Wounding: injuries and their interpretation

Wounding and the criminal law: England and Wales and Northern Ireland

Assaults

7.1   The law on wounding in England and Wales is governed by the Offences Against the Person Act 1861 ('the OAPA'), which itemises various offences:

Section 18   prohibits wounding or causing grievous bodily harm with intent to do so or with intent to resist lawful arrest and can be punished by imprisonment up to and including life imprisonment.

Section 20   prohibits maliciously wounding or inflicting grievous bodily harm, either with or without the use of any weapon or instrument. Injury may be 'inflicted' with or without the corollary of an assault. It can be punished by a maximum of five years' imprisonment.

Section 47   prohibits assault occasioning actual bodily harm. The maximum sentence is five years' imprisonment.

7.2   In addition, section 39 of the Criminal Justice Act 1988 prohibits the two common law offences of common assault and battery. The maximum sentence for each is six months' imprisonment. For section 39, an assault need not be physical – it may involve no more than causing a person, either intentionally or recklessly, to anticipate immediate violence. A battery, however, involves the infliction of personal violence, directly or through a weapon or instrument, albeit the violence may be no more than unwanted touching.

7.3   The nature of a 'wound' for the purposes of sections 18 and 20 of the OAPA is not defined, but must involve a break in the continuity of the whole skin,[1] and includes incised, punctured, lacerated or contused wounds, and gun-shot wounds. It would also include a similar injury to a contiguous mucous membrane. The point is relatively unimportant, as the alternative charges of *causing* actual or grievous bodily harm will cover bruising or more serious injuries, such as those that may result in a fracture without skin damage.

---

1   *R v Wood* (1830) 1 Mood 278, see also Archbold chapter 19 for definition of 'wound'.

Grievous bodily harm (GBH) is only defined as 'really serious harm', and the House of Lords has declined to give it further definition.[2] The distinction between the levels of injury is that, generally, fractures and wounds are charged as section 18 or 20 offences, whereas more than fleeting, but not serious, injuries (such as bruises or grazes) are charged as section 47. Actual bodily harm includes any hurt or injury calculated to interfere with the health or comfort of the victim. It need not be permanent but must be more than merely transient or trifling.[3] It can include momentary loss of consciousness, but more than that is likely to result in GBH being charged. Injury can include psychiatric injury but not mere emotions such as stress fear or panic.[4] A medical report will be necessary for the proof of more serious injuries, but is not a requirement if there are, for example, photographs. Generally, the CPS tends to charge injuries at common assault level unless there is medical evidence.

Homicide

7.4   Murder is defined as the unlawful killing of another person with intent to cause either death or grievous bodily harm. The victim of a homicide must be a person, and human life begins at birth. Thus a foetus cannot be the victim of murder or manslaughter, unless they are injured in the womb and born alive but die shortly afterwards from their injuries. (Further offences relating to children and foetuses are dealt with in Chapter 14.) The word 'unlawfully' relates to all assaults, including homicide, and allows a defendant to rely on self-defence. The defendant must *cause* the death, which means accelerate it by more than a negligible amount. The 'year and a day' rule has now been abolished.[5] An attempted murder is committed if the defendant does an act which is more than merely preparatory to murder, with intent to kill.

7.5   Manslaughter can be committed in a number of ways. The main distinction is between voluntary and involuntary manslaughter.

7.6   Voluntary manslaughter occurs when all the elements of murder are present but the crime is reduced due to particular extenuating circumstances. These include:

(i)   loss of control (the defendant committed the act having lost self control, which was caused by a 'qualifying trigger', and a normally tolerant and restrained person of the defendant's age and sex would have reacted the same way);[6]

(ii)   diminished responsibility (the defendant committed the act, but his or her acts are explained by an abnormality of mental functioning from a recognised medical condition which substantially impaired the defendant's ability to understand the nature of his or her conduct, form rational judgment and exercise self-control);[7] or

(ii)   a suicide pact.

---

2   *DPP v Smith* [1961] AC 290, HL.
3   *R v Brown (A)* [1994] 1 AC 212, HL, at 230, 242.
4   *R v Chan-Fook* (1994) 99 Cr App R 147.
5   Law Reform (Year and a Day Rule) Act 1996.
6   Coroners and Justice Act 2009, s 54.
7   Homicide Act 1957, s 2(1), as amended by the Coroners and Justice Act 2009.

7.7 Involuntary manslaughter is unlawful killing without intent to kill or cause grievous bodily harm. In turn, it can be committed in one of two ways:

(i) unlawful act manslaughter (the prosecution must prove that the defendant committed a criminal act which was physically dangerous and caused the death of the victim);[8] or

(ii) manslaughter by gross negligence (the prosecution must prove that: the defendant owed the victim a duty of care; the defendant breached that duty; the breach caused the death; and the breach was so gross as to justify a criminal conviction).[9]

Wounding and the criminal law: Scotland

Assaults

7.8 In Scotland, at common law, an assault is a deliberate attack on the person of another, meaning that the attack must be done either with the intent to cause personal injury or with the intent to place the victim in a state of fear of harm. No physical contact is necessary. Clearly, then, the offence can cover everything from a blow which misses its intended victim to an attack resulting in very serious injury. The range of offences is generally reflected in the seriousness of the sentence passed. However, at the trial stage, the law does recognise the concept of aggravated assault. There are no fixed categories of aggravated assault, but common examples include the extent of the injury on the victim (which can be libelled, i.e. specified on the indictment, as 'assault to severe injury'), assault aggravated by use of a weapon such as a knife or firearm, or by throwing corrosive substances, and the very severe forms of aggravation of assault 'to the danger of life', which can be specified whether or not there were injuries, and assault with intent to kill.

Homicide

7.9 In Scotland, the principal distinction is between murder and culpable homicide. Murder requires either an intention to kill or 'wicked recklessness' (not caring whether the victim lives or dies). The Scottish concept of 'wickedly reckless murder' has no place in English jurisprudence, where intention is essential to the crime, although it is sufficient that the intention was to cause grievous bodily harm only.

Culpable homicide is causing death without either of the two *mens rea* for murder (intent to kill or wicked recklessness). As in England and Wales, it can usefully be divided into voluntary and involuntary forms. Voluntary culpable homicide is usually committed when death was intended but there are mitigating factors affecting

---

8 *Attorney-General's Reference (No 3 of 1994)* [1998] AC 245, HL.
9 *R v Adomako* [1995] 1 AC 171, HL.

intention, such as diminished responsibility or provocation. Involuntary culpable homicide is, in turn, divided into unlawful act and lawful act/gross negligence forms, and each form is broadly similar to the unlawful act manslaughter/manslaughter by gross negligence forms of involuntary manslaughter in England and Wales.

Wounding and medicine: phraseology and overview

7.10   From the medical perspective, the terms 'wound', 'injury' and 'lesion' are often used interchangeably to indicate some form of deleterious consequence to the body. The use of lesion is advisably avoided as it has stronger connotations of natural disease and, as a result, may cause some confusion. In general, injuries can be separated into two broad types: blunt force injuries; and sharp force injuries. The former relates to injuries that arise when a blunt object or surface contacts the skin, whereas the latter relates to injuries that arise when a sharp-tipped or sharp-edged weapon contacts the skin.

Blunt force injuries to the skin surface

7.11   There are three main types of blunt force trauma injuries: abrasions, bruises and lacerations. Although invariably described separately, a single application of force may result in all three types being present.

Abrasion

7.12   An abrasion, commonly known as a graze or scratch, is widely encountered by the general public. Injury occurs only in the most superficial part of the skin, the epidermis. As abrasions require no specific treatment, they are of little clinical importance and, in general, are poorly documented by treating clinicians. They are, however, vital in the interpretative nature of forensic medicine, as they provide essential information about the agent or mechanism that inflicted them, as well as an indication of potential underlying damage.

An abrasion should, strictly speaking, not bleed, as the epidermis is free of blood vessels. However, the corrugated (undulating) nature of the epidermis ensures that bleeding is frequently encountered.

'Simple' abrasion

7.13   This occurs when a force is applied tangentially: the force 'scrapes' along the length of the skin, causing the abrasive damage. These are the types of the abrasions that are encountered on knees and elbows when an individual falls over, or as the fingernail is scraped across the skin producing a scratch (such as may be seen on the neck in strangulation caused by a finger or fingers).

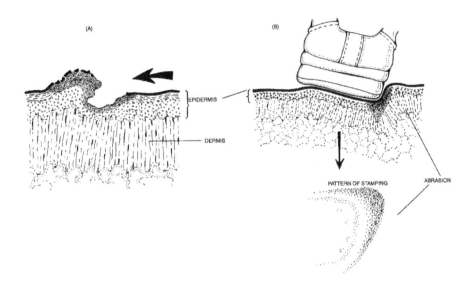

Figure 7.1 Abrasions of the skin. (A) Horizontal. The object struck moves along the surface and the broken epidermis 'piles up' as the force is applied. The direction of force is, thus, evident for some time after the event. (B) Vertical. As the skin is depressed, it is abraded by the sides of the striking object. A fairly faithful contour impression of the object remains. Contour bruising may also be seen.

Brush abrasion

7.14   If the tangential abrasion is relatively wide, it will often form within it multiple, broadly linear components. This type of abrasion is called a 'brush abrasion'. The finding of a brush abrasion is suggestive of a falling or dragging-type mechanism for its causation. Close inspection of the margins of the abrasion may reveal skin tags or 'pile-ups' of the epidermis at the terminal end of it, giving an indication of the direction of force across the skin. These tags are quite fragile, both in life and post-mortem, and are easily lost.

Crush abrasion

7.15   When the blunt force is applied perpendicular to the skin, the skin is crushed rather than scraped. As a result, an outline or imprint of the inflicting object can be produced. This imprint may precisely replicate the inflicting object but, if not, the broad pattern, particularly its outline, can assist. An example of this type of abrasion would be that seen with impact by footwear.

Parchmented abrasion

7.16   This refers to an abrasion or abrasions which are caused in the peri- or post-mortem period. Peri-mortem is defined as occurring just before death, at the point of death or after death. Such an abrasion inflicted around the time of death or after death has insufficient time to develop a vital reaction and, as such, takes on the appearance and texture of parchment (a dried translucent yellow): hence the term parchmented, or parchment-like. A classic example would be the ligature mark seen in a typical hanging case. Parchmented changes may also occur due to the slippage of skin that is encountered by decomposition. This is seen following body handling or even merely the pressure of the body weight in contact with the skin surface.

- An abrasion arises when the most superficial layer of the skin, the epidermis, is damaged.

- Force applied tangentially or directly perpendicular to the skin may cause an abrasion.

- An abrasion may arise as a post-mortem injury adopting an appearance known as 'parchmented'.

Bruising

7.17   Bruising is the result of bleeding into the tissues below the skin and arises when the vasculature is damaged. The application of blunt force to the body surface is the most common mechanism by which bruises appear, but bruising can be encountered in any situation where the vasculature is damaged, such as an incised wound slicing the skin and damaging vasculature (see below). However, in such a case, the extent of the localised bruising will be slighter in comparison to that caused by an equivalent application of blunt force.

Medical terminology regarding the bruise is relatively widespread, and a number of terms may be used, even in the same medical report. Clearly, 'bruise' is widely understood by both medical and lay alike and, as such, is the preferred term. Other words, such as haematoma, haemorrhage, contusions and ecchymoses, may be encountered. Strictly speaking, a haematoma tends to refer to discrete areas of haemorrhage which may be isolated.

Factors affecting the appearance of a bruise

7.18   There is considerable variability in the appearance of a bruise, and a number of factors – including the age of the bruise itself, the location of the injury, and the age and health status of the individual – are responsible for that. Some of these factors, such as the colour changes associated with the ageing of a bruise, are well recognised by the public but not necessarily that well understood.

BRUISING

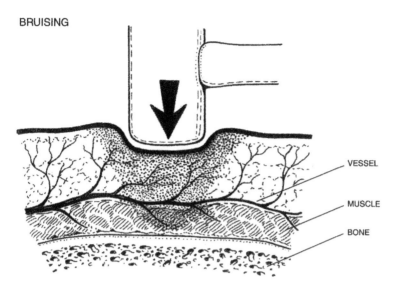

VESSEL

MUSCLE

BONE

Figure 7.2 Bruising. Subcutaneous capillaries may rupture when the skin is struck by a blunt object with insufficient force to break the skin; blood is then extruded into the surrounding tissues. A bruise is, therefore, a form of subcutaneous laceration.

Age of the bruise

7.19   It is common knowledge that the appearance of a bruise changes as the bruise ages. The fresh bruise will appear purple, red or blue. These individual colours give no specific information, and a bruise may comprise one colour or be a mixture of both. As the bruising ages, the colour changes to green then yellow then black as the haemoglobin within the red blood cells is converted to bile pigments before the bruise resolves completely. The precise length of time for the healing process is variable between individuals, and to some degree variable in an individual, depending on the location of the bruise. Despite much work, the only reliable feature is that a bruise that demonstrates yellow (or green) discolouration is at least 18 hours old in an individual under the age of 65 (Langlois and Gresham) and at least 24 hours old in a child (Stephenson and Bialas). It is important to stress that a bruise without yellow discolouration may be considerably older than 18 hours or, indeed, 24 hours.

More valuable evidence as to timing may be of a comparative nature: it can be reasonably stated that, in the same individual, one given bruise or group of bruises is older than another. This is of particular importance when chronicity of abuse, such as that involving children or the elderly, is the matter at hand. In general, bruises in similar anatomical sites will heal at more or less the same rates. However, healing of bruises is in part dependent on the extent of the blood supply to that region. For instance, a bruise of the distal foot may heal more slowly than one in a corresponding better-circulated, more proximal site in the leg.

The colour of a bruise does not provide any real additional information; in particular, it does not indicate its severity nor the extent of force use to create it.

The dating of injuries may be assisted by microscopic examination of bruises, based on the finding of iron by special histological stains or by identification of a certain compounds utilising more complex histochemical techniques. However, the relative appearance (or disappearance) of the various compounds is again somewhat variable and it is rarely possible to be specific. In general, the majority of forensic pathology textbooks suggest that the presence of iron-containing pigment in bruises arises after 48 to 72 hours. However, the strength of the supporting scientific work in these areas is not as robust as might be hoped, and some textbooks suggest that as little as 24 hours (or so) is the earliest timeframe by which iron-containing pigment is identified. In essence, where the ageing of injuries is paramount, early interaction between the appropriate medical witness and the legal professionals involved in the case is undoubtedly warranted.

Location and movement of bruises

7.20   The ease with which a location will bruise is heavily dependent on the underlying structures. Those regions of the body that are supported by close underlying bony support (such as the face) more readily bruise, as the solid bony support acts as an anvil facilitating localised vascular damage; whereas, by comparison, the abdominal skin and its underlying subcutaneous tissues are unsupported and, as result, are very difficult to bruise. As such, bruising of the abdomen (secondary to blunt force trauma) is usually a marker of very severe force being applied to the abdomen.

The laxity of the tissues is also important. The more lax the tissue, the easier for the blood to spread. For example, the tissues around the eye are relatively lax, and trauma to the eye socket region will result in bruising that will easily spread, resulting in the widespread characteristic 'black eye'. However, trauma to the soles of the feet and palms of the hands, where the skin and the underlying soft tissues are taut, will result, in comparison, with a small compact bruise.

7.21   Due to the laxity of tissues, bruises may 'move' to a different site or appear at a later point. In general, the escaped blood will move along the tissue lines of least resistance and under the effects of gravity. For example, a deep bruise of, say, the thigh muscles may be invisible on the surface until the blood tracks down the tissue planes and presents beneath the skin of the knee.

As such, the external evidence of bruising may alter with time; it is often most valuable to re-examine the victim or offender of an alleged assault some 24 hours or so after the event, as bruises that were originally indistinct or even invisible may become defined and 'come out'. In essence, if there is a delay between injury and examination, it may be that the site of bruising does not represent the site of trauma. Despite continued review, some bruises may never be visible on the surface of the skin. This is particularly true when the bruising is in the deeper tissues or when the bruise underlies the scalp, because the scalp is relatively thick and overlying hair will obscure it.

For the same reasons, deep tissue bruising, typically on the back of the body, may also appear several days after death. Dissection of the deeper tissues of the back of the body and limbs by the pathologist at the original post-mortem examination will identify such bruising.

Health

7.22   Age: The elderly bruise more readily, with bruising likely to be more extensive and to resolve over a much longer period. With increasing age, there is increased fragility of the vasculature as well as increased atrophy (thinning) of the skin, making the elderly more vulnerable to trauma and thus to bruising from conceivably innocuous trauma. Atrophy of the skin also increases the potential spread of the bruising into the surrounding tissues. Reduced functioning of components of the clotting system compound this further and, in particular, prolong the healing time significantly. In fact, healing may never be complete and residual bruising may develop the form of senile purpura, or old person's bruising, which demonstrates a characteristic more intense red/purple plaque-like appearance. Senile purpura conceivably can persist for many years and, although commonly encountered in the elderly, it can reveal a worrisome distribution raising the prospect of elder abuse.

7.23   Clotting abnormalities: Individuals who use alcohol to excess also have a propensity to bruise. This propensity clearly relates in part to the 'knocks and scrapes' situations that intoxication results in. However, alcohol can result in damage to the liver, which is an important factor in the production of proteins within the clotting cascade that manage clotting within the human body. It also results in a reduction in platelet numbers, a cell important in clotting.

For similar reasons, any persons with an inborn coagulation factor deficiency (such as haemophilia), diminished number of platelets, abnormalities of the small blood vessels or with liver disease will bleed more readily than normal and may give a false impression of the severity of injury.

Interpreting bruises

7.24   Intradermal (within the dermis of the skin) bruising is of special forensic importance as it is can be associated with interpretable reproduction of the outline of the inflicting object, as the bruising is 'held' in place by the relatively rigid epidermis.

Such patterned bruises include the following:

- Stamps with footwear, as the tread of the footwear is replicated.

- A characteristic pattern of bruising may be produced by a blow from an elongated rod or stick-like weapon, such as an iron bar or broomstick. This results in what is known as a 'tramline bruise' comprising of two parallel lines of bruising with pale skin between them. This pattern arises as the central area is compressed but the vasculature in that area is undamaged and, at the margins, the implement compresses the tissue but immediately adjacent tissue is uncompressed. This results in torsion or rupture of the vasculature of the margins.

- Clusters of small discs of bruising in close approximation can strongly raise the prospect of 'fingertip bruising' due to forceful gripping. Often concentrated on the arm, they rarely form a perfect line of evenly spaced bruises but, in the majority of cases, the pattern is quite characteristic and easily recognisable. It is important to note that, in the elderly, fingertip bruising can be encountered in the context of normal assistive handling.

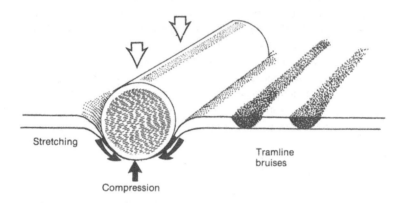

Figure 7.3 Tramline bruise. (From: *Lawyers' Guide to Forensic Medicine*, Knight, B., 1998, Cavendish Publishing Ltd, reproduced by permission of Taylor & Francis Books UK.)

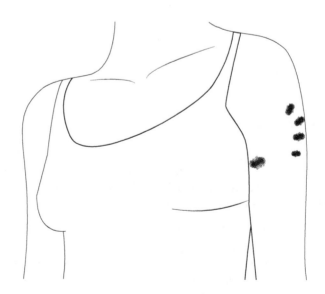

Figure 7.4 Gripping-type injuries on the upper limb. (Courtesy of Ruth Bowen, Medical Illustrator, Cardiff University.)

- Ante-mortem 'blushing' of the vessels beneath a pressure point may leave a distinct pattern, e.g. following a slap. This will invariably disappear by the time of any post-mortem examination in a deceased case.

Post-mortem bruises

7.25 Bruising should be considered an in-life phenomenon. Although 'bruises' can be caused after death, the size of the 'bruise' produced is disproportionately small in relation to the amount of force and associated damage (such as bony fractures and lacerations). The bruises arise as a result of localised vascular damage and leakage of blood out into the tissues.

Bruising of the soft tissues – deep bruising

7.26 Bruising principally involving the soft tissues (e.g. fat and muscle) may be sufficient to cause death without evidence of injury to internal organs or bleeding within the body cavities. This mechanism of death has been relatively well documented in the forensic pathology literature, but has remained, until quite recently, poorly appreciated by other medical practitioners. Death may result purely from a blood loss; however, other features (such as entry of breakdown products of fat and muscle into the blood system) may also play a role.

Smaller areas of bruising may also have catastrophic effects. For example, bruising within the eyeball may cause permanent blindness. Bruising over one of the coronary arteries may cause compression and prevent blood flow to the heart muscle.

- A bruise is the release of blood into the subcutaneous and/or deeper soft tissues following damage to the vasculature (blood vessels) that can be seen through the skin surface.

- The appearance of a bruise is dependent on a number of factors, such as the location of the injury, the age and health status of the individual, and the age of the bruise itself.

- The age of a bruise will affect its appearance. A fresh bruise is typically purple, red or blue, changing to green, yellow and then black.

- The location of the blunt force trauma upon the body affects its appearance on the skin surface.

- Bruises need not appear at the site of the trauma.

- Bruising may be patterned and demonstrate a profile of the implement that caused it.

- The location, distribution and architecture of bruising assists with its interpretation; for instance, in black-eye, gripping and defensive injuries.

- Bruising solely located in the soft tissues can be sufficiently severe to cause death in itself.

Lacerations

7.27   A laceration is the splitting or tearing of the whole skin by applied blunt force trauma. It is usually associated with abrasion (as the blunt force crushes the skin as a prelude to the splitting) and bruising (as there is concomitant damage to the vasculature). A laceration does not arise when a sharp-tipped or sharp-edged weapon is utilised (see **7.34** below).

Location

7.28   The location of the laceration has significant importance for the minimum amount of force required to cause it. For example, a blow over the cheekbone may result in a laceration, whereas an identical blow a few centimetres below on the cheek itself might well cause no more than an abrasion. Perhaps the classic laceration due to blunt injury is the boxer's 'cut eye', which is found in the eyebrow area. Equally, a laceration to the soft unsupported skin of the abdominal region requires an inordinate amount of force to lacerate in comparison to the scalp, where the firm bone lies close beneath. In essence, where bone lies close to the skin, less force is required.

The relative contour of the underlying bone is also important. The protuberant nature of the eyebrow ridge makes it more vulnerable to splitting than the flatter bones of the skull. This means that a punch may lacerate the skin of the face but is rarely, if ever, associated with causing a laceration to the scalp unless a ring or knuckleduster is worn.

Differentiation from an incised wound

7.29   The hallmark of a laceration, that allows differentiation from an incised wound, is the irregularity of the split including the presence of bridges of vessels and nerves across the deeper aspects of the wound, which gives a laceration a 'ragged' appearance. There is commonly associated bruising, abrasion and the potential for bony fracture.

On occasion, particularly to the scalp, without detailed examination, a linear laceration can mimic the appearance of an incised wound, as the underlying anvil effect can result in a relatively clean split.

Contacting surface

7.30   The nature of the contacting surface is important in the appearance of the laceration. For example, a broad surface (typically a fall) will often leave an irregular stellate (star-shaped) laceration frequently associated with widespread abrasion, whereas a projecting edge or linear object will result in a more linear laceration with limited abrasion.

Interpretation

7.31   A laceration does not give as much evidence as to the shape of the causative instrument as an abrasion does, but the two often coexist. However, the overall nature

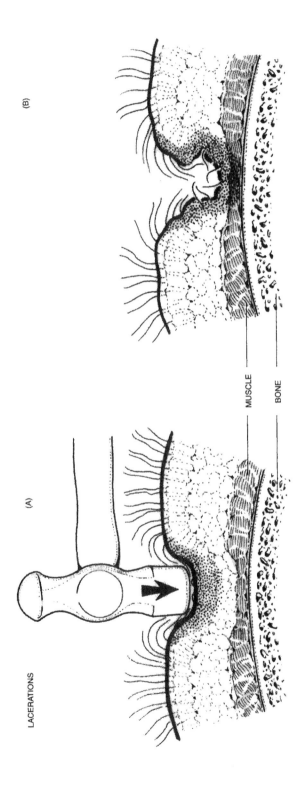

Figure 7.5 (A) The skin will split if it is compressed between an object and bone with sufficient force. (B) The split will, however, be irregular, there will be associated bruising and surface elements will be forced into the deeper parts of the lesion.

and grouping of the lacerations is very useful in terms of the interpretation that can be provided. For example, rounded or semi-circular lacerations can be suggestive of the use of a round-headed hammer. However, as the extent of the trauma (both in terms of severity of force and number of impacts) increases, the complex lacerations produced become more difficult to precisely interpret. The presence of multiple lacerations of a generally similar type, particularly if they are closely grouped but not identical in direction, must raise the suspicion of assaults. Unless they result from a fall, lacerations are seldom suicidal, because remarkable motivation would be needed to produce self-inflicted lacerations with blunt instruments; this has, however, been encountered (for example, when an individual repeatedly bashes their head against a wall or other item).

Lacerations due to more unusual objects

7.32 Lacerations may also take the form of penetrating wounds (that is, an injury that penetrates deeply but with more limited skin surface injury). An example of such a laceration would be the injury caused by a screwdriver being thrust into the body. Penetrating lacerations can bear some resemblance to a stab wound, and the sharper the tip of the object, the more difficult it becomes to distinguish between a laceration and a stab wound.

- A laceration is the splitting or tearing of the whole skin caused by the application of blunt force trauma.

- It generally occurs where bone lies close to the skin with little intervening soft tissue.

Sharp force injuries to the skin surface

7.33 A wide array of descriptive terms are utilised to describe sharp force injuries to the surface of the skin. These include phrases such as 'stab wounds', 'incised wounds', 'cutting wounds', 'slash wounds' and 'slicing wounds'. For example, some forensic pathologists utilise the phrase 'incised wound' to incorporate all forms of sharp force injury, whereas other forensic pathologists (including the authors) utilise it solely for slicing-type injuries. Undoubtedly, this can cause some confusion to legal professionals. For the purposes of this chapter, a stab wound refers to a penetrating injury caused by principally a sharp-tipped weapon producing a wound that is deeper into the body than the wound produced on the skin surface; whereas an incised wound refers to a sliced wound that is longer on the skin surface than it is deep and is the result of a sharp-tipped or sharp-edged weapon being drawn across the skin.

The use of the term 'slash wound' is best avoided by doctors and lawyers alike as somewhat emotive.

The matter is further complicated as it is well documented in the medical literature that clinical doctors and even some involved in the field of forensic medicine call incised wounds 'lacerations' on a frequent basis. This frequently arises when injuries are documented in hospital/casualty departments. The lawyer should pay particular attention to this error to avoid embarrassment when an appropriate expert is instructed.

INCISION

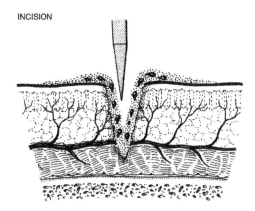

Figure 7.6 Incision. In some cases, there is a graduation from laceration to incision – a blow from a blunt axe will, for example, show features of both. In the typical incision from a sharp instrument, however, the wound is clean cut, there is no bruising and the vessels are divided to give rise to severe bleeding to the exterior. No superficial material is forced into the wound.

Incised/sliced wounds

7.34　　An incised wound results when a sharp-edged or sharp-tipped implement is drawn across the skin, resulting in a clean cut wound that is longer on the skin surface than it is deep into the body. The most common implement used in causing an incised wound is a knife, but any sharp-edged surface, such as broken glass, will cause this type of injury.

The dangers of such a wound are dependent upon its position on the body and its depth. For example, a deep incised wound to the buttock may cause little more than discomfort, whereas a comparatively superficial incised wound to the wrist (or neck) region may prove fatal due to division of major vasculature. It is important to appreciate that all pathologists undertaking autopsy examinations will have experience of fatalities caused by incised wounds to the wrists.

Incised wounds: manner of infliction

7.35　　Incised wounds may arise in all manners: accidental, suicidal/self-inflicted, homicidal/assault related, and defensive injuries.

7.36　　Accidental incised wounds are relatively common. Perhaps the most common accidental 'incised wound' is the paper cut, whereby extremely narrow paper is drawn across the skin at a considerable pressure, incising the skin superficially. Accidental incised wounds are also commonly sustained in the kitchen.

7.37　　Incised wounds are also commonly self-inflicted, whether to cause deliberate self-harm or for malfeasance (simulation of assault). There can be overlap between these patterns of injuries. In cases of malfeasance, the injuries are typically a cluster of delicate superficial incisions, invariably in parallel in non-sensitive parts (such as the cheek, the sides of the neck and back of the non-dominant hand).

So-called 'cries for help' may adopt a similar profile and frequently involve the wrist; but, if intent to endanger life is present, these wounds become increasingly severe.

In fatal cases, there is often a combination of superficial and deeper injuries. These deeper injuries may comprise either incised wounds or stab wounds. Superficial injuries often surround the deeper fatal injury and are termed 'hesitation' or 'tentative' marks. This distribution of injuries is characteristic, virtually pathognomonic, of self-infliction. However, on very rare occasions such a patterning may be found in an assault-type situation without planning or deliberately in some form of torture or similar episode.

7.38   The use of a bladed implement represents a common feature in assaults. In the majority of such incidents, confirming a third-party involvement is relatively straightforward, as the injuries are more widely distributed about the body. There is a lack of the more careful appearance of superficiality and regularity which is characteristic of self-inflicted injuries.

7.39   The presence of incised wounds to the upper limbs raises the possibility of self-defence or 'defensive injuries'. These can be defined as active or passive.

7.40   Active self-defence wounds typically consist of injuries to the palms of the hands, as active attempts are made to grasp the causative implement. The classic location where this injury is encountered is the webbing between the thumb and index finger extending onto the palm of the hand.

7.41   Passive self-defence wounds are more commonly encountered on the backs of the hands extending up the forearm and, at times, onto the upper arm. These are injuries that arise as the arms try and protect the vulnerable areas of the body such as the head. It is often forgotten that defensive injuries may arise in other body positions, such as to the back and the lower limbs, if the body adopts a foetal position. The distribution and depth of these wounds is usually somewhat irregular.

7.42   The presence of defence wounds indicates that an individual was at least conscious, and partially mobile. It is important to appreciate that the converse is not true, as an absence of defensive-type injuries does not indicate that the victim was unconscious or immobile. Defensive-type injuries are present in less than half of homicidal stabbings.

Defensive-type injuries are not just limited to sharp force assault. A similar distribution (comprising of bruising and laceration) may be encountered following blunt force assault (see **7.11** onwards above).

- An incised wound is caused by a sharp edge or tip being drawn across the skin resulting in a wound that is longer on the skin surface than deeper in the body.

- Incised wounds may arise in all manners: accidental, suicidal/self-inflicted and homicidal/assault-related.

- The presence of incised wounds to the upper limbs raises the possibility of self-defence or 'defensive injuries'. Their presence indicates that the individual was at least semi-conscious and able to move, to a greater or lesser extent.

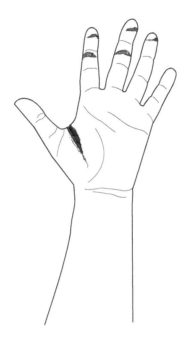

Figure 7.7 Defensive injuries. (Courtesy of Ruth Bowen, Medical Illustrator, Cardiff University.)

Stab wounds

7.43   A stab wound is a penetrating wound caused predominately by a sharp-tipped object penetrating the skin such that it forms a wound that is deeper into the body than the width of the wound on the skin. The skin surface characteristics are similar to that of an incised wound, comprising of a clean-cut, slit-type injury. Though most frequently associated with knives, any sharp-tipped implement, such as a piece of broken glass or needle, can result in a stab wound.

The appearance of a stab wound is heavily dependent on the implement that was utilised to cause the injury, and features such as the type of weapon and its dimensions can, to a certain degree, be interpreted from the wound characteristics.

Perhaps the most important feature that the lawyer will attempt to elicit from the medical witness is the level of force required to cause a stab wound. The force required to inflict a stab wound is dependent on the sharpness of the tip of the blade and also on the structures damaged on the passage of the blade through the body. Clearly, with increasing bluntness of the tip, increasing force is required.

Clothing is also important: for example, a thick leather jacket will require more force than a thin T-shirt for the blade tip to pass through it. This is more a matter of common sense, and the medical witness will not be able to expand on this significantly.

Forces involved in stab wounds

7.44 In relation to the human body, there is a wide array of literature and medical opinion regarding the forces involved in creating a stab wound. The literature to some extent contains contradictory findings due to the variety of approaches and techniques utilised in experimentation. Criticism and concerns regarding the various approaches are commonplace. A comprehensive overview can be found in review articles by Davison and Bohnert *et al.*

7.45 The skin is recognised to produce the most resistance to any weapon. In the body, bone and calcified cartilage require significant force. The remaining tissues of the body require less force to penetrate than the skin, although this does not mean that applied force of some degree is not required. In fact, some studies cast significant doubt on the lack of a resistive quality to muscle, but this is still less than skin. This area can be reviewed in the overview articles mentioned above. Ironically, it is far more difficult to remove a blade from a wound than to cause the wound in the first place.

7.46 Ultimately, force assessments in this field are subjective and unquantifiable. Most medical witnesses will separate force into three broad categories: (i) mild force/ gentle pressure; (ii) moderate force; and (iii) considerable/severe force.

In certain circumstances, a further category of extreme force is necessary, due to the severity of the injuries. Due to the subjective nature of the categories, most, but not all, medical witnesses will suggest that at least moderate force is required for a sharp-tipped blade to pass through the skin, and this is increased to the higher tier of considerable/severe force when bone is significantly damaged. However, some medical witnesses will adjust the boundaries between the categories, and a proportion will suggest that mild force is required to cause a stab wound penetrating skin.

Inevitably, most laymen (both lawyers and jurors alike) will have used 'normally' sharp kitchen knives in the course of preparing meat and therefore will to some extent be intuitively aware of forces involved.

At trial, when an expert witness is giving evidence in this area, the most frequent follow-up question by the judge is 'What is moderate force?'. This often causes difficulties to medical witnesses. The authors have heard colleagues provide a number of descriptions (and utilised some themselves); these include 'being similar to a reasonable punch' and 'knocking a nail into softwood'.

An important point to note is that the depth of the wound cannot be used to estimate the degree of force.

Description and interpretation of stab wounds

Knives

7.47 A stab wound caused by a knife will produce a clean incised wound, which, by virtue of the elasticity of the skin, will stretch to form an ellipse. A double-edged blade will normally produce a symmetrical surface pattern, whereas a knife with one sharp and one blunt edge may show at one end relative blunting, a fish-tailed appearance or even a sharp split. There will be less associated bruising and abrasion the sharper the blade, if indeed there is any.

It may be very difficult to tell if a particular wound has been caused by a single-edged or a double-edged weapon. Differential contraction of the skin and subcutaneous tissues may, on occasion, give a misleading impression of the cross-section of the weapon used. The weapon's characteristics are often more readily appreciated in internal organs, especially those lacking an elastic nature, such as the liver and the heart.

Further, entry and exit of the blade at different relative positions through rocking and twisting cause increasingly complex twisted and shelved wounds.

Other implements

7.48   Stab wounds caused by other implements will produce differing types of injuries. For example, stab wounds caused by scissors provide a wide array of complex injuries depending on the nature of the scissors and whether or not the blades are open or closed. Some knives are double-pointed at the tip.

Measurements

7.49   The dimensions of the wound on the skin surface are measured, including with the edges apposed (i.e. gentle pressure is placed on the ends of the wounds to draw the edges together), to counteract the effects of the natural elasticity of the skin.

In reality, the dimensions of the wound rarely reflect the dimensions of the blade, as it is exceptionally rare for the blade to be inserted and removed perfectly on the same plane. Retraction of the wound ends may shorten the length of the wound, suggesting a narrower blade was utilised. A stab wound seen where the skin is relatively stable – as in the chest – will sometimes demonstrate bruising or abrasion due to the blade guard of the knife. This is surprisingly rare.

The depth of the wound will be measured, typically by connecting the surface injury to the deepest identifiable point of injury within the body. In reality, this is no more than an estimate, as the hollow nature of the chest and abdominal cavities (combined with the non-fixed nature of the internal organs) poses significant difficulties. This is further compounded as, in solid tissue, there is often a mass of haemorrhage round the track of the wound, and the deep end may be difficult to ascertain with accuracy.

Due to the natural taper of the blade, the width of the internal injuries is generally related to the wound's relative depth in the body, but the same rocking and twisting movements that affect the surface appearance affect the internal components.

7.50   The depth of the wound is often extrapolated to provide an indication of the length of the blade. It is important to appreciate that this is no more than an indication only. A blade may not be inserted fully, so the depth may be shorter than the blade length. Due to the compressibility of the soft tissues, particularly surrounding the abdomen and to a lesser extent the chest, as well as the mobility of the internal organs such as the heart and the lungs, the wound track may be longer than the blade length.

7.51   Despite the obvious need for caution, the measurement of a number of stab wounds in a single body may enable the pathologist to give some description of the possible size and shape of the blade of the weapon used, especially in the case of a knife. The criminal justice system should nonetheless be wary of the medical witness who gives an apparently exact measurement of an alleged murder weapon. The pathologist will provide an estimate of the direction of the travel of the wound. This estimate, however, assumes that the body is in the upright anatomical position, which, in the reality of most situations of an assault, will not be the case. It is important in evidence to make this clear to the court.

Manner of infliction

7.52   Like most wounds, stab wounds can be accidental, suicidal or homicidal.

Accidental stab wounds are invariably single, unless a more complicated instrument is involved such as a double-pointed knife. Determining an accidental mechanism of causation is usually dependent on the circumstances surrounding it. In the majority of cases, distinguishing self-inflicted from assault-related stab wounds poses no difficulties, and the features described above can be utilised.

The site of a suicidal stab wound must have been accessible to the deceased. In practice, the great majority of single suicidal stab wounds are in an elective site: the neck, left side of chest and wrists. Tentative wounds – where an individual has created a number of small wounds around the main wound or wounds (possibly to ascertain the sharpness of the knife) – may be seen but are not invariably present. Clothing is more likely to have been removed to enable access of the knife.

Difficulties may arise, however, when the sole injury is a stab wound without the relevant accidental or self-inflicted background, or no background at all. Around two-fifths to half of homicidal stabbings are single-wound incidents, depending on the literature reviewed. Much will depend upon the findings at the locus of death and on the position and direction of the wound.

7.53   Essentially, due to the dynamic nature of assaults, precise attempts to reconstruct an assault are fraught with difficulty, but useful interpretation can be justified on occasion. However, utilisation of track directions to suggest, for example, right- or left-handedness, relative positions of the participants, or how the assailant was holding the blade, should be treated with some caution, and the appropriateness of such interpretations should be considered on an individual case basis with the medical witness prior to trial.

The most frequent area where this is important is when the proposition is advanced that the victim ran or fell onto a knife held by another individual – sometimes referred to as self-impalement – and that the holder of the knife provided no thrust.

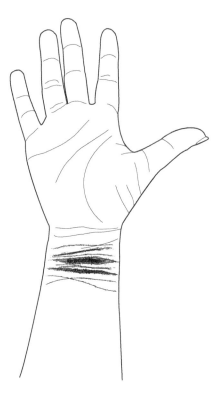

Figure 7.8 Self-inflicted injuries. (Courtesy of Ruth Bowen, Medical Illustrator, Cardiff University.)

In the vast majority of cases, the number of injuries, positioning, angle of entry, etc ensures that the account advanced by the defence can be easily dismissed. The scenario that poses most difficulty is the near single wound on the front of the torso moving from front to back within the body, the argument being that sufficient force can be generated by an individual moving or running forward for the knife to pass through the skin. *Knight's Forensic Pathology* indicates categorically that:

> 'When the knife penetrates the skin rapidly, for example if the body falls or runs onto the blade, the knife does not need to be held rigidly in order to prevent it being pushed backwards. Its inertia, if the tip is sharp, is quite sufficient to hold it in place while the body spears itself on the blade. It has been wrongly argued against a defence of falling or running onto a knife that the hilt would have had to have been supported against – for example, the hip.'

This viewpoint is unattributed but invariably ascribed to Knight's own experimental work (Dynamics of Stab Wounds). The latter paper is somewhat complicated and the methodology is perhaps open to criticism nearly 40 years later, but the topic of the non-fixed blade is not covered. It incorporates work on a falling body upon a fixed knife which is described as being 'firmly held' and the tip of the knife had been 'ground to the best possible edge'. Knight indicates it 'is thus very obvious that the moving body can readily transfix the knife, provided that the knife point is very sharp'. The current consensus is that the definitive statement in *Knight's Forensic Pathology* is not as clear-cut as suggested. An important corollary is that individuals presenting to hospital with non-fatal knife wounds, suggesting they walked onto or fell onto a knife, remain exceptional events.

- A stab wound is a penetrating wound caused predominately by a sharp-tipped object penetrating the skin such that it forms a wound that is deeper into the body than the width of the wound on the skin. The appearance is heavily dependent on the implement utilised to inflict the wound.

- The force required to cause a stab wound from a pathological/medical viewpoint is dependent on the structures injured on the passage of the implement through the body.

- Medical witnesses will suggest that, if the blade strikes and damages hard substance such as bone or calcified cartilage to some significant degree, increasing force is required, and, after bone and calcified cartilage, skin is the most resilient to blade passage.

- It is more difficult to remove a blade from a wound than to cause it.

- Force assessments are subjective and unquantifiable.

- Most (but not all) medical witnesses will suggest that it requires moderate force for a blade to pass through skin.

- A stab wound caused by a knife will produce a clean incised wound, which, by virtue of the elasticity of the skin, will stretch to form an ellipse. The depth of the wound will be measured, typically by connecting the surface injury to the deepest identifiable point of injury within the body.

- The depth of the wound should not be used to estimate the degree of force.

- The walking or running onto a knife 'defence' needs correlation with pathological features.

Chopping wounds

7.54   This a special category of intermediate wounds, with features overlapping sharp and blunt force injuries. The typical implements involved are items such as spades, axes, machetes and tomahawks. The precise appearances will depend almost entirely on the features of the weapon, in particular the bluntness; they can, however, usually be considered as incisions with lacerated edges and extensive injury to the underlying soft tissues and bone.

Facial injuries

7.55   Facial injuries are common, especially in the context of assaults, and are briefly discussed here. The surface anatomy of the face is demonstrated in Figure 7.9, and the underlying bony structure is demonstrated in Figure 7.10.

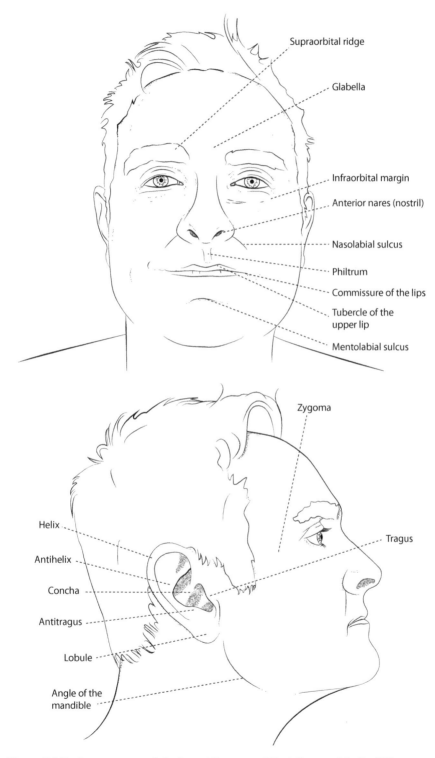

Figure 7.9 Surface anatomy of the face. (Courtesy of Ruth Bowen, Medical Illustrator, Cardiff University.)

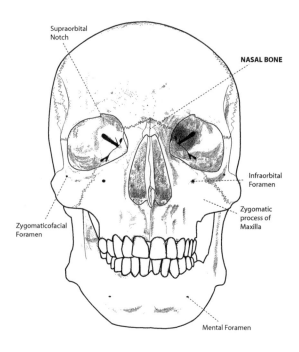

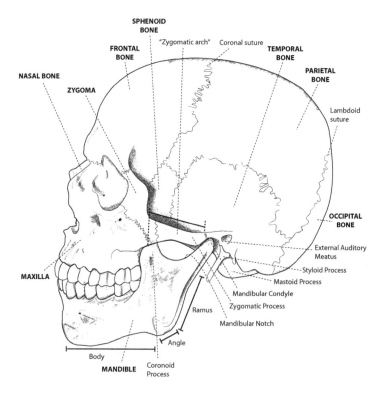

Figure 7.10 Anatomy of skull and facial bones. (Courtesy of Ruth Bowen, Medical Illustrator, Cardiff University.)

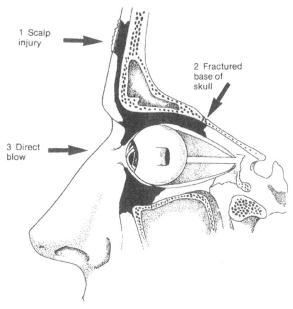

Figure 7.11 Sources of a black eye. (From: *Lawyers' Guide to Forensic Medicine*, Knight, B., 1998, Cavendish Publishing Ltd, reproduced by permission of Taylor & Francis Books UK.)

7.56　The 'black eye' is the archetypal injury in forensic medicine and pathology. It is usually encountered secondary to a direct blow, such as a punch, to the eye socket region, but a common alternative mechanism may arise to cause the black eye. Movement of the blood from basal skull fractures (racoon eyes), nearby facial injury (such as a nasal fracture) or from distant sites (such as the scalp) should always be considered. A simple falling mechanism to account for an isolated black eye would be unusual, due to the prominent contours of the face.

7.57　Blunt trauma to the nose readily results in injury. Fracturing of the nasal bridge is relatively common; cartilage damage, due to its flexibility, is less common. Bleeding into the respiratory system can occlude the airways (invariably in a concussed state), with the risk of respiratory impairment.

7.58　Blows to the mouth readily result in injury. Bruising and laceration can be encountered to the inner aspects of the oral cavity. The teeth may be damaged. A torn frenulum is an important injury in child abuse (see Chapter 14).

7.59　The mandible (lower jawbone) and maxilla (upper jawbones) may be fractured secondary to impact. The mandible may fracture in a number of patterns: these are particularly dependent on the point of impact and the direction of the applied force. It is important to appreciate that more than one fracture may arise secondary to a single impact to the mandible, particularly with an impact to the front in an anterior to posterior direction. Maxillary fractures are again common, and are classified by the Le Fort classification; this will be a common annotation in medical statements. In summary, the severity of injury increases from Le Fort I to Le Fort III, whereby the mid-facial skeleton is detached from the base of the skull. Punches can cause maxillary fractures but, as the complexity of the fractures increases, the forces involved increase, which raises the possibility of kicking or another mechanism.

Mode and causes of death following wounding

7.60   Rapid deaths are most frequently related to blood loss, entry of foreign substances into the hollow structures (e.g. air into the vasculature, blood and/or vomit into the airways, or blood into the heart sac), or destructive injury to a vital function of the body (e.g. brain or heart).

7.61   In sharp force injuries, haemorrhage is by far the most common of these potential causes of death and will be much more severe if an artery is penetrated than if only veins are affected (due to the high-pressure nature of an artery). The speed of death will depend upon the size of the vessel involved and on the secondary effects of the accumulation of blood. It is difficult to inflict a stabbing injury of 15cm depth without damaging an artery or vein of at least moderate calibre, and the direction of many stab wounds of the chest results in their frequent termination in the heart, aorta or major pulmonary vessels.

7.62   In blunt force injuries, it is more common that a combination of mechanisms is involved – for example, blunt force assault to the head may result in aspiration of blood as well as injury to the brain.

7.63   Rapidity of death and functioning following the infliction of ultimately fatal injuries are unpredictable. Some individuals with devastating internal injuries who would be expected to die rapidly, if not instantaneously, are documented to have significant post-injury activity, whereas others with more limited injury collapse and die immediately; in effect, they just 'drop down dead'. In general, those with more significant concomitant natural disease (and injury) are more likely to die rapidly.

Delayed deaths (attributable to wounds or injuries) need not initially present overtly to investigative officers. Common complications, especially following prolonged immobilisation, such as pneumonia or pulmonary thrombo-embolism, may occur in the population without assault. Blood loss may cause acute renal failure. Those of increasing old age may not be able to physiologically cope with relatively minor trauma.

7.64   Ultimately, a logical (medical) sequence originating from the assault to death needs to be shown. This will often be from the forensic pathologist, but assistance may well be required from ancillary experts. It is essential, in cases where causation is an issue, that the correct expert with the relevant expertise is instructed. Clearly, the prospect of any intervening medical negligence may need to be addressed.

- Deaths following wounding most frequently arise contemporaneous to the incident, but a proportion are delayed for periods up to many years. Causation in these cases may be an issue.

Further reading material

General textbooks

- Saukko, P. & Knight, B. *Knight's Forensic Pathology* (2004, 3rd Edition)
- Mason, J.K. & Purdue, B.N. *The Pathology of Trauma* (2000, 3rd Edition)
- Spitz, W.U. *Spitz and Fisher's Medicolegal Investigation of Death* (2006, 4th Edition)
- Shkrum, M.J. & Ramsay, D.A. *Forensic Pathology of Trauma* (2007)
- Payne-James, J., Jones, R., Karch, S.B. & Manlove, J. *Simpson's Forensic Medicine* (2011, 13th Edition)

Articles in update textbooks

- Bohnert, M., Huttemann, H. & Erbersdobler, A. 'Homicides by Sharp Force' in Tsokos, M., editor. *Forensic Pathology Reviews*. Volume Four. Humana Press; 2006. 65–89
- Davison, A. 'The Incised Wound' in Rutty, G.N., editor. *Essentials of Autopsy Practice, Recent Advances, Topics and Developments*. Springer; 2003. 187–220
- Shorrock, K. 'Chest and Abdominal Injuries' in Rutty, G.N., editor. *Essentials of Autopsy Practice, Current Methods and Trends*. Springer; 2006. 155–169
- Vanezis, P. 'Bruising Concepts of Ageing and Interpretation' in Rutty, G.N., editor. *Essentials of Autopsy Practice*, Volume One. Springer; 2001. 221–240

Articles in journals

- Cluroe, A.D. 'Superficial soft-tissue injury' *American Journal of Forensic Medicine & Pathology* 1995; 16(2):142–146
- Lee, K.A., Opeskin, K. 'Death due to superficial soft tissue injuries' *American Journal of Forensic Medicine & Pathology* 1992; 13(3):179–185
- Jones, R. 'Wounds and Injury Awareness amongst Students and Doctors' *Journal of Clinical Forensic Medicine* 2003; 10:131–134
- Milroy, C.M., Rutty, G.N. 'If a wound is "neatly incised" it is not a laceration' *BMJ* 1997;135:1312
- Nahum, A.M. 'The biomechanics of maxillofacial trauma' *Clin Plast Surg.* Jan 1975;2(1):59–64
- Knight, B. 'The Dynamics of stab wounds' *Forensic Sci.* 1975; 6(3):249–55
- Langlois, N.E., Gresham, G.A. 'The ageing of bruises: a review and study of the colour changes with time' *Forensic Science International* 1991; 50(2):227–238
- Stephenson, T., Bialas, Y. 'Estimation of the age of bruising' *Archives of Disease in Childhood* 1996; 74(1):53–55

Chapter 8

Ballistics: injury and death due to firearms

Firearms and the law

8.1   The law relating to firearms is statutory throughout the United Kingdom and is contained, in the main, in the Firearms Act 1968 ('the Act'), which has been heavily amended.[1] A firearm is defined in s 57(1) of the Act as any lethal barrelled weapon of any description from which any shot, bullet or other missile can be discharged.

Personal firearms are of three categories: (i) the smooth-bore weapon, or shotgun (i.e. a gun which does not have a rifled or grooved barrel); (ii) rifled weapons, which include revolvers, 'automatic' pistols and rifles; and (iii) in certain circumstances, air weapons.

Both shotgun and air weapons were devised primarily either for sporting activities or for the sport of killing small animals. Rifles, while being used in some forms of sport hunting, e.g. deer stalking, were mainly perfected for the killing of people. The regulations governing the possession and use of rifled weapons are, accordingly, far more strict than those which apply to either shotguns or airguns.

8.2   Section 1 of the Act defines, by exclusion, those weapons that it is unlawful to possess without simultaneously holding a firearm certificate. The section operates by defining a shotgun and an air weapon and stating that the requirement to possess a firearm certificate applies to every firearm which is not a shotgun or air weapon. By section 1(3)(a), a shotgun is a smooth-bore gun which: (i) has a barrel not less than 24 inches in length and does not have any barrel with a bore exceeding 2 inches in diameter; (ii) either has no magazine or has a non-detachable magazine incapable of holding more than two cartridges; and (iii) is not a revolver gun. By section 1(3)(b), an air weapon is an air gun, air rifle or air pistol which is not subject to the general prohibition on certain types of weapon contained in section 5 of the Act (such as, for air weapons, ones with a self-contained gas cartridge system) or one declared by the Home Secretary to be specially dangerous under section 53 of the Act.

8.3   Certificates are required for the possession of both shotguns and firearms. Under section 28(1) of the Act, a chief constable can grant or renew a shotgun certificate if he is satisfied that the applicant can be permitted to possess a shotgun

---

1   The Act itself applies to Scotland, England and Wales. Equivalent provisions apply to Northern Ireland via the Firearms (Northern Ireland) Order 1981.

without danger to the public safety or to the peace. Section 28(1A) entitles a chief constable to refuse a certificate if he or she has reason to believe that the applicant is prohibited by the Act from possessing a shotgun; or if he or she is satisfied that the applicant does not have a good reason for possessing, purchasing or acquiring one. The requirements for a firearms certificate are stricter: in addition to these requirements, the chief constable must be satisfied that the applicant is fit to be entrusted with a firearm (section 27). Fitness is not defined in section 27 itself, but will include consideration of factors such as whether the applicant is of unsound mind or intemperate habits (grounds for the revocation of certificates already issued: section 30A).[2] Very few categories of person are exempt from firearm certificate requirements – the commonest are members of approved rifle clubs and cadet corps, and race starters at athletic meetings (section 11). Persons in the service of the Crown or in the police are exempt from the requirements, but they are subject to rigid regulation by their parent authorities.[3]

Certificates to possess and use an airgun are not required, save that it is illegal to sell such a gun to anyone under the age of 18 or to present a young person under the age of 18 with an airgun for his possession. The relaxation of certification does not apply to 'specially dangerous air weapons'.[4]

8.4   There are over 70 criminal offences relating to the possession and use of firearms. Many relate to the need to strictly enforce the statutory regime on shotgun and firearms certificates, to prevent minors from possessing certain weapons, and to enforce the licensing regime both on the sale of such weapons and on their importation to the United Kingdom. However, the main offences which are likely to involve forensic investigation are set out in the Firearms Act 1968 and they include:

- the possession of a firearm or ammunition with intent to endanger life and also, in Scotland, to cause serious injury to property or to enable another person to do so (s 16);

- having possession of a firearm or imitation firearm with intent to cause, or to enable any other person to cause, any person to believe that unlawful violence will be used against him (s 16A);

- using a real or imitation firearm to resist arrest or possessing a firearm or imitation firearm at the time of committing (or being arrested for) a 'specified offence' (s 17);

- trespassing with a firearm (s 20);

---

2 Home Office guidance on the meaning to be given to these terms is set out in its Guide on Firearms Licensing Law 2014, available on www.gov.uk. No exhaustive definition of unsound mind is given, but chief constables are instructed to be alert to cases in which a General Practitioner's (GP) report reveals that an applicant has exhibited, or is exhibiting, signs of serious depression, suicidal tendencies, or long-standing or intermittent periods of either emotional instability or unpredictable behaviour (paragraph 12.24). 'Intemperate habits' means having a lack of self-control (paragraph 12.21).
3 Section 54 of the Act.
4 Defined as pump-action air rifles having a kinetic energy greater than 16 J (12 ft lb), or 8 J (6 ft lb) in the case of pistols – which are classified as 'section 1' firearms.

- carrying in a public place without lawful authority or reasonable excuse a loaded shotgun or any other firearm, whether loaded or not, together with appropriate ammunition (s 19); and

- shortening the barrel of a shotgun to less than 24 inches (60 cm) (section 4(1)) and possessing, purchasing or acquiring such a shotgun (section 4(4)).

To wound or cause grievous bodily harm with intent to do so by any means – which includes shooting – is a separate statutory offence in England and Wales.[5] In Scotland, wounding by shooting is a serious aggravation of an assault.

Gunshot injuries are of major pathological interest in that they can be interpreted with considerable objectivity; the pathologist (and, more importantly, the ballistics expert) can often give opinions that are soundly based and that are particularly valuable both to the police and to the lawyer.

Firearms

8.5   From the medical rather than legal viewpoint, there are two broad groups of firearms: those with smooth barrels (smooth-bore), which discharge pellets or cartridges that contain a number of 'shot', and those with rifled barrels (a series of grooved lines within the barrel), which discharge a cartridge which has, at its tip, a solid metal projectile or bullet. It is these two broad groupings that have most consequence on the appearance of discharge on the body.

Discharge is facilitated typically by the detonation of solid propellants into large volumes of gases forcing the shot or projectile forwards. However, the discharge can be also facilitated by compressed air (an air weapon). Although the projectile is invariably discharged, captive bolt and other humane veterinary weapons only discharge the projectile a few centimetres, and the projectile itself is still contained within the firearm.

Shotguns

8.6   Shotguns are normally smooth barrelled and may be single or double barrelled. Confusingly, shotguns with rifled barrels are available, but these invariably fire single shot (or slugs) for the purpose of hunting 'large game' over a longer range. Double barrelled shotguns may have the barrels 'side by side' or 'up and over'.

The shotgun discharges the pellets initially as a 'solid' mass but, as they pass through the air, the pellets diverge and spread from the solid mass. Manufacturers taper the barrel of the shotgun towards the muzzle. This is known as 'choking', which serves to lengthen the period during which the shot is restrained in a compact mass. The effective sporting range of a shotgun is approximately 50 metres.

The calibre of shotguns is expressed in unusual and somewhat complex terms. When the diameter of the barrel is less than ½ inch (1.25 cm), the calibre is given by that diameter – for example, a 'four-ten' shotgun has a barrel diameter of 0.410 inches. Guns larger than this are measured by their 'bore'. The bore is the number of

5   Offences Against the Person Act 1861, s 18 (see Chapter 7).

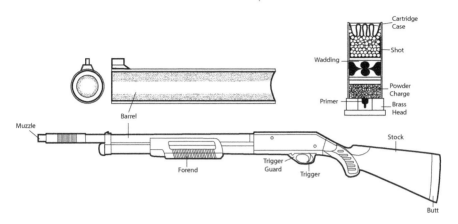

Figure 8.1 Shotgun with cartridge and cross-section of barrel. (Courtesy of Ruth Bowen, Medical Illustrator, Cardiff University.)

spherical lead balls with a diameter the same as the barrel that would it take to give a weight of 1 lb. In essence, the larger the diameter of the barrel, the less the number of balls that can be created out of the 1 lb. Thus, an '8-bore' gun is a larger and more powerful gun than the common '12-bore'.

The shotgun cartridge

8.7   The cartridge consists of a cardboard or plastic cylinder holding the shot attached to a brass plate, which contains the primer.

The shot within a shotgun cartridge consists of spherical metal balls of diameters ranging from 2 to 9 mm, and the number of shot can vary from eight to as many as 700, the size and weight being chosen according to the main purpose for which the gun is to be used. Some cartridges contain mixed shot (i.e. shot of varying sizes), especially homemade ammunition, which may simulate a double discharge on the skin surface.

The main powder charge and shot is separated now by plastic wads made of cups that hold each in place. These cups open out on discharge so as to form plastic sheets in the form of a George Cross (whereas the cups for the smaller 0.410 ammunition have three 'leaflets').

After discharge

8.8   The shot is propelled initially as a solid mass but begins to fan out as the compression by the wad is released. However, the shot and the wad are not the only things discharged: soot, propellant, flame, gases (including carbon monoxide) and other components of the cartridge case are also released.

These additional constituents have particular properties, particularly aerodynamically, and the identification of features associated with them in or around the wound assists with the interpretation of the discharge range.

The powder will continue to burn as the shot passes down the barrel, but some powder always remains unburnt.

Determining shot distance

8.9   The pathological evidence as to the distance from which the shot has been fired can be deduced based on the above factors, although variations occur between individual weapons, cartridges and other intrinsic factors.

A 'contact wound' is a wound that arises when the discharge occurs with the barrel end in contact with the skin surface.

A contact injury will show bruising and abrasion due to the recoil of the gun, and a perfect representation of the single or twin barrels may be formed on the skin; the shot will enter the body as a solid mass, so the entry wound will be approximate to the bore of the barrel.

The margins of the wound are often relatively clean. However, explosive gases will also enter the wound, so that the external wound may be ragged and heavily torn. This is especially the case when bone, such as the skull, closely underlies the wound, preventing the dissipation of the gases internally; and, in extreme cases, the head may be literally blown apart.

Internally, owing to the entry of flame into the wound, there may be burning of the wound track close to the skin as well as some pinkish discolouration, which would be attributed to the local effects of the discharged carbon monoxide. The wad should be located within the body. Internally, tissue destruction is usually widespread and solid organs are left unrecognisable.

Exit wounds are not a feature of shotgun injuries, other than in the contact situation, as the shot is rapidly halted within the tissues of the target. This does not apply in the case of large shot, which may be lethal at double the anticipated range.

At very short range, a few centimetres or so, the appearances described above are modified by the differing effects of the gases of combustion – these will not be forced into the wound but may still cause some irregularity of the entry hole.

Unburnt powder will be discharged into the skin surrounding the wound, leading to what is known as 'tattooing' as well as abrasion 'stippling' (where the skin is injured because unburnt powder damages, but does not penetrate, the skin). Soot

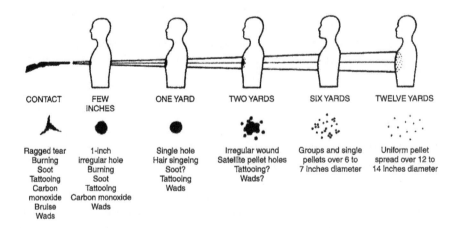

Figure 8.2 Effects of a shotgun injury related to distance. (Reproduced by permission of the author from B. Knight *Legal Aspects of Medical Practice*, 5th edn (Edinburgh, Churchill Livingston, Edinburgh, 1992), p. 195.)

staining is likely to be deposited around the wound. Hot gases will burn the skin or clothing, and carbon monoxide may similarly discolour the local tissues pink. The wad is identified within the body track and tissue destruction is widespread. However, the explosive nature of contact wounds is not present.

At medium range, these effects diminish as the distance from muzzle to wound increases. The critical distance is at about 2 metres as, at this distance, tattooing is scarcely visible and the wad fails to penetrate the wound. Modern plastic wads, however, become effective secondary missiles and may leave distinctive marks on the skin up to some 6 metres.

The shot begins to fan out and creates a pattern of entry in the clothing and on the skin.

Although the inclination of the body to the line of flight of the shot will alter the appearances, normally the pattern will be circular. The size of this circle depends to some extent on the degree of 'choking' (tapering) of the gun barrel, but British guns are sufficiently standardised to permit the use of a simple rule: the diameter of the shot pattern in centimetres is some two to three times the muzzle distance from the wound in metres (or the spread in inches is equivalent to the distance in yards).

Small shot tends to disperse more rapidly than does larger shot when both are fired from the same gun; estimates derived from such a formula must be checked by test firing whenever possible.

At longer range initially as the shot fans out it is still held relatively tight, such that injury is still broadly circular but the margins are scalloped, known commonly as a 'rat hole'. Figure 8.2 provides a graphical representation of shotgun injuries over various distances.

Internal injuries beyond around 2 metres are less drastic than those occurring at shorter distances and are caused by individual pellets damaging structures rather than being caused by a larger solid mass of them.

The effects of a shotgun injury are, as a result, more variable and depend upon the ability of individual pellets to penetrate either the heart, individual blood vessels or other organs liable to severe bleeding.

The interposition of solid matter between the gun and the skin leads to rapid dispersion of shot; thus, injury from a close-range discharge through a glass or wooden panel may give the impression of having been inflicted from a range of several yards.

Fatal injuries from a 12-bore shotgun are unlikely at a range of over 20 metres.

Unlawful shortening

8.10   Unlawful shortening of the barrel (say, to about 25 cm – the typical 'sawn-off' shotgun) is purely for purposes to conceal it and actually inhibits the performance of the discharge. Generally, the muzzle velocity of the shot is reduced by up to 20% and, in comparison to its full length equivalent, the spread of the shot may be up to double.

- The calibre of the shotgun is varyingly expressed according to the diameter of its barrel.

- The shotgun cartridge comprises of a cardboard or plastic cylinder attached to a brass plate and contains a wad separating the powder from the shot.

- A shotgun discharge will typically involve a cluster of shot that diverges over distance.

- The nature of the wound is significantly affected by the discharge distance.
- The 'sawn-off' shotgun is less effective and created solely for concealment.

Rifled weapons

8.11 Rifled weapons have a barrel that is spiral grooved and fires a single projectile at a time. The presence of the grooves (and the lands between them) results in the rotatory movement of the projectile, giving a gyroscopic stability to the projectile in flight, and produces a more accurate trajectory.

Rifled weapons are more variable than their shotgun counterparts and include variants such as pistols, revolvers, rifles and a variety of 'automatic' (self-loading) weapons.

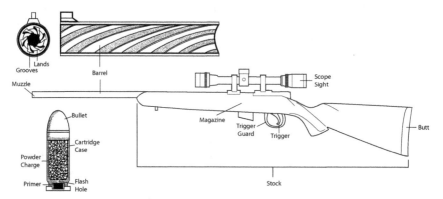

Figure 8.3 Rifled weapon with bullet and cross-section of barrel. (Courtesy of Ruth Bowen, Medical Illustrator, Cardiff University.)

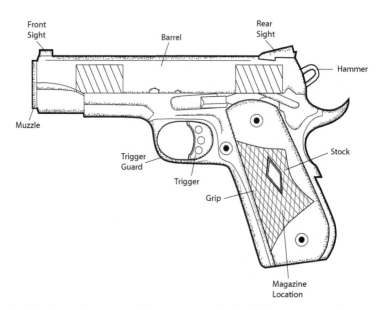

Figure 8.4 Handgun. (Courtesy of Ruth Bowen, Medical Illustrator, Cardiff University.)

Ammunition

8.12   The ammunition for the rifled weapon is more complex than that of the shotgun cartridge but is of a similar basic design of a metal cylinder (the casing) which has a percussion detonator at its base and houses the propellant and the projectile (bullet) internally. A number of modifications can be made to the various components to alter the relative properties. For example, the most famous modification is the full metal jacket where the soft core of the projectile (usually lead) is encased in a harder metallic substance (such as cupro-nickel), allowing higher muzzle velocities.

Wounds

8.13   The main difference between wounds from shotguns and those from rifled weapons rests on the fact that, whereas shot from a shotgun will certainly be found in the body, the bullet fired from a rifled weapon is equally likely to have exited the body. Contemporary entry and exit wounds are, therefore, a feature of wounds caused by rifled weapons.

Contact and close range entry wounds from rifled weapons have much the same characteristics as those from shotguns, albeit the wound is smaller. As in shotgun wounds, bruising, blast effects, soot deposition and tattooing will also be present.

Tattooing is typically found up to a range of 1.3 metres. However, the distance travelled by unburnt particles of gunpowder depends very much on the type of powder – whether of flake or ball type, the latter marking the skin at greater distance than the former – and also on the increasing calibre of the weapon used.

With regard to longer range, if the range was not so short as to cause explosive damage to the tissues, the characteristics of the entry wound will be governed by the gyroscopic stability of the bullet.

In the early phase of its flight (up to some 50 metres for a pistol or 150 metres for a rifle) and towards the end of its effective range (in the order of 460 metres for a pistol and 2.4 kilometres for a rifle), there is considerable 'tail wag', which results in a relatively large and ragged entry wound. In the most efficient phase of flight, the bullet will enter the body neatly 'nose on' and leave a regular small hole, which, because of the elasticity of the skin, may well not correspond exactly to the diameter of the missile and will generally be slightly smaller.

The entry wound will show inverted edges and is characterised by an abrasion ring, where the bullet has abraded the skin, which is more prominent the more the skin can be depressed.

The entry wound can be asymmetrical if the bullet has entered at an angle. The entry wound may demonstrate 'soiling' or 'bullet wipe'. A bullet will be contaminated as it passes down the barrel of the gun. This contaminated material is wiped off either by the clothing or skin on entry. It is found less frequently when the bullet has a hard metallic jacket.

As the bullet traverses the body, it may become deflected, deformed or fragmented, and it may create secondary projectiles as portions of tissue, particularly bone, are projected forwards.

The exit wound is likely to be irregular, its edges everted and without soiling.

The modern, very high-velocity rifle has unusual characteristics. It kills by virtue of the massive internal damage that results from the dissipation of large amounts of kinetic energy, but the entry and exit wounds are, however, small and are of very similar size.

The common tendency for the wound to enlarge from entry to exit is shown most clearly in bone, particularly the bones of the skull, in which the penetrating wound bevels outwards so that it is of larger diameter on the exit side.

This difference in size is useful in distinguishing a bullet wound from a surgical burr-hole in a skeletonised skull or fragment of skull bone presented for examination.

8.14   Two variations on the pattern of exit wounds deserve special mention.

The first is the so-called 'shored' wound, which is seen when the skin at the point of exit is supported by a solid surface such as a door or wall; the everted skin then tends to become compressed with the formation of an apparent abrasion ring; the shored exit wound can thus resemble an entry wound, the main distinguishing features being that there will be no soiling and the 'abrasion ring' will tend to be somewhat irregular.

Secondly, particularly where the skin is folded, an exit wound may be linear and sharply edged. On rare occasions, it may mimic a stab wound.

8.15   The force propelling a bullet in the body diminishes progressively, depending on which tissues it penetrates. With a low-velocity weapon, such as a pistol, the final obstacle is the skin at the point of exit, and it is not unusual to find a bullet immediately under the skin, or in the clothing of the victim.

The pathologist is likely to be able to give a very good opinion as to the direction of an injury from a rifled weapon as compared with shotgun injuries but has less evidence on which to base an estimate of range.

The recovery of a bullet from the body is, of course, of great importance to the investigation, as every rifled weapon leaves a characteristic pattern of scoring on the surface of the bullet; test firing of suspected weapons may then result in a convincing identification by comparison. Comparative evidence can be derived from spent cartridges recovered at the scene of a shooting: marks of an individual nature are made by the firing pin and hammer, the ejection mechanism and during extraction. Such methods of weapon identification are also available in the case of shotguns, but all lie in the province of the ballistics expert.

Morbidity

8.16   Bullets may kill by virtue of penetrating the heart, a major vessel or a vital centre of the brain.

The greatest damage is, however, caused, firstly, by the brute force of the bullet as it punches its way through the tissues and, secondly, by 'cavitation' in the track of the missile. The former is the predominant feature of low-velocity (and thus low kinetic energy) discharges, such as from handguns, whereas the former is a feature of high-velocity discharges.

Cavitation is a phenomenon resulting in the temporary formation of a expanding cavity (as opposed to punching through tissues) by transfer of energy, causing widespread tissue stretching and destruction. The effect of the resultant stretching of the tissues depends upon their density: the higher the density of a tissue, the more effective it will be at decelerating the projectile and thus the greater the transfer of energy. Thus, the passage of a bullet through, for example, the liver or brain will cause far more damage than will the same bullet passing through the less-dense bowel. This discharge of energy can tear structures removed from the actual path of the bullet.

Delayed death may result if a solid organ with a large blood supply is damaged; death from septic shock or sepsis may follow penetrating injuries of the bowel or similar structures.

- Rifled weapons have spiralled grooves along the length of the barrel. This provides stability to the projectile during the course of its flight.

- The discharged projectile may or may not travel through the body. It is often recovered just beneath the skin (i.e. prior to exit).

- The wound appearance, unless at contact or at near contact range, will be broadly similar, with little distinctive appearance to assist with range.

- Damage may result either from the projectile 'punching' through tissue or from cavitation.

- The entry wound will show inverted edges and is characterised by an abrasion ring – where the bullet has abraded the skin – which is more prominent the more the skin can be depressed.

- The exit wound is likely to be irregular, its edges everted and without soiling.

- The common tendency for the wound to enlarge from entry to exit is shown most clearly in bone, particularly the bones of the skull, in which the penetrating wound bevels outwards so that it is of larger diameter on the exit side.

Air weapons

8.17   As discussed above, an air weapon utilises the release of compressed air to facilitate the discharge of the projectile from the barrel rather the propellant used by shotguns and rifled weapons.

The projectiles are typically pellets of varying size, although more complex projectiles are available. Due to their lower-energy discharge, unless the pellet penetrates some vital spot, such as the eye or the brain, severe injuries from the normal air weapon (with a muzzle velocity of 80 to 105 ms^{-1}) are unlikely.

Nonetheless, pellets travelling at a speed of more than 110 ms^{-1}, when discharged from more powerful guns, will generally penetrate skin and even bone. The effect of those fired from these higher-velocity air weapons are comparably dangerous to those from small bullets from a rifled firearm.

The wound from an air weapon is similar to that of a rifled weapon, comprising typically a rounded hole with an abraded rim. However, as detonation of solid propellants does not occur, hot gases, propellant and other consequences of the detonation are not encountered.

The low velocity of the discharge means exit wounds are rare and airgun pellets rarely fragment.

Determination of the manner of discharge

8.18   The immediate need, in any case of fatal firearm wounding, is to distinguish between accident, suicide and homicide. The medical witness, in conjunction with the ballistics expert, will often be able to give an indication of the possibility of suicide or a self-inflicted injury.

Suicidal discharge

8.19   Barring unusual circumstances, the weapon must be within reach of the deceased and is typically retained in the grasp or close to his or her hand. On occasion, due to the recoil of the firearm it may be found out of reach of the individual, or some form of contraption for remotely firing the firearm may have been utilised.

The discharge also may not have proved immediately fatal or absolutely debilitating, and evidence of movement by the deceased may be evident in the form of bleeding around the scene.

The sites of election are also common, such as to the chest and the head (the temple, the forehead, within the mouth and under the chin being prime examples).

The most important question in determining discharge is the feasibility of the individual pressing the trigger in relation to the location of the wound, the length of the barrel and range of the discharge. Despite this, the possibility of a simulated suicide must always be considered.

Accidental and homicidal discharge

8.20   Accidental discharges involving a single individual are encountered and require significant 'work up' to exclude another party involvement, and it can be very difficult to exclude this.

Fatal accidental gunshot injuries may be 'self-inflicted', as in the classic 'cleaning the gun' situation, or involve another party, such as when a moving fellow hunter is mistaken for game. The former situation may closely simulate suicide. The latter type of fatal accident injury, if the injury shows no more than the effect of a relatively long-range discharge, is (on pathological evidence alone) indistinguishable from homicide.

The interpretation may rest upon both an examination of the locus by forensic scientists (in conjunction with the post-mortem findings) combined with circumstantial evidence. It will likely not be resolved by the medical witness alone. Certain features are strongly indicative of homicide. A single wound of contact or very close range type in an inaccessible position is an obvious example (the back, the nape of the neck or behind the ear being the commonest sites). Similarly, the existence of more than one fatal injury will be very strong evidence against both suicide and accident; but, despite this, on very rare occasions, multiple gunshot wounds may be found in suicidal deaths, including in the head.

The medical expert should be very wary of estimating the survival time following a fatal gunshot injury. The victim may be capable of considerable activity, despite sustaining an injury which might well be judged likely to have caused immediate death, and most people who have actually shot someone have been surprised at the apparently slight immediate effect. There are no absolutes.

Examination of victims

8.21   The initial autopsy in any suspicious death from firearms injury should ideally be performed by the forensic pathologist in the presence of a ballistics expert. Radiographic examination of the body before autopsy is considered mandatory (and is incorporated into most regulatory guidelines), and no post-mortem examination should be undertaken in circumstances where no radiology facility is available.

Currently, conventional radiography is being replaced with computed tomography (CT scanning), to allow more precise location of any remaining projectiles to be established. Computed tomography can also provide increased information about the relative trajectory within the body.

The clothing and possible entry wounds must be carefully examined, under the guidance of the ballistics expert.

Samples for 'firearms residue' are taken as per the protocol of the kit supplied (see **8.23** below).

8.22   Once the position of the projectile(s) have been established, the track can be dissected, measured, and its angle determined. It is essential that every (rifled) projectile is found and recovered for the ballistics expert. This may be very difficult when multiple wounds are present, and the use of fluoroscopy (a form of radiographic examination in which the image is intensified and shown on a screen) during the course of the post-mortem examination can assist. This is not available in most mortuaries. In the case of shotgun injuries, only a sample of pellets are typically taken.

When there are numerous injuries close together, such as from an automatic rifle, it is often impossible to define each separate track, and a general approximation of the angle of trajectory is usually only possible.

The angle of trajectory through the body represents the angle of trajectory through the body in its anatomical position, and this is not the same as the position of the body in relation to the weapon. For example, if the victim ducks or bends forward as a shot is fired, the angle of the wound may give the false impression that the shot was fired from above. This does not preclude useful interpretation, especially when the projectile traverses limbs or head/torso together and the tracks can be aligned.

Examination of suspects

8.23   The medical examination of a suspected firearm assailant is directed, mainly, to the demonstration of firearm residues on his or her hands. Clearly, visible soot may be present; this derives from the burning – or destruction – of the gunpowder and, while it may indicate that the examinee has fired a gun, it provides comparatively little evidence as to the precise firearm used. Other residues may be invisible and yet provide something akin to a gun's 'signature'; a main function of the examining doctor will be to provide suitable specimens for analysis by the ballistics expert.

Metallic residues, derived from the primer mixture contained within the rim or the primer cap of the cartridge, can be quantified in this 'dermal residue' test. These include compounds of mercury, antimony, barium and lead in varying proportions. The residues are removed by a variety of methods, including swabbing with moistened filter paper or with something resembling sticky tape.

The interpretation of these swabs is a complex scientific exercise, and issues regarding 'natural' contamination, cross-contamination and false negative rates are possible and are a matter for the instructed ballistic experts.

Further reading material

General textbooks

- Saukko, P. & Knight, B. *Knight's Forensic Pathology* (2004, 3rd Edition)

- Mason, J.K. & Purdue, B.N. *The Pathology of Trauma* (2000, 3rd Edition)

- Spitz, W.U. *Spitz and Fisher's Medicolegal Investigation of Death* (2006, 4th Edition)

- Shkrum, M.J. & Ramsay, D.A. *Forensic Pathology of Trauma* (2007)

- Payne-James, J., Jones, R., Karch, S.B. & Manlove, J. *Simpson's Forensic Medicine* (2011, 13th Edition)

- Di Maio, V. *Gunshot Wounds* (1999, 2nd Edition, CRC Press)

Articles in update textbooks

- Karger, B. 'Forensic Ballistics' in Tsokos, M. *Forensic Pathology Reviews*. Volume Five, 2008

Articles in journals

- Introna, F., Smialek, J.E. 'Suicide from multiple gunshot wounds' *Am J Forensic Med Pathol* 1989, vol. 10, p. 27

- Levy, V., Rao, V. 'Survival times in Gunshot and Stab Wounds Victims' *Am J Forensic Med Pathol* 1988, vol. 9, p. 215

- Home Office Guide on Firearms Licensing Law (October 2014). www.gov.uk

Chapter 9

Head injury and other brain pathology

9.1   Head injuries are a major common cause of morbidity and mortality in medico-legal work. They are one of the most difficult areas for interpretation of both the type and causation of injury. This may have significance in relation to the cause of death as well as the potential for contributing to death.

There have been a number of advances in recent years in understanding of head injury, particularly in the field of alleged non-accidental head injury in children, as well as issues such as timing and severity of head injury. Much of this work has been undertaken due to advances in microscopy of brain tissue. In most, if not all, fatal medico-legal cases, involvement of a neuropathologist is frequently necessary. Details of the post-mortem examination are covered in Chapter 3. The points below relate specifically to head injury cases.

Approach to the examination in head injury cases

9.2   In those patients who survive for a while after injury, the pathologist/ neuropathologist should undertake detailed assessment of the clinical and radiological findings. This is particularly so in relation to radiological findings, where scans performed during life may well reveal important findings. Expert opinion of a neuroradiologist rather than a general radiologist is advisable.

It is important to assess any therapeutic measures which have been undertaken, such as a craniotomy (opening of the skull to facilitate neurosurgical procedures) as well as burr holes (creation of small openings in the skull to release pressure, monitor the condition of the brain or remove a haematoma).

Photographs may have been taken in hospital which should be sought. These may either be when the patient is admitted and/or during operative treatment.

Therapeutic procedures may cause a number of artefactual injuries (for example, areas of bruising in relation to surgery not related to trauma). It is essential that these are noted.

At post-mortem examination, all features noted should be photographed for record purposes. It is not uncommon to identify extensive areas of sub-scalp bruising where none or minimal is observed on the surface of the skin. Shaving of the hair is useful in terms of identification of potential sites of bruising.

The skull should be examined prior to removal of the brain and subsequent to removal of the brain.

External injuries to the scalp

9.3 Interpretation of these may be difficult. The general appearance of wounds is covered in Chapter 7. If a weapon is used, there may be a characteristic pattern (for example, in the case of a hammer producing a round bruise/abrasion). Other patterned bruising may occur which potentially can be correlated with an implement. Kicking/stamping may produce patterned injury which has the potential for footwear identification. There may be difficulty in differentiating between an assault and an accident, particularly where injuries are not extensive. As a generalisation, the more lacerations (open wounds to the scalp) that are present, the likelihood of an assault increases versus an accident. In a simple fall onto the back of the head, bruising with or without a laceration in that region is commonly found. In that scenario, the presence or absence of facial bruising should be sought to identify possible areas of punching or other blunt trauma.

Difficult areas in terms of interpretation of scalp injuries occur in particular where an individual is found at the bottom of, or part way down, a flight of stairs. In this case, multiple areas of bruising may be present; however, it would be uncommon to have extensive areas of lacerational injury. Likewise, a fall from a height may also produce difficulties. Other evidence may need to be sought in terms of, for example, an individual hanging on to a balcony who sustains damage to the hands.

9.4 'Black eyes' can have a number of explanations, including direct blows to the area. It should be noted that, in a simple fall to the ground, such bruising is not common, as injury tends to occur over the forehead/eyebrow regions. Caution should be exercised where there is evidence of skull fractures at the base of the skull, and blood may track down from inside to 'pool' around the orbital regions, giving the appearance of a 'black eye'. This is not related to a direct blow. In this scenario, the 'bruising' is confined to the orbit (bony opening around the eye). In some cases, particularly in the living, differentiation may be difficult.

In the scenario of traumatic subarachnoid haemorrhage (see **9.17** below), identification of both external and internal injuries should particularly concentrate on the neck region.

- Hair may hide bruises and lacerations.

- Falls downstairs from a height may be difficult. The more lacerations, the more worrying the case.

- 'Black eyes' may represent a direct blow or be secondary to a fracture at the base of the skull.

Skull fractures

9.5 Skull fractures indicate that there has been impact to the head. It should be recognised that the presence of a skull fracture does not necessarily imply significant brain damage. Conversely, the absence of skull fracture in a head injury case does not mean that there may not be significant brain injury. This is particularly so in the context of road traffic collisions.

Linear fracture

9.6   This is particularly common where the head strikes a flat surface, such as the pavement or road. This type of linear fracture usually originates at the point of impact and travels across well-recognised paths of the skull. A typical and relatively common example is an impact of the occipital region (back) of the head. The skull fracture then travels in an anterior (going forwards) direction across the base of the skull and may be seen with associated orbital (part of the skull lying next to the eye sockets) fractures. These are the type of fractures that may give rise to 'black eyes'. Sometimes the fracture may travel in atypical form, going around the side of the skull. There may be more than one fracture line giving a complex pattern. Linear fractures may also occur at other sites, for example in the thin squamous part of the temporal bone, where an associated extradural or epidural haematoma may be identified (see **9.10** below).

Depressed fractures

9.7   A depressed fracture is one where a portion of the skull is driven inwards as opposed to the linear variety described above. These are most frequently seen where there has been contact of the skull with an object such as a hammer. In the case of a hammer blow, a typical rounded area of depressed fracture may be seen. It should be noted that depressed fractures typically cause focal (localised) brain damage, the damage being worse beneath the site of the impact.

This damage is less severe than where the moving head strikes a surface, such as falling onto the back of the head on the pavement or road, where the forces of acceleration/deceleration are much more significant than those associated with an object hitting the stationary head. This causes diffuse injury affecting many areas of the brain.

3.   Other types of fracture

9.8   These include the following:

(a)   Ring fracture

This fracture involves the foramen magnum (at the base of the skull joining the vertebral column). It may be complete or partial, and results from a fall from height, but may also be seen in road traffic incidents.

(b)   Hinge fracture

This extends across the base of the skull from one side to the other. It is seen in road traffic incidents.

(c)   Contre-coup fractures

These are transmitted fractures opposite the site of impact. They commonly involve the orbital roofs, such as in the scenario of the fall onto the back of the head where there is contre-coup brain injury.

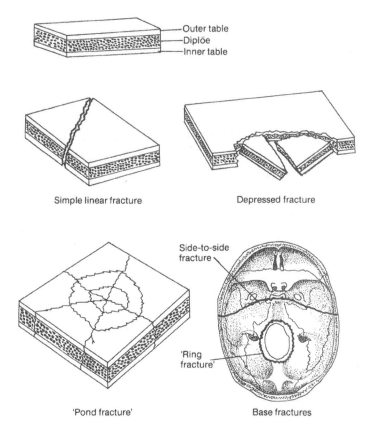

Figure 9.1 Skull fractures. (From: *Lawyers' Guide to Forensic Medicine*, Knight, B., 1998, Cavendish Publishing Ltd, reproduced by permission of Taylor & Francis Books UK.)

- A linear fracture occurs with broad blunt impact; a typical example is a fall with the head hitting the ground. It may be simple or complex.
- A depressed fracture indicates contact with a weapon or object such as a hammer.

Intracranial haematomas (bleeding within the skull cavity including the brain)

9.9   These comprise:

- Extradural haematoma.
- Subdural haematoma.
- Subarachnoid haemorrhage.
- Intracerebral haemorrhage.
- Haemorrhage in association with contusional ('bruising') injury.

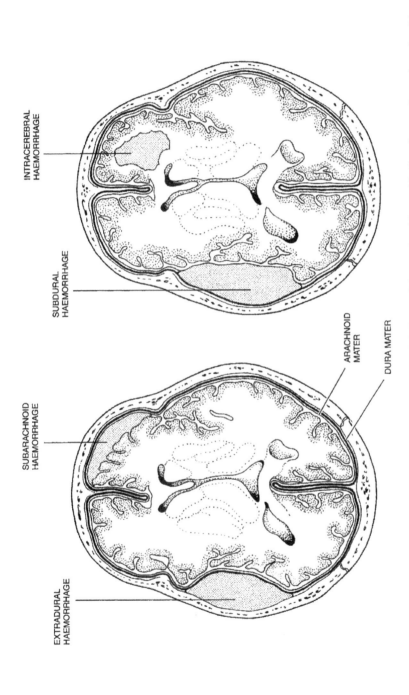

Figure 9.2 Four forms of intracranial haemorrhage. The dura is shown as a thick line and the arachnoid as a thin line. In practice, subarachnoid haemorrhage is more diffuse than is shown here. (The central structure is the normal ventricle of the brain.)

In all these types of haemorrhage, it is the effect on the surrounding brain which is of significance, in particular where the brain becomes compressed and unable to fit into the skull cavity, which forms a rigid box. The different types of haemorrhage are illustrated diagrammatically in Figure 9.2.

Extradural haematoma (also known as epidural haemorrhage)

9.10   Haemorrhage occurs as a result of injury to the middle meningeal artery which overlies the dura beneath the skull but outside the brain. Bleeding occurs in a localised area. The major problem of this type of haematoma is that bleeding expands and the brain subsequently becomes compressed, both to the opposite side of the skull and also downwards causing brain stem compression. This type of haemorrhage is not infrequently associated with a fracture of the squamous part of the temporal bone.

Problem areas

9.11
(1)   Delayed or incorrect diagnosis of extradural haematoma. An extradural haematoma is a treatable condition, as the underlying brain may be uninjured or only slightly injured. Neurosurgical intervention, with draining of the haematoma, is necessitated. Clinically, an individual usually loses consciousness for a brief period of time and recovers with subsequent deterioration over a period of hours which, if untreated, may lead to death. A patient may appear well, with no signs of injury, but then experience subsequent deterioration, which may be rapid.

Problems may arise where a skull fracture is missed in the casualty department, as any fracture is recognised to be associated with a higher incidence of underlying brain injury or haematoma.

Extradural haematoma in children is less frequently associated with a skull fracture, and difficulties may arise with an unclear history.

(2)   Timing of injury. This may be important in the medico-legal setting; however, other than giving a rough time estimate from a pathological point of view, it is not possible to accurately time injury. Detailed clinic-pathological correlation may assist with signs/symptoms such as headache, vomiting, drowsiness and weakness. Rarely, an extradural haematoma may take some time to develop over several days, probably due to slow bleeding from a small artery branch. Again, this has implications in the timing of injury.

(3)   Spontaneous extradural haematoma is rare but well recognised, usually in association with vascular abnormality.

(4)   In the forensic setting, heat haematoma (where the head is exposed to intense heat) may lead to bilateral extradural haematomas over the vertices of the skull as opposed to being unilateral over the side of the skull. Differentiation from ante-mortem injury may be difficult in bodies which have sustained extensive fire damage.

- Acute extradural haematoma is a treatable condition: death is due to an expanding haematoma within the skull overlying the surface of the brain causing compression of the brain.

- Bleeding typically occurs from the middle meningeal artery.

- Extradural haematoma may be missed if a skull fracture is not identified.

- A brief period of concussion with recovery and subsequent rapid deterioration typically occurs.

Subdural haematoma

9.12   In this situation, bleeding occurs between the dura and the brain. This is caused by the tearing of veins travelling from the dura into the brain. There are various types of subdural haematoma, and a simple classification comprises acute and chronic.

Acute subdural haemorrhage most commonly occurs in the context of falls/assaults and road traffic collisions. Unlike extradural haematoma, subdural haematoma is much more likely to be associated with underlying brain damage, whether this be contusional ('bruising') in nature and/or with varying degrees of traumatic axonal injury (see **9.22** below). Acute subdural haematoma may occur as a solitary 'pure' haematoma, in particular where there are underlying predisposing conditions such as anti-coagulant therapy and brain atrophy (shrinkage). In this context, the degree of trauma may be less, there may be little or no underlying brain injury, and there may be a lucid interval in some cases. Acute subdural haemorrhage in infants is covered in Chapter 14.

Problem area

9.13   In the medico-legal context, such issues as underlying brain abnormality, alcohol and role of previous head injury may become important in the assault situation. Issues include degree of trauma required to cause the subdural haematoma as well as increased vulnerability.

Chronic subdural haematoma

9.14   These typically occur in the elderly either after a fall or assault. In a number of cases, the history of trauma may be minimal or absent. This is characterised by bleeding over the surfaces of the brain and the formation of membranes with multiple episodes of re-bleeding. This occurs as the healing process of the haematoma takes place. This haematoma generally takes three to four months to become clinically present. It is particularly common in the elderly where there is a degree of brain atrophy. It can be difficult to diagnose, particularly in the elderly, as symptoms and signs similar to dementia and stroke-like illness may occur.

A number of underlying conditions may also contribute to the formation of chronic subdural haematoma such as brain atrophy (shrinkage of the brain), which may be seen in neurodegenerative conditions such as dementia and chronic alcoholics. Coagulation disorders (abnormalities of blood clotting) also predispose with increased risk of bleeding.

Problem area

9.15   In cases of trauma, the trauma may be at some time distant from presentation, leading to difficulty in isolating a particular incident. Bruising may be minimal or absent. It should be noted that bruising in the elderly can persist for a while. Pathologically, it is possible to give the rough age of a chronic subdural haematoma by examining the areas of bleeding/membrane formation; however, as in most things pathological, broad time frames only can be obtained. At trial, the defence may well be that a known episode of assault may not be the cause of the haematoma, with other episodes of trauma suggested, for which there may or may not be supporting evidence. Chronic subdural haematoma in infants is covered in Chapter 14.

- Subdural haematoma is bleeding between the dura and surface of the brain as a result of tearing of bridging blood vessels.

- Acute subdural haematoma occurs in the background of accelerated falls/ assaults and road traffic collisions.

- Acute subdural haematoma is likely to be associated with a degree of underlying brain injury which may be severe.

- 'Pure' subdural haematoma may arise in the background of anticoagulant therapy and/or brain atrophy with minimal trauma.

- Chronic subdural haematoma is bleeding between the dura and brain characterised by multiple episodes of re-bleeding from friable blood vessels – common in the elderly with brain atrophy.

- Chronic subdural haematoma usually takes some months to become apparent.

Subarachnoid haemorrhage

9.16   Subarachnoid haemorrhage occurs beneath the meninges, a thin film material covering the brain surface. Subarachnoid haemorrhage has a number of causes, the commonest of which is rupture of a cerebral aneurysm. A cerebral aneurysm (also known as a 'berry' aneurysm) is an abnormal swelling of one of the blood vessels which cover the base of the brain (see Figures 9.2 and 6.2). Bleeding from such an aneurysm accounts for the majority of cases of natural subarachnoid haemorrhage. Other less common causes include vascular malformation (congenital abnormality of blood vessels). Post-mortem identification of such an aneurysm is usually relatively simple. It is likely, however, that in the past so-called 'aneurysm negative' post-mortem examinations (where there is subarachnoid haemorrhage but no aneurysm is found) may be related to traumatic subarachnoid haemorrhage (see below) rather than an underlying aneurysm. There are rare but recognised reported cases of an assault precipitating bleeding from a natural aneurysm. In reported cases, the assault and subsequent collapse are instantaneous. Whether or not this is due to transient increase in blood pressure and/or direct trauma as a result of a blow to the head is unknown. The temporal relationship in these cases is an essential part in medico-legal proceedings.

- Subarachnoid haemorrhage is most commonly due to natural causes as a result of a rupture of a cerebral (or 'berry') aneurysm.

- Commonly presents with headache and sudden collapse.

Traumatic subarachnoid haemorrhage

9.17   This entity has become increasingly recognised over the last few decades. Bleeding occurs beneath the meninges and over the surface of the brain. In this instance, the bleeding is predominantly over the base of the brain.

The typical circumstances are sudden collapse arising following a punch or other blow to the head usually, although not invariably, associated with a degree of alcohol intoxication which, however, may not necessarily be great. The mechanism currently favoured is that a blow, in particular to the side of the head, produces sudden rotational movement of the head/neck and tearing of an intracranial portion of a cranial artery in the posterior circulation. In cases where the patient survives and makes it to hospital, these haemorrhages are sometimes misinterpreted as being due to a ruptured berry aneurysm rather than trauma. However the vast majority of cases do not survive admission to hospital, usually dying at the scene. Around 50–60% will show signs of external injury, such as imprint of a foot or bruising externally. It is unclear as to how severe the trauma needs to be to cause such a haemorrhage. Some cases show underlying abnormalities of the blood vessels.

Problem areas

9.18

(1)   Degree of trauma. There are isolated reported cases where sudden jerking of the neck to avoid a blow has resulted in such a haemorrhage. Clearly, there should be assessment of external and internal injuries in these cases, as they may in themselves indicate a much more significant degree of trauma.

(2)   Survival time. Most cases die immediately at the time of the assault. The precise mechanism is unclear but it may be due to disturbance of the brain stem directly. There are, however, reported cases where there has been a delay in presentation and, from a medico-legal aspect, it may be difficult to isolate a particular incident as the cause of the haemorrhage, especially if there are a number of alleged assailants.

(3)   The role of alcohol. There is a strong association with a degree of alcohol intoxication. The alcohol levels need not necessarily be very high. It is thought that alcohol may have a direct role on blood vessels causing bleeding to occur more commonly and also have an effect on the elasticity of the neck muscles. There are rare cases where an individual is unconscious prior to the alleged assault. This is probably because, in the unconscious person, the neck is relatively unprotected by the usual mechanisms of muscle contraction.

- Traumatic subarachnoid haemorrhage is caused by a rupture of a blood vessel over the base of the brain following trauma to the head/neck region.

- It occurs commonly in the context of an assault, with bruising to one side of the neck.
- Death occurs rapidly, probably due to disturbance in brain stem function.
- There is a strong association with alcohol intoxication rendering neck muscles more vulnerable to excess movement/stretching.

Intracerebral haemorrhage

9.19   There are a number of causes of intracerebral haemorrhage (haemorrhage within the brain), and they characteristically occur at different locations within the brain:

- Intracerebral haemorrhage in association with contusional injury.
- Intracerebral haemorrhage in association with traumatic axonal injury.
- Natural intracerebral haemorrhage, the most common being in association with hypertension or cerebral amyloid deposition.

Contusional brain injury

9.20   Contusional brain injury, in simple terms, is 'bruising' to the surface of the brain. This commonly occurs in brain injury and may or may not be seen in association with skull fractures. Bleeding occurs over the surface of the brain (subarachnoid haemorrhage) and within the grey matter (the outer structure of the brain containing neurons). Small haemorrhages are seen. In some cases, these haemorrhages may become large, giving rise to the term 'intracerebral haemorrhage in association with contusional brain injury'. Contusional injury may occur directly beneath an impact of the head, in particular where the skull is depressed into the brain – coup contusion. Contre-coup contusion is a term given where contusions occur opposite the site of impact. These most commonly involve the frontal and temporal regions. A typical scenario in this case is an impact to the rear of the head, such as when the head strikes the pavement, with the majority of brain injury occurring towards the front of the brain. The precise mechanism of this injury is not known, but it may be related to movement of the brain within the skull giving rise to different strain forces or potentially a 'vacuum-type' effect.

A fracture contusion occurs where the brain is damaged by an overlying skull fracture, such as a hammer blow.

Lacerations may be seen in contusional injuries of all types. A laceration is where the surface of the brain is physically disrupted.

Table

Coup contusion – damage beneath the impact site
Fracture contusion – damage beneath and/or in association with a skull fracture
Contre-coup contusion – damage opposite the impact site (commonly temporal and/or frontal)
Laceration – 'tearing' of the brain tissue

Problem areas

9.21

(1) Differentiation between natural intracerebral haemorrhage and haemorrhage in association with trauma. This may be a problem where there is a large intracerebral component of a contusional injury, and the question of underlying hypertension (raised blood pressure) or other natural disease arises. These cases can usually be differentiated, as an intracerebral component of a contusional haemorrhage is normally in continuity with the surface component in the brain tissue. Likewise, an intracerebral haemorrhage due to hypertension usually occurs deep within the brain rather than in the frontal or temporal regions. There may also be a history of hypertension as well as changes in other organs, including heart enlargement of the left ventricle.

(2) Ageing of contusional injuries. Histological examination may aid. However, for practical purpose in medico-legal cases it may not add to the overall picture. Histology, however, may reveal old contusions indicative of a previous head injury.

- Contusional brain injury is 'bruising' to the brain, usually on the surface but there may be areas of intracerebral haemorrhage.

- A common situation is a fall onto the back of the head, with contre-coup contusional injury involving the frontal and temporal regions opposite the site of impact.

- Coup contusions occur beneath the site of impact such as caused by a weapon.

- Fracture contusion occurs beneath the site of a skull fracture.

- Differentiation between a natural intracerebral haemorrhage such as caused by hypertension and that associated with a contusional injury may be difficult. A history of hypertension should be sought.

Traumatic axonal injury

9.22   Traumatic axonal injury has become increasingly recognised over the last number of decades. It is recognised to be the basis of severe structural brain injury in head injury. The circumstances are those of road traffic collisions, significant assaults and falls. The axons ('telegraph wires') arise from neurons (nerve cells) in the grey matter. The axons pass through the white matter, exiting down through the brain stem. Microscopic examination of the brain in cases of axonal injury will identify alterations in the protein transport by the axons, and this can be picked up by use of a stain called amyloid precursor protein (APP). This stain is used in microscope preparations and damaged axons (nerve fibres) stain brown (see Figure 9.3). It is important to recognise that traumatic axonal injury is a spectrum, ranging from small areas of damaged axons through to severe widespread damage to axons in the hemispheres, cerebellum and brain stem. This latter may also be called 'diffuse traumatic axonal injury' when it affects all parts of the brain, and it is recognised to be associated with coma and a high morbidity/mortality. Any head injury will give

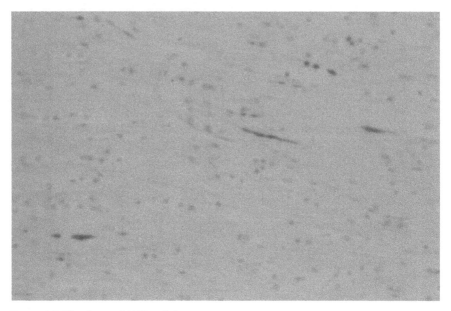

Figure 9.3 Histology of APP staining.

rise to damaged axons. Some cases of traumatic axonal injury at the severe end of the spectrum show areas of haemorrhage, usually multiple, within the brain – so-called 'tissue tear' haemorrhages. A brief period of unconsciousness is thought to be associated with small areas of damage to axons. Post-mortem studies have identified individuals who sustained a relatively minor head injury but died several days or weeks later of completely unrelated causes, such as a myocardial infarction. Areas of damaged axons corresponding in time to the head injury can be identified.

Detailed neuropathological examination of suspected cases of traumatic axonal injury is necessary. This may either show no axonal injury or show traumatic axonal injury from mild to severe. It is important to recognise that axonal injury may not necessarily be traumatic, as the staining of axons can occur where there is significant brain swelling and/or hypoxic-ischaemic damage (damage due to lack of blood/oxygen). This is a difficult area and requires specialist neuropathological examination.

Problem areas

9.23

(1) Accurate diagnosis as to whether axonal injury is traumatic or not may be difficult, particularly in the presence of brain swelling. This is because the typical areas in the brain which are vulnerable to axonal injury are also those which are vulnerable where there is damage due to brain swelling/lack of blood.

(2) Timing of injury. There are numerous articles relating to the evolution and staining of axons when they are injured. It used to be thought that it took an hour and a half to two hours for staining to become positive, but it is now well recognised that this may take place earlier. Caution should be given in expressing survivability purely on the neuropathological aspects alone – for

example, the findings of isolated positivity within the brain when a victim has been strangled and has clearly died within a very short period of time.

(3) Interpretation of haemorrhages in cases of diffuse axonal injury. These may vary in location and are also known as 'tissue tear' haemorrhages. They are common in the white matter adjacent to the midline as well as in the deep brain, the corpus callosum (bridge of tissue between the hemispheres of the brain) and the brain stem. Differentiation from a primary hypertensive haemorrhage, in particular in the context of a road traffic collision, may be difficult. This has medico-legal significance relating to the potential cause of any collision, both in the criminal and civil setting.

- Traumatic axonal injury is damage to the axons or 'telegraph wires' which pass through the brain.
- It varies from mild to severe – which is known as 'diffuse traumatic axonal injury', where much of the cerebral hemispheres and brain stem are involved.
- It is possible to time frames for injury using immunocytochemical stains.
- Differentiation of traumatic axonal injury from ischaemic brain damage and swelling may be difficult.

Brain swelling

9.24 By definition, this is an increase in the volume of brain, commonly as a result of increased blood within the blood vessels. Care needs to be taken at post-mortem examination that this is not confused with true cerebral oedema (see below).

Cerebral oedema

9.25 Cerebral oedema is due to excess fluid within the brain. The water content of the brain tissue is increased. Cerebral oedema commonly occurs as a reaction to many conditions, including meningitis, encephalitis, trauma to the brain, contusional injury and subarachnoid haemorrhage. It may be a clinical problem, as severe oedema can be resistant to treatment. The cerebral oedema causes variable degrees of swelling of the brain. As the brain is in a closed rigid cavity (that is, the skull), there is limited room for expansion. At the severe end of cerebral oedema, various herniations of parts of the brain occur, including herniation or movement of the brain into the top part of the spinal column. This may lead to irreversible compression of the brainstem, which includes the vital structures to serve the brain.

Concussion

9.26 Concussion in association with a head injury is categorised as loss of consciousness. Concussion ranges from mild, lasting a short period of time, to severe with prolonged unconsciousness. Concussion may be caused in circumstances such as a blow or other trauma to the head during boxing or other sporting activity as well as falls and road traffic collisions. It is now recognised that even minor forms of concussion produce damage to the axons within the brain. In medico-legal terms, concussion may produce a retrograde amnesia (no memory of the events shortly before or shortly after the incident). This has implications for evidential purposes. In addition, minor neuropsychiatric sequelae are common in association with concussion. There has recently been considerable debate as to the second impact syndrome and the implications for contact sports such as rugby. There is increasing evidence that the brain is more vulnerable to further injury if this occurs following initial impact. Aside from the neuropsychiatric issues, concussion itself is a prognostic factor in indicating underlying brain injury. Neuropsychiatric sequelae include headache, loss of concentration, giddiness and memory loss.

- Concussion is loss of consciousness after a head injury; if prolonged, it is known as coma.

- Even minor forms of concussion produce damage to the axons.

- Neuropsychiatric sequelae are common in association with concussion.

- It is important to recognise, in sports injuries, that the brain is more vulnerable after a previous episode of concussion.

Sudden death in head injury

9.27 Clearly, this may occur in the context of a number of circumstances, including where there is massive disruption of the brain such as by gunshot wounds or significant falls. It also occurs in the setting of traumatic subarachnoid haemorrhage (previously discussed).

More recently, sudden death has been reported to occur where there has not been significant trauma. In these circumstances, there may be an impact or impacts to the head and death follows rapidly. It is noted that, in virtually all of these cases, there is a degree of alcohol intoxication. The mechanism proposed is that of direct brain stem injury akin to that seen in concussion but producing prolonged post-injury apnoea (cessation of breathing).

Coma

9.28 Evaluation of the conscious state of a patient is extremely important in assessing evidence of brain injury. A deteriorating conscious level may initially present as drowsiness, as the level of consciousness decreases and drowsiness and confusion increase. In clinical practice, a numerical scale is used for assessing the state of consciousness. This is known as the Glasgow Coma Scale (GCS). Evaluation of three different responses is undertaken. These are: eye opening; motor response; and verbal response. A score is given to each, with a total score being recorded. Fifteen is the best score and three is the worst score. This is covered in more detail in Chapter 18.

Long-term effects of head injury

9.29 These range from relatively mild neuropsychiatric sequelae (as commented above) to severe brain damage including permanent vegetative state. They may also include physical sequelae. Complications of the head injury include meningitis or sepsis in relation to skull fractures allowing infection to spread from outside into the brain. These may be delayed for weeks or months. Post-traumatic epilepsy is a significant complication which, again, may occur shortly after recovery or be delayed. Linkage between post-traumatic epilepsy and death may be problematical in terms of causation.

Brain death

9.30 Brain death is defined as irreversible cessation of brain function which has been diagnosed by the absence of brainstem reflexes. Pathologically, perfusion of the brain ceases, thus no blood flow occurs. Blood stagnates within the circulation and brain tissue, in simple terms, 'dies'.

Prior to the clinical diagnosis of brain death, various criteria must be met to exclude the effect of biochemical abnormalities as well as drugs which may be therapeutic or, in some cases, illicit. The body temperature should also be above 35 degrees, as it is well recognised that the body functions, including that of the brain, are significantly depressed in hypothermia.

The following table indicates the tests:

(1)	Pupils unreactive to light.
(2)	Absent corneal reflex (this refers to the contraction of the muscles to stimulation of the cornea).
(3)	Absent oculocephalic reflex – doll's eye position. If the head is moved sidewards, the eyes stay centrally positioned.
(4)	Absent vestibulo-ocular reflex – injection of iced water into the external ear does not give rise to any eye movements.
(5)	Absent cough reflex.
(6)	Absent contraction of facial muscles to painful stimuli.
(7)	Absent respiratory movements on ventilation disconnection.

Other tests which may also be used include angiography (injection of dye into blood vessels in the brain) which shows no blood flow, as well as electroencephalogram (EEG) which shows no electrical activity.

Permanent vegetative state

9.31 This may arise following severe brain damage as a result of which part of the brain, the cortex which contains neurons (grey matter), dies. These neurons cannot regenerate. The cortical cells appear to be more susceptible to hypoxia than those of the brainstem. Brain stem function is maintained, with basic functions such as eye opening, eye movement and swallowing continuing. There are multiple causes of hypoxia, which include asphyxia such as crush asphyxia. This was the basis of the brain damage in a long-surviving Hillsborough victim (*Airedale NHS Trust v Bland* [1993] UKHL 17). Other conditions include drug overdose, incorrect administrations of anaesthetics and respiratory failure.

163

Natural intracerebral haemorrhage

9.32   A natural intracerebral haemorrhage may occur in any part of the brain spontaneously. It is commoner in the older age group and there is a strong association with underlying hypertension (raised blood pressure) – see Chapter 6. Treatment of hypertension has reduced the incidence of this condition.

Hypertension comprises approximately 50% of all cases of intracerebral haemorrhage. This occurs usually within the deep brain structures and to a lesser extent in the hemispheres, cerebellum and pons.

These haemorrhages are due to rupture of small vessels within the brain giving rise to haemorrhage. Histological examination may show features of long-standing hypertension or other vascular pathology in the brain and other organs.

Problem areas

9.33
(1)   Ageing of haemorrhage may be difficult but is not usually significant in the context of the medico-legal case, aside from identifying a potential underlying natural disease.

(2)   The role of stress in the causation of an intracerebral haemorrhage is complex. There are well-recognised cases where an individual is subject to either emotional or physical stress, with subsequent intracerebral haematoma. The role of underlying disease such as hypertension in these cases may be difficult to establish.

Intracerebral haemorrhage – other causes

9.34   Cerebral amyloid is a protein-like material deposited in the small blood vessels of the brain, the meninges and brain, and is an increasingly recognised cause of intracerebral haemorrhage. The blood vessels become rigid, fragile and prone to rupture. In a number of cases, there may be hypertension as an additional feature. The location of this type of haemorrhage is slightly different to that seen in a primary hypertensive haemorrhage, in that it involves the parietal or occipital region extending towards the surface. Histological examination confirms the presence of amyloid.

Problem areas

9.35
(1)   As with hypertension, the relationship of haemorrhage to 'stress' is problematical. Timing with any episode is essential – for example, in the case of an individual in a fight suddenly suffering from a brain haemorrhage at the same time.

(2)   There is association with warfarin treatment (anticoagulant treatment) which is a contributory factor, particularly with cerebral amyloid.

Further rare causes of intracerebral haemorrhage

9.36 The main point to remember is that it may be important to differentiate these from trauma. These include vascular malformations of varying types, as well as haemorrhage into a tumour.

Disorders of blood flow and/or lack of oxygen to the brain including stroke

9.37 Hypoxia is a low level of oxygen within the blood or in the brain tissue. There are a number of ways that this can be caused (see table below). These include reduced oxygen in the blood as a result of lung disease, various blood abnormalities and reduced blood flow to the brain caused by reduced cardiac output or interruption to local supply to the brain, such as that caused by a thrombus or blood clot blocking a blood vessel to the brain. In this latter circumstance, cerebral infarction occurs (which is discussed below). Ischaemia refers to the failure of blood flow to the brain, thus there is not only a lack of oxygen but also accumulation within the brain of toxic products of metabolism. This can be classified as focal ischaemia (where one part of the brain is affected) or global ischaemia (which results in failure of blood flow to the brain).

Table

Hypoxia – Low oxygen levels in the blood or brain
Ischaemia – Failure of focal or generalised (global) blood flow to the brain

9.38 Cerebrovascular accident (CVA) covers both cerebral haemorrhage as well as cerebral infarction as a cause. Cerebral infarction occurs where there is damage to brain tissue caused by blockage of one of the major arteries supplying the brain. This may cause what is known, in laymen's terms, as a stroke. A stroke may also be caused by a haemorrhage such as due to hypertension rather than infarction. The underlying pathology with cerebral infarction is most commonly atherosclerosis, with occlusion or narrowing of a major blood vessel, which may be complicated by superadded thrombosis. As a result of the lack of blood flow/oxygen to the brain, the brain tissue becomes ischaemic. Common sites include the branches of the Circle of Willis, carotid arteries and the vertebrobasilar arteries.

- A stroke is damage caused by either haemorrhage or ischaemia (lack of blood flow) to an area of the brain.

- A haemorrhage occurs commonly where there is a history of hypertension.

- A cerebral infarction as a result of arteriosclerosis arises where there is occlusion to one of the major blood vessels supplying the brain.

- Rarer causes of a stroke are due to haemorrhage as a result of amyloid, where the blood vessels are friable and prone to rupture.

Meningitis

9.39   Meningitis is inflammation or infection of the meninges. The commonest cause is bacterial meningitis, with the bacteria including streptococcus pneumonia, neisseria meningitidis and, in children, haemophilus influenzae. In fatal cases, it can be identified as pus over the surface of the brain. There are other rarer causes of meningitis, including tuberculosis. The onset of meningitis may be extremely rapid, particularly in children. Failure to diagnose and rapidly give appropriate antibiotics may result in fatalities or, as a result of severe septicaemia, loss of limbs.

Cerebral abscess

9.40   This is an abscess within the brain which can be caused by multiple organisms. Associated findings are dental infections, middle ear infections, intravenous drug users and HIV-infected individuals. A cerebral abscess presents as a space occupying mass with the potential for compression of vital structures.

Encephalitis

9.41   This is a rare condition and is defined as inflammation of the brain structure, in particular the neurons. The commonest cause is herpes simplex encephalitis, which can be fatal as well as leaving long-term debility – in particular, problems with short-term memory. HIV can also cause encephalitis.

Dementias

9.42   Dementia is an increasing problem, particularly in the western world including the United Kingdom. With an ageing population, the incidence is rising, with implications for long-term care. In the medico-legal setting, dementias may cause abnormal behaviour including aggressive behaviour, as well as issues in road traffic collisions.

Dementias are caused by neurodegenerative (nerve cells become abnormal and non-functional) conditions. Dementia can only be diagnosed by histological examination of the brain, although some dementia types have different symptoms and signs in contrast with others. The increased use of detailed scanning has also refined the diagnosis of a precise type. The pathologist may be limited on examining the brain, as the differentiation between normal ageing and a neurodegenerative condition may be difficult, if not impossible, to detect. Thus, detailed clinic-pathological correlation is necessary.

Alzheimer's disease

9.43   This is the commonest type of dementia, usually occurring after the age of 65, although there are early onset cases. The brain macroscopically shows atrophy or shrinkage, particularly of the temporal regions.

The histological hallmark is the presence of neurofibrillary tangles and amyloid plaques. A neurofibrillary tangle is seen within the neuron by special stains, and comprises tangles or disorganised fibrils within the neurons. Amyloid plaques are also identified histologically.

Vascular dementia

9.44   This is a less common cause of dementia and is often found in conjunction with other pathology such as Alzheimer's disease. Multiple small and large infarcts occur within the brain, and the blood vessels show underlying abnormalities with thickening and narrowing.

Rarer causes of dementia include Lewy body dementia, which may be associated with Parkinson's disease, as well as dementia caused by Creutzfeldt-Jakob Disease and HIV.

Iatrogenic pathology

9.45   A number of medical procedures may cause pathology (that is, iatrogenic pathology) within the central nervous system and raise the issue of potential negligence. For a detailed description of these, the reader should refer to specific texts.

Such medical procedures include anticoagulant therapy, with increased risk of bleeding, procedures related to treatment of cerebral aneurysms using coils, as well as surgery on the head, spinal surgery or manipulation.

Further reading material

General textbooks

- Leestma, J.E. *Forensic Neuropathology* (2009, 2nd Edition, CRC Press)

- Oehmichen, M., Auer, R.N., Konig, H.G. *Forensic Neuropathology and Associated Neurology* (2009, Springer)

- Whitwell, H.L. *Forensic Neuropathology* (2005, Hodder Arnold)

Articles in update textbooks

- Hausmann, R. 'Timing of Contusions' in Tsokos, M. *Forensic Pathology Reviews*. Volume One, 2004

Articles in journals

- Adams, J.H., Jennett, B., McLellan, D.R., Murray, L.S. and Graham, D.I. 'The neuropathology of the vegetative state after head injury' *J Clin Pathol* 1999; 52, 804–6

- Al-Sarraj, S., Mohamed, S., Kibble, M. *et al.* 'Subdural hematoma (SDH): assessment of macrophage reactivity within the dura mater and underlying hematoma' *Clin Neuropathol* 2004; 23, 62–75

- Black, M., Graham, D.I. 'Sudden unexplained deaths in adults caused by intracranial pathology' *J Clin Pathol.* 2002; 55; 44–50

- Blumbergs, P.C., Scott, G., Manavis, J., Wainwright, H., Simpson, D.A. and McLean, A.J. 'Staining of amyloid precursor protein to study axonal damage in mild head injury' *Lancet* 1994; 344, 1055–6

- Leadbeatter, S. 'Extracranial vertebral artery injury – evolution of a pathological illusion' *Forensic Sci Int* 1994; 67, 35–40

- McCrory, P., Davis, G., Makdissi, M. 'Second impact syndrome or cerebral injury after sporting head injury' *Current Sports Medical Reports* 2012; 11(1):21–3

- Maxeiner, H. 'Detection of ruptured cerebral bridging veins at postmortem examination' *Forensic Sci Int* 1997; 89, 103–10

- Ramsay, D.A. & Shkrum, M.J. 'Homicidal blunt head trauma, diffuse axonal injury, alcoholic intoxication and cardiorespiratory arrest: a case report of a forensic syndrome of acute brainstem dysfunction' *Am J Forensic Med Pathol.* 1995; 107–113

- Reichard, R.R., Smith, C. and Graham, D.I. 'The significance of beta-APP immunoreactivity in forensic practice' *Neuropathol Appl Neurobiol.* 2005; 31, 304–13

Chapter 10

Major blunt impact trauma: road traffic collisions and falls

Introduction

10.1 Deaths due to road traffic collisions and accidental falls form a high proportion of medico-legal practice. There is an additional public health issue within this group of deaths, in that accident investigation has a role in identification of causes, thus potentially reducing morbidity and mortality rates. This has been demonstrated within the car industry, with the development of airbags and other safety features, as well as in the urban environment with the introduction of more restrictive speed limits.

The law and road traffic collisions

10.2 The criminal law on road traffic offences is extensive. Offences may be broadly divided into two categories: general criminal offences, which will apply to all road users; and more specialist, regulatory offences, such as those which regulate the haulage industry or the use of heavy goods vehicles. The latter category of offences will rarely involve forensic investigation; an outline of the law that applies to such offences can be found in specialist works on road traffic offences.[1] In respect of general criminal offences, these are, for the most part, set out in the Road Traffic Act 1988 ('the Act') (which applies to Scotland, England and Wales and, in substance, to Northern Ireland through the Road Traffic (Northern Ireland) Order) 1995). The offences covered by the Act range from minor road traffic offences – such as driving without insurance (section 143) and driving while disqualified (section 103(1)) – to more serious offences, such as causing death by dangerous driving (section 1).

10.3 The main offences which tend to involve forensic investigation and/or road traffic collisions are those set out in sections 1 to 5 of the Act. The main demarcation in those sections is between those offences which involve careless driving and those which involve dangerous driving. Careless driving – driving without due care and attention – is the less serious, and is defined in section 3ZA as driving in a way which falls below what would be expected of a competent and careful driver. Dangerous driving, the more serious, is defined in section 2A as driving in a way which falls *far* below what would be expected of a competent and careful driver (section 2A(1)(a)),

---

1 See, for instance, *Wilkinson's Road Traffic Offences* (2014, Sweet and Maxwell).

and it would be obvious to a competent and careful driver that driving in that way would be dangerous (section 2A(1)(b)). By section 2A(3), the dangerous driving may also be committed if a person drives a vehicle when it would be obvious to a competent and careful driver that driving the vehicle in its current state would be dangerous.

The substantive offences which follow from the two definitions are the following: where death results from dangerous driving, the likely charge will be under section 1 of the Act (causing death by dangerous driving);[2] where serious injury results, the charge will be under section 1A (causing serious injury by dangerous driving). Serious injury for this purpose will be physical harm amounting to grievous bodily harm in England and Wales and severe physical injury in Scotland (section 1A(2)(a) and (b) – see Chapter 7). In the absence of either death or serious injury, the charge will be simply dangerous driving contrary to section 2 of the Act.

Where death results from careless driving, the appropriate charge is causing death by careless, or inconsiderate, driving contrary to section 2B of the Act; or, when the driver is unfit to drive through drink or drugs, causing death by careless driving when under the influence of drink or drugs contrary to section 3A. There is no equivalent offence of causing serious injury by careless driving; all cases of careless driving, where death does not result, amount to the offence of careless driving contrary to section 3 of the Act.

10.4   Finally, the last main category of offence under the Act is the criminalisation of driving having consumed drugs or alcohol. Section 4 creates the offence of driving, or being in charge of a vehicle, when under the influence of drink or drugs. It can include attempting to drive. Section 5 creates the offence of driving, or being in charge of a vehicle, with an alcohol or drug concentration above the prescribed limit.[3] The main difference between sections 4 and 5 is that a specimen of alcohol/controlled drug concentration in blood, breath or urine needs to be obtained to support a charge under section 5; other forms of evidence of unfitness will suffice for section 4. Failure to provide a specimen is a separate offence under section 7(6) of the Act.[4] The Act, and various statutory instruments made under it, govern police powers for the taking of specimens of breath, blood and urine, licensing and regulation of 'breathalysers', the circumstances in which blood and urine samples may be taken, and means by which defendants can either challenge the reliability of specimens or provide further specimens (see sections 6–10 of the Road Traffic Act 1988 and sections 15 and 16 of the Road Traffic Offenders Act 1988). By section 11 of the Road Traffic Act 1988, the prescribed limits are 35 micrograms of alcohol in 100 millilitres of breath, 80 milligrams in 100 millilitres of blood, and 107 milligrams in 100 millilitres of urine. Greater quantities will affect the severity of the sentence passed, which ranges from a fine at the lowest level (breath at 36–59 mg) to 26 weeks' imprisonment (breath at 120–150 mg and above).

---

2 If the criminal conduct is serious enough, it is still possible to charge manslaughter or, if the requisite intent is present, murder. Section 3ZB also creates the separate offence of causing death by driving if, at the time of the incident, the driver was unlicensed, disqualified or uninsured.

3 Section 5A creates the parallel offence of driving, or being in charge of, a vehicle with a concentration of a specified controlled drug above the specified limit. The section was added by the Crime and Courts Act 2013, which came into force on 2 March 2015.

4 Failure to co-operate with a preliminary (i.e. roadside breathalyser) test is an offence under section 6(6).

Road traffic collisions including pedestrian deaths

10.5   The death rate for vehicular occupants such as car drivers and passengers has reduced over the last several decades. This is in part due to improvements in car safety as well as speed reduction, seat belt wearing and the introduction of the drink-drive offences (see Chapter 17).

Car occupants

10.6   Both driver and passengers may be injured or killed during road traffic collisions. This may involve other vehicles in head-to-head or side impact, as well as impact of a vehicle with a stationary object such as a tree or wall. Less common are rear and side impacts.

Injuries

10.7   Chapter 7 on wounding covers the general features of injuries, such as laceration and bruises. However, there are particular points that should be noted, both in pedestrians and cyclists including motorcyclists.

Car occupants may show the following injuries:

External injuries

- Multiple lacerations due to fragmented glass, particularly in front seat occupants, especially if there has been no restraint by a seat belt either not worn or failing. These have the appearances of 'bird's feet' and are more common over the face and other exposed areas. Windscreen glass is of laminated form so that, instead of cracking into large pieces, it cracks into small chips that are held together to some extent by the laminated nature.

- Lacerations of the palmar skin between the thumb and the index finger are almost diagnostic of having been caused from the steering wheel or other control column at the time of impact. This may involve underlying fracture of the bones.

- Seat belt injuries. These comprise abraded and bruised areas over the shoulder, anterior chest and abdomen in a pattern resembling that of the seat belt. Clothing will modify the appearances. The pattern of clothing may be replicated on the skin with severe impacts. The presence or absence of, and patterns of, seat belt injury are not only important in terms of the restraint effect but also may confirm or otherwise the relative position of the individual in the vehicle. This may be of particular importance in identifying the driver.

- Air bag injuries or fatalities. Air bags are present in most modern vehicles. These may be at the front of the vehicle but also to the sides and, increasingly, other locations. Air bags work due to an explosive production of gas cushioning the impact. Abrasions and superficial chemical burns may occur to exposed areas. Fatalities are rare but recognised and include severe spinal injury and abdominal injuries with damage to internal organs. These injuries are more common in conjunction with lap-only seat belts. Fatalities have been reported in infants as a result of air bags due to the airbag enveloping/suffocating the child. They have been reported in infants who are either front or rear facing.

Internal injuries

- Head injuries. Head injuries are a major cause of death in road traffic collisions, either as a result of impact with part of the vehicle or as a result of being propelled externally and coming into contact with items such as trees or walls. Due to acceleration/deceleration speeds, there is a high incidence of severe primary brain damage, with traumatic axonal injury as well as subdural haematoma and other cerebral haemorrhages. Skull fractures are frequently seen and are either linear or, if there is contact with a protrusion, depressed. Head injury fatalities may not occur immediately in the context of a road traffic collision but after a period of survival, which can be variable. Particularly in the younger age group, head injury is a severe and common cause of continued debility which may necessitate continual lifelong care. Detailed discussion of the various types of head injury is covered in Chapter 9.

- Chest and abdominal injuries. In severe road traffic collisions, injury may be transmitted to the internal organs without corresponding visible external damage. In particular, this involves compression of the chest or abdomen as well as spinal injury. Compression of the chest may result from impact against an object such as the steering wheel of the car. There may be fracturing of the sternum and ribs. Abrasions in the skin overlying the injuries may be identified. Compression may also occur as a result of forcible flexion of the upper body, with the head and knees being thrown towards each other. This may occur when a lap seat belt is worn without a shoulder strap. However, it is more commonly seen in aircraft accidents, where there may be rupture of the heart due to compressive injury in particular of the atria. Likewise, the aorta, which is tethered to tissues surrounding the spine and unable to move, may also rupture. In this instance, the heart is torn away from the aorta. This may also be seen in falls from a height and aircraft accidents.

   The liver is particularly susceptible to blunt injury and, depending on the extent of damage, may be fatal or life threatening. The spleen may also be ruptured, as may the kidneys. Rupture of the mesentery (the fatty flap of tissue housing the blood supply of the intestine) may occur, in particular where there has been the use of a simple lap seat belt. Rupture of the bowel, particularly of the junction between the retroperitoneal duodenum and mobile duodenum, is also seen.

- Bony injuries. Spinal injuries are common in both car and aircraft accidents. This is due to sudden body flexion. The most vulnerable areas are the cervico-thoracic region and, secondarily, the lower thoracic region, in particular in that area where there is a simple lap seat belt. Pelvic fractures may also occur, as well as lower limb fractures. These are probably more common in pedestrian or cycling incidents.

- The death rate for vehicular occupants has reduced over the last several decades due to increase in safety aspects.

- The major external injuries include lacerations to exposed parts and areas of abrasion from seat belts or airbags.

- The major fatal injuries related to road traffic collisions are head injuries, blunt trauma to the abdomen and chest, and spinal injuries.

Whiplash injury

10.8   The cause of this condition is a true whiplash movement of the head, as shown in Figure 10.1. It is typically due to a rear-ended impact, with a hyperextension rather than flexion injury. It should theoretically be mitigated by an efficient headrest. Common signs include neck stiffness, pain and headache. The symptoms may be delayed and chronic disability may occur. This is a huge source of potential litigation. From a clinical viewpoint, symptomatology may result from a complex amalgam of physical and psychological factors. These cases may be difficult to diagnose from the clinical aspect and there is the potential for false or exaggerated claims.

- Whiplash injury is a common scenario in medico-legal practice, with symptoms ranging from minor to chronic disability.

- It is due to movement of the head/neck in a 'whiplash' manner.

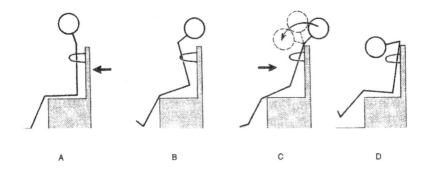

| | | | |
| A | B | C | D |

Figure 10.1 Mechanism of the specific whip-lash injury to the neck: (A) force is applied from the rear; (B) the body is accelerated against the harness but inertia leads to extension of the neck: (C) the vehicle and body are stopped but the head continues to accelerate, leading to a wide arc of unnatural forces on the neck, with the head finishing in forced flexion (D).

Pedestrian injuries

10.9   There has been a proportionate increase of pedestrian deaths/injuries over the last few decades, partly as advances in vehicle, driver and road safety have taken place with a resultant fall in vehicle occupant deaths. The elderly, young and intoxicated are more vulnerable. The majority of pedestrian fatalities arise from

Figure 10.2 Primary, secondary and tertiary injuries from road traffic collision. (Courtesy of Ruth Bowen, Medical Illustrator, Cardiff University.)

contact with a single vehicle. The source of any abrasions may be obvious, such as patterns of radiator grills or tyres. Scaled photography (photography of an injury with a measurement scale) allows for the potential to correlate with part of a vehicle, which is particularly useful in the 'hit and run' type of incident.

(1) Primary impact is where the front of the vehicle impacts with the pedestrian, with subsequent lifting up of the pedestrian into the air, to facilitate the secondary impact by contact with bonnet, windscreen or roof. Detailed evaluation can be difficult in these cases, due to the severity of the injuries involved. However, injuries to the legs, knees and thighs should be particularly sought as a result of bumper injuries and these can be correlated with measurement of relevant heights and parts of the vehicle. These may not always be visible externally, but internally may be associated with fracturing, bruising and laceration of musculature. The classic fracture is a fracture of the tibia in the form of a triangular wedge shape indicating the point of the contact (the rear of the wedge) and the direction of the impact (in line with point), but this is not present in all cases. Correlation with the accident investigator may assist.

(2) Additional (or tertiary) impact injuries may result from ground contact after impact with the vehicle. These components often leave the most significant injuries as the body comes rapidly to rest. There may be prominent brush abrasions as the body slides across the ground.

(3) Run over injuries may be exceptionally severe and involve de-gloving (lifting of the skin from the underlying tissues) with extensive abraded/ lacerational injury when dragging or run over by a vehicle has occurred. Internal injuries are variable and include skull/head injuries, compressive abdominal and chest injuries, as well as spinal injuries and other fractures. Patterned tyre injury may be seen on the body. Correlation with any clothing is extremely useful, as is identification of any paint/glass or other material.

- The incidence of deaths in pedestrian injuries has increased over the last several decades.

- The elderly, young and those under influence of either drugs or alcohol are more vulnerable.

- Primary impact sites are commonly the lower limbs, with or without fractures.

- Additional impact injuries may occur either on parts of the car, including bonnet and windscreen, or on ground contact.

- Run over injuries may be severe and necessitate differentiation from accidental or homicidal (i.e. where the individual is dead prior to any contact with a vehicle).

- Forensic examination of clothing and vehicle may be useful.

Cycle injuries including motor cycles

10.10   Injuries to cyclists have gained increasing national prominence over the last few years. There is an increasing number of fatalities associated with pedal cycling. Injuries sustained include, in particular, head injuries (there is no mandatory requirement in this country to wear a helmet unlike other jurisdictions, such as New Zealand). There is good evidence that this reduces the incidence of serious head injuries. Head injuries tend to arise when the individual is propelled on to the road surface. In addition, spine and other fractures may occur. If an individual becomes entangled with a vehicle, further injuries of varying types may be caused. Rarely a cyclist may become entrapped beneath a vehicle which produces a multiplicity of injuries.

- Fatal cycle injuries are increasing.

- The commonest cause of death are head injuries as well as multiple injuries.

- Injuries due to trapping/dragging may be seen.

Aircraft injuries

10.11   These produce similar injuries to occupants of vehicles but, in addition, there are additional vertical forces leading to increased severity of injury. Death may also result from smoke inhalation or fire which, in aircraft that land, is one of the major hazards. If the aircraft sustains damage with exposure to the atmosphere, rapid decompression may occur, with expulsion of victims and/or barotrauma (physical injury caused by differences in atmospheric pressure).

- Injuries in aircraft fatalities are variable, including multiple severe trauma.

- Death may occur as a result of fire or smoke inhalation.

Falls from a height

10.12   This includes falls down stairs as well as falls from greater heights such as bridges, apartment buildings or other high structures. The incidence of falls from high buildings varies according to jurisdiction. In Singapore, it is a relatively common method of suicide.

Falls down stairs are an important cause of injury. They are particularly prevalent in the older age group, who may have additional physical disease. In the younger age group, there is association with drugs or alcohol.

Death by falls down stairs may be difficult to interpret in the forensic setting, as the mere presence of a body at the base of the stairs does not necessarily mean that the individual fell or was somehow propelled down the stairs (where the push, in itself, would likely leave no injury). Other injuries should be sought. The major type of injuries seen in falls are head injuries of various types as well as other blunt trauma such as rib fractures and spinal injuries. Bruising may be variable and there may be brush abrasion reflecting the direction of fall. Multiple lacerations should raise the possibility of assault, as should other injuries such as signs of strangulation.

Falls from a height are associated with increasingly significant injury as the distance fallen increases. Homicidal falls from a height are rare; however, they are reported.

Careful examination of the hands of the deceased is essential, as this may indicate damage due to attempting to hold on to part of a building.

- Falls down stairs are relatively common as a cause of death.

- Other injuries should be sought in case of concealed homicide, such as neck injuries or multiple head lacerations.

- Examination for drugs/alcohol should be undertaken.

Relationship of natural disease and accidents

10.13   Natural disease may be the precipitating cause of a road traffic collision or other accident. It is important to identify any natural disease which may be the cause of death prior to any injuries sustained. Such natural causes of death include acute onset of ischaemic heart disease, as well as epilepsy and primary brain haemorrhage such as due to hypertension. Other conditions include diabetes with hyper- or hypoglycaemic coma.

Natural disease in the context of other accidents – in particular, accidents suffered by pedestrians as well as accidental falls – may comprise visual impairment as well as limited mobility. Fatal accidents in the home are common, particularly in the elderly. These may involve stairs or a simple fall. Again, natural disease may play a role (for example, transient hypertension causing dizziness or faintness). Injuries caused vary; the elderly are, however, particularly vulnerable to fractures of the femur (hip) as well as head injury.

- Natural disease may cause or contribute to any accident or collision.

- Natural diseases of significance include heart disease, epilepsy and intracerebral haemorrhage.

- The elderly are particularly prone to falls due to physical debility or natural disease.

Fat embolism

10.14   This is a recognised cause of death in association with trauma. It particularly occurs where there have been fractures of the long bones. There is a release of fat from the bone marrow cavity which passes into the blood system and becomes caught in the small blood vessels within the lungs. In this situation, it can precipitate 'adult respiratory distress syndrome', which is also known as 'shock lung'. Fat can also pass through the lungs and lodge in the small blood vessels/capillaries of the brain and kidneys. This can lead to coma and death.

- Fat embolism is recognised as a cause of death, in particular in association with long bone fractures.
- Death may occur as a result of fat lodging in the brain and/or lungs.

Deep vein thrombosis

10.15　This is covered in Chapter 6. It is well recognised that immobility predisposes to deep vein thrombus which may lead to pulmonary embolus. The presence of natural disease, such as heart disease, may further complicate the picture in terms of a direct link of pulmonary embolism and injury.

- Immobility predisposes to deep vein thrombosis and possible pulmonary embolism.
- Medico-legal issues may relate to causation and the interaction of natural disease.

Further reading material

General textbooks

- Saukko, P. & Knight, B. *Knight's Forensic Pathology* (2004, 3rd Edition)
- Mason, J.K. & Purdue, B.N. *The Pathology of Trauma* (2000, 3rd Edition)
- Spitz, W.U. *Spitz and Fisher's Medicolegal Investigation of Death* (2006, 4th Edition)
- Shkrum, M.J. & Ramsay, D.A. *Forensic Pathology of Trauma* (2007)
- Payne-James, J., Jones, R., Karch, S.B. & Manlove, J. *Simpson's Forensic Medicine* (2011, 13th Edition)
- Whitwell, H.L. *Forensic Neuropathology* (2005, Hodder Arnold)

Articles in update textbooks

- Turk, E.E. 'Fatal Falls from Height' in Tsokos, M., editor *Forensic Pathology Reviews*. Volume Five. Humana Press; 2008. 25–38

Articles in journals

- Beale, J.P., Wyatt, J.P., Beard, D., Busuttil, A. and Graham, C.A. 'A five-year study of high falls in Edinburgh' *Injury* 2000; 31, 503–8

- Clark, D. 'Effects of repeated mild head impacts in contact sports: adding it up' *Neurology*. 78(22): e140-2, 2012 May 29

- Cooper, J., Balding, L. and Jordan, F. 'Airbag mediated death of a two-year-old child wearing a shoulder/lap belt' *J Forensic Sci* 1998; 43, 1077–81

- Karger, B., Teige, K., Buhren, W. and DuChesne, A. 'Relationship between impact velocity and injuries in fatal pedestrian car collisions' *Int J Legal Med* 2000; 113, 89–97

- Lau, G., Ooi, P.L. and Phoon, B. 'Fatal falls from a height: the use of mathematical models to estimate the height of fall from the injuries sustained' *Forensic Med Pathol* 1998; 21, 32–5

- Lau, G., 'Homicidal and dyadic falls from a height: rarities in Singapore' *Med Sci Law* 2004; 44, 93–106

- Macpherson, A.K., and Macarthur, C. 'Bicycle helmet legislation: evidence for effectiveness' *Pediatr Res* 2002; 52, 472

- Preub, J., Padosch, S.A. and Dettmeyer, R. *et al.* 'Injuries in fatal cases of falls downstairs' *Forensic Sci Int* 2004; 141, 121–6

- Ryan, G.A., McClean, A.J. and Vilenius, A.T.S. *et al.* 'Brain injury patterns in fatally injured pedestrians' *J Trauma* 1994; 36, 469–76

- Yanagida, Y., Fujiwara, S. and Mizoi, Y. 'Differences in the intracranial pressure caused by a "blow" and/or a "fall" – an experimental study using physical models of the head and neck' *Forensic Sci Int* 1989; 41, 135–45

Chapter 11

Asphyxia, pressure to the neck and similar entities

11.1   Any textbook on forensic medicine or pathology will invariably have a chapter entitled 'Asphyxia', in which a number of broad mechanisms perceived to involve interference with respiration are considered. This collective approach results in confusion to lawyer and medical practitioner alike. These deaths are best considered as separate entities but with the potential for some limited overlap. Ultimately, when asphyxia is discussed, it is often assumed that the findings, complications and mechanism of death are related to deprivation of air to the lungs (the target area) but, in reality, the findings in an asphyxial death relate to obstruction to venous return. The mechanisms of death are variable.

Legal aspects

11.2   Where death occurs as a result of others' actions, deliberately or otherwise, murder and manslaughter (or culpable homicide in Scotland) charges may ensue. Normally, a murder charge will be appropriate. However, in certain cases, forensic evidence may be crucial in determining whether murder or manslaughter/culpable homicide is the appropriate offence. For instance, where it is accepted that death occurred as a result of interference with the respiratory chain, but it is denied that there was any intent to kill, such as where the possibility of death by vagal inhibition is raised (see **11.27** onwards below), forensic evidence as to the presence or absence of any contributory factors affecting the likelihood of this occurring will be necessary. Where the third party has deliberately asphyxiated but not killed the victim, the specific offence of attempting to choke, suffocate or strangle with intent, contrary to section 21 of the Offences Against the Person Act 1861, is rarely used, and such behaviour more usually forms the subject of assault charges (see Chapter 7). The same is true in Scotland where the likely charge will be aggravated assault, libelled in this case as assault 'to the danger of life'. If there was an intention to kill but the victim survived, there remains, of course, the possibility of charging the perpetrator with attempted murder.

Pressure to the neck

11.3   Pressure may be applied to the neck by a number of methods. These include the hands, as in manual strangulation, and ligature, either placed by another or by the individual party such as in hanging.

In spite of the mechanisms involved in these cases, the medical doctor will attempt to identify two broad groups of findings: the localised injury to the neck; and the effects of that pressure to the neck on other areas of the body. It is the latter category that are often called the asphyxial signs (or perhaps more appropriately, given that they are not caused by a deprivation of oxygen but obstruction to venous return, the 'so-called' asphyxial signs).

The 'asphyxial' signs

11.4   The asphyxial signs are a group of changes that are identified away from the neck and include the following:

(1) Petechial haemorrhages: These are small dot-like haemorrhages that are most often evident in the whites (sclera) of the eyes, the eyelids and elsewhere on the face, particularly where the skin is relatively loose. Typically, they are no more than a few millimetres in diameter, but with intensity can coalesce to form larger, coarser haemorrhages, most frequently within the sclera.

(2) Congestion: This is the accumulation of blood in the vasculature of the face and head. Invariably, this is associated with movement of fluid into the tissues resulting in swelling (oedema). Bleeding may also be encountered from the ears and the nasal passages as a result of rupture of small blood vessels.

(3) Cyanosis: This is the bluish discolouration of tissues of the face that accompanies congestion. Commonly explained as being secondary to de-oxygenation of oxygen-carrying haemoglobin, at post-mortem in reality it may be more of a passive phenomenon caused by diffusion (or movement through tissues) in extensive congestion. In a way, it can be considered a reflection of the extent of the congestion.

There is usually a demarcation or a tide line between areas of asphyxial change and those without. In ligature strangulation, the demarcation can be pronounced, with changes prominent in the head and neck about the ligature mark.

Mechanism and effects of asphyxial signs

11.5   The presence of these so-called asphyxial signs relates not to asphyxia or lack of oxygen but is due to obstructed venous return. As described in Chapter 1, blood is moved from the heart to target organs via the arteries, and de-oxygenated blood is returned to the heart via the veins. Simplistically, the arteries are relatively thick walled in comparison to the veins and, to some degree, can resist compression (by the external neck pressure), whereas veins do not. This means that blood can enter the head but its return to the heart is prevented. As a result, there is a build-up of blood in the head region (congestion) and a small, thin-walled type of vein, known as a venule, can rupture due to engorgement, resulting in small haemorrhages (petechial haemorrhages).

It is the presence of these findings that raises the prospect of pressure to the neck but the findings in themselves are not confirmatory of such, either in isolation or combination. Petechial haemorrhages are not diagnostic of pressure to the neck.

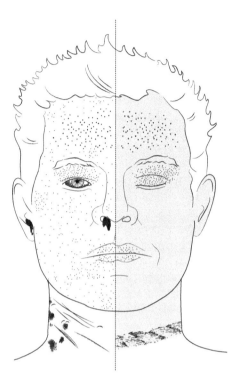

Figure 11.1 Asphyxial signs with manual strangulation injuries (L) and ligature strangulation (R). (Courtesy of Ruth Bowen, Medical Illustrator, Cardiff University.)

For example, petechial haemorrhages may be encountered in situations associated with 'straining' such as sneezing, coughing, vomiting or childbirth. In this situation, pressure forces blood from the intrathoracic (chest) region into the head, but this increased pressure also prevents return of blood from the head. For similar mechanical reasons, it has been suggested that cardiopulmonary resuscitation may also result in the presence of petechial haemorrhages; however, there is no absolute scientific support for this proposition. In these latter scenarios, the frequency and extent of petechial haemorrhages is slight and occasional in comparison with the intense and florid nature in the majority of pressure to the neck cases.

Congestion may also be seen in individuals with a degree of cardiac failure with impaired venous return.

11.6   Although considered an in-life sign, it is well-recognised amongst pathologists that the asphyxial signs may become apparent in the hours (or possibly days) after death (or, in reality, more pronounced) and this is often evident during the autopsy, with the extent of petechial haemorrhages significantly increasing as the post-mortem examination progresses. The extent of the congestion can also wane, as the agent obstructing venous return is not present. This may also apply in survivors of neck compression.

Other findings – non-specific

11.7   Internally the organs, particularly the lungs, may also be congested. This finding is non-specific and is encountered in nearly all deaths, although the intensity is somewhat greater when part of the asphyxia signs. Haemorrhages may be encountered on the pleural surface of both lungs and the epicardium of the heart. These are traditionally called Tardieu's spots and are not specific to 'asphyxia' and can arise as a consequence of terminal cardiac failure congestion.

Historically, other features – such as engorgement of the right side of the heart and the fluidity of blood – have been proposed, but are of such limited value with no scientific basis that they can be disregarded without comment.

The coarse dot haemorrhages on the internal aspects of the scalp were considered historically as 'petechial haemorrhages' and markers of asphyxia. They are, in fact, bleeding associated with mechanical tearing of vasculature during the process of removing the scalp from the skull. They are not a sign of obstructed venous return, and no importance should be placed upon them, but in a congested scalp they may be more prominent.

- 'Pressure to the neck' is the archetypal 'asphyxia', and it can be applied by a number of means.

- The (so-called) asphyxial signs are a group of changes that are identified away from the neck and include petechial haemorrhages, congestion and cyanosis.

- Asphyxial signs are not to do with asphyxia or a lack of oxygen but are caused by obstructed venous return.

- The presence of pronounced asphyxial signs by itself does not equate to pressure to the neck.

- Asphyxial signs are an in-life phenomenon; however, they may not be present immediately after death, and they may wane with increasing post-mortem interval.

- A number of historical signs of 'asphyxia' are obsolete.

Injuries to the neck in manual strangulation

11.8   Pressure to the neck may result in damage to the surface of the skin, underlying soft tissue (principally the musculature), the bony structures of the neck and ancillary structures such as the thyroid gland and the lymph nodes. The broad appearances of the injuries to the neck tend to reflect the means by which the pressure was applied.

Manual strangulation involves the hand or hands being utilised to apply pressure to the neck. It can be facilitated with one or two hands and from any relative position to the victim. It is rarely possible, however, to come to a firm conclusion in particular as to the relative position of the assailant/defendant, size or one/two hands.

Surface injuries

11.9   Injuries may result from the following: the fingernail edge compressing the skin, producing short curvilinear abrasions (and, to a lesser extent, bruises); the fingernail being dragged across the skin, producing a more elongated, coarser linear abrasion; or the finger pads (and the palms of the hands) contacting the skin, producing discoid abraded or bruised marks to more irregular and ill-defined marks. See Figure 11.1.

The 'textbook' manual strangulation demonstrates extensive and widespread injury and, although the majority of cases are far less severe, the pattern is quite characteristic. A proportion of the injuries, particularly those related to fingernails, will have been caused by the victim attempting to remove the assailant's hands. As a result, scrapings of the fingernails may provide just as useful information as swabbing of the neck.

Deep injuries

Haemorrhage/bruising

11.10   The musculature of the anterior neck are commonly known as the 'strap muscles', because they are relatively narrow bands of muscles that travel from the bony supports of the sternum and clavicles to various structures in the neck up to the level of the jaw bone. Bruising typically extends to involve both the superficial and deeper musculature and is usually prominent in the form of discrete clusters. Bruising may also been seen in the thyroid gland and the lymph nodes, but this is often superimposed on congestion.

Artefactual or erroneous bleeding may be encountered in the musculature of the neck and the posterior aspect of the oesophagus (the Prinsloo-Gordon lesion). The artefactual musculature haemorrhage can be prevented by drainage of venous engorgement prior to their examination. This can be achieved if the brain is removed prior to the layered examination of the neck muscles; and it is also wise to remove the chest organs at the same time, as this improves the venous drainage. The Prinsloo-Gordon lesion is associated with more prolonged post-mortem interval but the above techniques can prevent it to some extent. Its importance is that, as an *isolated finding*, an alternate, more plausible explanation for its presence (i.e. artefact) is evident rather than neck trauma.

Hyoid-laryngeal complex injuries – deep injuries

Anatomy

11.11   The hyoid-laryngeal complex comprises three main elements: the hyoid bone; the laryngeal cartilage; and the cricoid cartilage. The larynx is a V-shaped

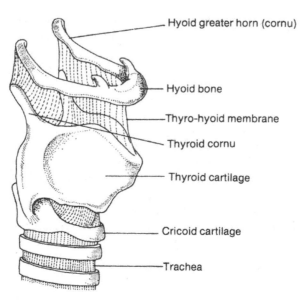

Anatomy of the larynx

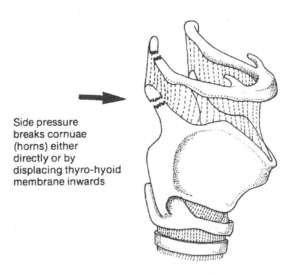

Side pressure
breaks cornuae
(horns) either
directly or by
displacing thyro-hyoid
membrane inwards

Mechanism of hyoid fracture in strangulation

Figure 11.2 Hyoid and larynx with common fracture points. (From: *Lawyers' Guide to Forensic Medicine*, Knight, B., 1998, Cavendish Publishing Ltd, reproduced by permission of Taylor & Francis Books UK.)

structure that is identified on the skin surface in post-puberty male with some ease as the Adam's apple. From the superior and inferior lateral margins are four slender projections, known as the superior and inferior horns.

Immediately superior to the laryngeal cartilage is the hyoid bone which is joined to it by the thyrohyoid membrane. The hyoid bone is broadly U-shaped and has the same orientation as the V of the laryngeal cartilage. The anterior aspect of the hyoid bone is horizontal and is known as 'the body'. There is invariably a joint at either side of this body, which corresponds to the location of small, short, superiorly placed projections known as the lesser horns. The greater horns are the long and slender ones, running backwards from anterior to posterior. On occasion, a small cartilage may be present between the ends of the greater and superior horns known as the triticeous cartilage.

The cricoid cartilage is a modified cartilage ring similar to the cartilage rings of the trachea. It sits below the laryngeal cartilage and is in close contact.

Findings in neck compression

11.12   In strangulation, fracturing of the hyoid bone and laryngeal cartilages most frequently involves fracturing of one or both tips of the greater and superior horns respectively. These regions are relatively avascular (lacking a blood supply), so an in-life fracture need not always be associated with bruising. However, trauma to adjacent soft tissue invariably arises and haemorrhage is seen with the fracture.

Another common fracture is a vertically orientated fracture of the V-shaped laryngeal plates, but this is more in keeping with a heavy impact to the front of the neck splaying the larynx against the vertebral column than a strangulation-type process, but clearly there can be overlap.

The presence or absence of fracturing to the hyoid-laryngeal complex is dependent in part on the age of the victim.

11.13   The use of the words 'cartilage' and 'bone' often causes confusion. In youth to early middle age, both the laryngeal cartilage and hyoid bone are predominantly relatively soft and cartilaginous but, beyond this age, both structures ossify (turn into bone) and become hardened. This has an important consequence, as cartilaginous structures are relatively pliable and resist traumatic breakage. Therefore, strangulations involving those of young age do not typically demonstrate fracturing unless very severe force has been utilised.

- Pressure applied to the neck may result in damage to the skin surface and the deeper tissues.

- Manual strangulation involves the use of the hand or hands to apply pressure.

- Artefactual bleeds may be seen and appropriate techniques must be used.

- Injury to the hyoid-laryngeal complex is considered the archetypal injury in pressure to the neck.

- The presence or absence of fracturing to the hyoid-laryngeal complex is dependent in part on the age of the victim – younger victims may show no fractures.

Injuries to the neck in ligature strangulation

11.14   Ligature strangulation may be facilitated with virtually any material, and the appearance of the neck is heavily dependent on its nature.

Surface injuries

11.15 A fine but firm, narrow ligature will typically leave a narrow depressed furrow. Patterning may be encountered to the mark if the ligature itself was patterned. Although bruising may be evident within the ligature mark, by far the most common appearances are those of either parchmented or reddened abrasions. See Figure 11.1.

A parchmented abrasion has a translucent yellow appearance said to resemble parchment paper and is the hallmark of a peri-mortem injury (that is, an injury that arose shortly before the time of death, at the time of death or after death) as insufficient time has passed to allow the early stages of healing to commence. The parchmented appearance progresses after death and becomes harder and stiffer.

11.16 If the ligature does not completely encircle the neck, a single linear profile almost on the same plane is seen. However, relative movements of deceased and assailant mean that such simplicity is relatively rare. Defensive-type fingernail injuries may be present in the vicinity of the ligature mark, as attempts to facilitate removal of the ligature are made.

The ligature may be wrapped around the neck on multiple occasions, and knots may be incorporated to retain its position on the neck. Unsurprisingly rare, these result in somewhat complex injuries to the skin surface but usually some interpretation can be provided.

11.17 A broad soft ligature, such as a scarf, is less damaging to the surface of the neck and may leave no skin injury whatsoever. Injuries may be present as clusters of fine linear bruises, as the underlying skin is 'nipped' extending to more pronounced (often) linear bruises at the margin. Interposed objects, such as a necklace, may form a pseudo-ligature mark. This may also apply to manual strangulation.

Internal injuries

11.18 Internal injury, particularly injury to the hyoid-laryngeal complex, is usually less severe for ligature strangulation than for manual strangulation, but it is clearly dependent on the nature of the ligature involved. Ultimately, this cannot be used for any diagnostic purposes.

Asphyxial signs

11.19 So-called asphyxial signs are usually very pronounced, more often with larger areas of coalescing petechial haemorrhages. A tide-line is more likely to be evident, with pronounced changes above the ligature mark but none or very limited below it.

- Ligature strangulation may be facilitated with virtually any material, and the appearance of the neck is heavily dependent on its nature.

Self-strangulation

11.20   Self-strangulation may be facilitated by ligature, provided the ligature has the ability to self-grip and lock around the neck – in essence, maintain its own tension. This is a relatively rare death, and asphyxial changes tend to be very prominent. This type of death may be seen in the custodial setting, or similar.

Arm locks

11.21   The pathological appearance of arm locks or neck holds is similar to broad ligature strangulation.

Two main types are classically described, namely the 'carotid sleeper' and the bar arm 'choke hold':

(a)   In the carotid sleeper, the bend of the upper limb is positioned anteriorly such that the arm and forearm compress the lateral aspects of the neck, compressing vasculature of the carotid bundle (carotid arteries and jugular veins).

(b)   In the choke hold, the forearm compresses the front of the neck such that the trachea is compressed but also the base of the tongue is elevated to occlude the throat region.

In the majority of situations involving arm locks, neither type is perfectly applied and, with struggle, pressure is applied broadly to various sites in the neck. In 'perfect conditions' the choke hold is considered safe, and is utilised in a number of martial art sports. Findings in this situation are variable – ranging from pronounced asphyxial features to minimal or absent. The findings following an arm lock or broad neck hold are often similar to broad soft ligature strangulation, and fractures of the laryngeal structures are not as common as in manual or ligature strangulation. See also **19.25** onwards.

Hanging

11.22   Three broad types are usually considered: full suspension, partial suspension and judicial hanging.

Hanging – full suspension

11.23   In a complete, full suspension hanging, the body weight is totally supported by the neck. The appearance of the ligature mark is clearly dependent on the nature of the ligature, but the mark is relatively characteristic and is situated slightly higher over the front of the neck than ligature strangulations, with a more prominent parchmented abrasion extending upwards towards the back of the head.

An area devoid of injury is often seen that arises broadly diametrically opposite to the horizontal component, as the ligature does not completely encircle the neck due to the way in which pressure is applied. This area is often termed the 'suspension point'.

The ligature marks are usually more pronounced than in strangulation, as the ligature is in contact for a longer period of time with the skin of the neck. If a slip (or self-tightening under pressure) knot has been fashioned, the suspension point and the rising nature of the ligature may be lost.

Bruising to the musculature of the neck is less common, although fracturing within the hyoid-laryngeal complex is relatively frequent.

Asphyxial changes are invariably absent, as the pressure applied by the body weight is sufficient to occlude the arteries. As a result, this appearance of this form of hanging is often described as being one of a 'pale face'. Indeed, the presence of asphyxial features is more associated with a horizontal component (see below).

Hypostasis (see Chapter 4) may be evident to the soles of the feet and the hands with prolonged suspension, as well as to the internal organs.

Hanging – partial suspension

11.24 In partial suspension hanging, part of the body weight is supported by other means (for example, by the parts of the torso resting on the ground if the ligature is secured around a door handle). As a result, the extent of the force applied to the neck is significantly reduced and compression of the arteries is not seen, resulting in more pronounced asphyxial signs and less frequent, deeper neck injury (muscle or bone).

Judicial hanging

11.25 Judicial hanging is associated with a significant drop and is more commonly associated with mechanical disruption (breakage) of the contents of the neck, particularly the cervical spine at the level of C2–C3.

- Suspension deaths (hanging) are a special form of ligature-type 'strangulation' whereby the body weight is utilised to place pressure upon the neck.
- Hangings are broadly separated into three types: full suspension, partial suspension and judicial hanging.
- An area of absence of mark, known as a 'suspension point', may be encountered.

Mechanism of death in cases of pressure to the neck

11.26 The precise mechanism or mechanisms by which pressure to the neck results in death are not fully established. Historically, airway occlusion was considered to be the principal mechanism. It is for this reason that asphyxia and interference with the respiratory function have become synonymous. In reality, deaths arise more quickly than in pure oxygen deprivation. The consideration of the 'choke hold' being utilised in regulated sport again points to the likely more limited role that it plays.

Subsequently, more focus has been placed on the effects of interruption of the (inflow and outflow) vasculature of the brain, as well as effects of pressure on nearby nerves. Although an interplay between all mechanisms seems likely, interest by some quarters has been placed upon cardiac effects caused by interference with various neural reflexes (in essence, automatic brain responses to stimuli). This concept has been utilised in court as part of the 'vaso-vagal' defence.

Carotid bodies and 'vaso-vagal' events

11.27 There is a specialist cluster of neural cells called the carotid bodies in close approximation to the bifurcation of the carotid arteries. The carotid bodies are often described as baroreceptors (or pressure receptors) but, in fact, are more complex and are involved in assessing the passing blood for a number of parameters, including levels of oxygen and carbon dioxide.

In response to changes, a reflex arc is established whereby the stimulus travels along the glossopharyngeal nerve to the medulla oblongata of the brain stem, before being transmitted to the heart from the brain via the vagus nerve (which extends to the heart via the neck).

11.28 It has been suggested that possible interference with the carotid body's normal functioning, by the application of pressure to or near the carotid body, occurs by interfering with the homeostatic or normal functioning of the reflex. It has been *suggested* that the reflex is compromised and this, in turn, can result in the development of arrhythmia or complete cessation of cardiac output. This is known variably as a 'vagal reflex', 'vagal inhibition', 'vaso-vagal shock' or 'reflex cardiac arrest'.

As an extrapolation of this reflex or inhibition, it has been suggested that the application of neck pressure could result in immediate death, without the need for prolonged application of pressure. For instance, British forensic medicine and pathology always highlight the scenario of death being caused by a 'playful tweak' rather than prolonged manual forceful compression. In doing so, similar cases without reference seemingly involving 'wartime dances' are invariably invoked, which can only raise concern. The literature, as well as other texts noted in the reference list, is inconclusive if not somewhat dismissive, especially from overseas.

This area was reviewed by Schrag *et al* (2011). The authors' review concluded that 'reflex cardiac arrhythmia due to carotid bifurcation stimulation cannot provoke death without the presence of contributory factors'. Those contributory factors were cardiac pathology or abuse of cardio-stimulatory drugs such as cocaine. This viewpoint is broadly in keeping with clinical data suggesting that those who have inherently hypersensitive carotid sinuses are at no increased risk of mortality. This is evidenced in a number of papers in the literature. Deaths have been encountered following therapeutic carotid sinus stimulation for bradycardia (a slow heart rate); but, where presented in the literature, they are related to individuals with pre-existing carotid artery disease.

In essence, if such a special category of cases does exist, then they will, by definition, present with a complete absence of asphyxial signs and neck injury, except perhaps localised minor abrasion (otherwise, there would be evidence of the application of more prolonged application of pressure). Such minor abrasions, if present at all, would combine with either cardiac pathology or abuse of cardio-stimulatory drugs. The pathological picture is normally exclusionary of this phenomenon.

- The mechanism by which pressure to the neck causes death is not fully established.

- Possible interference with the carotid body's normal functioning, by the application of pressure to or near the carotid body, is suggested as playing a role (vaso-vagal) by inducing immediate cardiac death through vagal inhibition. The evidence to support this in the literature is not strong. If it occurs, other pathology is usually present.

Problem areas in cases of pressure to the neck

The duration of the applied neck pressure in fatal cases

11.29   The length of time for which neck pressure was applied is an essentially unanswerable question. This is further compounded if one accepts that pressure to the neck deaths can never be a stylised continuous application of pressure but are, in reality, a more complex incident where the nature and extent of the pressure is varied throughout.

The findings of asphyxial features (in particular, of petechial haemorrhages) are generally accepted to develop after 15 to 30 seconds of neck pressure. There is no precise scientific basis for this, but their mechanism of creation requires a period of time to pass (unlike that associated with other, more instantaneous mechanisms such as sneezing). In the majority of cases, the extreme nature of the asphyxial changes ensures that this timeframe can be proposed without significant difficulty. Ultimately, the presence of 'asphyxial' signs suggests that the death arose, as a minimum, after 15 to 30 seconds. However, in any individual case this may be over a longer time period.

Degree of force

11.30   The extent of forces involved can never be precisely stated. The amount of force required to compress the individual structures (e.g. arteries, veins, etc) are provided in a number of journal articles. They are difficult to interpret and, in isolation, are of limited value to the court.

The only opinion that can be provided relates to the nature of the traumatic damage to the musculature and hyoid-laryngeal complex. Fracturing of uncalcified hyoid or larynx is indicative of relatively severe trauma, whereas bruising in the musculature is indicative of less significant force in comparison to the bony structures, but the forces involved are still reasonable. Quantitative figures, again, are difficult for the lawyer, layman and medical doctor to use effectively. An area that may assist practitioners is that, if the forces involved were so slight, the necessary causation for criminal liability would be absent.

The presence of other injuries to the body may also assist in the totality of the force involved in the incident.

Decomposition in the face down position

11.31   A body that is maintained in a prone position (face down) after death can mimic both asphyxial signs and traumatic features. Pronounced hypostasis (red discolouration – see **4.6** onwards) in the facial region can mimic congestion, although areas of pallor secondary to contact of the face with a surface can ease recognition. Coarse haemorrhages may occur in the hypostasis, and these can resemble petechial haemorrhages. They are commonly known as 'vibices'. These haemorrhages may also mimic skin surface and musculature bruising in the neck region. In the majority of cases, the appearances of the coarser nature of the changes, combined with similar changes elsewhere (e.g. to the front of the torso and limbs), assist in interpretation. However, if the body has been prone with the head significantly dependent (e.g. head off the edge of the bed) for a few days then, in the absence of ligature marks, abrasions and bony injury, distinguishing decomposition-related changes from strangulation may be extremely difficult if not impossible. This area is covered by Pollanen and colleagues (2009).

Deaths associated with limited findings

11.32   Where findings are extensive, the proposition that pressure to the neck has caused death is relatively straightforward. Where findings are limited (more often, the broad neck hold or in soft ligature strangulations), the pathologist will be more circumspect. For both prosecution and defence counsel, it is important that the report of the pathologist, in all cases of pressure to the neck, is considered in some detail in order to understand the confidence of the pathologist's opinion. Case conferences are highly advised.

Live victims of neck pressure

11.33   It can be difficult to provide interpretation on survivors of applied pressure to neck. Rather than being examined by medical doctors with forensic medicine training, medical evidence in assault cases is often provided by treating physicians. Specialist police photography is usually undertaken days later, or simply not all. The role of the treating physician is treatment rather than evidence accumulation. Subtle signs can easily be missed or not appreciated.

Live victims can complain of symptoms including a sore throat, a hoarse voice and localised pain and tenderness.

The injuries to the skin surface will undergo healing changes and, invariably within a day or so, demonstrate a degree of crusting infection, making interpretation difficult.

11.34   Asphyxial signs are usually poorly documented by treating clinicians, as they are not aware of their significance. Congestion (as the venous return is restored) and oedema are lost relatively rapidly. Petechial haemorrhages may remain for a longer period and will often coalesce with passage of time and, as a result, can be more pronounced.

In comparison to post-mortem examination, review of the deeper structures may not be available by direct inspection. Radiological investigation (by CT scan) may have been undertaken and, if so, it should be reviewed by a radiologist with expertise in forensic radiology to identify (if possible) bruising and bony injury. Examination by a specialist in ear, nose and throat (ENT) medicine may be able to visualise some internal injuries on direct inspection.

Restriction of chest movements/crush asphyxia

11.35   Crush asphyxia may occur in fixation of the chest by crushing caused by building collapse or crowd. It may also arise homicidally when an assailant sits upon the chest to prevent respiratory movement, and will often involve some form of other potentially lethal component. For example, 'burking' (named after the methodology of Burke and Hare) involves chest fixation combined with smothering. Crush asphyxia has been previously known as 'traumatic' asphyxia, but the use of 'crush' is now preferred.

Similar to pressure to neck, the signs of crush asphyxia relate to trauma and asphyxial signs.

Localised trauma

11.36   Clearly, the nature of the trauma will affect the extent of the localised injury, which can range from relatively slight injury, limited to localised bruising and abrasion, to more widespread injury, with fracturing of the bones of the torso.

Asphyxial signs

11.37   These develop because the increased intrathoracic (and intra-abdominal) pressure increases to such an extent that arterial blood is forced into the head and venous return is prevented. In comparison to death due to neck pressure, the asphyxial changes are more marked due to the extent of the pressure, but it is also likely that the relative time of pressure is more prolonged. It is not currently understood at what stage such deaths become inevitable in these cases. The extent of the asphyxial signs in cases of pressure to the chest may increase and, conversely, it is also possible that the congestion may wane to some extent if the chest compression is removed close to death or immediately after.

Survivors

11.38   In those that survive the initial phase, complications secondary to muscle and other tissue breakdown products entering the blood stream, resulting in renal failure or 'hypoxic-ischaemic' encephalopathy (brain damage due to lack of oxygen), may develop, causing delayed death.

- Crush asphyxia arises when significant pressure is applied to the chest and/ or abdomen to prevent effective respiratory movements of the chest, by crushing caused by building collapse or crowd.

- The appearances are variable and dependent on the extent and length of the crushing.

The other 'asphyxias'

Occlusion of the external airways (smothering)

11.39   Occlusion of the nose and mouth by a variety of means is known as 'smothering'. It can be achieved by a variety of means, such as pillow or hand. Material that is pervious to air, such as most cloth-type material, becomes rapidly impervious as moisture is absorbed. Although considered a means of causing death to the very young or the very old, it can be utilised against those with significantly reduced consciousness, such as those who are intoxicated.

Smothering is an exceptionally difficult diagnosis to make at post-mortem examination, as it potentially leaves no pathological signs. The frequency of smothering in the population is thus a great 'unknown unknown' in forensic pathology.

11.40   Injuries may be encountered to the peri-oral and peri-nasal region as well intra-oral region around the gum margins. This typically comprises small abrasions and bruises and, ultimately, is a reflection of haphazardly forceful smothering or resistance by the victim to the smothering episode.

Asphyxial signs are the exception and not the rule. When present, they usually comprise a few petechial haemorrhages. Although a smothering episode may encompass a degree of pressure to the neck, the physiological effects of a Valsalva-like manoeuvre (forced expiration against the closed airway increasing cardiac output and reducing venous return) may be a more likely explanation.

11.41   The frequency of findings is probably far less in infants than adults, often limited to a few coarser haemorrhages to the thymus, lungs and heart that arise in the majority of infant deaths anyway. See **14.12**.

In prosecuted cases of smothering, the vast majority of causes of death will be 'unascertained' (although some supportive pathology may be evident) on a background of (strong) other evidence. Even when supportive pathology is evident, alternative explanations for them, notably resuscitation, should always be considered. Invariably, recovery of the smothering agent (such as a pillow) may well be of more value than the pathological report.

Overlay in infants

11.42   This is the death of an infant co-sleeping in an unsafe environment, such as a sofa or bed, with an adult. Deaths in this situation may pathologically overlap with the internal findings encountered in infant smothering but are often absent. The mechanism of death is more complex and may include a combination of occlusion of the external airways, re-breathing of carbon dioxide and overheating. See **14.8**.

Deaths associated with irrespirable atmospheres and suffocation

Irrespirable gas deaths

11.43   Entry into an abnormal atmosphere can occur in a variety of situations, such as fire. However, this type of death usually relates to sudden death on entry to an irrespirable atmosphere, such as are encountered in nitrogen-rich grain silos, ship's tanks and other industrial equipment. Deaths occur extremely rapidly, and certainly no more than limited movement is evident in the vicinity. These deaths cannot be related to asphyxia but are likely to relate to a reflex cardiac arrest associated with overstimulation of the respiratory centres. No pathological features are encountered, so the diagnosis is completely dependent on the circumstances.

Plastic bag asphyxias (or suffocation)

11.44   These are similar in that they are associated with extremely rapid deaths and have no pathological features. If the bag is removed then, on the pathology alone, such a death cannot be attributed to this mechanism of death. The mechanism of death is unclear, but a reflex cardiac arrest related to re-breathing of the localised atmosphere is considered most likely. The bag need not be tied at the bottom, and plastic sheeting over the front of the face can have the same effect.

Obstruction of the mouth (gagging) and throat (choking)

11.45   This arises when the airways are occluded, either intentionally by a gag or accidentally by a food item, denture plate or even vomit. Death may arise when the mouth has been stuffed with material to stifle calls for help. Suicidal gagging must be considered very rare. If removed prior to examination, there may be localised injury, such as tearing of the frenulum, or the tongue may be pushed backwards within the mouth; a similar effect is often encountered by the insertion of emergency airways by paramedics.

Accidental gagging – and, invariably, choking – can also follow impaction of a bolus of food in the larynx. This may be associated with drunkenness but is most commonly seen in elderly persons. Young children may choke by the impaction of a small object in the larynx – such deaths can occur due to inhalation of buttons, of beads and of a 'baby aspirin', as well as various items of food.

Diagnosis may depend on the history alone if the obstruction has been removed.

- Other forms of asphyxia more classically associated with interference of respiration include smothering, overlay, suffocation and gagging/choking.

Positional asphyxia

11.46   Positional asphyxia is a catch-all term used to describe deaths where the body's position prevents effective respiration and the body is prevented from escape, usually by intoxication (or other causes of stupor and neurological disease). Crush asphyxia can be in a way considered part of a positional asphyxia, but the two should not be used interchangeably. Other examples include significant flexion of the neck obstructing the internal airways as well as deaths arising in the head-down, inverted position. The latter is somewhat tenuous in its inclusion, as death is more likely to relate to the effects of obstructed venous return (due to gravity).

The pathological features are extremely variable and are dependent on the nature of events. For example, deaths associated with significant obstructed venous return are likely to have prominent asphyxial signs, whereas deaths associated with marked flexion of the neck are likely to have none (except for some potentially associated with a Valsalva-like effect).

Special types of deaths: autoerotic deaths

11.47   Autoerotic deaths may involve a wide variety of lethal paraphilia, including anaesthesiophilia (sexual arousal and pleasure from volatile substances such as chloroform), electrophilia (similar arousal from electricity), and masochism. The most common autoerotic deaths relate to those associated with the 'asphyxial' types, including use of ligatures, inverted suspension, plastic bags, gags and masks, and invariably relate to failure of safeguards in solo activity. The majority of the deaths relate to accidents in the context of reckless behaviour rather than attempts at suicide, and close inspection of the scene assists with this. Deaths involving more than one party are much rarer, given the presence of an effective additional 'safety mechanism'. On occasion, given the intimate nature of strangulations, a defendant will suggest that the death arose in a consensual 'sex game'. Pathological review may be able to assist to a certain degree in determining whether this is the case.

Further reading material

General textbooks

- Saukko, P. & Knight, B. *Knight's Forensic Pathology* (2004, 3rd Edition)

- Spitz, W.U. *Spitz and Fisher's Medicolegal Investigation of Death* (2006, 4th Edition)

- Shkrum, M.J. & Ramsay, D.A. *Forensic Pathology of Trauma* (2007)

- Payne-James, J., Jones, R., Karch, S.B. & Manlove, J. *Simpson's Forensic Medicine* (2011, 13th Edition)

- Di Maio, V., Di Maio, D. *Forensic Pathology* (2001, 2nd Edition, CRC Press)

- Vanezis, P. *Pathology of Neck Injury* (1989, Butterworths)

Articles in textbooks

- Seidel, S. 'Accidental Autoerotic Death' in Tsokos, M. *Forensic Pathology Reviews*. Volume One, 2004

- Schafer, A.T. 'Death in the head down position' in Tsokos, M. *Forensic Pathology Reviews*. Volume Three, 2005

Articles in journals

- Hampton, J.L., Brayne, C., Bradley, M. *et al.* 'Mortality in carotid sinus hypersensitivity: a cohort study' *BMJ Open* 2011;1:e000020

- Maxeiner, H., Jekat, R. 'Resuscitation and conjunctival petechial hemorrhages' *J Forensic Leg Med.* 2010;17:87–91

- Pollanen, M., Perera, S., Clutterbuck, D. 'Hemorrhagic lividity of the neck: controlled induction of postmortem hypostatic hemorrhages' *Am J Forensic Med Pathol.* 2009 Dec;30(4):322–6

- Schrag, B., Mangin, P., Vaucher, P., Bollmann, M. 'Death caused by cardioinhibitory reflex: what experts believe' *Am J Forensic Med Pathol* 2012;33: 8–12

- Schrag, B., Vaucher, P., Bollmann, M., Mangin, P. 'Death caused by cardioinhibitory reflex cardiac arrest – a systematic review of cases' *Forensic Sci Int.* 2011;207:77–83

Chapter 12

Drowning and hypothermia

Immersion deaths

12.1   Immersion deaths are deaths where a body is recovered from water. It is important to realise that death in these circumstances may or may not have resulted from true drowning. In addition, pathologically it may be difficult or, indeed, impossible to prove that a true drowning death has occurred. This is particularly so where decomposition is marked. Table 1 simplifies the classification of deaths from bodies found in water:

Table 1

Deaths from natural causes, either before being in water or whilst in water
Death as a result of injuries, either before or after in water
Deaths from drowning, either true drowning or 'rapid' drowning

Signs of immersion

12.2   The body may show signs of immersion, whether or not a true drowning has occurred, and independently of other features such as signs of injury. These features are:

- Maceration of the skin. This commences in the exposed hands and feet areas, and early signs include 'washer woman's' change. Here the skin becomes wrinkled, pale and odematous (swollen). This change may occur within 30 minutes to an hour after immersion. With the passage of time, the skin sloughs off, often in a 'glove and stocking' manner. How long this takes is dependent on the conditions in which the body is found. As a general rule, cold water slows down this process.

- Gooseflesh. Here the erector pilae (the muscles attached to the hair follicles) contract. This is related to the cold and produces a 'gooseflesh' appearance. It is non-specific for drowning – it is a reflection of cold.

- Hypostasis (pooling of the blood) may be seen; however, it should be noted that this has no diagnostic significance in terms of positioning of the body after death. In drowning deaths, it can be variable due to movement of the body in water.

- Mud, sand and other components of water (such as seaweed and algae) may be found on the body, at times adherent to the body. Mud and dirt may be present within the mouth and air passages; however, it should be noted that, in terms of diagnosing a true drowning, this has limited diagnostic significance, as water and its contents can passively enter into the airways and stomach.

Deaths from drowning

12.3   These may be accidental, suicidal or homicidal. Accidental drowning may occur in a variety of circumstances, including both salt water and fresh water. Swimming pools, water tanks, rivers and in the domestic setting are the major locations for fresh water drowning. Deaths in sea water occur either from beaches or as a result of falling in from a ship or boat. In many cases, the circumstances will be clear as to the accidental nature; however, in others it may be difficult to differentiate between suicide and homicide. Alcohol or other drugs are associated with a higher incidence due to predisposition to falling but also reduced inability to extricate from the water. Likewise, if an individual is knocked unconscious as a result of falling into water, this will impede extrication.

Death may occur as a result of drowning in the bath although, in these circumstances, other findings should be sought, such as electrocution, poisoning from carbon monoxide as a result of a faulty water heater, as well as a previous history of epilepsy. Epileptics are particularly prone to dying in the bath. Death from other natural causes, such as heart disease, may also occur whilst in the bath.

12.4   Suicidal drowning may be associated with the placing of weights in the pockets, but this also occurs in homicidal drowning. Distribution of clothing or other belongings may prove helpful – for example, an individual leaving most of their clothes and personal possessions on the beach or riverside tends to occur in suicides. Again, intoxication and effects of drugs should be sought.

Homicidal drowning occurs for a number of reasons. It is important to identify features of injury which may have occurred either before or whilst being in water and, indeed, deaths may have resulted from these injuries rather than true drowning. Circumstances are likely to aid in interpretation; however, where an individual is pushed from a boat in the open sea, for example, differentiation between accident and suicide may well be impossible. Homicidal drowning was a feature of the so-called 'Brides in the Bath' case.

Features of drowning

External features

12.5

- When a fresh body is recovered, classical features are a large mushroom-like plume of froth present over the mouth and extending into the airways (champignon de mousse). This may disappear after the passage of time. It is usually white but may be blood-tinged. It is not diagnostic of drowning, as it is recognised to occur in acute drug overdoses and external pressure to the neck; however, the circumstances of a body retrieved from water showing this feature is a strong indication of true drowning. Any degree of decomposition may make the diagnosis of a true drowning death difficult and, with extensive decomposition, impossible.

- Petechial haemorrhages are not a feature of drowning deaths and, if present, should alert that other pathology may be present. Signs of strangulation should be sought, as the body may have been dumped in water in an attempt to hide the true cause of death.

Internal findings

12.6

- The lungs are over-inflated and, on average, heavier than normal. They fill the chest cavity and appear 'crepitant', showing irregular areas of haemorrhage. Markings of the ribs may be present. Microscopy may show that the walls of the alveoli (airspaces) have broken down and are distended. In addition, pale fluid may be seen within the airways which may be blood-stained. This is as a result of pulmonary oedema.

- Other organs may show congestion (distention of blood vessels with blood), in particular of the kidneys, liver and heart, but these are non-specific findings. The stomach frequently shows contents of water and sand/or silt; however, this can occur by the body simply being in water and, on its own, cannot be taken as diagnostic of drowning.

Difference between fresh water and salt water drowning

12.7   Drowning in salt water tends to occur over a longer period than that in fresh water, due to the differences in the chemistry of the water and the effect in the blood. It is said that this occurs in around 5 to 8 minutes and is probably closest to a true 'asphyxial' death. In fresh water, drowning water is transferred from the lungs into the blood stream much more quickly than in sea water. This dilates the plasma, and water passes into the cells of the blood, releasing potassium. This acts on the heart causing fatal arrhythmia (rhythm disturbance). It is said, as commented above, to be much more rapid than drowning in salt water, occurring in a few minutes.

- Signs of immersion include skin maceration, 'gooseflesh' and adherent mud/dirt.

- The cause of death in immersion may be drowning or from other causes including natural disease, as well as injuries occurring prior to entering the water.

- True drowning deaths classically show froth around the mouth and nose, with over-inflation and crepitant lungs.

- Petechial haemorrhages are not a feature of drowning deaths.

- Injuries should be sought to exclude assault prior to entering the water.

So-called 'dry drowning'

12.8   Death in these cases occurs very rapidly and the features of true drowning are absent. It is thought that death occurs in these circumstances due to a sudden rush of cold water into the upper air passages resulting in reflex cardiac arrest. Likewise, a sudden rush of water into the trachea would have the same effect. This type of death commonly occurs when cold water is involved and commonly with a degree of alcohol intoxication. The individual is typically surprised or unprepared. The pathological findings of froth and internal findings are absent. Care must be taken in excluding other causes of death, such as natural causes or drug overdose, as well as causes of occult homicide such as strangulation. Investigation of the circumstances is important.

- Dry drowning is where typical drowning and other causes of death are excluded.
- It is thought to be due to sudden entry of cold water into the air passages.
- A degree of alcohol intoxication is common.

Other findings of immersed bodies

12.9   As noted above, it is important to observe for signs of injury. It is not uncommon in a homicide for the body to be disposed of in water after being subject to other trauma, such as strangulation or head injuries. If death has occurred before the body enters the water, signs of drowning will be absent. Clearly, if an individual survives for a period of time, features of true drowning may be present.

Injuries sustained whilst in the water

12.10   These can be difficult to interpret. Injuries can occur from various structures such as bridges or wharfs. These show the features of blunt trauma or lacerational injury. Features may also be seen as a result of contact with components of a boat, such as a propeller or other part. Animal predators (e.g. fish) also may cause injury. In these cases, it is important to differentiate post-mortem wounds from ante-mortem wounds.

Natural death in water

12.11   The presence or absence of natural death should be sought. If the individual suffers from an underlying natural disease, such as cardiac pathology, this may cause death, either on its own or as a result of drowning due to the physical activities whilst in water.

Deaths in the bathtub (referred to above) may be associated with epilepsy. Toxicology may show the presence of alcohol and/or low levels of anti-convulsant therapy. Homicidal bath tub deaths are rare; however, they are not unheard of, as recognised in the 'Brides in the Bath' series of deaths, where death occurred as a result of sudden immersion in water by the deceased's feet being suddenly being pulled upwards with the head going beneath the water.

12.12   Channelopathies are cardiac diseases associated with abnormalities in channels in cell walls that facilitate the entry and exit of ions (such as potassium and sodium) into the cells. As the electrical conduction signal of the heart is propagated by these channels, arrhythmia is common. The heart is itself structurally normal and devoid of overt abnormality. Although some changes can be encountered dependent on the abnormality on ECG, post-mortem diagnosis is precluded bar genetic testing. Given the wide genetic abnormalities, such analysis is variably successful. There seems an interesting association between drowning deaths and ion channelopathies, quite possibly due to physical exertion in essentially an 'unsafe' environment. It is suggested that as many as 30% of swimming-related drowning deaths had a cardiac channel mutation (Tester, 2011).

Diagnosis of drowning

12.13   The pathological features are noted above. Care should be taken to differentiate between true drowning deaths and those where the body has been immersed in water.

Various biochemical tests on body fluids have been undertaken over the years, but none have shown to improve the diagnosis of drowning. These include biochemistry of the heart blood for electrolytes and other substances.

Diatoms in the diagnosis of drowning

12.14   These are unicellular microscopic organisms, of which there are multiple varieties. They are predominantly found in rivers and seas. They are useful in limited circumstances, in particular where the body has undergone a degree of decomposition. Diatoms enter into the air passages from the water and are absorbed into the lungs, passing into the blood stream. The presence of diatoms in lung tissue is of no diagnostic significance, as they can enter by passive absorption.

12.15   If the diatoms pass through into the blood stream, they enter the circulation and thus may be found in other organs of the body. The circulation ceases after death, so the presence of diatoms in organs/bone indicate that the circulation was present and the individual alive. Diatom testing is a specialist area of pathology, and there are a number of technical issues which are important as regards collection of the various samples of tissue and water. Samples are taken at post-mortem examination of various organs including lung, liver and bone marrow. Diatoms may also be assessed in stomach contents. Comparison with the diatoms from the water at the scene of the body is essential. The procedure is very technical, and issues may arise such as contamination of samples from the surround.

Delayed death from drowning

12.16   Death following near-drowning may occur as a result of post-immersion pneumonitis. This is due to structural damage on the lungs by inhaled water. This may present hours after an apparently successful rescue. It is associated with a high mortality.

- Injuries sustained whilst in water may be difficult to differentiate from true injury, as well as from ante-mortem wounds.

- Death from natural disease in water includes cardiac disease as well as epilepsy.

- Diatoms are unicellular microscopic organisms which enter the blood stream if an individual is alive.

- Diatoms may positively prove a true drowning death if identified in liver and bones.

Problem areas of bodies in water

12.17

- Is death due to true drowning? This may be difficult to determine, and care must be taken in giving a firm diagnosis, particularly in the presence of decomposition, as this can lead to such features as over-inflation of lungs.

- Is death due to dry drowning? This is a diagnosis by exclusion, together with examination of the circumstances. The presence of drugs/alcohol, natural disease and other injuries should be taken into account.

- Is death as a result of injuries other than drowning? This can only be ascertained by careful assessment and, in some cases, it may not be possible to establish with any degree of certainty, particularly in cases of decomposition as well as where there is extensive injuries that could have been caused by items such as a boat or other structures. There are, albeit rare, cases where a combined mechanism is present, such as strangulation and drowning.

- Has the death been caused by other causes, including natural disease? A particularly common scenario is death in a bathtub, where other causes need to be excluded such as electrocution, carbon monoxide poisoning and other natural disease. Epilepsy is usually diagnosed by the history of the deceased and is supported by low anti-convulsant levels and raised alcohol levels; as might be expected, the incidence of sudden death in epilepsy is raised in these situations. Neuropathological examination may show features of previous epilepsy; however, this may be supporting evidence rather than definitely diagnostic.

- Disposal of a body at sea. This may be lawful – burial at sea – or unlawful. Various locations are recognised for sea burials which may aid, along with other items with a body, such as a shroud.

Hypothermia

12.18 In general, hypothermia is the reduction of the core body temperature below 35°C, although significant clinical effects are encountered typically with much lower core body temperatures. In contrast to its relatively good defences against a hot environment, the human body adapts very poorly to cold; the protective mechanism of shivering operates only when the body temperature has actually fallen.

The warmest clothing, and not artificially heated, will fail to protect a person at rest from a fall in body temperature when that of the ambient temperature is –20°C; it will not keep him in comfort at an ambient temperature of 0°C or less. The subject is at grave risk when the body temperature falls to 30°C; evidence of life is difficult to detect at a body temperature of 27°C; and recovery from a fall in body temperature to 24°C is unlikely. Shivering ceases when the body temperature has fallen to 33°C and, after that, the only defence open to the body is one involving shifts of blood from the periphery to the deep core. This causes profound physiological changes to which the body may be unable to adapt. On the contrary, as metabolism approaches zero, so do the body's requirements for oxygen; sufficient quantities of the gas may, in fact, be dissolved in the plasma. States of 'suspended animation' can therefore occur, and these are potentially reversible in the hospital setting.

Risk factors

12.19   The risk factors for the development of hypothermia are well-recognised, and relate to those within the body and those that are external. For example, extrinsically poor environmental conditions and inadequate social conditions form the basis of the majority of hypothermic deaths. Having said that, cold (weather) is not a prerequisite for hypothermia, and hypothermia is encountered in temperate environments. In general, ill-health, emaciation, alcoholism and the extremes of age predispose to heat loss and also a reduced ability to escape environmental conditions. In addition, direct irregularity of the body's thermoregulatory system, such as infection or disorders of the hypothalamus, may also play a role. Alcohol intoxication and long-standing alcohol misuse, in particular, are very significant risk factors. The risk is multi-fold and includes such factors as clouding of consciousness, peripheral vasodilatation and various deregulations of internal systems.

12.20   The clinical diagnosis of hypothermia is relatively straightforward, reliant on measuring the core body temperature. In comparison with the in-life diagnosis, the post-mortem diagnosis is, by converse, fraught with difficulties and reliant on assessment of the scene, autopsy findings and the result of additional investigations. Despite this, a death from hypothermia may arise without any recognisable signs, and any signs present are somewhat unpredictable in their occurrence. These are discussed below.

In general, hypothermic signs are associated with higher environmental ambient temperature deaths, suggesting that they may be not a marker of hypothermia per se but a marker of a more prolonged period of hypothermia. Survival in hospital typically leads to resolution of signs, and pathological findings in immersion-related hypothermic deaths are invariably absent.

The scene of a hypothermic death

12.21   The scene of the hypothermic death to the inexperienced police officer always raises the matter of the criminality. Two features, 'paradoxical undressing' and 'hide and die' syndrome, result in a chaotic scene, whereby the deceased is naked or partially clothed and there is significant disorder of the scene environment, with furniture dislodged and often pulled onto the body of the deceased. The latter feature is suggestive of some form of terminal 'burrowing' akin to an early animalistic evolutionary response combined with ongoing confusion. Additional features may be present at the scene related to risk factors for the development of hypothermia, which can range from merely the nature of the environmental conditions to evidence of neglect and habitual intoxication.

For similar reasons to the inexperienced police officer, it is not unheard of for the family, often after finding the deceased, to become convinced of criminality in the death, requiring significant reassurance during the inquisitorial process. The more worrying development is the experienced police officer, aware of the scene of hypothermic deaths, overlooking a truly homicidal death.

Signs of hypothermia at autopsy

12.22   Two autopsy findings in particular raise the prospect to the pathologist of a hypothermic death: 'frost erythema' and 'Wischnewski ulceration'.

Frost erythema are areas of reddish or violet discolouration over the extensor surfaces of the large joints, such as the knees, elbows and hips, as well as cheeks, chin, nose and ears. They are not associated with haemorrhage below the skin surface and the histological profile is unclear.

12.23   Wischnewski ulcers are multiple small areas of submucosal bleeding to ulceration within the stomach and, on very rare occasions, the duodenum. These haemorrhages often form a 'predictable' series of lines of approximate equal spacing along the length of the stomach. Although not unique to hypothermia, the sheer frequency of their number is characteristic. The precise mechanism of their formation is not clear.

Other features, such as alteration of the colour of hypostasis, pancreatitis, perivascular haemorrhages and pulmonary oedema, are so non-specific, or often more likely completely unrelated to hypothermia, that their presence or absence does not assist in the diagnosis of hypothermia. Risk factors pre-disposing to the development of the hypothermia, such as general physique, extent and nature of natural disease and stigmata of drug or alcohol misuse, are frequently present.

Mechanism of death

12.24   The precise mechanism of death in hypothermia is unclear, but arrhythmia compounded by increased circulating catecholamines, electrolyte disturbances and generalised deoxygenation is suggested.

Physical injury due to cold

12.25   Frostbite most commonly affects the extremities and exposed areas and arises due to direct injury caused by the freezing combined with reduced blood flow to peripheral vasoconstriction. The latter component explains the propensity of the extremities to develop frostbite. The initial stages, often called frostnip, are associated with white and numb skin that becomes reddened and painful on warming. As it progresses to its worst severity, drying out and necrosis become increasingly involved and the frostbite is dark and mummified.

If the cold exposure occurs in a wet environment, 'immersion foot' rather than frostbite develops. This injury has historic recognition through its alternative name, 'trench foot'. In comparison with frostbite, where direct injury from cold predominates, immersion foot is more associated with repeated cooling and re-warming, resulting in an ischaemic reperfusion injury. The injury is moist and associated with significant nerve damage.

Post-mortem freezing

12.26   Freezing of the human body occurs after death on a relatively frequent basis, in an attempt to preserve the body condition in the mortuary environment. It can also arise as a secondary consequence of an illicit attempt to conceal a body, although this is far more frequent in detective fiction than real life. Two areas need raising in the context of post-mortem freezing. The first relates to the defrosting of the body that must be undertaken prior to examination. This has the peculiar consequence of accelerated decomposition of the surfaces and superficial tissues, often despite being still frozen centrally. During the course of the autopsy examination, it is not unheard of for a relatively 'fresh' appearing body to be markedly decomposed by the end. The second relates to artefact caused by the freezing process, particularly affecting histological examination. On occasions, areas mimicking bruising can appear in a variety of sites. However, the artefacts if identified (in the right circumstances) can be used to suggest a prior episode of illicit freezing and defrosting of a body.

Problem areas of a hypothermic death

12.27

- Is death due to hypothermia? Due to the transient and variable nature of the findings, an autopsy examination will often fail to reveal any positive findings. As such, care is required in opining the diagnosis.

- Increasing awareness of scenes encountered in hypothermia may give false reassurance to the police.

- Hypothermia is a potentially fatal condition associated with reduction of the core body temperature.

- Deaths may arise and no signs of it may be present. The most common findings are frost erythema (reddish violet discolouration of the skin surface of joints) and Wischnewski ulceration (coarse haemorrhages to the stomach wall).

- Unusual behaviours may be encountered at the scene, and the body may be (paradoxically) undressed or hidden away.

- Cold may result in physical injury to the body.

Further reading material

General textbooks

- Saukko, P. & Knight, B. *Knights' Forensic Pathology* (2004, 3rd Edition)

- Mason, J.K. & Purdue, B.N. *The Pathology of Trauma* (2000, 3rd Edition)

- Spitz, W.U. *Spitz and Fisher's Medicolegal Investigation of Death* (2006, 4th Edition)

- Shkrum M.J. & Ramsay, D.A. *Forensic Pathology of Trauma* (2007)

- Payne-James, J., Jones, R., Karch, S.B. & Manlove, J. *Simpson's Forensic Medicine* (2011, 13th Edition)

Articles in update textbooks

- Rothschild, M.A. 'Lethal Hypothermia' in Tsokos, M. *Forensic Pathology Reviews*. Volume One. 2004

- Lunetta, P. & Modell, J.H. 'Macroscopical, Microscopical, and Laboratory Findings in Drowning Victims' in Tsokos, M. *Forensic Pathology Reviews*. Volume Three. 2005

- Madea, B.M., Tsokos, M. & Preuss, J. 'Death due to Hypothermia' in Tsokos, M. *Forensic Pathology Reviews*. Volume Five. 2008

Articles in journals

- Albiin, N., Eriksson, A. 'Fatal accidental hypothermia and alcohol' *Alcohol.* 19:13–22, 1984

- Davis, J. H. 'Bodies found in the water. An investigative approach' *Am. J. Forensic Med. Pathol.* 7:291–297, 1986

- Foged, N. 'Diatoms and drowning – once more' *Forensic Sci Int* 21; 153–9. 1983

- Giertsen, J.C. 'Drowning while under the influence of alcohol' *Med. Sci. Law* 10:216–219, 1970

- Gordon, I. 'The anatomical signs in drowning. A critical evaluation' *Forensic Sci.* 1:389–395, 1972

- Grieve A.W., Davis, P., Dhillon, S., Richards, P., Hillebrandt, D., Imray, C.H. 'A clinical review of the management of frostbite' *Journal of the Royal Army Medical Corps* 2011; 157(1):73–7

- Hirvonen, J. 'Necropsy findings in fatal hypothermia cases' *J. Forensic Sci.* 8:155–164, 1976

- Lunetta, P., Modell, J. H., Sajantila, A. 'What is the incidence and significance of "dry lungs" in bodies found in water?' *Am. J. Forensic Med. Pathol.* 25:291–301, 2004

- Mallet, M.L. 'Pathophysiology of accidental hypothermia' *QJM* 2002; 95(12):775–785

- Modell, J.H., Bellefleur, M., Davis, J.H. 'Drowning without aspiration: is this an appropriate diagnosis?' *J Forensic Sci.* 1999, 44:1119–1123

- Peabody, A.J. 'Diatoms and drowning – a recent review' *Med Sci Law* 20; 254–61. 1980

- Pollanen, M.S. 'Diatoms and homicide' *Forensic Sci Int* 91; 29–34. 1998

- Schafer, A.T., Kaufmann, J.D. 'What happens in freezing bodies? Experimental study of histological tissue change caused by freezing injuries' *Forensic Sci Int* 102(2-3):149–158. 1999

- Taylor, J.J. 'Diatoms and drowning—a cautionary case note' *Med. Sci. Law* 34:78–79, 1994

- Tester, D.J., Medeiros-Domingo, A., Will, M.L. & Ackerman, M.J. 'Unexplained drownings and the cardiac channelopathies: a molecular autopsy series' *Mayo Clin Proc.* 86:941–7. 2011

- Wedin, B., Vanggaard, L., Hirvonen, J. '"Paradoxical undressing" in fatal hypothermia' *J. Forensic Sci.*; 24(3):543–553. 1979

Chapter 13

Heat, fire and electricity

13.1   The application of 'heat' to the body represents a major constituent of forensic medicine and comprises a wide array of modalities of injury, including burns, scalds and electricity. Heat itself has consequent indirect effects, most notably the development of smoke or explosion.

Legal aspects

13.2   The unlawful application of heat to the body will normally amount to an offence against the person and, as such, depending on its severity, constitute assault or wounding, or, where death results, either murder or manslaughter (or culpable homicide in Scotland). See the relevant legal framework set out in Chapter 7.

13.3   Further offences may include:

- Where criminal damage also results (and that damage is caused by fire), arson contrary to section 1(3) of the Criminal Damage Act 1971[1] (the offence of arson is aggravated when it is done with intent to endanger life, or recklessness as to whether life would be endangered).

- In cases of the deliberate infliction of severe burning, scalding or electrocution (where that is done by a person in an official capacity), torture contrary to section 134 of the Criminal Justice Act 1988.

- In cases of injury caused by explosions or other corrosive substances (such as acid), the offences prohibiting such conduct under sections 28, 29, 30 and 64 of the Offences Against the Person Act 1861.

- The commission of further offences under the Explosive Substances Act 1883 (for instance, causing explosion likely to endanger life or property under section 2 of that Act).

- Where such injuries are sustained in the workplace, prosecutions brought by the Health and Safety Executive for non-compliance with the relevant industry standard.

---

1   Fire-raising in Scotland.

Burns

13.4   A burn arises when the substance of the skin (and underlying tissues) is damaged by heat or an exothermic (heat-generating) process.

The source of the heat may be due to dry heat (e.g. open flames and fire), moist heat (a scald), corrosive substances (such as acids), electricity, solar radiation (e.g. sunburn) or ionising radiation (e.g. X-rays), but the ultimate consequence is transfer of energy and localised damage.

The epidemiology or distribution of types of burns varies significantly with age. Under the age of three years, a high proportion are due to scalding; scalding also occurs in later childhood, but setting light to clothes is more important in this age group and is the most significant source of burning in old age. In normal adult life, the great majority of accidental burns stem from house fires and industry.

Dry heat

13.5   External heat applied to the body will result in damage dependent on its intensity and duration of application. A lower temperature over a long period of time can be as damaging as a much higher temperature over a short period of time. A classic example of this is a burn from prolonged hot water bottle contact. The minimum temperature recognised to burn skin is 44°C and this is over a six-hour period (Mortiz *et al* 1947).

Burn injuries (of all types) are classified, according to the relative depth of the injury, into three (and, more recently, four) broad categories:

- **First Degree Burns**. These involve the epidermis only and are associated with redness but not blistering. Sunburn is a common example. Injuries of this severity may not be appreciated at post-mortem. The burn will resolve without scarring.

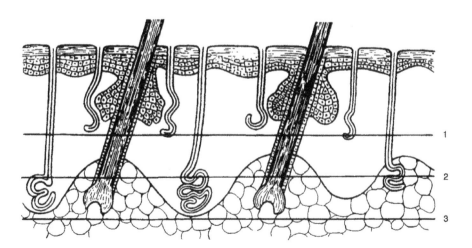

Figure 13.1 Skin showing 'degree' of burns. (Reproduced with permission from J K Mason and B N Purdue (eds) *The Pathology of Trauma* (3rd edn, 2000), and amended)

- **Second Degree Burns**. These are sub-divided into partial involvement and full-thickness involvement of the dermis. The burning is more severe with skin loss, reddening and blistering. The burn will resolve invariably without scarring.

- **Third Degree Burns**. These involve burn extension into the subcutaneous tissues. They have a leathery dried appearance and can be charred. Skin elasticity is lost and the burn will heal with scarring.

- **Fourth Degree Burns**. These are a variant of third degree burns with damage involving the musculature and bone. Charring is commonplace.

The anatomy of the skin is discussed in Chapter 1.

Scald

13.6   A scald is a burn that arises secondary to contact with a heated liquid or steam and is an exceptionally common injury in childhood.

The appearance of a scald is similar to a first degree or second degree dry heat burn and, even with severe damage, lacks charring (unless involving some form of superheated oil).

It has a well-demarcated border (unlike a dry heat burn) and this feature assists with the interpretation of the scald's causation. For example, a different distribution will arise from an body being placed into hot water in comparison to a child pulling hot water onto them.

Corrosive substances

13.7   Injury resulting from contact with corrosive substances secondary to assault is becoming increasingly more common. Corrosive substances, including acids and alkalis of varying types, can be doused (similar to scalds or immolation, discussed later) or can be drunk. In both cases, significant damage can arise both internally and externally. Deaths may be delayed, particularly in cases of more limited injury associated with spillage into the lungs, causing pneumonia and oedema. It is said that subtle differences (for example, in colouration of the injured skin) may arise, but in reality it is very difficult for the medical doctor to provide significant evidence of the substances involved.

Clinical consequences of burns

13.8   Clinical assessment of the burn injury is based predominately on the extent, or the relative surface area, of burn involvement. For ease, regions of the body are sub-divided into areas, based on the value '9' (hence it is known as the 'Rule of Nines'), with the front of the torso, the back of the torso and each lower limb scoring 18% respectively, each upper limb and the head scoring 9% and the perineum scoring

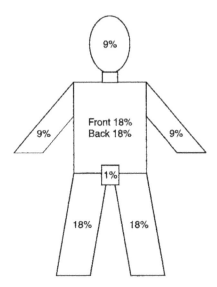

Figure 13.2 The area of burning is generally assessed using the 'Rule of Nine'; the percentage of the whole body area of the various components is as shown. (From R.F. Brown, 'Injury by Burning' in J.K. Mason (ed.), The Pathology of Trauma, 2nd edn (1993) by permission of the author.)

1%. The regions of burning are totalled to give an indication of the extent of the surface area of burn injury.

The surface area of the burn involvement gives an indication of the clinical prognosis, but other factors, such as the age of the victim (and, in conflagrations, whether or not there has been inhalation of smoke gases and damage to the lining of the respiratory tract), are involved. The surface area of burn injury is of particular importance, as it indicates the extent of the likely loss of body fluids, a factor related to the area rather than the depth of burning. With widespread burning, the loss of the skin's integrity allows massive loss of water, protein and electrolytes, and severe surgical shock arises if treatment is inadequate.

A secondary complication of burn injury is the development of overwhelming infection. This is often related to organisms that are commensal (bacteria – and other organisms – that reside normally on the skin, and elsewhere, without causing harm), and the loss of integrity of the skin allows easy access of the bacteria to the blood.

Another factor is pain, and the susceptibility to pain is dependent on the depth of the burning. Paradoxically, the superficial burn, in which sensory nerve endings are left exposed, is far more painful than is the deep partial-thickness burn in which the nerve endings are destroyed.

- A burn arises when the substance of the skin (and underlying tissues) is damaged by heat or an exothermic process. External heat applied to the body will result in damage dependent on its intensity and duration of application.

- Burn injuries (of all types) are classified according to the relative depth of the injury.

- A scald is a burn that arises secondary to contact with a heated liquid or steam and is an exceptionally common injury in childhood. The appearance of a scald is similar to a first degree or second degree dry heat burn.

- The surface area of the burn involvement gives an indication of the clinical prognosis, but other factors, such as the age of the victim (and, in conflagrations, whether or not there has been inhalation of smoke gases and damage to the lining of the respiratory tract), are involved.

- Pain, and the susceptibility to pain, is dependent on the depth of the burning.

Electricity

13.9 Electricity is used on a vast scale, in the majority of cases by individuals with negligible understanding of its behaviour. The fact that it causes few deaths is an indication of the safety engineering and regulation of the electrical components industry.

Physics of electricity

13.10 The outcome of an electrical shock is dependent on the physical factors of the discharge (the nature of the electrical current) as well as the physical course of the electrical current through the body.

Electricity is the movement of electrons from areas of high to low concentration. The difference between the two points (potentials) is known as the potential difference or voltage ('V', measured in Volts). The current ('I', measured in Amperes) is a measure of the electron flow. The voltage and current are linked by Ohm's Law ($V = IR$) by a constant known as the resistance ('R', measured in Ohms), which measures the resistance of the 'circuit' to electron flow.

The electrical charge is a measure of the current and time over which the electrical discharge is passed, and is measured in Coulombs.

Electron flow can be uni-directional (direct current (DC)) or rapidly changing direction (alternating current (AC)). Alternating current is, for example, used for the domestic supply of electricity, and the frequency of alternations is in the order of 50 Hz to 60 Hz (i.e. alterations per second), dependent on country. Alternating current is considered more dangerous than direct current. With alternating current, the risk is increased, in part, due to muscular spasm being initiated that can prevent release of the conductor, allowing long exposure to the electrical current.

If the voltage is sufficiently high, the electrical current may *jump* from one solid conductor to another solid conductor through the air. This is known as 'arcing' and can cause 'flash and flame'-type injury.

13.11 The resistance of the human body is variable between individuals, individual tissues and situations. Wetness of the skin is a classic example, whereby dry skin has a resistance of 100,000 Ohms whereas wet skin's resistance may be as low as 100 Ohms. Given the constraints of Ohm's Law, a significantly reduced resistance in the context of the same (fixed) potential difference (voltage) will result in a significantly elevated and potentially fatal current through the body (if voltage stays the same, and resistance decreases, current must increase).

In general, the electrical current will flow down the path of least resistance and will enter at one point on the skin surface, travel through the body before exiting at another point on the skin surface. At the point of entry, exit or both, an 'electrical burn' may be encountered due to the electrical energy being converted into heat.

Pathological findings

13.12   The entry and exit marks are similar to each other and may be faint, and a determined search may be needed for their identification. Electrical burns are not present in every case of electrocution and are heavily dependent on a number of factors, such as the current, voltage, area of contact, and the length of time over which the current was discharged. It is important to stress that, in fatal cases, no burn injury may be present and, in itself, an electrical burn does not equate to a fatal electrocution.

The electrical burn (from a low voltage circuit) is typically a small blistered erythematous (or reddened) area. The blistered area is often lost, leaving a greyer central crater. Keratin within the skin may melt, particularly if the contact is not tight, and form a raised hard brown nodule. Microscopically, the electric burn shows 'bubbling' of the keratin layer due to the liberation of steam together with 'streaming' of the basal nuclei. The appearances are typical of electricity only in that they result from intense localised heat; there is no reason why similar changes do not follow heat of any type delivered in a similar fashion.

Metallic deposits may also be deposited in the burn and can be identified with special investigative techniques.

A rare form of multiple flash burning, spread over a wide area, results from long-distance arcing from a very high voltage source; the appearances are known as 'crocodile skin'.

Charring in electrocutions is encountered with increasing voltage or increased contact time, and the extent of the injury can be substantial.

Electrocutions in water are not associated with burn injury.

Mechanism of death in electrical fatalities

13.13   The mechanism of death is predominately related to the structures that the current travels through.

Passage through the heart is associated with the development of ventricular fibrillation, whereas muscular and respiratory paralysis may be encountered when the current passes through the chest. Electrical interference within the cardio-respiratory centres of the brainstem is also recognised to cause death.

Burns and secondary trauma (for example, following falls from a height) may also be involved.

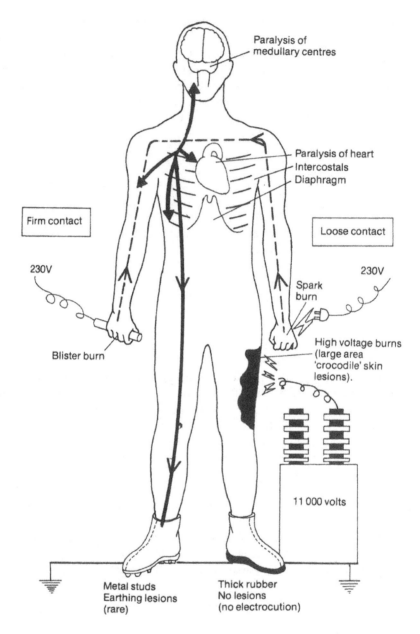

Figure 13.3 Electrocuting pathways. (From: *Lawyers' Guide to Forensic Medicine*, Knight, B., 1998, Cavendish Publishing Ltd, reproduced by permission of Taylor & Francis Books UK.)

Manner of death in fatal electrocutions

13.14   The manner of death in fatal electrocutions may be related to homicide, suicide or accident. Suicidal electrocution is uncommon, despite the ready availability of the method; the diagnosis can seldom be in doubt, owing to the complexity of the arrangements made. Homicide by electricity must be equally rare. It must be admitted, however, that homicide or fabrication may be suspected in an apparent suicide without elaborate preparations. The difficulty invariably lies in proof. The same applies to the distinction between accident and homicide, particularly in cases of death in the bathroom; there have been several reports of electric apparatus falling into the bath water; proof that this was done deliberately may depend on an expert examination of the apparatus.

Accidents are overwhelmingly responsible for death due to electricity and are of several types.

Industrial accidents are kept to a minimum by stringent safety precautions, but nevertheless continue to occur as a result of genuine mishap or flouting of the regulations.

Direct contact may not be necessary, if very high tension cables are involved, as arcing may occur at a considerable distance depending on the voltage (2–3 cm for every 10,000 V is frequently suggested), and the zone of danger may be very much wider when the air is damp (Settle, 2000).

Domiciliary accidents are more common and are of three main types: the electrical apparatus may be defective, often due to fraying of insulation; attempts may be made to repair equipment without disconnecting it from the mains supply while using makeshift tools; or apparatus may be dangerously used – the most common example involves the use of electric equipment in the bathroom, where conditions for electrical conduction are optimal.

Neutral fusing, which can give a false indication that the apparatus is 'dead', is a hazard peculiar to older apparatus of British manufacture. On occasions, the use of electricity as part of autoerotic stimulation may result in death.

- The outcome of an electrical shock is dependent on the nature of the electrical current and its physical course through the body. In general, the electrical current will flow down the path of least resistance and will enter at one point on the skin surface, travel through the body before exiting at another point on the skin surface.

- If the voltage is sufficiently high, the electrical current may jump from one solid conductor to another solid conductor through the air. This is known as 'arcing' and can cause 'flash and flame'-type injury.

- The resistance of the human body is variable between individuals, individual tissues and situations.

- At the point of entry, exit or both, an 'electrical burn' may be encountered due to the electrical energy being converted into heat.

Lightning

13.15   Lightning is a high voltage electrical discharge to the ground secondary to atmospheric conditions. Deaths associated with lightning strikes remain an unusual and, in themselves, a newsworthy event. Death occurs in less than half of strikes.

Lightning strikes typically result in the passage of an electrical current through or near the body, as well as primary 'flash' and secondary thermal burning and the pressure effects of a high-intensity blast wave.

Despite the significant potential of extensive injury, the extent is often quite slight. Most frequently, this is limited to Lichtenberg figures, which are painless fern-like branching linear marks. These are a temporary phenomenon and disappear after a few hours to a few days, both in life and after death. These marks will often demonstrate interesting morphology, beginning or ending at metallic objects, even those (such as electrocardiogram pads) that have been placed on the body after death.

In the most extreme cases, the subject struck may sustain injuries of traumatic type, including fractures, and the clothes may be torn; the appearances initially mimic those of assault or road traffic collision. The tearing of clothing relates to flashover, as the electrical discharge occurs over the entire body.

- Lightning is a high voltage atmospheric discharge of electricity, with injury extent being typically limited, but can result in significant destructive changes.

Fire

13.16   The consequences of fire are a common occurrence in forensic medicine, especially forensic pathology. Fire has a particular importance, as it is often utilised to facilitate body disposal or obscure a homicidal death through attempts to suggest that death arose in the course of the fire, or to destroy injuries (in part, increasingly, in an attempt to remove forensic evidence of direct contact between the deceased and other parties involved in the death).

Despite media suggestions, recognition is often reasonably straightforward, but the destructive nature of fire can cause substantial difficulties.

Nature of fires

13.17   Fire is a chemical reaction that results in the production of heat, light and by-products of various complexities.

The chemistry of fire is a branch of science in its own right and far too complex for this book's scope. The danger of fire to life relates to six factors: (i) reduced oxygen concentrations accompanied by increased carbon monoxide concentrations; (ii) extremely high temperatures; (iii) presence of smoke; (iv) direct consumption by fire; (v) other toxic gases; and (vi) fear. The consequences of heat and smoke gases are the principal factors.

Autopsy examination

13.18   Prior to the autopsy examination in the significantly heat damaged victim, radiological investigations should be undertaken to assist in identification of projectiles and similar trauma. It may be that the radiological investigation also assists in the identification of the deceased. Increasingly, CT scans are undertaken and can provide more useful information to the pathologist than conventional radiology. CT scanning is preferential in showing soft tissue and organ injury.

External findings

13.19   The initial part of the autopsy examination involves an assessment for the extent and severity of the burns. It is important to realise that burns may be ante-mortem or post-mortem, and it is rarely possible to indicate which, even with histological examination. This is because death occurs very rapidly before any reaction can take place in the tissues. For example, the presence of an erythematous (reddening) rim to the burn is not an indicator of an ante-mortem burn. Histological changes of an in-life reaction to a burn invariably require a period of survival far beyond that of a typical fire death; and, even with prolonged survival, a significant proportion will not demonstrate a histological response.

The hair will also undergo heat-related changes. A characteristic appearance is the keratin bulb, as the hair melts before reforming as a brittle red-brown bulb on cooling; although, with increased heat, either by intensity or time, the hair will simply be lost.

Heat will also have other effects on the body, the classic effect being the pugilistic posture. In this, the elbows and hands flex, adopting a 'fighting' stance. In reality, the heat shrinkage of tissues that cause the posture affects all muscle groups, but it is most noticeable around elbow joints, knee joints and hands, which become flexed.

13.20   Fire may also result in 'open' wounds that may mimic traumatic injuries. These are typically most prominent in areas of heavy heat damage, particularly charring, on the extensor surfaces and the head. The wound margins are relatively clean and the ends are pointed. There is no bleeding of any significance, although some oozing can be seen. The internal aspect of the wound will have little or no soot deposition, suggesting that the splitting of the skin arises as part of cooling. Blood may ooze from the mouth and nose, as blood is moved from the lung into the airways.

In a typical fire, the most significant destruction of the body is concentrated initially to the limbs and the head, and the torso is 'broken' apart between 50 and 80 minutes. Additional damage may be caused by rescue personnel attempting to extinguish a fire.

Internal findings

13.21   Internal examination can often demonstrate surprisingly intact and undamaged organs, despite significant external heat damage; but, as the conflagration increases, the extent of the internal damage increases significantly. The appearances are variable to the organ systems, but a feature of all systems is heat shrinkage producing shrunken, firm, hardened and cooked organs.

Unsurprisingly, bones are far more resistant to heat than the other body parts. Even with legal cremations, a quantity of bone will still remain. With increasing heat exposure, the bones become grey and brittle. Due to their brittle nature, they easily fracture, and distinguishing between ante-mortem and post-mortem heat-related fracturing is not always straightforward. Typically, heat-related fractures are in areas of greatest heat damage and often involve the skull adopting a variety of profiles. The most difficult fracture to distinguish is perhaps a linear one, but fractures resembling the entry and exit of a gunshot wound have been reported rarely.

Another artefact of heat is the development of a collection of blood in the extradural space (the space between skull and dura), colloquially known as a 'heat haematoma'. This arises as blood is pushed out from the skull and also from collections of venous blood from sinuses. The appearance is rather different from a true extradural bleed, as it has a crumbly spongy brown appearance. It is suggested, in German-language literature, that similar bleeds can be seen in other areas within the skull, including within the brain. However, there is no real experience of this elsewhere, and the finding of bleeding elsewhere intracranially should be treated with significant caution.

Spontaneous human combustion

13.22   Spontaneous human combustion is an area that warrants a brief mention, if only to allay media (and, occasionally, legal) exaggeration. Spontaneous human combustion is often used to describe a body that demonstrates significant heat damage where the majority, if not all, of the body is burnt away, yet the surrounding vicinity (and even parts of the body) is relatively spared.

The profile of complete incineration of the torso, with sparing of the extremities, is at odds with the typical conflagration, where the limbs and head are often preferentially affected, and is a rare event. In reality, the 'wick effect' – with the body fat burning slowly, assisted by clothing and adjacent furniture providing the wick function – is well described.

Common features of these deaths are that the individuals are more frequently the overweight, elderly or alcoholics, with a classic description of an overweight elderly female. A source of ignition, such as an open fire or cigarette, is invariably present. Death in these cases can arise secondary to factors such as smoke inhalation and burns.

- Fire is a chemical reaction that results in the production of heat, light and by-products of various complexities.

- Prior to the autopsy examination in the significantly heat damaged victim, radiological investigations should be undertaken to assist in identification of projectiles and similar trauma.

- Heat will also have effects on the body, the classic effect being the pugilistic posture, but it will also split the skin and destroy the body. The internal organs can be surprisingly spared.

- Another artefact of heat is the development of a collection of blood in the extradural space (the space between skull and dura), colloquially known as a 'heat haematoma'.

Smoke

13.23   The smoke generated during the course of a fire plays both a direct and an indirect role in the causation of death. Indirectly, smoke obscures the vision, reducing the capacity for escape and also rescue, as well as causing disorientation. The toxicity associated with its respiration is the most recognised mechanism of death in fire. Smoke inhalation far more commonly causes death than burns in fires.

Smoke is produced during the course of any fire, but the nature of the smoke varies considerably between fires.

Smoke is a mixture of gases and solid particles. Smoke (due to the combustion itself) has significantly reduced levels of oxygen in comparison to the normal environment, which in itself can result in incapacitation, but is typically insufficient to account for death.

Staining of the airways (and, less frequently, the oesophagus) by the inhaled solid particles is used as a sign of vitality, or that the deceased breathed or swallowed smoke. It is also a very strong indicator that death has arisen as a result of smoke inhalation.

For similar reasons, the presence of soot staining is also a useful indicator that carbon monoxide and other smoke gases have been inhaled. Although the presence of an elevated carboxyhaemoglobin and soot staining can be utilised as sign of vitality in a fire, an absence of carboxyhaemoglobin (or soot staining) does not mean that a death must have arose before the fire started.

Carbon monoxide

13.24 Carbon monoxide is the archetypal (but not necessarily predominant) gas produced in fire and arises secondary to the incomplete combustion of organic compounds. Carbon monoxide combines with haemoglobin in the red blood cell to produce carboxyhaemoglobin (COHb). Carbon monoxide has an affinity for haemoglobin in the order of 200 to 300 times greater than oxygen, and thus preferentially displaces oxygen (reducing the oxygen-carrying capacity of haemoglobin), but it also has some effects on the residual oxygen that is bound with haemoglobin.

Sources

13.25 The most common sources of carbon monoxide poisoning are from fire and internal combustion engines.

With regard to fires, solid-fuel, gas or oil fires fitted with inadequate flues or used in rooms without sufficient ventilation, oil heaters in bedrooms (including caravans) or geysers in bathrooms are obvious examples. Although domestic gas now contains no carbon monoxide, the toxic gas can still be generated through inadequate combustion. An increasingly common means of suicide or accidental death is the use of disposable barbecues in a confined environment. Death can even occur where the barbecue is left in close proximity outside the tent or other enclosed place and the toxic gas leaks in.

Internal combustion engines may have defective exhaust systems, or operate within closed garages. The motor car exhaust is a reasonably frequent source of carbon monoxide for suicidal purposes. The suicidal nature is likely to be shown by the intricate arrangements made. Even with catalytic converters, car exhaust gases contain sufficient carbon monoxide to cause death in a matter of minutes.

Toxicology

13.26 As well as the level of carboxyhaemoglobin, other factors affect the individual's susceptibility to death following carbon monoxide poisoning. For example, the elderly are likely to succumb more easily than the young, and the presence of concomitant disease, such as ischaemic heart disease or anaemia, can also increase susceptibility. Similarly, the symptoms of carbon monoxide poisoning will also depend on the physical state of the individual. Thus, it is generally stated that conversion of 30% of the haemoglobin to carboxyhaemoglobin results in dizziness and headache, lack of coordination appears at 50% saturation, unconsciousness at 60%, and death at 70% to 80%.

However, deaths are encountered with much lower levels. For example, carboxyhaemoglobin levels encountered in fire are considerably lower than in cases of so-called 'pure' carbon monoxide toxicity, due to the presence of other toxic and destructive factors.

Hydrogen cyanide and other gases

13.27 Hydrogen cyanide is another important gas that is produced in fire, although it is less frequently measured than carboxyhaemoglobin, as it is relatively unstable at post-mortem and also subject to post-mortem generation secondary to decomposition.

Given this relative instability, the true importance of hydrogen cyanide in fire deaths is probably not appreciated. A wide array of other potentially toxic compounds, such as hydrogen chloride and formaldehyde, are also produced, and the nature of these compounds is dependent on the combustible materials involved.

- Smoke is a mixture of gases and solid particles, and the presence of soot in the airways and oesophagus is used as a sign of vitality. The converse is not true, as an absence of soot by itself does not mean that death arose before the fire commenced.

- Carbon monoxide is the archetypal (but not necessarily predominant) gas produced in fire and arises secondary to the incomplete combustion of organic compounds. It represents the most common mechanism of death in fire deaths.

- The effect of carbon monoxide levels is enhanced by increasing age and disease.

- Hydrogen cyanide is another important gas that is produced in fire, although it is less frequently measured than carboxyhaemoglobin, as it is relatively unstable at post-mortem and also subject to post-mortem generation secondary to decomposition.

Survivors of fires

13.28 In those that survive with significant burns and smoke inhalation to reach hospital, a significant proportion will die, either due to untreatable burns or the consequences of burns/smoke inhalation, such as multi-organ failure or sepsis. The length of survival correlates with the extent of the burn injuries, and multi-organ failure accounts for a significant proportion of these deaths.

Immolation

13.29   In immolation, individuals (usually at their own hands) douse themselves in a flammable liquid and set themselves on fire.

The individual typically demonstrates third degree burns, and the pattern of this burning may assist with interpretation as to how the individual was doused. The majority will die at the scene, although a proportion will die later in hospital.

Due to the nature of the flash fire, signs of vitality (such as evidence of inhalation of products) are relatively variable.

At post-mortem examination, retention of materials, such as lungs, in a nylon bag (or similar protective material) for volatile analysis should be made.

Heat stroke

13.30   The human body is fairly well adapted to hot climates and exertional activity; sweating is the main protective mechanism.

Physiological abnormalities are encountered, including three overlapping conditions: heat cramps; heat exhaustion; and heat stroke. Hyperthermia, an elevation of the body temperature, may form part of heat stroke, but it is not exclusive to heat stroke.

Heat cramps are painful muscular spasms that often follow exercise (in warm climates) due to loss of fluids and electrolytes.

Heat exhaustion represents the general progression of prolonged exposure to heat, with increased core temperature and symptoms of exhaustion.

As the core temperature increases, heat stroke develops and physiological changes are pronounced; sweating stops as thermoregulatory control is lost and a shock-like picture ensues.

Death is common with heat stroke, and direct pathological features (bar an elevated body temperature) are absent. Findings that are evident arise as a consequence of the physiological stress changes, such as disseminated intravascular coagulation (a condition associated with inappropriate consumption of clotting factors that is followed by a bleeding tendency).

- Physiological abnormalities are encountered, including three overlapping conditions: heat cramps; heat exhaustion; and heat stroke.

Explosions

13.31   Explosions may occur in the home or industry, but in the main they are most associated with armed conflicts and terrorist offences. The nature of the events (and, thus, injuries) is heavily dependent on the energies and also the environment involved.

Primary effects

13.32   After the explosion occurs, a large volume of gas is generated, which is significantly expanded by the associated heat of the explosion. This results in a primary air blast, or a blast wave resulting in blast effect injuries.

The effects of blast are due to a combination of positive pressure, the blast wave itself and the subsequent negative pressure. The effects, which are exaggerated in an enclosed space, are seen particularly in those organs capable of elastic recoil and containing multiple gas/fluid or fluid/solid interfaces.

Thus, the lungs in particular are the subject of disruption and haemorrhage; the eardrums are also very sensitive to pressure changes.

Blast effects are well transmitted in water; the hollow viscera, such as the intestines, are particularly vulnerable to underwater explosions and, since there are no injuries due to secondary impacts, those killed in these circumstances often present with little external but massive internal damage.

Secondary effects

13.33 Secondary effects of the explosion are also frequently encountered. These include missile injuries, as the casing of the explosive or nearby objects are splintered into fragments.

As well as larger objects, dust, glass fragments and other similar material are propelled and may tattoo the skin irregularly with small wounds.

The classic injury that results consists of the triad of punctate bruises, abrasions and small puncture lacerations (see Chapter 7). The addition of dust impaction onto and into the skin adds a virtually diagnostic picture.

Other consequences

13.34 Burn injuries may be seen either directly from the explosion or from secondary fires. Buildings and furniture may be dislodged, resulting in further injury from falling masonry and similar.

In individuals extremely close to the detonation site, significant disintegration of the body arises, especially with military explosive devices. Despite the fact that homicidal bombing in a civilian context occurs in very diverse circumstances, the pattern of injuries is surprisingly reproducible. As compared with their military equivalents, terrorist bombs are relatively inefficient, and the severe damage that they cause may be comparatively localised; disintegration of the body is rare unless the victim is in direct contact with the device.

Pathological consequences

13.35 The pathological diagnosis of death due to explosion is usually straightforward. The cause of the explosion, e.g. bomb detonation or domestic gas ignition, may, however, be unknown and the pathologist has not discharged his responsibility by merely recording a relatively self-evident cause of death. Thus, the most important evidence to be obtained from the post-mortem dissection lies in the search for and recovery of fragments of bomb casing, which will not only demonstrate the cause but, much as in the case of firearm wounds, will provide information of value to investigators; the importance of X-ray study as a means of localising such fragments is stressed.

- After the explosion occurs, a large volume of gas is generated, which is significantly expanded by the associated heat of the explosion. This results in an air blast or a blast wave, causing blast effect injuries.

- Secondary effects include missile injuries, as the casing of the explosive or nearby objects are splintered into fragments.

- Burn injuries may be seen either directly from the explosion or from secondary fires. Injuries are also encountered from falling masonry and similar.

Further reading material

General textbooks

- Saukko, P. & Knight, B. *Knight's Forensic Pathology* (2004, 3rd Edition)

- Mason, J.K. & Purdue, B.N. *The Pathology of Trauma* (2000, 3rd Edition)

- Spitz, W.U. *Spitz and Fisher's Medicolegal Investigation of Death* (2006, 4th Edition)

- Shkrum, M.J. & Ramsay, D.A. *Forensic Pathology of Trauma* (2007)

- Payne-James, J., Jones, R., Karch, S.B. & Manlove, J. *Simpson's Forensic Medicine* (2011, 13th Edition)

- Di Maio, V., Di Maio, D. *Forensic Pathology* (2001, 2nd Edition, CRC Press), 367–387 (Fire deaths)

Articles in update textbooks

- Bohnert, M. 'Morphological Findings in Burned Bodies' in Tsokos, M., editor *Forensic Pathology Reviews*. Volume 1. Humana Press; 2004. 3–27

Articles in journals

- Bohnert, M., Rost, T., Pollak, S. 'The degree of destruction of human bodies in relation to the duration of the fire' *Forensic Science International* 1998; 95(1):11–21

- Einhorn, I.N. 'Physiological and toxicological aspects of smoke produced during the combustion of polymeric materials' *Environmental Health Perspectives* 1975; 11:163–89

- Hausmann, R., Betz, P. 'Thermally induced entrance wound-like defect of the skull' *Forensic Science International* 2002; 128(3):159–61

- Moritz, A.R., Henriques, F.C. 'Studies of Thermal Injury: II. The Relative Importance of Time and Surface Temperature in the Causation of Cutaneous Burns' *American Journal of Pathology* 1947; 23(5):695–720

- Tsokos, M. 'Heat-induced post-mortem defect of the skull simulating an exit gunshot wound of the calvarium' *Forensic Science, Medicine & Pathology* 2011; 7(2):227–228

Chapter 14

Child injuries and deaths

14.1 Child injuries and deaths are among the most difficult area of both clinical forensic medicine and pathology, and they pose particular problems in the medico-legal sphere. There have been significant controversies in a number of cases within the judicial system over the last few years with a number of high-profile cases.[1] In addition, advances within the field, in particular head injury in infants and children, have led to re-evaluation of both the clinical and pathological understanding of this area. There have been fundamental changes in the knowledge base about the nature of injury, as well as specific areas including the 'triad' (see **14.38** below) and the issue of birth injury.

These cases may be highly complicated in a number of areas, and the reader is advised to consult the wide range of literature available in such cases. This is an overview covering essential aspects.

Current practice in the UK is for post-mortem examinations to be undertaken jointly with a paediatric pathologist and forensic pathologist in infant/paediatric deaths where there are potential judicial proceedings. Guidelines with regard to these examinations are published by the Royal College of Pathologists and the Royal College of Paediatrics and Child Health.

The law

14.2 Cases involving child death will usually be charged as murder or manslaughter (or culpable homicide in Scotland), or one of the child-specific lesser offences. These latter are particularly used where it is difficult to identify the perpetrator or the cause of the death. Injuries caused to children will be charged either as an assault or, again, under the child-specific offences. In the case of more minor injury (akin to actual bodily harm or common assault), the various overlapping offences within child cruelty (section 1 of the Children and Young Persons Act 1933 or section 12 of the Children and Young Persons (Scotland) Act 1937 ('the 1937 Act') – see below) attract higher maximum sentences than simple assaults and are easier to

---

1   Essential case law:
   - *R v Cannings (Angela)* [2004] 1 All ER 725;
   - *R v Kai-Whitewind (Chaha'oh Niyol)* [2005] 2 Cr App R 31;
   - *R v Harris (Lorraine)* [2006] 1 Cr App R 5;
   - *R v Holdsworth (Suzanne)* [2008] EWCA Crim 971;
   - *R v Allen* [2005] EWCA Crim 1344;
   - *R v Henderson (Keran Louise), R v Butler (Ben), R v Oyediran (Oladapo)* [2010] 2 Cr App R 24.

   See also the 'Report of a meeting on the pathology of traumatic head injury in children', 10 December 2009 by the Royal College of Pathologists.

prove, so they are more frequently charged. Where the identity of the perpetrator is not clear, but the injuries are at least grievous bodily harm or death, in England and Wales and in Northern Ireland the offence of causing or allowing a child to suffer serious harm (section 5 of the Domestic Violence, Crime and Victims Act 2004) is available. General assaults and homicides are dealt with in Chapter 7.

Child-specific offences

14.3   Section 5 of the Domestic Violence, Crime and Victims Act 2004 created a new offence of 'causing or allowing a child or vulnerable adult to die', and that offence was amended in 2012 to include 'death or suffer serious physical harm'.[2] It is generally an offence used to charge both parents, where it is not clear who caused the death or injury, and it carries a maximum sentence of 14 years where death has resulted and 10 years otherwise. The elements to be proved include:

- The defendant was a member of the same household as the child, and had frequent contact with him.

- The child suffered death or serious physical injury (akin to grievous bodily harm).

- The child's death or serious injury was caused by the unlawful act of a member of the same household who had frequent contact with him.

- There was a significant risk of serious physical harm being caused by the unlawful act of such a person.

- Either the defendant did the unlawful act, or the defendant foresaw or ought to have foreseen the circumstances and appreciated the risk and failed to take reasonable steps to protect the child.

  The section does not require the prosecution to prove whether the defendant did the unlawful act or was the person failing to protect the child. Furthermore, there are special provisions in relation to this offence which make remaining silent more difficult for defendants.[3]

14.4   Child cruelty, contrary to section 1 of the Children and Young Persons Act 1933/section 12 of the 1937 Act, is a widely drafted and widely used offence. It is charged, even where the child has died, when it is difficult to prove the cause of the death, particularly where there has been a failure to seek timely medical attention. It is commonly used in the criminal courts because it allows the prosecution to be non-specific about when or how a child came by its injuries, when one or both carers have failed to seek medical advice. It carries a maximum penalty of 10 years.

  It applies to a person over 16, who has responsibility for a child under 16, who:

  'wilfully assaults, ill-treats, neglects, abandons, or exposes him, or causes or procures him to be assaulted, ill-treated, neglected, abandoned, or exposed, in a manner likely to cause him unnecessary suffering or injury to health (including

---

2   Domestic Violence, Crime and Victims (Amendment) Act 2012.
3   Sections 6, 6A and 7 of the 2004 Act.

injury to or loss of sight, or hearing, or limb, or organ of the body, and any mental derangement).'[4]

Some specific ways of committing the offence are set out in the section, including failing to provide food, clothing, accommodation or medical aid, and sleeping in the same bed as an infant while under the influence of alcohol and the infant dies.

14.5   Section 58 of the Children Act 2004[5] precludes the defence of reasonable chastisement in relation to this offence or any of the more serious assault offences, actual or grievous bodily harm (sections 47, 20 and 18 of the Offences Against the Person Act 1861). It remains available as a defence to common assault, if such correction 'be moderate in the manner, the instrument and the quantity of it'.[6]

For Scotland, the legality of physical punishment of children carried out by parents or others[7] is governed by section 51 of the Criminal Justice (Scotland) Act 2003, which provides that, in determining whether physical punishment of a child is justifiable (in the language of the statute, a 'justifiable assault'), the court must have regard to the nature of what was done, the reason for it and the circumstances in which it took place. Consideration must also be given to its duration and frequency, any effect on the child, the child's age, and the child's personal characteristics. Section 51(3) expressly prohibits blows to the head, shaking and use of an implement.

14.6   Other specific and rare offences which may arise in relation to children include:

- the prohibition on female genital mutilation, contained in sections 1–3 of the Female Genital Mutilation Act 2003;[8]

- abandoning or exposing children under two years of age whereby life is endangered, contrary to section 27 of the Offences Against the Person Act 1861;

- abduction, contrary to sections 1 and 2 of the Child Abduction Act 1984;[9]

- child destruction, contrary to sections 1 and 2 of the Infant Life (Preservation) Act 1929;[10]

4   Section 12 of the 1937 Act is identical to section 1 of the 1933 Act, save that the words 'assaults' and 'assaulted' were deleted as part of the enactment of section 51 of the Criminal Justice (Scotland) Act 2003 on the physical punishment of children.
5   For Northern Ireland, Article 2 of the Law Reform (Miscellaneous Provisions) (Northern Ireland) Order 2006.
6   1 Hawk c 60, s 23; c 62, s 2; *R v Hopley* (1860) 2 F & F 202.
7   That is, within section 51(1), 'physical punishment carried out in exercise of a parental right or of a right derived from having charge or care of the child'.
8   For Scotland, sections 1–3 of the Prohibition of Female Genital Mutilation (Scotland) Act 2005.
9   For Scotland, section 6 of the same Act; for Northern Ireland, Articles 3 and 4 of the Child Abduction (Northern Ireland) Order 1985.
10 There is no Scottish equivalent to this Act, nor does it extend to Northern Ireland; for the latter, the offence is contained in section 25(1) of the Criminal Justice Act (Northern Ireland) 1945.

- infanticide (usually charged nowadays as murder or manslaughter), contrary to section 1 of the Infanticide Act 1938;[11]

- concealment of birth, contrary to section 60 of the Offences Against the Person Act 1861;[12] and

- use of poison or instruments to cause miscarriage (illegal abortion), contrary to section 58 of the Offences Against the Person Act 1861.[13]

'Sudden infant death syndrome' (SIDS), 'sudden unexpected death in infancy' (SUDI) and 'unascertained'

14.7 By definition, SIDS is the sudden death of an infant under one year of age which remains unexplained after a thorough case investigation, including performance of a complete autopsy, examination of the death scene and review of the clinical history. In the UK, at least 300 babies die suddenly and unexpectedly every year, the majority occurring between the ages of one week and a year, with most being under six months. There has been much confusion over the terminology in this area, with the use of such terms as 'cot death' and 'crib death' in the United States. The term 'sudden infant death syndrome' or 'SIDS' came into being in the late 1960s and 1970s. This was defined as an infant put to bed in a cot/crib and subsequently found dead by the carers. Sudden unexpected death in infancy (SUDI) is a phrase which has become more prevalent following the Kennedy report which was published in 2004. This report recommended that investigation of such deaths should follow a standard protocol, with involvement of a multi-agency team including police, paediatricians, other medical personnel, social and community health services as well as pathologists. It should be noted that the terms 'SIDS' and 'SUDI' are sometimes confused. In this book, 'SIDS' is used to mean an infant who is put to bed in a cot and later found dead; 'SUDI' is used in the category of sudden deaths in infants with atypical features. These include age – either younger or older than the typical SIDS, as well as unusual circumstances or pathological features. Strictly speaking, SUDI is not a recognised cause of death, and the term 'unascertained' is often used in such circumstances.

Epidemiology

14.8 The rate of SIDS has fallen progressively, particularly since the 'back to sleep' campaign which encouraged parents to lie an infant on its back rather than a prone position. Thus, there has been a proportional increase in those cases where

---

11 Again, the Act has no Scottish equivalent: the equivalent is child murder, though very often diminished responsibility will be recognised, reducing the offence to culpable homicide. The Northern Irish offence is contained in section 1 of the Infanticide Act (Northern Ireland) 1939.

12 For Scotland, a slightly different offence is contained in the Concealment of Birth (Scotland) Act 1809. Contrary to section 60 of the 1861 Act, the concealment must be for the whole period of the pregnancy. As with the other provisions of the 1861 Act, it applies to Northern Ireland.

13 Subject to the provisions of the Abortion Act 1967, abortion is a common law offence in Scotland.

death results from other causes, including potentially unnatural causes such as co-sleeping deaths where an infant shares a sofa or bed with an adult or other individual. Such deaths are associated with smoking and alcohol/other intoxicant substance in the adults. The precise mechanism of death in these cases is unclear and they frequently show no pathological features to indicate a mechanism.

Pathological findings in SIDS and SUDI

14.9   These are non-specific and non-diagnostic. Petechial haemorrhages to the face and conjunctiva (dot-like haemorrhages) are not a feature, but they may be seen on the lungs, heart and thymus gland. Intrapulmonary haemorrhage should not be seen to any great extent.

Theories relating to the causation of SIDS

14.10   The current favoured theories arise in the area of respiratory dysfunction within the brain stem, various inflammatory markers within the blood and cardiac arrhythmia. There is some evidence that infants with SIDS do not demonstrate the normal respiratory pattern and show a reduced arousal response to hypoxia (that is, lack of oxygen within the blood). An increasing number of genes are now recognised to predispose to fatal cardiac arrhythmias. It is essential to look at the family history in these cases and undertake genetic investigation. Low birth weight and prematurity are known risk features for SIDS.

Other causes of death

14.11   Death in infancy, aside from SIDS or unascertained, may also result from natural causes, such as underlying heart disease or lung disease such as pneumonia, as well as traumatic conditions including both accidents or homicides.

- Sudden infant death syndrome (SIDS) is the death of an infant under one year of age where death is unexplained, typically where an infant is put to bed in a crib/cot.

- Atypical features which may classify a death as SUDI/unascertained, rather than SIDS, include the circumstances and pathological findings not usually seen in a true SIDS case, such as facial petechiae and minor injuries.

- The cause of SIDS is not yet positively identified; however, central nervous system respiratory dysfunction and cardiac arrhythmias are possibilities.

- A detailed family history and genetic testing should be undertaken in all of these cases.

Suffocation

14.12 This is a particularly difficult area within forensic pathology because, frequently, there are no physical abnormalities such as bruising or petechial haemorrhages.

The commonest method is smothering, either with a hand or an item such as a pillow.

Findings

14.13 External examination may show petechial haemorrhages on the conjunctiva or inside the mouth; there may be congestion or cyanosis of the face, as well as unusual areas of pallor. Abrasions and facial bruising may be identified. However, there may be no external findings of note.

Internal examination

14.14 This may show fresh lung haemorrhage, which is said by some to point to upper airway obstruction as a cause of death.

Extensive areas of haemorrhage within the lung alveoli (air sacs) should raise this possibility, although caution is required as extensive resuscitation may produce similar findings. As in all cases of infant death, natural diseases such as a bleeding disorder should be excluded.

An area of contention is the presence of haemosiderin containing macrophages. Macrophages are 'scavenger' cells which take up iron, a breakdown product of red cells seen in blood. A finding of large numbers of these cells was thought to indicate previous lung haemorrhage; however, whilst some attention should be paid to their presence, the finding cannot be taken as in any way diagnostic of upper airway obstruction.

- Suffocation in infants is an extremely difficult area in forensic pathology.
- It is commonly impossible to differentiate a true suffocation from SIDS or SUDI.
- The presence of facial bruising and petechial haemorrhages, as well as extensive lung haemorrhages and/or haemosiderin macrophages, should raise the level of suspicion.

Problem areas

Differentiating upper airway obstruction/suffocation from a true SIDS

14.15 This is an extremely difficult area. Airway obstruction, whether deliberate or otherwise, may show identical features to those identified in a true SIDS case. The findings in a true SIDS are non-specific.

Petechial haemorrhages to the eyes or face are not generally found, although scattered occasional ones may be seen in a true SIDS. In some, but by no means all, instances, more extensive petechial haemorrhages on both the face and conjunctiva may be seen in upper airway obstruction. In some cases, upper airway obstruction/ suffocation pallor may be noted around the face. In addition, any marks around the mouth or bruising to the frenulum or face should be treated with caution as, whilst they may occur in upper airway obstruction, they may be as a result of resuscitation, either by a carer or professional. In the absence of explanation, the level of suspicion becomes raised.

The presence of iron-containing macrophages was said to indicate previous haemorrhage in the lungs which may occur with upper airway obstruction. When seen in large numbers, the possibility of previous lung haemorrhage is raised, but there are a number of potential causes including natural disease.

Large areas of fresh haemorrhage within the lungs are unusual in a true SIDS case and raise the suspicion of suffocation, but may be seen in the background of resuscitation.

The presence of other injuries, recent or old (for example, unexplained healed rib fractures), raises the level of suspicion. For more information on fractures, see **14.29** below.

Munchausen Syndrome by Proxy or Fictitious Illness by Proxy

14.16 This term was coined by Professor Sir Roy Meadow, Consultant Paediatrician, in 1977.[14]

It has been defined by a form of child abuse where a parent artificially causes symptoms of disease in a child and may lead to the child's death. It may also be referred to as fictitious or induced illness. Covert video surveillance has indicated that this syndrome is genuine; however, others have raised doubts as to the validity of the diagnosis. Common causes of methods of harm include imposed upper airway obstruction, administering noxious substances, as well as producing artefactual bleeding (for example, in the urine). This diagnosis has come under increasing scrutiny over the previous decades with a number of high-profile cases.

- Munchausen Syndrome by Proxy is a contentious diagnosis.

- An infant or child may be harmed in a number of ways, including upper airway obstruction, artefactual bleeding and administering other toxic drugs or substances.

Stillbirth

14.17 A still-born child is defined in England and Wales as a 'child which has issued forth from its mother after the twenty-fourth week of pregnancy and which did not at any time after being completely expelled from its mother breathe or show

---

14 Professor Meadow also hit the headlines after giving misleading statistical evidence in the multiple SIDS death cases (*Sally Clarke*, *Angela Cannings* and *Donna Anthony*).

any other signs of life'.[15] Most stillbirths either die in utero or during the early stages of delivery, rather than after expulsion from the birth passage.

A number of natural conditions are recognised to cause stillbirth. These include asphyxia, infection, severe congenital abnormalities and (rarely, with good obstetric care) birth injury.

14.18   The burden of proof, in terms of any criminal charge, lies with the prosecution to prove that the infant had a separate existence. Whether there are incontrovertible signs of post-natal survival is an area which has given rise to considerable controversy in forensic pathology. In addition, if the pathologist has identified positively that there is a separate existence for a live birth, the death must be shown to have occurred either by commission or omission (for example, an infant deliberately stabbed or abandoned where survival is not possible without intervention) for any potential prosecution. Clearly, if death is due to natural causes, this is not an issue. Indeed, it may be impossible to prove, with a significant degree of certainty, that death has occurred by commission (for example, stabbing) or omission (for example, abandonment). Most deaths occur immediately or shortly after (i.e. within hours of) birth.

Circumstances

14.19   In terms of the range of cases seen, the most common scenario is when the body of an infant is concealed in items such as a dustbin, cupboard or suitcase. Mummified remains may be found many years later, having been stored in a wardrobe or suitcase. In some cases, multiple deaths may have occurred. Identification of a potential mother may be assisted by newspapers or other items at the scene. Here the difficulty may lie in showing that there has been a separate live existence, especially when there has been any significant decomposition or putrefaction. Concealment of birth, where it is not possible to prove that the infant was born alive, is a relatively minor crime, as opposed to the situation where there is positive proof that an infant has been born alive and then additional trauma has occurred. The more common causes of additional trauma, if born alive, include suffocation, drowning and abandonment, where the infant dies through lack of food and water and/or hypothermia/hyperthermia. Head injuries and penetrating injuries are less common. Not uncommonly, there is a background of concealed pregnancy, particularly in younger mothers.

Live birth or not?

14.20   The whole area is fraught with difficulty, and expert assistance in such cases will be required.

Various findings have been used in the past to indicate or, at least, suggest a live birth. These include the flotation test (to assess if air is in the lung tissues), where pieces of lung tissue are placed in fluid to see if they float – if so, it was said that the infant had breathed and was born alive. However, gases created on

15 Section 41 of the Births and Deaths Registration Act 1953.

decomposition and resuscitation can cause false results and the test is unreliable. Signs of a stillbirth might include meconium in the airways, maceration, appearance of the lungs, presence of vernix, or discolouration of the umbilical cord. An estimate is made of the gestational age of the infant in order to ascertain the potential of a live birth using, for example, weight, crown heel, crown rump, head circumference as well as foot length. Maceration (decomposition of the infant in utero following intra-uterine death) may affect some of these parameters. Radiological assessment should also be undertaken, for age assessment, identification of air in the lungs and stomach, inflation of the lungs and the presence of food in the stomach. Putrefaction (decomposition) may leave artefactual changes within the body. Traumatic injury may be identified, and toxicological assessment on blood or other available material should be performed to exclude foetal drug intoxication. Tests for infection in-utero should be undertaken. The pathologist should also take DNA samples, as there may be disputes over parentage.

If the placenta is available, this should be examined. It may aid in gestational age as well as if there is underlying placental pathology. If the infant has survived for 24–48 hours, the cord will show signs of separation from the infant, with evidence of inflammation. The cord may also show signs of cutting or tearing.

Accidental death in childhood

14.21   The causes of accidental death in childhood are multiple and various. They include drowning, fire deaths, road traffic collisions and falls, as well as other types of head injury. Pedestrian deaths are also relatively common in this age group. Drowning deaths may occur in both the younger and older age group, such as in the bath, lake or swimming pool. Death may occur very rapidly in these cases with a 'vaso-vagal mechanism', which may influence any judicial proceedings (see Chapter 12).

Accidental 'asphyxial' deaths include an infant being trapped by the side of a bed or cot, as well as accidental strangulation with a harness or blind cord. Other causes of accidental asphyxia include swallowing a balloon or other object (see also Chapter 11). Legal issues include lack of care and death in institutional settings which may come under gross negligence manslaughter, as well as criminal proceedings relating to homicide, such as in fire deaths and road traffic collisions.

- Accidental death in childhood includes drowning, fire deaths, road traffic collisions (in particular, as pedestrians) as well as falls.
- Accidental asphyxia may occur in a cot by trapping or as a result of strangulation by a cord/blind.

Non-accidental injury/child abuse

14.22   This is an area which has become increasingly important. There have been considerable advances in understanding of paediatric head injury in recent years. Child abuse is one of the commonest causes of morbidity and mortality in this age group. The major causes of death are head injury and thoracic/abdominal trauma.

Other injuries seen in both fatal and non-fatal cases include rib fractures and other bony injury, as well as abdominal trauma and a variety of surface injuries. 'Adult' modes of injury, such as stabbing and strangulation, may also be seen.

Child abuse is an important area in the clinical field where, most often, a paediatrician will be involved in assessment of any injuries as well as the clinical management. In medico-legal proceedings in these cases, it will most often be that the witness is a paediatrician. It is essential that the experience of any witness is determined by the court or instructing party. On many occasions, inexperienced treating physicians may find themselves giving, or being asked to give, expert evidence on causation.

In fatal cases, a joint examination with a paediatric pathologist is recommended. The forensic pathologist should lead on injury interpretation, and the paediatric pathologist on the many diseases of childhood.

Investigation

14.23   Many of these cases survive with variable long-term morbidity. In the fatal group, there may be a period of survival. It is imperative that as much detail of the background, including presenting history and details of medical findings whilst in hospital, are sought. Photographic documentation is essential and this may need to be done on a serial basis. Skeletal survey is mandatory. CT/MRI scanning may be invaluable in the head injured patient, particularly if survival is for some time, as the findings early on admission may prove to be the best indicator of the state of the brain. Previous medical history, as well as birth history, should be obtained.

- Child abuse is a common cause of death as well as long-term disability.

- The major cause of death relates to head injury.

- Detailed investigation including the clinical history and joint examination with a paediatric pathologist is best practice.

General injuries in child abuse

14.24   Features of injuries, including bruises, abrasions and lacerations, are covered in Chapter 7.

More specific issues related to the child are covered in the next section.

Bruises

14.25   An older child who is mobile will often show bruises to the legs whilst walking/crawling. Unexplained bruises over other areas, such as the neck, face, ears, trunk, buttocks and genitalia, particularly in the younger, less-mobile age group, should raise concern. Objects such as a rod or stick may leave tramline bruises. Grip marks leave multiple small bruises, often to the limbs or trunk. Bruising to the ears is said to be particularly suspicious of non-accidental injury.

Ageing of bruises is difficult, and the features are covered in Chapter 7. Full haematological screening should be undertaken to exclude disorders of blood clotting.

Abrasions

14.26   Occasional cases may show a patterned abrasion which can be matched with an object such as a ring. Bite marks are dealt with in Chapter 16.

Oral injury

14.27   The features of suspected smothering/suffocation have been covered earlier.
A characteristic finding in a child of a blow to the mouth is injury to the frenulum (the tissue between the gum and upper lip on the upper part). Features vary from minor bruising to lacerational injury. This may be due to a blow or excessive force from a bottle in the mouth.

Burns

14.28   The features have been described in Chapter 13.
These include immersion burns, spill burns as well as contact burns with cigarettes or bars of a fire. Old scars from cigarette burns may be seen.

Bony injuries

14.29   A skeletal survey is essential in evaluation of bony injury in both living and fatal cases of suspected child abuse. Additional radiological assessment by CT and/ or MRI may also be used. Careful assessment for underlying natural disease should be sought. For example, rickets is known to be in the differential diagnosis in suspected child abuse cases – this has been increasingly recognised over the last few years.[16] This is known to occur with lack of sunlight/Vitamin D. Other conditions include osteogenesis imperfecta, as well as disorders of collagen.
The common types of fracture are described below.

Metaphyseal fractures

14.30   There has been considerable debate over the diagnosis and specificity of these over the last several years. Historically, they have been regarded as at least suspicious of inflicted injury, although latterly this has been questioned. For a detailed discussion, the reader should consult the appropriate expert – see **14.44** below).
Metaphyseal fractures occur across the metaphysis of a long bone: the femur, tibia and humerus most commonly. The mechanism is understood to be torsion/traction when the grabbing of a limb occurs.

Rib fractures

14.31   These are most commonly seen in the posterior position near the articulation of the rib to the vertebra. They may also be seen anteriorly. Thoracic compression/

---

16 *Islington LBC v Al-Alas* [2012] 2 FLR 1239.

squeezing is the underlying mechanism. Resuscitation may be an explanation, particularly if prolonged.

Long bone fractures

14.32 Unexplained fractures are highly suspicious of abuse in a child who is not mobile. Accidental falls in the older age group are more frequent.

Skull fractures

14.33 These have been covered in Chapter 9. Less common fractures may be seen, including epiphyseal and vertebral (spinal) fractures.

Head injury in the young

14.34 This area has shown significant advances in both aetiology and understanding of the head injury.

Of particular significance is the so-called 'shaken baby syndrome' (which is covered at **14.47** below). It is difficult to determine the true incidence of head injury in abuse. Variation between 11.2 and 24.6 per 100,000 children has been noted.

Blunt head injury

Mechanism

14.35 This is the commonest cause of death in child abuse cases. Mechanisms include slamming the child against a wall or floor, direct blunt trauma with fists or a weapon.

External and internal findings

14.36 It should be noted that hair protects against bruises being noted externally; even in their absence, when there is deep (beneath the skin) bruising, this should be taken as evidence of impact.

There may or may not be skull fractures. Linear fractures may occur both in the accidental and non-accidental setting; however, multiple complex depressed fractures are highly suggestive of child abuse in the absence of explanation.

Subdural haematoma, brain swelling, oedema and hypoxic ischaemic damage, with varying degrees of contusional and traumatic axonal injury, are seen. These are covered in detail in Chapter 9.

- Head injury, with impact on a surface or by an object, is the commonest cause of death in child abuse.

- A variety of findings, including skull fracture, subdural haematomas, brain swelling, hypoxic ischaemic injury and primary brain injury, may be seen.

'Shaken baby syndrome'

14.37   This term has been widely used in many cases of inflicted head injury to include blunt trauma to the head. It should be reserved for those cases where there is no evidence of impact, in that there is no evidence of scalp bruising, deep (sub-scalp) bruising or skull fracture. In general terms, the 'syndrome' tends to occur in the younger age group of three or four months of age. The presentation typically is of sudden collapse with respiratory arrest which is thought to be due to interference with vital structures in the brain stem at the cranio-cervical junction giving rise to respiratory arrest.

The findings may also be referred to as the triad, which comprises: bilateral acute thin-film subdural haematomas; abnormal brain function/brain swelling with variable degrees of hypoxic-ischaemic damage (encephalopathy); and retinal haemorrhages. The thin-film subdural haematomas are, by definition, patchy small collections of blood in the subdural space. They are different in volume and appearance from the subdural haematomas seen in other cases, which may be space-occupying and larger.

In the triad cases, differentiation from birth trauma is essential, particularly in the early post-natal period up to a month or so in age.

In the older infant/child (i.e. several months), there is almost invariably evidence of impact injury. Impact alone is sufficient in these to produce the findings without the need to postulate additional 'shaking'. Any impact will produce a degree of neck movement. In a number of cases, there may be evidence of older injury.

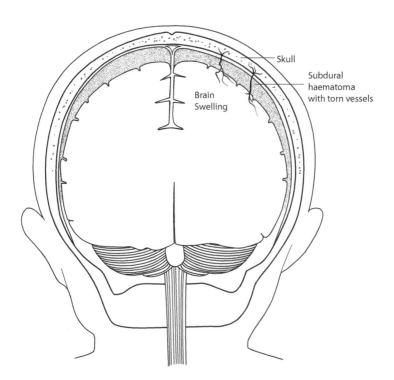

Figure 14.1 Acute thin-film subdural haematoma. (Courtesy of Ruth Bowen, Medical Illustrator, Cardiff University.)

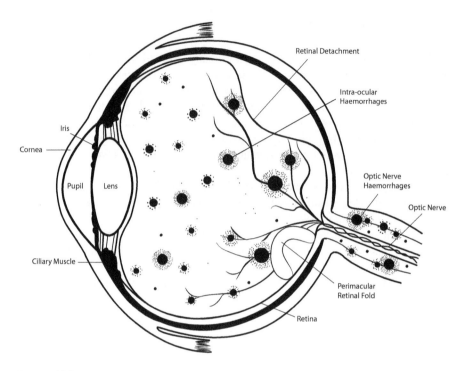

Figure 14.2 Intra-ocular haemorrhages including retinal haemorrhages. (Courtesy of Ruth Bowen, Medical Illustrator, Cardiff University.)

There are rare but well-recognised causes of subdural haematomas, either arising de novo or predisposing to subdural haematomas. These include bleeding disorders, septicaemia and various metabolic disorders.

Problem areas in infant head injury

Triad or so-called 'shaken baby syndrome' (SBS)

14.38   The triad comprises subdural haematoma, brain swelling (encephalopathy) and retinal haemorrhages.

Both medical and legal practitioners should consider the case law in this area generally, and specifically the Court of Appeal's directions as to case management in such cases in *Henderson.*[17]

There has been much discussion over the last few years with the introduction of immunocytochemistry on brain tissue. Immunocytochemistry (APP) – covered in Chapter 9 – identifies damage to axons. Initially, the axonal injury in the so-called shaken baby or triad cases was thought to be at the severe end of the spectrum (that is, diffuse traumatic axonal injury); however, both pathological and radiological studies have more recently shown that this is not the case, and the major pathology seen is that of hypoxic-ischaemic brain damage with cerebral swelling (hypoxic-ischaemic encephalopathy).

17 See footnote 1 above.

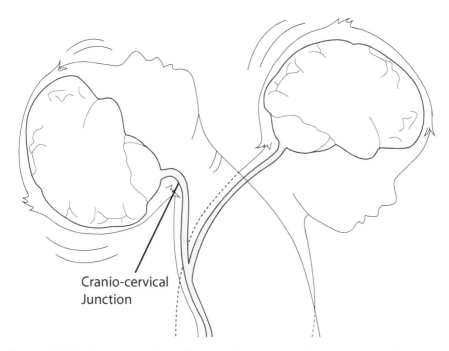

Figure 14.3 'Shaking' mechanism of injury with damage to the cranio-cervical junction. (Courtesy of Ruth Bowen, Medical Illustrator, Cardiff University.)

The subdural haematomas in these cases are typically thin-film in nature. There is some controversy over the origin of these as to whether they are truly traumatic, with rupture of the bridging veins, or whether they are secondary to severe brain swelling with hypoxia (damage due to lack of oxygen). This has led to a debate as to the degree of 'shaking' or trauma required to cause injury in the so-called triad cases, or if trauma is necessary at all. It is now generally accepted that, whilst the pathology of the triad alone may be a strong pointer to there being traumatic injury, other factors within the history/circumstances should be taken into consideration in the overall picture.

Low-level falls – accidental or non-accidental?

14.39   The question here is, 'How far does an infant or child need to fall to cause injury?'. This is of particular importance where the sole presenting feature is that of a single impact head injury. It is generally accepted that the vast majority of infants/ children do not die or sustain serious injury from a simple fall. However, there are well-documented cases where fatalities have occurred. The same issue applies to stairway falls. It is essential that a detailed history, scene examination as well as assessment of other injuries is undertaken. Increasingly, biomechanical assessment is being obtained.

Re-bleeding in subdural haematomas

14.40   Re-bleeding of existing subdural haematomas is recognised to occur in adults, most commonly in the background of sub-acute and chronic subdural haematomas (see Chapter 9). Over the last several years, it has been established that many newborns have asymptomatic subdural haematomas not infrequently associated with assisted delivery births. This raises the issue of the potential for re-bleeding in the background of such subdural haematomas. In the older infant/ child, as to whether re-bleeding may occur spontaneously or with minimal trauma is debatable at the current time. Genuine cases no doubt exist which have been supported by pathological evidence.

Intra-ocular haemorrhages

14.41   Retinal haemorrhages are commonly seen, in particular in the triad cases, as well as in cases of blunt inflicted head injury in children. They are commonly bilateral. Retinal folds and detachment may also be seen. Indeed, some authors would suggest that, in the absence of retinal haemorrhage, a case should not be classed as a triad case. There has been considerable debate as to the severity and extent of the retinal haemorrhages and intra-ocular haemorrhages as to their significance in terms of the severity of the head injury. The same applies to haemorrhage of the optic nerve root. It is recognised that intra-ocular and optic nerve haemorrhages may occur with severe cerebral swelling and may not necessarily be associated with traumatic brain injury. In addition, they can be seen in other non-traumatic conditions, such as bleeding abnormalities and infections.

- The triad comprises subdural haematoma, brain swelling (encephalopathy) and retinal haemorrhages.

- 'Shaken baby syndrome' implies a mode of 'injury'. This term is often misused in the context of child abuse head injury. A 'triad' case, on the pathology alone, cannot definitively be said to be caused by trauma, and other factors should be taken into account.

- The cause of a single impact head injury in an infant or child may be difficult to identify in terms of distinguishing accidental fall from inflicted injury.

Thoraco-abdominal trauma

14.42   Abdominal trauma is the second most common cause of death in child abuse cases, particularly so in the older infant and child. It is often found where there are other findings of abuse. Injuries occur in particular to the liver and bowel, as well as other organs including the pancreas. Compression injury to the abdomen is common, where the bowel impacts against the vertebral column and there may be multiple areas of injury. Injury to the liver may also occur, although this is more common in the non-accidental situation, such as road traffic collisions. Intra-abdominal haemorrhage and bowel rupture are common sequelae of intra-abdominal trauma. Damage to the pancreas may also occur, with pancreatitis and chronic scarring.

Chest injuries include rib fractures (see **14.31** above). Injury to the heart and major blood vessels may also occur; however, this type of severe injury is more common in the accidental scenario, such as a road traffic collision.

- Abdominal trauma is the second most common cause of death in child abuse cases.

- Injuries commonly occur in the liver, bowel and pancreas.

Starvation and neglect

14.43   This is a relatively rare but well-recognised cause of death, and is also seen in the living child. Infants and children may be affected. Infections, as well as dehydration and features of starvation (severe underweight, muscle atrophy) in varying degrees, are features. Natural disease as well as toxicological causes should be sought.

In conclusion

14.44   Child abuse is one of the most difficult areas of forensic medicine. It is essential that, in these cases, appropriate experts are consulted. These specialities may include radiology, paediatrics, pathology, neurosurgery and others. It is also important that any such expert has the relevant experience and expertise in this area.

Further reading material

General textbooks

- Byard, R.W. *Sudden death in the young* (2010, 3rd Edition, Cambridge University Press)

- Collins, K.A., Byard, R.W. *Forensic pathology of infancy and childhood* (2014, Springer)

- Whitwell, H.W. *Forensic Neuropathology* (2005, Hodder Arnold)

Articles in update textbooks

- Byard, R.W. 'Medicolegal Problems with Neonaticide' in Tsokos, M. *Forensic Pathology Reviews*. Volume One, 2004

- Byard, R.W., & Krous, H.F. 'Diagnostic and Medico-Legal Problems with Sudden Infant Death Syndrome' in Tsokos, M. *Forensic Pathology Reviews*. Volume One, 2004

- Collins, K.A. 'Intentional starvation/malnutrition and dehydration in children' in Griest, K., editor *Pediatric Homicide. Medical Investigation* (Boca Raton: CSC Press) pp. 169–85

- Langlois, N.E.I. & Byard, R.W. 'Sudden Natural Deaths in Infancy and Childhood' in Turk, E.E. *Forensic Pathology Reviews*. Volume Six, 2011

- Griest, K.J. 'Supporting evidence in physical child abuse' in Griest, K.J., editor *Paediatric Homicide, Medical Investigation* (2010, CRC Press)

- Whitwell, H.L. 'Non-accidental injury in children' in Lowe, D.G. and Underwood, J.C.E., editors *Recent Advances in Histopathology* (2001, Edinburgh: Churchill Livingstone)

- Weber, M.A. & Sebire, N.J. 'Post-mortem investigation of Sudden Unexpected Death in Infancy: Role of Autopsy in Classification Death' in Turk, E.E. *Forensic Pathology Reviews*. Volume Six, 2011

Articles in journals

- Atwal, G.S., Rutty, G.N., Carter, N. *et al.* 'Bruising in non-accidental head injured children: a retrospective study of the prevalence, distribution and pathological associations in 24 cases' *Forensic Sci Int* 1998; 96:215–30

- Becroft, D.M.O., Thompson, J.M.D., Mitchell, E.A. 'Nasal and intrapulmonary haemorrhage in sudden infant death syndrome' *Arch Dis Childh* 2001, vol. 85, pp. 116–20

- Byard, R.W., Blumbergs, P., Rutty, G., Sperhake, J., Banner, J., Krous, H.F. 'Lack of evidence for a causal relationship between hypoxic-ischaemic encephalopathy and subdural haemorrhage in fetal life, infancy and early childhood' *Pediatr Dev Pathol* 2007; 10:348–350

- Caffey, J. 'On the theory and practice of shaking infants. Its potential residual effects of permanent brain damage and mental retardation' *Am J Dis Child* 1972; 124:161–3

- Carpenter, R.F. 'The prevalence and distribution of bruising in babies' *Arch Dis Child* 1999; 80:363–6

- Chiesa, A., Duhaime, A.C. 'Abusive head trauma' *Pediatr Clin North Am* 2009; 56:317–331

- Clouse, J.R., Lantz, P.E. 'Posterior rib fractures in infants associated with cardiopulmonary resuscitation' in *American Academy of Forensic Sciences, 60th annual meeting*. 2008 Feb; Washington, DC, 2008

- Coats, B., Margulies, S. 'Potential for head injuries in infants from low height falls' *J Neurosurg Pediatrics* 2008; 2:321–30

- Cohen, M.C., Scheimberg, I. 'Evidence of occurrence of intradural and subdural hemorrhage in the perinatal and neonatal period in the context of hypoxic Ischemic encephalopathy: an observational study from two referral institutions in the United Kingdom' *Pediatr Dev Pathol* 2009; 12(3):169–76

- Drago, D.A. 'Kitchen scalds and thermal burns in children 5 years and younger' *Pediatrics* 2005; 115(1): 10–6

- Dwek, J.R. 'The radiographic approach to child abuse' *Clin Orthop Relat Res.* 2011; 469(3):776–89

- Ehsani, J.P., Ibrahim, J.E., Bugeja, L., Cordner, S. 'The role of epidemiology in determining if a simple short fall can cause fatal head injury in an infant' *Am J Forensic Med Pathol* 2010; Vol. 31, pp. 287–298

- Geddes, J., Hackshaw, A.K., Vowles, G.H., Nickols, C.D., Whitwell, H.L. 'Neuropathology of inflicted head injury in children. 1. Patterns of brain damage' *Brain* 2001; 124:1290–8

- Geddes, J.F., Vowles, G.H., Hackshaw, A.K. *et al.* 'Neuropathology of inflicted head injury in children. 2. Microscopic brain injury in infants' *Brain* 2001; 124:1299–306

- Geddes, J.F., Tasker, R.C., Hackshaw, A.K, Nickols, C.D. *et al.* 'Dural haemorrhage in non-traumatic infant deaths: does it explain the bleeding in "shaken baby syndrome"?' *Neuropathol Appl Neurobiol* 2003; 29:14–22

- Hobbs, C.J. 'Abdominal injury due to child abuse' *Lancet* 2005; 366(9481):187–8

- Kemp, A.M., Dunstan, F., Hanson, S., Morris, S. *et al.* 'Patterns of skeletal fractures in child abuse: systematic review' *BMJ* 2008; 337:a1518

- Kennedy, H. 'Sudden Unexpected Death in Infancy. A multi-agency protocol for care and investigation. The report of a working group convened by The Royal College of Pathologists and The Royal College of Paediatrics and Child Health': The Royal College of Pathologists and The Royal College of Paediatrics and Child Health, 2004

- Kleinman, P.K. 'Problems in the diagnosis of metaphyseal fractures' *Pediatr Radiol* 2008; 38 (sup 3): S388–S394

- Leestma, J.E. 'Case analysis of brain injured admittedly shaken infants: 54 cases, 1969-2001' *Am J Forensic Med Pathol* 2005; 26:199–212

- Matshes, E.W., Lew, E.O. 'Do resuscitation injuries kill infants and children?' *Am J Forensic Med Pathol* 2010; 31(2):178–85

- Matshes, E.W., Lew, E.O. 'Two handed cardiopulmonary resuscitation can cause rib fractures in infants' *Am J Forensic Med Pathol* 2010; 31(2):303–7

- Maxeiner, H., Jekat, R. 'Resuscitation and conjunctival petechial haemorrhages' *J for Leg Med* 2010; 17:87–91

- Plunkett, J. 'Fatal pediatric head injuries caused by short-distance falls' *Am J Forensic Med Pathol* 2001; 22:1–12

- Ryan, M.P., Young, S.J., Wells, D.L. 'Do resuscitation attempts in children who die, cause injury?' *Emerg Med J* 2003 Jan:20(1):10–12

- Sugar, N.F., Taylor, J.A., Feldman, K.W. 'Bruises in infants and toddlers. Those who don't cruise rarely bruise' *Arch Pediatr Adoles Med* 1999; 153:399–403

- Togioka, B.M., Arnold, M.A., Bathhurst, M.A., Zeigfeld, S.M. *et al.* 'Retinal haemorrhages and shaken baby syndrome: an evidence-based review' *J Emerg Med.* 2009; 37:98–106

- Weber, M.A., Risdon, R.A., Offiah, A.C., Malone, M., Sebire, N.J. 'Rib fractures identified at post mortem examination in sudden unexpected deaths in infancy (SUDI)' *Forensic Sci Int.* 2009; 189(1): 75–81

- Whitby, E.H., Griffiths, P.D., Rutter, S. *et al.* 'Frequency and natural history of subdural haemorrhages in babies in relation to obstetric factors' *Lancet* 2004; 363:846–51

Chapter 15

Sexual assaults

With Bernadette Butler and Anna Riddell

Sexual offences in adults

Introduction

15.1   In England and Wales, in the year 2013/2014, a total of 64,200 sexual offences were reported to the police, of which 20,725 were rape.[1] This is a rate of 1 per 1,000 head of population.

Many changes have been introduced in recent years in the investigation of sexual allegations. Guidelines for the investigation of sexual assault allegations have been produced for police forces.[2]

The law

15.2   The Sexual Offences Act 2003 radically redrafted the law on sexual offences in England and Wales, and most cases are now prosecuted under its provisions. Historical allegations, pre 1 May 2004, however, will fall under the pre-2003 provisions. Readers are referred to the practitioners' texts for explanations of the differences. This chapter will focus on the main 'contact' offences under the 2003 Act; offences such as grooming and child pornography are, of course, unlikely to result in the need for medical evidence.

Many sexual offences were also redefined in the Sexual Offences (Scotland) Act 2009 and the Sexual Offences (Northern Ireland) Order 2008.

Consent

15.3   A person consents if they agree by choice and have the freedom and capacity to make that choice.[3]

Thus, if the complainant has consented to sexual activity while drunk or under the influence of drugs, this does not vitiate consent unless the effect of the alcohol

---

1 See www.ons.gov.uk/ons/rel/crime-stats/crime-statistics/period-ending-march-2014/stb-crime-stats.html#tab-Sexual-Offences-.
2 See www.cps.gov.uk/publications/agencies/cps_acpo_rape_protocol.pdf.
3 Sexual Offences Act 2003, s 74.

or drugs was such as to render the complainant temporarily without the capacity to choose whether to engage in sexual activity or not.[4]

Some complainants with mental disabilities may not have the capacity to consent. Complainants with mental disorders are specifically protected by sections 30 to 33 of the Act. Children are specifically protected by sections 5 to 13 of the Act.

The main offences

15.4   Rape (contrary to section 1 of the Sexual Offences Act 2003) is defined as the defendant intentionally penetrating, with his penis, the vagina, anus or mouth of the complainant, to which penetration the complainant did not consent and the defendant did not reasonably believe that he or she did consent. It is in contrast to the previous definition under the Sexual Offences Act 1956, in that the belief in consent must be reasonable.

Penetration of the vagina includes the vulva,[5] and has been said to include the labia of the pudendum.

Assault by penetration (contrary to section 2 of the 2003 Act) is defined as the defendant intentionally penetrating with a part of his body, or anything else, the vagina or anus of the complainant, where the penetration is sexual, to which penetration the complainant did not consent and the defendant did not reasonably believe that he or she did consent.

Sexual assault (contrary to section 3 of the Act) is defined as the defendant intentionally touching the complainant and the touching is sexual, to which touching the complainant did not consent and the defendant did not reasonably believe that he or she did consent.

Section 4 of the Act prohibits the defendant from intentionally causing the complainant to engage in an activity, where the activity is sexual, to which activity the complainant did not consent and the defendant did not reasonably believe that he or she did consent.

In Scotland, rape can be committed by intentional or reckless penetration.[6]

Examinations

15.5   If the complaint is first made to the police, it is standard practice to obtain early evidence; this may include, but is not limited to, early evidence kits (EEKs).[7] Such kits are carried by police officers on patrol, whereby mouth (oral) samples and

---

4   *R v Bree* [2007] 2 Cr App R 13.
5   Sexual Offences Act 2003, s 79(9).
6   Sexual Offences (Scotland) Act 2009, s 1.
7   National Police Improvement Agency, Association of Chief Police Officers (Now National Police Chief Council). Professional Practice. Briefing Note on First Response to Rape (www. app.college.police.uk/app-content/major-investigation-and-public-protection/rape-and-sexual-offences).

urine may be obtained as soon as possible. Other evidence obtained might include clothing and non-intimate samples, e.g. swabs from face, hands, nails.

The forensic medical examination, in terms of obtaining evidence in the form of samples for DNA or toxicology, is also time dependent (see below). Of complaints made to the police, 46% were made within 24 hours of the incident and almost 70% within seven days. Complainants under the age of 16 were less likely to present early.[8]

Sexual assault referral centres

15.6   In some areas, the provision of a 'non-police' or 'self' referral forensic medical service enables complainants ('complainers' in Scotland) to present to a sexual assault referral centre (SARC, an examination facility) and undergo an examination, but without having to involve the police first. The evidence is obtained with the necessary chain of evidence, to ensure that it is sufficiently robust for court purposes, should a complaint be made to the police at a later date. A chain of evidence is a robust audit trail which demonstrates the integrity of that evidence, from its source to presentation in court.[9]

The staff of a SARC are trained in obtaining and recording an account of an allegation, including the importance of first disclosure, taking contemporaneous notes and avoiding leading questions.

The forensic medical examination

15.7   The preparation for a forensic medical examination (FME) involves a balance between the medical (physical and psychological) needs of the individual and the potential loss of evidence as a result of any delay.

The FME is conducted by a doctor or nurse (clinician) who should have received specialist training in the examination of an individual who has alleged – or been accused of – a sexual offence. In the United Kingdom, the Faculty of Forensic & Legal Medicine (FFLM) produces quality standards and guidance to develop and support best clinical forensic practice. UK-based clinicians will use FFLM publications to inform and support their practice.[10] In many SARCs, the clinician is assisted in the examination by a trained crisis worker. Some clinicians will have acquired qualifications in forensic medicine (see Box 1).

8   Feist, A., Ashe, J., Lawrence, J. *et al*. Investigating and Detecting Recorded Offences of Rape. Home Office Online Report 18/07. London: Home Office, 2007. http://library.npia.police.uk/docs/hordsolr/rdsolr1807.pdf.
9   College of Policing, Authorised Professional Practice (APP). Prosecution & Case Management. Section 2.3: Exhibits. November 2013 (www.app.college.police.uk/app-content/prosecution-and-case-management/hearing-and-trial-management/#exhibits).
10 Faculty of Forensic and Legal Medicine's quality standards: http://fflm.ac.uk/upload/documents/1378397186.pdf   http://fflm.ac.uk/upload/documents/1393326841.pdf   http://fflm.ac.uk/upload/documents/1395839844.pdf.

Box 1

DMJ	Diploma in Medical Jurisprudence
DFCASA	Diploma in Clinical & Forensic Aspects of Sexual Assault
LFFLM/MFFLM/FFFLM	Licentiate, Membership or Fellowship of the Faculty of Forensic & Legal Medicine
DFMS	Diploma in Forensic Medical Sciences
DFMB	Post-graduate Diploma in Forensic Medicine & Bioethics
PG Dip or MSc FLM	Post-graduate Diploma or Master of Science in Forensic & Legal Medicine

15.8   The clinician will need to assess the appropriateness or otherwise of conducting a forensic medical examination, which will depend upon:

- The nature of the allegation.

- The time elapsed since the incident.

- Consent of the examinee.

- In some situations, the complainant's pubertal status (see Table 1 at **15.15**, Box 6 at **15.37** and Box 8 at **15.40** below).

The doctor or nurse will need to make a preliminary assessment based on information from the police officer or the complainant; this is essentially a triage process and may also involve prioritisation of one referral ahead of another. Details of the allegation, the nature of the assault, and the date and time at which it is believed to have occurred, along with comprehensive information about the complainant, must be obtained (see Box 2).

Box 2

Name
Age
Gender
Language issues and need for interpreter
Learning disability
Medical and psychological problems, including mobility issues
Substance misuse or dependence
For those <16 years, details of parental responsibility or the need for a 'responsible' adult
Child or adult safeguarding issues
Acute injury and need for assessment in an emergency department
Recent alcohol or substance use, or dependency on alcohol or drugs
Capacity to consent and other issues which may affect it e.g. intoxication, injury, distress, tiredness, dementia, learning disability

15.9 In general, a forensic medical examination would be conducted as soon as is feasible, but it may have to be delayed to allow the patient to become sober, have some sleep, or have medical treatment in hospital, if necessary. Sometimes, it may be too late to obtain biological evidence, but an examination to record injury (or its absence) is appropriate.

The examination would usually be conducted in a suitably equipped room or suite which is appropriately cleaned and decontaminated between examinations; this will include facilities for staff to wash and change their clothing. However, where the complainant cannot come to the SARC, e.g. if unconscious, in prison, or in a secure psychiatric ward, the SARC staff will conduct an 'off-site' examination.

Investigating symptoms and injuries

15.10 The investigation of symptoms and injuries starts with obtaining a history of the incident. In adults, this may be from the specialist police officer, the complainant or both.

The history and examination findings will usually be recorded within a proforma, a pre-printed document the aim of which is to ensure a systematic record of the findings. Examples of proforma are available from the FFLM and from the World Health Organisation (WHO).[11]

It is essential that the individual understands and gives consent to the examination and its implications, especially in relation to confidentiality, as, in order to support an investigation and possible prosecution, information must be shared, e.g. with the police, forensic scientists and the defence.

The history

15.11 The history will include:

- The date and time of the allegation.

- The alleged act(s), including any physical assault or use of weapons.

- Condom use and whether ejaculation is believed to have occurred.

- Information about the alleged assailant, e.g. ethnicity, age, relationship to the victim.

- Whether any drugs (prescribed, over-the-counter, alcohol or illicit) were involved, before, during or after the incident, whether voluntarily taken, or thought to be covertly administered.

- Any injuries noted and whether any other acute medical care has already been provided.

---

11 a) Faculty of Forensic & Legal Medicine. Proforma for adult female and male forensic sexual assault examination. London: FFLM, 2010. http://fflm.ac.uk/upload/documents/1276183431.pdf.
b) World Health Organisation. Guidelines for medico-legal care for victims of sexual violence. Geneva: WHO, 2003 http://whqlibdoc.who.int/publications/2004/924154628x.pdf.

A more detailed history should be obtained from the complainant, including:

- Post-assault activities, e.g. washing, bathing, defecating, urinating.

- Post-assault symptoms (complaints or changes which the examinee has noticed), e.g. pain, bleeding form the vagina or anus/rectum.

- Injuries noted to be present prior to the allegation and any noted since.

Such information will assist the clinician in deciding what forensic samples may be appropriate. The clinician must be objective (forensic role), notwithstanding their duty to the examinee as a patient (therapeutic role). The clinician records anything which the examinee says, and this is explained as part of the consent process. This approach is essential for the clinician to fulfil his or her duty of impartiality to the criminal justice system and the court.

15.12   In terms of other information, the following would usually be recorded:

- A relevant past medical history, which will include details of serious illness or injury and skin disorders.

- A mental health history, including any psychiatric illness, self-harm, treatment and admission, a history of learning disability.

- Any treatments which might impact on the examination findings.

- Details of recent drug and alcohol use and dependency.

It is also necessary to take a relevant sexual and reproductive history (see Box 3).

Box 3

Women
– Menstrual history: last period, cycle length, age at first period or date of menopause
– Contraception and adherence to it
– Tampon use
– Number of children and mode of delivery
– Genital trauma, e.g. related to childbirth, female genital mutilation (FGM), genital surgery
– Date and nature of last sexual intercourse or activity, or any previous history of any (receptive) penetrative sexual activity and when
Men
– Genito-anal trauma, e.g. from surgery
– Date and nature of last sexual intercourse or activity, or any previous history of any (receptive) penetrative sexual activity and when

The examination

15.13   The forensic medical examination will usually consist of a 'top-to-toe' examination, according to consent, recording both positive and negative signs (the physical findings).

The general findings recorded may include:

- Weight (kg), height (cm), body mass index (BMI in kg/m^2).

- If relevant, pubertal development (Tanner staging).

- Demeanour, e.g. quiet, withdrawn, tearful, angry.

- Any signs of intoxication or substance misuse, e.g. smell of alcohol, constricted pupils, injection ('track') marks.

- Dominant hand, damage to nails.

- Skin colour.

- Skin conditions, e.g. eczema, psoriasis, scars, piercings and tattoos.

A record of other physical findings may include:

- Disability/limitation or impairment of function (whether pre-existing or recent).

- Tenderness (a subjective observation by the examinee of pain or discomfort), which may be present in the absence of any obvious injury.

- Transient findings (see also Box 4).

- Injuries (see also Box 4).

- The absence of injury which might have been expected, based on the history.

The physical findings may be recorded in the forensic medical notes or proforma or, along with the injuries, on body diagrams or body maps.[12]

15.14 Important and relevant details of an injury which should be recorded are shown in Box 4.

Box 4

Type of injury, e.g. abrasion (scratch or graze), bruise, laceration (tear), burn, or a 'mixed' injury
Transient or associated findings and signs of healing or treatment, e.g. oedema (swelling), erythema (redness), bleeding, scab, signs of treatment such as sutures
Measurements in metric units, cm or mm
Site: distance from a reference point/body landmark
Size: length × width, or diameter
Shape, e.g. oval, circular, linear
Colour
Pattern: may be discernible if a weapon/implement has been used
Additional details, e.g. a round-shaped injury consisting of bruising, laceration might be a bite mark; information from the complainant about how/when injury caused/noticed

12 For examples of body maps, see the FFLM website at http://fflm.ac.uk/librarydetail/4000095.

Forensic samples

15.15   Clinicians based within the UK will use the FFLM's *Recommendations for the Collection of Forensic Specimens from Complainants and Suspects.*[13] This document is updated every six months and is available in the publications area of the website. It is important to note that such documents are guidelines and should be adapted to suit the individual circumstances of each case. A clinician may properly choose not to follow the guidance if there is justification for so doing.

Table 1 The July 2015 guidance to persistence data in relation to DNA or toxicology.

Nature of activity	Other details	Persistence (likely maximum limit)
Penile-vaginal intercourse	Post-pubertal female	7 days
	Pre-pubertal female	3 days (72 hours)
Penile-anal intercourse	Female	3 days (72 hours)
	Male	3 days (72 hours)
Penile-oral intercourse	Female	2 days (48 hours)
	Male	2 days (48 hours)
Digital penetration	Of the vagina	2 days (48 hours)
	Of the anus	2 days (48 hours)
Samples from skin		Up to 48 hours (2 days)
	If not washed	Up to 7 days
Samples from the penis		Up to 3 days (72 hours)
Toxicology		
Blood		Up to 3 days (72 hours)
Urine		Usually up to 5 days
	If drug facilitated sexual assault	Possibly up to 14 days
Hair		Obtain at 4–6 weeks

Documentation of physical findings

Injuries

15.16   Minor injury occurs to the body in everyday activity, e.g. bruises and abrasions on the limbs, particularly to those who play sport or have manual jobs. The presence, or absence, of an injury is dependent on a number of factors:

- The force used.

- The length of time it was applied.

- Resistance, if any, by the complainant.

13 Faculty of Forensic & Legal Medicine. *Proforma Body diagrams*. London: FFLM, July 2015 at http://fflm.ac.uk/upload/documents/1439981280.pdf.

- The susceptibility of the individual to injury, which may include:

    – the loss of supporting tissue (collagen) in skin, which may be as a result of ageing process or a consequence of treatment with steroids;

    – the pubertal status of a child;

    – the post-menopausal woman;

    – previous injury, scarring or infection; in the ano-genital region, this might include female genital cutting (mutilation, FGM), childbirth, an anal fissure or fistula;

    – treatment with drugs which interfere with the clotting mechanism, e.g. heparin, warfarin and aspirin; or

    – more rarely, congenital and other skin conditions.

For the definitions of types of injury, see Chapter 7.

The prevalence of injuries

15.17   The research which is available worldwide has shown a very wide range in the prevalence of physical (body) and oral, genital or ano-rectal injuries. This is partly due to differences in examination and recording techniques, as well as variations in practice.

Ideally, medical knowledge would be informed and supported by scientific research. There are practical difficulties to conducting such research, including consent and ethics approvals, and collating a study group (i.e. those who had been sexually assaulted and a 'control' group who had not), but clinicians will use such research to assist the explanation and interpretation of their findings.

Interpreting findings

15.18   The presence of an injury, or other physical finding, must be interpreted in context, e.g. it may be co-incidental or have pre-dated or post-dated the alleged incident. It may not be possible for a clinician to be precise as to causation or age of an injury.

The absence of injury may be a neutral finding, unless it directly contradicts the history. The presence of injury, particularly when there are multiple injuries, may support a complaint but may also be neutral: interpretation in context is essential. Evidence of possible defence injuries may support a complaint (see Chapter 7 for examples).

As the sexual acts in alleged assault or rape may be identical to those of consensual activity, the findings may be similar, e.g. no injuries, or findings such as petechial bruising on the neck or breasts (colloquially, a 'hickey' or 'love bite'). Therefore, it may be impossible for the clinician to assist the court in terms of distinguishing whether the activity was consensual or not.

Oral, genital and ano-rectal injury

Oral injury following alleged oral rape

15.19   Penetration of the mouth with the penis (fellatio) may result in (petechial) bruising on the roof of the mouth (palate), or in the throat (pharynx), or injuries to the frenula within the mouth or on the lips. Such injuries may not distinguish between consensual or non-consensual penetration.[14] Bruises on the face or head may be found where the head has been forcibly held. Again, it is possible for those to have been caused consensually but, depending on the history, may be suggestive of non-consensual activity.

There are several postulated mechanisms for the causation of petechiae or palatal bruising, some or all of which may be relevant:

- The negative pressure caused by the suction.

- Through retching or vomiting due to pharyngeal irritation (gag reflex).

- Direct trauma.

Genital injury following alleged vaginal rape

15.20   Research conducted in the UK, Europe and Australasia shows that the majority of complainants of vaginal rape have no genital injury. Overall genital injury rates are of the order of 24–30%; thus, about two-thirds to three-quarters of complainants will not have any injuries.[15]

There are several reasons why a true complaint may not result in such injuries:

- The time elapsed since the incident; minor abrasions or petechial bruising may have resolved (within a few days).

- The anatomical structures are designed to accommodate penetrative sexual activity.

- Some women can deliver a baby vaginally without injury.

- There may have been some consensual activity prior to the incident, such that sexual stimulation resulted in increased vaginal lubrication.

14 a) Schlesinger, S.L., Borbotsina, J., O'Neill, L. 'Petechial hemorrhages of the soft palate secondary to fellatio' *Oral Surg Oral Med Oral Pathol.* 1975; 40(3):376–8.
b) Worsaae, N., Wanscher, B. 'Oral injury caused by fellatio' *Acta Derm Venereol.* 1978; 58(2):187–8.
c) Brew-Graves, E., Morgan, L. 'Injuries and allegations of oral rape: A retrospective review of patients presenting to a London sexual assault referral centre' *J Forensic Leg Med.* 2015 Aug; 34:155–8.
15 a) Bowyer, L., Dalton, M. 'Female victims of rape and their genital injuries' *Br J Obstet Gynaecol.* 1997; 104(5):617–20.
b) Kerr, E., Cottee, C., Chowdhury Hawkins, R., Jawad, R., Welch, J. 'The Haven: a pilot referral centre in London for cases of serious sexual assault' *BJOG*, March 2003; 110: 267–71.
c) Palmer, C.M., McNulty, A.M., D'Este, C., Donovan, B. 'Genital injuries in women reporting sexual assault' *Sexual Health* 2004; 1(1) 55–9.
d) Hilden, M., Schei, B., Sidenius, K. 'Genito-anal injury in adult victims of sexual assault' *Forensic Sci Int.* 2005; 154(2-3):200–5.

- A woman does not resist or is incapable of resisting, e.g. through the effects of sleep, unconsciousness, alcohol or drugs.

In adolescents or young women, it is often assumed that there will be genital injuries, especially if the allegation is also the first ever episode of penetrative vaginal intercourse. However, a study of adolescent complainants of sexual assault (aged 12–17 years) compared two groups described as 'non-virgins and 'virgins'; 53% of the virgin group had a genital injury, and 32% of the non-virgin group had a genital injury. Of those who were described as 'virgins', just under 50% had an injury to the hymen.[16]

15.21 The absence of hymenal injury may be due to the following:

- Increases in reproductive hormones, especially oestrogen, in puberty causes the hymen to become more elastic and better able to accommodate penetration by an object, e.g. finger, tampon or penis, without any acute injury or lasting sign.

- Penetration may not have reached the hymen, i.e. between the labia only.

- Healing may occur and leave no residual sign.

- No penetration took place.

Conversely, the presence of hymenal injury may be due to:

- Penetration by penis or other object.

- Other non-sexual activity; theoretically, straddle injury or a gynaecological examination could injure the hymen, but there is no evidence base to say how common this might be.

It is important to note that the use of the term 'intact' in relation to the hymen is unhelpful and may be misleading.

15.22 Where multiple assailants are involved, one might expect genital injuries to be found more frequently, but they are not an inevitable finding.[17]

In the post-menopausal woman, body injury may be more likely to occur due to the loss of collagen in the skin. Similarly, due to the relative lack of oestrogen causing atrophic changes in the genital tissues, including the vagina, genital injury is more likely than in a pre-menopausal woman.[18]

Similarly, genital injuries in allegations of assault by penetration are not particularly common. In one study of 249 women, 18 alleged an assault by penetration and only one was found to have a genital injury.[19]

---

16 White, C., McLean, I. 'Adolescent complainant of sexual assault; injury patterns in virgin and non-virgin groups' *J Clin Forensic Med*, 2006; 13: 172–80.

17 Morgan, L., Brittain, B., Welch, J. 'Multiple perpetrators sexual assault. How does it differ from single perpetrator assault?' *J Interpers Violence* 2012; 27(12); 2415–36.

18 a) Bowyer, L., Dalton, M. 'Female victims of rape and their genital injuries' *Br J Obstet Gynaecol*. 1997; 104(5): 617–20.
   b) Morgan, L., Dill, A., Welch, J. 'Sexual assault in post-menopausal women: a retrospective review' *Br J Obstet Gynaecol*. 2011; 118:832–43.

19 a) Hilden, M., Schei, B., Sidenius, K. 'Genito-anal injury in adult victims of sexual assault' *Forensic Sci Int*. 2005; 154(2-3):200–5.
   b) Sturgiss, E.A., Tyson, A., Parekh, V. 'Characteristics of sexual assaults in which adult victims report penetration by a foreign object' *J Forensic Leg Med*. 2010; (17) 140–2.

Anecdotal reports and published small series show that genital injury can occur after consensual intercourse. For example, a UK-based study looked at the frequency of genital injury in women examined within 48 hours, following consensual vaginal intercourse and in allegations of vaginal rape. In the 500 complainants of rape, 114 (22.8%) had a genital injury; and in the 68 women who had consensual intercourse, 4 (5.9%) had a genital injury.[20]

Injury following alleged anal rape

15.23   The latest National Survey of Sexual Attitudes and Lifestyles showed that, within a year, 13–19% of men and women aged 16–44 had anal sexual intercourse.[21]

Following alleged anal rape in women, genito-anal injury is more often recorded, as compared with allegations of vaginal rape.[22] In one study, 38 women alleged anal rape, and 20 (52.6%) had an ano-genital injury.[23]

Research into the prevalence of ano-rectal injury, following anal rape in men, shows a range from 18–39%.[24] However, it must be noted that the study groups were relatively small, and not all men alleging anal rape had a forensic medical examination, which might result in an underestimate.

Again, it is difficult to put these figures into context, as the prevalence of injury in any control group of sexually naïve individuals, or of those engaging in consensual anal intercourse, is not known. Other explanations or causes of injury may be relevant, e.g. constipation, haemorrhoids ('piles') or inflammatory bowel conditions, some of which may be associated with anal fissures.

In summary, clinical forensic practice shows that most body and ano-genital injuries are minor and do not require medical interventions, e.g. admission to hospital or sutures.[25] The absence of ano-genital injuries cannot be interpreted as evidence that the alleged rape or sexual offence did not take place; and, conversely, the presence of an ano-genital injury cannot be interpreted as proof that it did.

Other sources of medical or clinical evidence

15.24   Evidence comes in a variety of forms; in sexual offences, evidence may include the consequences of the sexual act.

20 McLean, I., Roberts, S.A., White, C., Paul, S. 'Female genital injuries resulting from consensual and non-consensual vaginal intercourse' *Forensic Sci Int.* 204 (2011) 27–33.
21 Sexual attitudes and lifestyles in Britain. Natsal3 (www.natsal.ac.uk/media/823260/natsal_findings_final.pdf).
22 Bowyer, L., Dalton, M. 'Female victims of rape and their genital injuries' *Br J Obstet Gynaecol.* 1997; 104(5): 617–20.
23 Hilden, M., Schei, B., Sidenius, K. 'Genito-anal injury in adult victims of sexual assault' *Forensic Sci Int.* 2005; 154(2-3):200–5.
24 a) McLean, I., Balding, V., White, C. 'Forensic medical aspects of male-on-male rape and sexual assault in greater Manchester' *Med Sci Law.* 2004; 44(2): 165–9.
   b) Reeves, I., Jawad, R., Welch, J. 'Risk of undiagnosed infection in men attending a sexual assault referral centre' *Sex Transm Infect.* 2004; 80(6): 524–25.
25 a) Bowyer, L., Dalton, M. 'Female victims of rape and their genital injuries' *Br J Obstet Gynaecol.* 1997; 104(5): 617–20.
   b) Palmer, C.M., McNulty, A.M., D'Este, C., Donovan, B. 'Genital injuries in women reporting sexual assault' *Sexual Health* 2004; 1(1) 55–9.

Pregnancy

15.25   Pregnancy may result from allegations of rape. Dating a pregnancy by means of a positive pregnancy test and an ultrasound scan may allow it to be linked to an allegation, or excluded from any association.

Genetic material may be obtained from the products of conception, if there is a termination of the pregnancy or a miscarriage. At delivery, blood from the umbilical cord or a DNA sample from the infant may be obtained. The genetic evidence may then be compared with that of the alleged assailant as the putative father.[26]

Clearly, such evidence has a greater probative value in those who are deemed unable to consent to intercourse, e.g. children, those who are unconscious or who have a significant learning disability.

Sexually transmitted infections

15.26   Sexually transmitted infections (STIs) may arise following allegations of rape and, in some situations, they may have evidential value. STIs are of greater significance in those who could not have consented to the intercourse, e.g. children, the elderly, or where the allegation involves a type of intercourse which has never occurred before (thus limiting another partner as the source of infection). An example might be of a male who has never had 'receptive' ano-rectal intercourse, who alleges an anal rape, and is later found to have Chlamydia trachomatis or Neisseria gonorrhoeae (N. gonorrhoeae). If the same infection is demonstrable in the alleged assailant (who cannot be compelled to undergo tests for sexually transmitted infections), there may be scope for further tests to see if, for example, both the complainant and alleged assailant have the same strain (serovar) of N. gonorrhoeae.[27] In adults, if the strain is the same, expert advice from a consultant physician in genito-urinary (GU) medicine should be sought about how this should be interpreted. In children, expert advice should be sought, as an assessment will need to be made as to the likelihood of alternative explanations for an infection, e.g. vertical transmission (mother to baby, during pregnancy) or via fomites, inanimate objects, e.g. towels.[28]

26 Faculty of Forensic & Legal Medicine, Association of Chief Police Officers, Forensic Science Service. *Guidance in Criminal Paternity Cases.* 2010. London. http://fflm.ac.uk/upload/documents/1280843586.pdf.

27 a) Rogstad, K., Thomas, A., Forster, G. *et al.* 'UK National Guideline on the management of sexually transmitted Infections and related conditions in children and young people'. London: BASHH, 2010. www.bashh.org/documents/2674.pdf.
b) Royal College of Paediatrics & Child Health (RCPCH) in collaboration with the Royal College of Physicians (RCP) and its Faculty of Forensic & Legal Medicine (FFLM). *The Physical Signs of Child Sexual Abuse*: an evidence-based review and guidance for best practice. London: RCPCH, 2nd edition, 2015.

28 a) Rogstad, K., Thomas, A., Forster, G. *et al.* 'UK National Guideline on the management of sexually transmitted Infections and related conditions in children and young people'. London: BASHH, 2010. www.bashh.org/documents/2674.pdf.
b) Royal College of Paediatrics & Child Health (RCPCH) in collaboration with the Royal College of Physicians (RCP) and its Faculty of Forensic & Legal Medicine (FFLM). *The Physical Signs of Child Sexual Abuse*: an evidence-based review and guidance for best practice. London: RCPCH, 2nd edition, 2015.
c) Kelly, P. 'Childhood gonorrhoea in Auckland' *NZ Med J* 2002 115 (1163).
d) Goodyear-Smith, F. 'What is the evidence for non-sexual transmission of gonorrhoea in children after the neonatal period? A systematic review' *J Forensic Legal Med* 2007 14 (8) 489–502.

By contrast, an allegation of rape from a complainant who suggests that they have never previously had consensual vaginal, oral or anal intercourse may be undermined by the existence of, for example, anal warts or other STIs, although other possible explanations would need to be considered and excluded where possible.

Clinical samples taken with the possibility that they may have evidential value should be done with the same attention to chain of custody procedures and guidance is available to clinicians who may be taking such samples.[29]

Differential diagnoses

15.27   The differential diagnoses of the findings may include:

- Co-incidental causation of injury.
- Self-inflicted injury.
- Co-existing conditions which may mimic or exacerbate a finding.
- Skin appearances which may mimic injury, e.g. birthmarks or naevi, classically 'the Mongolian Blue spot', which may mimic a bruise.
- Congenital abnormalities which may be mistaken for acute or healed injury.
- In a non-acute examination, considering alternative explanations for findings, e.g. a healed peri-anal scar, could be explained by trauma from a fissure due to constipation or infection, not only by sexual assault.

Occasionally, some issues which may lead to confusion can be assisted by reviewing the patient, e.g. what might be thought to be petechial bruising on the roof of the mouth (palate) is still present two to three weeks later, and so is likely explained as pre-existing pigmentation; or what might be a blue/purple, but non-tender, bruise is unchanged on review after two weeks, and so is likely to be a blue naevus.

In relation to genital injuries, if a colposcopic recording has been taken, this can be reviewed by the examining doctor, together with an expert for the defence.

The alleged assailant

15.28   In broad terms, the examination of the alleged assailant will follow similar principles as that of the complainant. The suspect has the same rights of withholding informed consent as any other patient; however, a court may 'draw such inferences from the refusal as appear proper'.[30] It is important for a clinician to explain to a suspect whether they are seeing them as part of an evidence-gathering procedure or as a patient, or both. A detainee has the same right to health care as any other individual, although the same duties of confidentiality may not apply. The detainee should be explicitly informed of this.[31] For further information on the care and examination of detainees, see Chapter 18.

29 Royal College of Pathologists and the Institute of Biomed Science. Guidelines for handling medico-legal specimens and preserving the chain of evidence. London: RCPath, 2008. www.rcpath.org/Resources/RCPath/Migrated%20Resources/Documents/G/G047_ChainOfEvidence_Jul08.pdf.
30 Police and Criminal Evidence Act 1984, s 62.
31 Health care of detainees in police stations, BMA & FFLM 2009 (https://fflm.ac.uk/upload/documents/1236269117.pdf).

Samples

15.29   The principles of sample-taking will be the same, including samples for toxicology; but, whilst the forensic physician may advise what may or may not be appropriate, what is taken is usually the decision of the Senior Investigating Officer (SIO).

For an alleged assailant, obtaining intimate samples requires the sanction of a police officer of at least the rank of Inspector (Police and Criminal Evidence Act 1984, Code C).

A defendant may claim that it was not possible for him to have penetrative sexual intercourse due to pre-existing erectile dysfunction, often termed 'impotence'. This is an area for expert evidence.[32]

Sexual offences in children and young people

Introduction

15.30   The clinical examination of a child or young person (CYP) who has been subject to a sexual offence is often the key focus for social workers and the police. However, important though it may be for the criminal investigation, it is only part of the detailed multidisciplinary assessment of the child and family. Recognition of sexual abuse is analogous to completing a jigsaw puzzle. It is rare that a single physical sign will be diagnostic, but rather that a collection of signs in the context of the history and observation of the child's behaviour lead to a diagnosis. The assessment of the child or young person aims to ensure a holistic examination to identify health needs, provide necessary treatments, start the therapeutic process and contribute to the ongoing safeguarding of the child, as well as collection and recording of forensic evidence. Quality standards have been defined by the Royal College of Paediatrics and Child Health and the Faculty of Forensic & Legal Medicine.[33]

The law

Age of consent

15.31   Consensual activity is lawful for both heterosexual activity and homosexual activity from the age of 16,[34] unless in a position of trust. Under that age, it is not an offence for the pre-16-year-old to have sexual activity, but such sexual activity is not lawful for their partner, no matter what their age. So, two consenting 15-year-olds are *both* actually committing an offence.[35]

---

32 Mostyn, P., Morgan, L. 'Are men with erectile dysfunction able to ejaculate? A survey' *JFLM* 2013; 20(4):239–41.

33 FFLM 2014 quality standards http://fflm.ac.uk/upload/documents/1393326841.pdf; 2012 examination guidance: http://fflm.ac.uk/upload/documents/1352802061.pdf; Royal College of Paediatrics & Child Health: 2009 Service Specification for the Clinical Evaluation of Children & Young People who may have been sexually abused (Draft); Royal College of Paediatrics and Child Health and the Faculty of Forensic and Legal Medicine. Guidelines on Paediatric Forensic Examination in Relation to Possible Child Sexual Abuse, 2007. This most up-to-date version is from 2012; see http://fflm.ac.uk/upload/documents/1352802061.pdf.

34 Sexual Offences (Amendment) Act 2000.

35 Sexual Offences Act 2003, ss 9–13.

Under-13s

15.32   Each of the main four contact offences is replicated in relation to children under 13 years of age. Because an under-13-year-old *cannot*, in law, consent, the prosecution do not have to prove lack of consent or reasonable belief in consent. Section 5 of the Sexual Offences Act 2003 prohibits rape of a child under 13; section 6 refers to sexual assault by penetration of a child under 13; section 7 refers to sexual assault of a child under 13; and section 8 refers to causing or inciting a child under 13 to engage in sexual activity.

These offences are essentially strict liability, in that there is no need for the prosecution to prove lack of consent, or lack of reasonable belief in consent, nor is it a defence to have a reasonable but mistaken belief that the complainant was over 13, even where the offender is under 16 themselves.[36]

There are also additional offences, similar to those under sections 6 to 8, created by sections 9 to 12 of the Act which are specific to those over 18, and can be committed against under-16s and under-13s.

Finally, section 13 creates a catch-all offence for young persons under 18 committing offences against under-16s or under-13s.

The main non-consensual offences, as described above, can, of course, be committed against persons of any age. Offences against under-13s will often be prosecuted under sections 5 to 10 because it is not necessary to prove consent. If the offence is committed by a young adult and there is ostensible consent, that fact will be reflected in sentence (on a sliding scale, according to the age of the offender). Offenders under the age of 18 may be prosecuted under section 13 but remain liable.

The medical assessment

15.33   A medical practitioner called upon to assess a child suspected of being the victim, or the perpetrator, of sexual abuse is duty bound to consider issues other than simply forensic evidence. The assessment of the child or young person aims to ensure a holistic examination to identify health needs, provide necessary treatments, start the therapeutic process and contribute to the ongoing safeguarding of the child, as well as collection and recording of forensic evidence.

The standards for practice in the examination are set out in guidelines published jointly by the Royal College of Paediatrics and Child Health (RCPCH) and the Faculty of Forensic & Legal Medicine (FFLM). These documents give detail on the competencies and qualifications required to examine a child for sexual abuse.[37] Single or joint examinations can be conducted between paediatricians and sexual offence examiners or other practitioners, such as genito-urinary physicians or GPs. Increasingly, examinations of adults who have been sexually assaulted are being

---

36 *R v G* [2008] UKHL 37, [2009] 1 AC 92.

37 Royal College of Paediatrics and Child Health and the Faculty of Forensic & Legal Medicine. Guidelines on Paediatric Forensic Examination in Relation to Possible Child Sexual Abuse, 2012.

carried out by enhanced skilled nurses. For examinations of children and young persons (CYP), practitioners must also demonstrate competencies specific to the assessment of children.

Consent and confidentiality

15.34   The General Medical Council has clear guidance in regard to obtaining consent from children and their carers.[38] This can be particularly challenging in the context of a child or parent with learning disability. In order to obtain informed consent to a procedure or examination from a CYP, their 'Gillick' competence must be established. This is dependent not only on their developmental stage but also on their ability to understand the procedure being undertaken and the possible complications and consequences arising from it. In order for a carer to give consent for the examination, they must have parental responsibility as defined by the Children Act 1989. If a disclosure of sexual abuse is made during the process of the assessment, the doctor has a duty to report this, even though it may breach confidentiality.

A failure to obtain the requisite consent may call into question the validity and robustness of the entire examination.

'Peer review' describes the process of a person(s) of the same ability or expertise providing an impartial evaluation of the work of others. It is increasingly used by medical practitioners working in the field of sexual abuse to obtain consensus on interpretation of physical findings and ensure appropriate evidence-based management as part of continuing professional development. This process is very different from that of obtaining an expert witness review of a case and cannot replace it.[39]

The history and examination

15.35   In order to ensure that the history and examination are comprehensive, it is good practice to use a proforma.[40] If appropriate, the CYP should have the opportunity to speak to the doctor without the carer present. Aspects to history taking which are different in the case of a CYP are given in Box 5. A child's interpretation of events may be very different from an adult's, particularly for a CYP who has not previously been sexually active. For example, a child who states that the perpetrator has 'put a stick up my bottom' may actually have been anally raped. It is important, therefore, to assess the CYP's developmental stage, whether they have learning disability, and confirm previous involvement with social services.

---

38 '0–18 years: Guidance for all doctors' GMC 2007.
39 There is guidance developed by the FFLM and the CPS regarding this; see http://fflm.ac.uk/upload/documents/1396515960.pdf.
40 The Child Protection Companion (RCPCH 2006).

Box 5

Assessment requirements for children and young people
• Obtaining informed consent, taking into account confidentiality issues, competence and parental responsibility.
• Consultation with the child/young person.
• A comprehensive paediatric assessment, including consideration of emotional, psychological welfare and physical development.
• Past medical and family history.
• A general physical examination, including assessment for abuse, neglect and injuries, both old and acute.
• Examination of the genital and anal areas.
• Obtaining forensic samples.
• Pregnancy testing, if required.
• Assessment for STI, including swabs for screening, deferred in acute cases in view of incubation periods and according to local arrangements in the genito-urinary medicine service.
• Plan for immediate healthcare (e.g. emergency contraception, antibiotic and or HIV/ Hepatitis B prophylaxis).
• Recording of the assessment, including (with consent and if appropriate) still or video/DVD/Digital CD ROM photo documentation.
• Comprehensive documentation of all of the above.

Aspects of the history and examination which may increase concern that abuse has occurred include:

• An allegation.

• Ano-genital symptoms which are persistent and associated with emotional changes.

• Genital or anal injury.

Changes in normal routine and behaviour could result from sexual abuse and need to be explored (for example, new bed-wetting, nightmares or truancy from school).

Concerns may be raised if they have sexual knowledge and curiosity inappropriate to their age.

15.36 The examination technique will vary depending on sex and pubertal stage. Detail on examination methods are set out in the 'Purple Book' published in May 2015 by the Royal College of Paediatrics and Child Health.[41] The Purple Book is the review and guideline for best practice and is a revision of the 2008 edition. The handbook focuses on evidence for the physical signs of child sexual abuse in the following areas: female genitalia; male genitalia; anal signs; oral signs; and sexually transmitted infections. It is a vital tool and a standard text for examining health practitioners, and recommended reading for lawyers involved in child sexual abuse cases.

Physical manifestations may change according to the position and technique of the examination. In order to be able to rely on research evidence to support findings, it is vitally important that standard positions and examination techniques are used. There are

---

41 'Physical Signs of Child Sexual Abuse' (or the Purple Book), RCPCH 2015 (www.rcpch.ac.uk/ physical-signs-child-sexual-abuse).

three standard positions for examination of the ano-genital area in girls: supine (frog leg), prone (knee chest) and left lateral (particularly used for examining the anal region).

If signs are observed in other positions, such as supine (knee chest), these need to be confirmed using standard positions.

Similarly, the examiner should clearly state whether separation or traction (the labia majora are held between the thumb and forefinger and gently pulled outwards) has been used. Upwards traction is used to visualise the urethra, and downward traction to visualise the margins of the hymen and fossa navicularis).

15.37 CYP pubertal status influences timing of assessment for acute sexual assault (see Table 1 at **15.15** above).

Pubertal status also changes the appearance of the female genitalia on examination. Under the age of two years, maternal oestrogen may still be present. The hymen may be thick, somewhat convoluted and waxy in appearance. Between two years of age and puberty, the hymen becomes very thin and vascular. During puberty, the hymen enlarges, thickens and becomes more opaque with overlapping redundant tissue. The opening increases in size, although this is not readily apparent, as the thickened hymen covers it more completely. Signs, such as tears, can become hidden within folds, and therefore different techniques are required to visualise the entire rim of the hymen. Again, in order to rely on research, examination techniques need to be adapted according to pubertal stage, as set out in Box 6

Box 6

Pre-pubertal	Pubertal
Always use prone position to check findings in the posterior hymen	Consider use of a damped cotton wool swab to identify the hymenal margin
	Flood the vestibule with sterile water to clarify the hymenal edge
	Foley catheter to reveal injuries in hidden folds
	A speculum can be used in older girls and those who have been sexually active

15.38 Examination under a general anaesthetic may be required to identify the cause of internal bleeding and whether there is a foreign body or vaginal wall damage. A small cystoscope or hysteroscope would be used and photo-documentation made.

When examining younger boys, the foreskin (if present) may not be retractable. As with examination of girls, it is important to understand the changes in male genitalia with age. It is good practice to state the Tanner pubertal stage in the medical notes and any statement.

The anal region would normally be examined in the left lateral position for both genders. Buttock separation is used to assess for tone of the external anal sphincter and inspection of any injuries. Observation should be recorded for at least 30 seconds and any evidence of reflex anal dilatation recorded. Digital examination is unpleasant for the child and generally not helpful. If there is a suspected injury higher up in the anal canal, this should be assessed under a general anaesthetic using a proctoscope.

15.39 In order to identify abnormal findings, the examiner obviously needs to have an understanding of what is normal for the developmental age. Normal genitalia, with labelling of the normal anatomy, are shown in Figure 15.1 for girls and Figures 15.2 and 15.3 for boys. The examiner should comment on the demeanour of the child and note any appearance of anxiety, distress or whether they are withdrawn.

15.40   The evidence base around the significance of abnormal findings is covered in detail in the Purple Book.[42] As previously stated, the majority of findings, on examination for sexual abuse, are non-diagnostic. Some findings give good evidence of abuse. These are detailed in Box 7, along with issues for their identification in practice. See also Box 9 below.

Box 7

Good evidence	Issues for practice
Hymenal findings in pre-pubertal girls	Early examinations are more likely to detect these signs, as they can heal quickly, often leaving no residua
• Hymenal transections	
• Deep clefts/notches of the hymen	
• Hymenal bruising	Measurements of the hymenal orifice diameter vary considerably and are of little use in the diagnosis of sexual abuse
• Hymenal abrasions	
• Laceration/tears of the hymen or posterior fourchette	Measurement of posterior hymenal width is not accurate
• Scars to the hymen or posterior fourchette	Interpretation is aided by follow-up and re-examination for resolution/persistence
• Reduced posterior hymenal tissue	
Anal bruising, lacerations and scars	Forensic and microbiological evidence needs to be supported by chain of evidence procedures and robust laboratory quality control
Presence of semen in the vagina, anal canal or on the external genitalia	
Presence of an STI	

Recording of findings

15.41   Standard notation is detailed in the Purple Book,[43] as well as how to interpret findings, according to the research.

A colposcope is an instrument which allows visualisation of the ano-genital region at a distance, providing a light source and magnification, and with the facility to record both still and moving images of the examination. It is common practice to use a colposcope in the examination of children where sexual abuse is alleged. It is particularly important when single-examiner examinations are conducted. As the child relaxes during the examination, dynamic changes can be seen better on video.

There is detailed guidance on the use of intimate images as evidence at court.[44] The images should be of sufficient quality to support the examination findings. It is good practice for the images to be viewed at the host institution by both the examining doctor and the expert, so that differences of opinion can be explored in advance of the court hearing.

Common pitfalls include over-interpretation of minor signs and inability to appreciate depth in the two-dimensional image provided by a colposcope recording.

---

42 See note 41 above.
43 See note 41 above.
44 'Guidance for best practice for the management of intimate images that may become evidence in court' (FFLM and RCPCH 2010).

Patient's name:
Doctor's name:
Hvn number:
Exhb number:
Date:

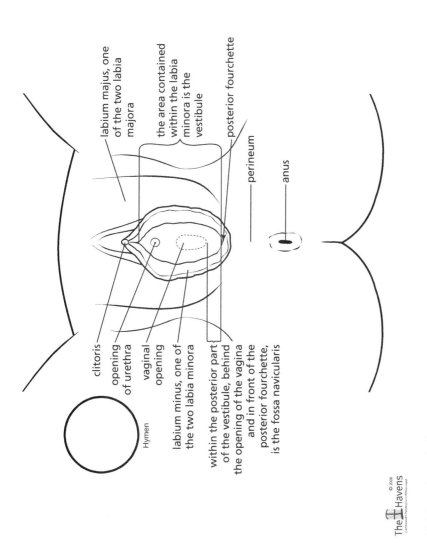

labium majus, one
of the two labia
majora

the area contained
within the labia
minora is the
vestibule

posterior fourchette

perineum

anus

clitoris

opening
of urethra

vaginal
opening

labium minus, one of
the two labia minora

within the posterior part
of the vestibule, behind
the opening of the vagina
and in front of the
posterior fourchette,
is the fossa navicularis

Hymen

The Havens
© 2006

Figure 15.1 Female genitalia. (Reproduced with kind permission of the Haven Clinic.)

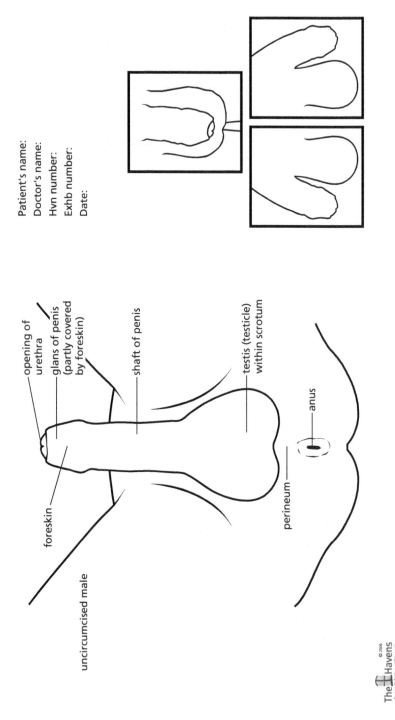

Patient's name:
Doctor's name:
Hvn number:
Exhb number:
Date:

opening of
urethra
glans of penis
(partly covered
by foreskin)

shaft of penis

testis (testicle)
within scrotum

anus

foreskin

perineum

uncircumcised male

The Havens
© 2006

Figure 15.2 Male genitalia (with foreskin). (Reproduced with kind permission of the Haven Clinic.)

Patient's name:
Doctor's name:
Hvn number:
Exhb number:
Date:

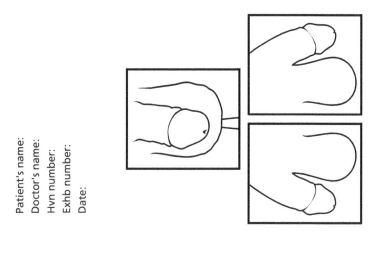

opening of
urethra

glans of
penis

shaft of penis

testis (testicle)
within scrotum

coronal
sulcus

anus

perineum

circumcised male

The Havens
© 2006

Figure 15.3 Male genitalia. (Reproduced with kind permission of the Haven Clinic.)

It is good practice for the examiner also to record their findings on a body map including interpretation.

Follow-up after the initial examination is important to ensure that all the evidence for the case is collected. It is good practice to conduct a 'healing examination', whenever injuries and positive physical findings are found, to confirm if signs have disappeared as a result of healing or are naturally occurring variations.

Investigations

15.42 If forensic samples have been taken, the practitioner should consider the timing and location of the examination and the demands of forensic evidence collection (e.g. whether the location is capable of being forensically cleaned and capable of storing forensic samples). Samples should only be taken by an examiner with the appropriate training. SARCs are forensically clean and have procedures in place for collection and storage.

Testing for sexually transmitted infections (STIs) should be conducted in all cases where abuse is suspected, and in particular when vaginal or anal penetration has occurred. STIs should be considered when the CYP has signs and symptoms consistent with an infection (for example, penile or vaginal discharge, genital ulceration or vulvitis). The presence of an STI may be of medico-legal significance in a pre-pubertal child or a pubertal child who has not been voluntarily sexually active. Newer microbiological techniques can be used to link a perpetrator to a victim when an STI has been detected.

Note that nucleic acid amplification test (NAAT) techniques to identify chlamydia and gonorrhoea are unlicensed for use with oropharyngeal, rectal and genital tract specimens in children. Therefore, their interpretation should be done in collaboration with specialists in the field. The only samples valid for children for such testing are urine and high vaginal swabs (the latter being very invasive, so to be avoided if possible).

As STIs have a lead time before they are detectable, it may be forensically important if a complainant has negative test at baseline (i.e. at the time of the incident/report) and a positive test some time later. Tests for Neisseria gonococcus (GC) and Chlamydia trachomatis (CT) should be repeated at two weeks. Tests for blood-borne viruses (BBVs), such as HIV, hepatitis B and C, and for Syphilis should be conducted at three months after the last exposure or assault.

15.43 Microbiological detection techniques are rapidly changing. The latest information can be obtained from the BASHH Children and Young People guidelines (www.bashh.org.uk). The current recommended testing is outlined in Box 8.

Box 8

Pre-pubertal females
Vulvovaginal swab 1: microscopy and culture for GC, *Trichomonas vaginalis*, Candida, Streptococci
Vulvovaginal swab 2: NAAT for GC and CT
First pass urine for GC and CT NAAT

Pubertal females (using a speculum)
High vaginal swab for microscopy and culture for GC, *Trichomonas vaginalis*, Candida, Streptococci
Endocervical swab 1: microscopy and culture for GC, *Trichomonas vaginalis*, Candida, Streptococci
Endocervical swab 2: NAAT for GC and CT
Vulvaginal swabs if endocervical swabs cannot be obtained
Males
Urethral or meatal swab 1: microscopy and culture for GC
Urethral or meatal swab 2: CT culture if available
First pass urine for GC and CT NAAT

Other sites, such as the oropharynx or anus, should be sampled as indicated by the history. If there are genital blisters or ulcers, viral swabs should be taken for Herpes simplex virus (HSV) PCR. The virus causing genital warts (Human papilloma virus or HPV) can be identified by PCR from histological specimens. HPV typing can be used for evidential purposes in specific cases. Although these infections are not uniquely caused by sexual activity, they may be strong pointers.

Pregnancy testing should be conducted in all pubertal girls where vaginal penetration has been alleged.

Differential diagnoses

15.44   When assessing a child or young person for sexual abuse, certain differential diagnoses should be considered. These are medical conditions which can look similar, on physical examination, to injuries associated with sexual abuse (Box 9).

Box 9

Sexual abuse	Medical condition	Reference
Laceration or transection secondary to penetrative abuse	Accidental genital injury such as a straddle injury, seatbelt injury	Heppenstall-Heger, A. *et al.* (2003)
Usually involves protected areas such as the hymen and posterior fourchette	Normally involves the anterior external genitalia (labia majora, labia minora and the clitoral hood)	
Genital erythema	Vulvovaginitis secondary to nappy dermatitis, Candidiasis and poor hygiene	Adams, J.A. *et al.* (2003)
Recurrent vulvovaginitis or vaginal bleeding secondary to sexual abuse	Group A beta- haemolytic Streptococcal infection	Pokorny, S.F. (1992)
	Coagulation disorder	
	Embryonal rhabdomyosarcoma (rare)	Mogielnicki, N.P. (2000)
Vaginal discharge secondary to a sexually transmitted infection	Vaginal discharge secondary to vulvovaginitis due to poor hygiene or a Group A beta- haemolytic Streptococcal infection	Herman-Giddens, M.E. (1994)
	Presence of a foreign body	

Genital bruising /haemorrhage	Lichen sclerosus et atrophicus Hallmark is the associated white plaques and atrophic friable skin. Typically a 'figure of eight' configuration Haemangioma	Isaac, R., *et al.* (2007)
Urethral bleeding or bruising	Urethral prolapse	Johnson, C.F. (1991)
Anal laceration secondary to sexual abuse	Anal fissure secondary to chronic constipation (often associated with an anal tag)	Pierce, A.M. (2004) Agnarsson, U. *et al.* (1990)

Controversies to consider

15.45   Listed in Box 10 are areas of practice which are controversial or may be subject to variable interpretation.

Box 10

Consent:
- Clear consent should be recorded for the examination and use of photo-documentation (failure may indicate a careless and non-systematic approach).
- Failure to obtain valid consent by a practitioner could constitute an assault.
- The examination is not necessarily for the benefit of the patient but is a vehicle for obtaining evidence for prosecution of the perpetrator.
- An examination can only proceed without consent if providing care is the primary purpose of the examination and if the injuries are life-threatening.

Conduct of the assessment:
- The approach to history-taking during the medical assessment should not jeopardise the ascertaining best evidence interview (ABE) if it has not already taken place. Check leading questions have not been asked.
- Consider carefully the robustness and transparency of the history-taking:
  - Is it systematic?
  - Is the note-taking robust and accurate?
  - Leading questions should always be avoided, particularly if exam is before ABE.
  - Particular risk in very young children and those with learning difficulties. Has sufficient care been taken to consider language and cognitive development?
  - Who had taken the history? Good practice ensures clarity in recording who has given the information (eg Haven centres have a proforma based on the Child Protection Companion).
  - Who had given the history?
- During the examination, anything disclosed by the child may form evidence in court. Disclosures should be documented verbatim.

The examination:

If the child is examined using non-standard methodologies, the findings may be different. Therefore:

- Standard positions must be used for ano-genital examination in order to validate findings; e.g. the finding of a deep notch in the hymen could be called into question if it is seen in a non-standard position, as it may be artefactual.
- The use of techniques such as the dampened swab for inspecting hymenal findings in peri-pubertal girls, and the use of foley catheters for the same purpose in post-pubertal young women, have no evidence base but are in common use by expert practitioners.

Investigations:

- If forensic samples have been taken, consider the location, timing and demands of forensic evidence collection (was the location capable of being forensically cleaned and capable of storing forensic samples?).
- Note that NAAT techniques are unlicensed for use with oropharyngeal, rectal and genital tract specimens in children. Therefore, their interpretation of positive results should be made in collaboration with specialists in the field.
- There should be a chain of evidence for all specimens, including those for STI, pregnancy testing etc taken in the examination context.

Photo-documentation:

- Clear consent must be obtained for photo-documentation, ensuring that the CYP understands who may have access to the images (court, peer review, teaching etc).
- Images taken must be of sufficient quality to be a clear representation of the clinical findings. This can be validated by an expert witness.
- Consider the validity of the history taken from CYP with learning difficulties.
- Ensure that protocol has been followed regarding recording, storage and confidentiality of digital images.

Judgement and opinion:

- Differential diagnosis and non-abuse diagnoses should be included, wherever possible.
- Always remember that there is a clear RCPCH statement that the absence of any ano-genital sign does not exclude the possibility of abuse.

Further reading material

- Adams, J.A., Girardin, B., Faugno, D. 'Adolescent sexual assault: documentation of acute injuries using photo-colposcopy' *J Pediatr Adolesc Gynecol.* 2001 Nov; 14(4):175–80

- Agnarsson, U., Warde, C., McCarthy, G., Evans, N. 'Perianal appearances associated with constipation' *Arch Dis Child.* 1990 Nov; 65(11):1231–4

- Bowyer, L., Dalton, M. 'Female victims of rape and their genital injuries' *Br J Obstet Gynaecol.* 1997; 104(5):617–20

- Brew-Graves, E., Morgan, L. 'Injuries and allegations of oral rape: A retrospective review of patients presenting to a London sexual assault referral centre' *J Forensic Leg Med.* 2015 Aug; 34:155–8

- Goodyear-Smith, F. 'What is the evidence for non-sexual transmission of gonorrhoea in children after the neonatal period? A systematic review' *J Forensic Legal Med* 2007 14 (8) 489–502

- Heppenstall-Heger, A., McConnell, G., Ticson, L., Guerra, L., Lister, J., Zaragoza, T. 'Healing patterns in anogenital injuries: a longitudinal study of injuries associated with sexual abuse, accidental injuries, or genital surgery in the preadolescent child' *Pediatrics* 2003 Oct; 112(4):829–37

- Herman-Giddens, M.E. 'Vaginal foreign bodies and child sexual abuse' *Arch Pediatr Adolesc Med.* 1994 Feb; 148(2):195–200

- Hilden, M., Schei, B., Sidenius, K. 'Genito-anal injury in adult victims of sexual assault' *Forensic Sci Int.* 2005; 154(2-3):200–5

- Isaac, R., Lyn, M., Triggs, N. 'Lichen sclerosus in the differential diagnosis of suspected child abuse cases' *Pediatr Emerg Care.* 2007 Jul; 23(7):482–5

- Johnson, C.F. 'Prolapse of the urethra: confusion of clinical and anatomic characteristics with sexual abuse' *Pediatrics* 1991 May; 87(5):722–5

- Kelly, P. 'Childhood gonorrhoea in Auckland' *NZ Med J* 2002 115 (1163)

- Kerr, E., Cottee, C., Chowdhury Hawkins, R., Jawad, R., Welch, J. 'The Haven: a pilot referral centre in London for cases of serious sexual assault' *BJOG*, March 2003; 110: 267–71

- McLean, I., Balding, V., White, C. 'Forensic medical aspects of male-on-male rape and sexual assault in greater Manchester' *Med Sci Law.* 2004; 44(2): 165–9

- McLean, I., Roberts, S.A., White, C., Paul, S. 'Female genital injuries resulting from consensual and non-consensual vaginal intercourse' *Forensic Sci Int.* 204 (2011) 27–33

- Mogielnicki, N.P., Schwartzman, J.D., Elliott, J.A. 'Perineal group A streptococcal disease in a pediatric practice' *Pediatrics* 2000 Aug; 106(2 Pt 1):276–81

- Morgan, L., Brittain, B., Welch, J. 'Multiple perpetrators sexual assault. How does it differ from single perpetrator assault?' *J Interpers Violence* 2012 27(12); 2415–36

- Morgan, L., Dill, A., Welch, J. 'Sexual assault in post-menopausal women: a retrospective review' *Br J Obstet Gynaecol.* 2011; 118:832–43

- Mostyn, P., Morgan, L. 'Are men with erectile dysfunction able to ejaculate? A survey' *JFLM* 2013; 20(4):239–41

- Palmer, C.M., McNulty, A.M., D'Este, C., Donovan, B. 'Genital injuries in women reporting sexual assault' *Sexual Health* 2004; 1(1) 55–9

- Pierce, A.M. 'Anal fissures and anal scars in anal abuse – are they significant?' *Pediatr Surg Int.* 2004 May; 20(5):334–8. Epub 2004 Jun 24

- Pokorny, S.F. 'Prepubertal vulvovaginopathies' *Obstet Gynecol Clin North Am.* 1992 Mar; 19(1):39–58

- Reeves, I., Jawad, R., Welch, J. 'Risk of undiagnosed infection in men attending a sexual assault referral centre' *Sex Transm Infect.* 2004; 80(6): 524–25

- Schlesinger, S.L., Borbotsina, J., O'Neill, L. 'Petechial hemorrhages of the soft palate secondary to fellatio' *Oral Surg Oral Med Oral Pathol.* 1975; 40(3):376–8

- Sturgiss, E.A., Tyson, A., Parekh, V. 'Characteristics of sexual assaults in which adult victims report penetration by a foreign object' *J Forensic Leg Med.* 2010; (17) 140–2

- White, C., McLean, I. 'Adolescent complainant of sexual assault; injury patterns in virgin and non-virgin groups' *J Clin Forensic Med*, 2006; 13: 172–80

- Worsaae, N., Wanscher, B. 'Oral injury caused by fellatio' *Acta Derm Venereol.* 1978; 58(2):187–8

Chapter 16

Forensic odontology

With Catherine Adams

Introduction

16.1 Forensic odontology (dentistry) expert opinion should be provided by a registered dental surgeon, with additional postgraduate training in providing such opinions for the court. The areas in which a forensic odontologist may assist the court are: identification of human remains; bite mark analysis and comparison; and, in some cases, aiding with human age estimation. However, there exists controversy in the areas of bite mark analysis and dental age estimation, and this is briefly discussed later in the chapter.

Dental identification, on the other hand, is recognised by INTERPOL as one of the primary identifying techniques for disaster victim identification, by comparing and analysing post-mortem and ante-mortem dental features, in order to provide assistance in achieving the dignity of a name for the deceased. Identification of the deceased – whether of an individual or multiple bodies – is an important standard of a civilised society, and dental identification has long been regarded as reliable and accurate.

It is important that legal professionals have an understanding of the human dentition as a basis for understanding cases that involve forensic dental evidence.

Basic dental anatomy

16.2 Human teeth are essentially made up of mineralised tissue surrounding the central pulp of teeth, as follows:

- The dental crown of a tooth is the part of the tooth that, when erupted, is visible in the mouth and is involved in biting and mastication. The roots of teeth are underneath the gingiva (gum), and they anchor the tooth in its socket within the jawbone.

- Enamel is 96–98% mineralised, making it the hardest tissue in the human body, and it is the outermost layer of the dental crown.

- Dentine lies beneath the enamel of the dental crown and the cementum on the root of the tooth.

- Cementum is the outermost layer of the root of the tooth.

- The dental pulp is the innermost part of the tooth and consists of a pulp chamber in the centre of the dental crown and pulp canals travelling through the tooth root/s. The pulp tissue contains neurovascular bundles, neural receptors, lymphatics and connective tissue.

All teeth have their own morphology, and there are differences between species. Human anterior teeth (incisors and canines) are single-rooted teeth, whereas the posterior teeth (pre-molars and molars) are multi-rooted. Single-rooted and multi-rooted teeth with convergent roots are easily lost (as a result of decomposition of the soft tissues securing them into tooth sockets, or trauma), and care should be taken to search thoroughly for these teeth at a scene, and they should be given to the forensic odontologist rather than replaced by anyone else into any available sockets. The forensic odontologist is an expert in tooth morphology and will be able to replace the teeth in their correct positions. This is particularly important when photographic comparison of the anterior tooth features may be used to supplement the ante-mortem dental record information for identification purposes.

16.3   The child human dentition (deciduous dentition) consists of 20 teeth, and the adult human dentition (permanent dentition) consists of 32 teeth (see Figures 16.1 and 16.2).

Deciduous Teeth

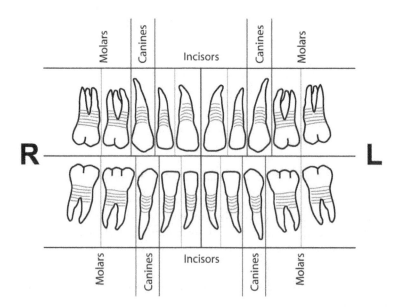

Figure 16.1 Deciduous dentition. (Courtesy of Ruth Bowen, Medical Illustrator, Cardiff University.)

Permanent Teeth

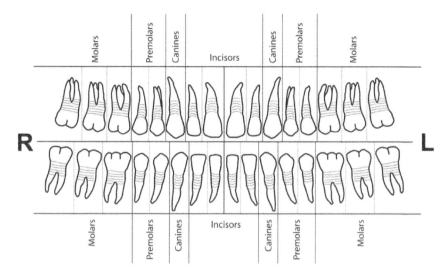

Figure 16.2 Permanent dentition. (Courtesy of Ruth Bowen, Medical Illustrator, Cardiff University.)

16.4 The deciduous dentition differs from the permanent dentition in the following ways (adapted from *Oral Anatomy, Histology and Embryology*):

- Deciduous teeth are smaller and the dental arches are smaller.

- Deciduous teeth have a greater constancy of shape.

- The crowns of deciduous teeth appear bulbous.

- The enamel of deciduous teeth bulges at the cervical margin of the tooth rather than gently tapering.

- The cusps of newly erupted deciduous teeth are more pointed than corresponding permanent teeth.

- Crowns of deciduous teeth have less enamel than permanent teeth and appear whiter.

- The roots of deciduous teeth are shorter and less robust.

- The roots of deciduous incisors and canines are longer in proportion than permanent incisors and canines.

- The roots of deciduous molars are widely divergent and extend beyond the dimensions of the crown.

- The pulp chambers of deciduous teeth are proportionally larger than permanent tooth chambers.

- The root canals of deciduous teeth are very fine.

16.5 The human dentition develops sequentially (see Figures 16.3 and 16.4), but the timings may be variable within a population and even between the same dental phenotype in an individual. Generally, the crowns of the deciduous dentition start to mineralise before birth, and tooth eruption begins between six months and three years of age. Full root development is normally complete approximately one year after eruption of the crown of the tooth. At six years of age, the deciduous dentition begins to exfoliate, beginning with the incisor teeth and then progressively around the mouth, until, by the age of 12, all the deciduous dentition will have been lost and replaced by the succeeding permanent dentition. The age of 12 is an important consideration when related to human bite mark analysis as, legally, a child is defined as under 18 years of age but, dentally, a child above the age of approximately 12 may have an adult (permanent) dentition. Finally, by the age of 18–23, the third molars (wisdom teeth) will most likely be fully developed and, if there is room, will have erupted into the mouth. Often, there is not sufficient room for the wisdom teeth (and sometimes other teeth) to erupt into the mouth, even though they are fully formed, and this is referred to as the teeth being 'impacted'. Complete root development of permanent teeth normally occurs two to three years after eruption into the mouth of the dental crown.

16.6 In 2009, AlQahtani produced an updated, illustrated atlas of tooth development and eruption that may be used in conjunction with radiographs of the developing dentition. An example of an orthopantomogram (OPT) is shown in

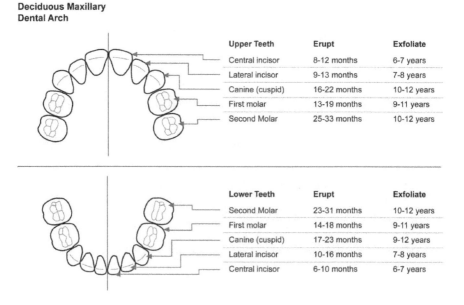

Deciduous Maxillary Dental Arch

Upper Teeth	Erupt	Exfoliate
Central incisor	8-12 months	6-7 years
Lateral incisor	9-13 months	7-8 years
Canine (cuspid)	16-22 months	10-12 years
First molar	13-19 months	9-11 years
Second Molar	25-33 months	10-12 years

Lower Teeth	Erupt	Exfoliate
Second Molar	23-31 months	10-12 years
First molar	14-18 months	9-11 years
Canine (cuspid)	17-23 months	9-12 years
Lateral incisor	10-16 months	7-8 years
Central incisor	6-10 months	6-7 years

Deciduous Mandibular Dental Arch

Figure 16.3 Sequence and timing of human deciduous tooth eruption. (Courtesy of Ruth Bowen, Medical Illustrator, Cardiff University.)

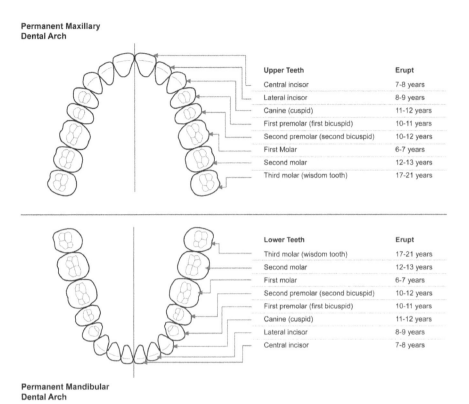

Permanent Maxillary
Dental Arch

Upper Teeth	Erupt
Central incisor	7-8 years
Lateral incisor	8-9 years
Canine (cuspid)	11-12 years
First premolar (first bicuspid)	10-11 years
Second premolar (second bicuspid)	10-12 years
First Molar	6-7 years
Second molar	12-13 years
Third molar (wisdom tooth)	17-21 years

Lower Teeth	Erupt
Third molar (wisdom tooth)	17-21 years
Second molar	12-13 years
First molar	6-7 years
Second premolar (second bicuspid)	10-12 years
First premolar (first bicuspid)	10-11 years
Canine (cuspid)	11-12 years
Lateral incisor	8-9 years
Central incisor	7-8 years

Permanent Mandibular
Dental Arch

Figure 16.4 Sequence and timing of human permanent tooth eruption. (Courtesy of Ruth Bowen, Medical Illustrator, Cardiff University.)

Figure 16.5. It is a clear and useful aid to determining biological age at death of neonates and children up to the age of full dental development. Adult dental ageing past the completion of dental development is a complex matter, and the variation of results is considerably wider than those for younger age groups. For adult ageing, the removal of a tooth for histological quantification of age-related deposition of sclerotic dentine, or amino-acid racemisation biochemical analysis, is necessary. This clearly has issues, as the removed tooth tissue is often destroyed, and so the coroner's permission is required.

Dental identification of the deceased

16.7   Teeth are the hardest tissue in the human body and are capable of withstanding biological, chemical and thermal insult better than any other part of the body. This makes the human dentition an invaluable resource as a means of identifying the deceased in single or multiple events, particularly where there has been extensive body disruption. Dental identification provides a quick, economic and reliable method, provided that ante-mortem dental records are available for comparison. Due to their resilience to insult, teeth are also invaluable as a source of DNA when the body decomposition is so advanced that soft tissue and bone samples are unreliable (Pretty, 2007).

Dental identification is recognised by INTERPOL as one of the primary methods of disaster victim identification (DVI). Noteworthy examples where dental identification proved particularly valuable, in a mass fatality situation, include: the Lockerbie air disaster (1988); the Asian tsunami (2004); the London bombings (2005); the Dhow boat disaster (2006); and the Christchurch earthquake (2011).

Forensic odontology contributes to identification by way of comparison and reconstruction methods (Pretty and Sweet, 2001). Ultimately, identification will rely on comparison between post-mortem dental examination and ante-mortem dental records. However, when records are not initially available, such as when there is no putative name for an individual, characteristics of the oro-dental structures may be used to indicate age, sex, medical or dental history etc.

16.8   Dental post-mortem and ante-mortem dental record examination will detail the following:

- Fillings – crown or root, number, shape, position and material.

- Fixed prosthodontics – crowns, bridges, implants.

- Dentures – full or partial, and material.

- Orthodontic appliances.

- Missing teeth – extracted or developmental.

- Congenital/developmental anomalies – supernumerary teeth, microdontia, hypoplasia, retained deciduous teeth.

- Anatomical features – root and pulp morphology, position of the inferior alveolar canal and mental foramen, shape of the maxillary sinus floor in relation to the roots of the upper teeth, bony trabeculae.

- Oral pathology – caries, periodontal disease, retained roots, cysts, periapical or periodontal cysts, bone pathology.

The value of dental radiographs cannot be over-emphasised (see Figure 16.5). Dental fillings are now often recorded as covering whole surfaces of the tooth on digital and written records whereas, in the past, it was commonplace for the shape of the filling to be drawn on records. Not all identifying information will be seen on the crown of the tooth, such as root morphology, anatomical relationships, pathology and any iatrogenic features that are not visible to the naked eye (for example, the shape of the floors of any fillings made by the dentist's drill, pin retainers, root fillings and implants).

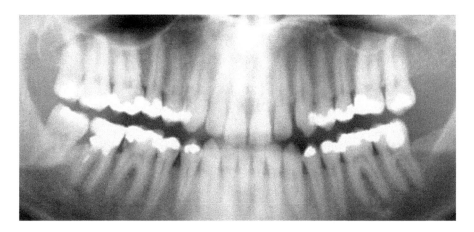

Figure 16.5 Orthopantomogram radiograph of an adult human showing the morphology of the permanent dentition, anatomical relationships, dental restorations and root fillings.

Retrieval of dental records

16.9   Ante-mortem dental records may include all recorded information, including handwritten and/or digital clinical information, dental and/or facial radiographs, clinical photographs and dental models, and possibly also specific information from relatives and friends. Commonly, it is the handwritten or digital clinical information, dental radiographs and an ante-mortem smiling photograph that are most readily available.

Features of the dentition may contribute to either the comparison or reconstructive methods, depending upon the quality of the ante-mortem dental records and photographs available. There are some circumstances where ante-mortem smiling photographs may be of tremendous help in comparing post-mortem dental findings, such as discolouration or missing (and malformed or misaligned) anterior teeth. This information may have been recorded on the dental records, but experience shows that this is not always the case. However, it is becoming more common, with the advent of digital software for record keeping by dentists, to take images of the dentition; and there will be dental images taken if the deceased has had orthodontic treatment, for example, or other aesthetic dentistry procedures, such as crown and bridge work or tooth whitening or dental implants, at a specialist practice or as a hospital referral.

16.10   Once a putative identification of an individual is obtained, it is normally the Coroner's Officer, Family Liaison Officer (FLO) or police officer who is tasked with obtaining the ante-mortem dental records, and the standard operating procedure recommended by the British Association for Forensic Odontology DVI team for obtaining these records is shown below:

(1)   Immediate contact with lead odontologist to join team that is managing and co-ordinating procedure.

(2)   When a dental practice is visited, the FLO should try to speak to the dentist, or at least the practice manager, rather than the receptionist or nurse.

(3)   All ORIGINAL records should be provided, regardless of date – if the records are computerised, they should be printed in colour (often, computerised records have a colour coding denoting the treatment done) and any X-rays or photographs copied onto CD. If the records have treatment that is colour coded, the key of explanation should also be printed.

(4)   Please make sure that contact details for the dentist providing the records are clearly recorded and provided with the records to the odontologist.

(5)   Dental records are anything produced by a dental professional (dentist, dental hygienist, dental therapist) or doctor in relation to examination and/or treatment of teeth or jaws; and may be in the form of written examination records, X-rays, photographs, dental models, treatment plans, and clinical investigation results. ALL records should be collected, even if they are not recent.

(6)   Dental treatment means anything seen by a dentist:

   –   Dental examination, scaling (seen by hygienist), fillings, crowns, bridges, dentures, fractured teeth, extractions, bleaching, cosmetic dentistry.

   –   Includes tooth extraction under an anaesthetic in a hospital or local specialist practices providing sedation or general anaesthetic.

   –   Includes dental assessment for patients with medical problems or being treated for medical problems, e.g. heart disease, clotting disorders, complex illnesses, cancer etc.

   –   Includes tooth straightening (orthodontics).

   –   Includes facial and jaw trauma, e.g. in an accident or assault, so hospital records may be very helpful.

(7)   Ask relatives and friends if they know whether or not the missing person has had any dental treatment, and if they know where it was provided and by whom.

(8)   Ask relatives and schools if missing person saw the school dentist or community dental service.

(9)   Ask colleagues at school, at college or at workplace if they know if missing person had been seen by a dentist and/or had any dental treatment.

(10)   Check on whether the missing person has been seen in a hospital following an accident or facial injury. X-rays may have been taken.

(11)   If the answer is 'yes', the following need to be approached:

   –   General dental practice (NHS and private). Check, if necessary, with NHS Dental Services in Eastbourne (NHS patients) and the Scottish and Northern Irish equivalents.

   –   Dental hospitals – Cardiff, Bristol, Birmingham, Kings, Guys, Royal London (London), Newcastle, Manchester, Sheffield, Liverpool, Glasgow, Edinburgh, Dundee.

- Hospital (non-dental) with dental units / Oral and Maxillofacial departments / Orthodontic departments / Restorative departments.

- Community Dental Services. These treat children, and people with physical or mental disorders, and provide emergency care.

- Employers (e.g. Boots, Marks and Spencer) who may provide dental care for their employees.

- The Armed Forces.

- Dental Access units on street corners or any emergency treatment centres.

- DENPLAN – offices at Winchester, tel 0800 328 3223. They will have a database of patients paying direct debits to DENPLAN, and this should link to date of birth and who the dentist is.

- PRACTICE PLAN – similar to above, tel 01691 677966.

- Primary Health Care Trusts in each region. These will have lists of dentists in the area and will manage primary dental care and emergency dental treatment.

(12)   It is the responsibility of the Forensic Odontologist alone to fill in the details in F1 and F2 forms. Please resist the temptation to allow the deceased's dentist, dental nurse, practice manager, receptionist, or even yourselves to fill in the details.

Post-mortem dental examination

16.11   Dental examination of the deceased should be carried out before comparison with ante-mortem dental records is undertaken. There are circumstances, however, when information from ante-mortem dental records indicating unusual dental features may be useful to expedite the process of reconciliation in a DVI scenario with a limited number of bodies.

Ante-mortem dental records

16.12   Forensic odontologists are comprehensively involved throughout the identification process. To avoid unnecessary confusion and misinformation, it is advisable that the odontologist be contacted at the initial stages of any identification process where it is thought that a dental identification may be possible.

   Although it is preferable for the ante-mortem dental records to be contemporaneous, this is not essential, and neither is it essential that obvious dental work is present. A lot of dental fillings are tooth coloured, and excellent quality of restorative work may make it difficult for non-dentists to identify that any is present. The presence or absence of dental restorations does not preclude a dental identification, particularly if radiographs are available for comparison and there have been recent extractions.

Dental reconciliation

16.13 The dental reconciliation process is the process undertaken by the odontologist of comparing the information obtained in the post-mortem clinical dental examination with that contained in the original ante-mortem dental records. After legal ratification by the coroner (or equivalent), the deceased may be repatriated to their loved ones.

There is an accepted range of conclusions available to the coroner (or equivalent) in human identification, namely:

- Insufficient information – there is insufficient information to enable a comparison to be undertaken.

- Exclusion – the post-mortem examination and ante-mortem dental records show irreconcilable differences, such that the individual concerned cannot be that person.

- Possible – there are features that are comparable between the post-mortem examination and ante-mortem dental records, but either the post-mortem remains are fragmented and incomplete, or the ante-mortem dental records are lacking in information such that confirmation of ID cannot be established.

- Probable – there are no irreconcilable discrepancies between the post-mortem examination and the ante-mortem dental records, but there may only be a fragment of mandible or maxilla with a few teeth, or the ante-mortem records are a few years old.

- Established – there is complete correlation between the post-mortem examination and ante-mortem dental records, such that identity may be confirmed.

The odontologist will compare all the information and determine if there are any discrepancies; and, if there are discrepancies, whether they are explainable on the grounds of expected dental deterioration (if the records are old), expected treatment (due to evidence of referral for specialist treatment) or human error in the records.

Young children often will not necessarily have dental records and, if they do, the changes due to tooth eruption mean that the dentition may change rapidly. However, as mentioned previously, tooth development is sequential and may be extremely helpful in ageing the deceased child and contributing information to other identification specialities as a secondary identifier.

16.14 Where there are no ante-mortem dental records available, facial mapping techniques may be employed by appropriately trained odontologists as a secondary identification method. These techniques compare facial anatomical points and teeth, utilising anthropometric measurements and relative proportions, or photographic superimposition of an ante-mortem smiling photograph with an equivalently positioned post-mortem facial photograph. Although these techniques have been accepted by the criminal court and used to establish identity (*R v Rosemary Pauline West*, 1996), they are generally accepted as more valuable to exclude or provide a possible identification. An additional identification method may then be used to establish an identity.

Bite mark analysis and comparison

16.15   Human bite marks occur in a minority of forensic investigations, usually as a result of human beings biting one another offensively or defensively. Mostly, cases involve violent crimes, such as assault, rape, murder, manslaughter and child abuse. Occasionally, bite marks may be observed in food stuffs or other inanimate objects.

MacDonald (1994) defined a bite mark as 'a mark caused by the teeth alone or in combination with other mouth parts'. Human bites on skin may be important features in establishing contact between the dentition of the biter and the skin of the recipient. Bites do not, however, establish that other injuries or contact necessarily occurred, and they do not prove intent.

Typical bite mark appearances

16.16   A human bite mark typically consists of a circle or oval of two opposing arcades of small impact marks due to the biting surfaces of the teeth. These normally make up an overall oval shape, with gaps at the base (widest part) of the arcades. Normally, each of the arcades is made up of six separate marks representing four incisor and two canine teeth. However, there may be an extra tooth mark or teeth marks or missing teeth.

The impact marks may be distinguished from one another and may cause injuries in the form of bruises, lacerations, abrasions, puncture wounds or a combination of the aforementioned. In the centre of the arcades, there may be a reddened area of petechial haemorrhage (spot bleeding/ bruising) that may be caused by sucking, tongue thrusting or the bunching up of soft tissue between the arcades of teeth. It is not known what the precise mechanism of this spot bleeding or bruising is, and whether it is an effect of pushing down on or pulling up of the tissue between the arcades of teeth (i.e. may be positive or negative pressure involved).

In a bite made by adult (permanent) teeth, the distance across an arcade of upper teeth (i.e. canine to canine tooth) is typically over approximately 2.5cm to 4cm; in a bite made with baby/child (deciduous) teeth, it may be approximately 2cm up to 3cm. These are approximate dimensions and it is not sufficient to rely purely on inter-canine distance to determine adult and child teeth. Other features, such as dimensions of individual marks and pattern of the marks, also need to be taken into consideration. It is often difficult to distinguish between a dentition under the age of 12 years and that of a person over the age of 12 years.

Taking into account many factors – such as the shape of the surface on which a bite mark is inflicted, underlying structures, medical conditions, the age of the injury etc. – any given bite mark may have all or some of these features present.

Bite mark analysis

16.17   Bite mark analysis is not an empirical science. It relies on the opinion of experienced experts comparing the pattern of marks on, for example, skin with the arrangement of the dentition of a possible suspect. The field of bite mark analysis is controversial.

Skin is well recognised as being an imprecise impression medium and, consequently, it is not often possible to safely attribute marks to an individual perpetrator. There is a body of opinion that believes that bite mark analysis may only reliably be able to come to a 'possible biter' conclusion as far as identifying an individual perpetrator is concerned, and there is no literature available that can reliably quantify the presence of dental anomalies in the general population. It is believed by some practitioners (including the author) that it may be possible, in a few circumstances, to achieve a higher level of conclusion within a known pool of possible perpetrators. These caveats are essential for the court to keep in mind when considering bite mark analysis evidence (Bush, 2011).

In essence, bite mark analysis is the comparison of a pattern of marks with the dentition of an individual to determine if his/her teeth may have features that are comparable or not with the features observable in the marks. The analysis relies ideally on clinical examination of the marks and examination of photographs of the marks, taken with a rigid right-angled scale according to a standard protocol (British Association for Forensic Odontology, 2005), which requires experience and expertise. This analysis may reveal important information relating to features within the arrangement of the marks. Clinical examination findings, photographs and impressions of a suspect's dentition are then compared with the pattern of the marks, if appropriate. Overlays of the suspect dentition's dental models (using either transparent acetates or appropriate software) are then used to compare more fully with the marks at the same magnification. When the marks are diffuse bruising only, it may be unnecessary to undertake overlay comparison if there is insufficient evidence to compare.

16.18   There is a professionally accepted protocol for bite mark analysis imaging compiled by the British Association for Forensic Odontology (BAFO) (2005). This protocol should be used as a guide for bite mark analysis, as it is recognised as best practice in the UK and is based on the American Board of Forensic Odontology (ABFO) equivalent. The BAFO protocol may be found at www.bafo.org.uk. Ideally, for maximum evidence gathering, the photographs need to be taken as soon as possible. But, when there is an injury that requires medical attention, the evidence available is often reduced as a result of needing to prioritise treatment required.

Injuries, such as bite marks on the human body, present many problems in interpretation due to distortion of the tissues occurring as a natural physiological process at the site of the injury, body position, and also as a result of difficulty in accurately imaging these injuries for reliable analysis.

Conclusion levels available for bite mark analysis adopted by the American Board of Forensic odontology and accepted by the British Association for Forensic Odontology (2005):

- 'Exclusion': the injury is not a bite mark.

- 'Possible': an injury showing a pattern that may or may not have been caused by teeth; the injury may have been caused by other factors but biting cannot be ruled out.

- 'Probable': the pattern of the injury strongly suggests or supports an origin from teeth but could conceivably be caused by something else.

- 'Definite': there is no reasonable doubt that teeth created the injury.

Conclusions available when describing the results of bite mark comparison with an individual (according to BAFO (2005) protocol):

- 'Excluded': there are discrepancies between the bite mark and the suspect's dentition that exclude the individual from having made the mark.

- 'Inconclusive': there is insufficient forensic detail or evidence to draw any conclusion on the link between the suspect's dentition and the bite mark injury.

- 'Possible biter': teeth like those of the suspect could be expected to create a mark like the one examined but so could other dentitions.

- 'Probable biter': the suspect most likely made the bite; most people in the population would not leave such a mark.

- 'Beyond reasonable doubt': the suspect is identified for all practical purposes by the mark. Any expert with similar training and experience, evaluating the case evidence, should come to the same conclusion.

Dental age estimation of the living

16.19   Knowledge of your age is a basic human right (UNICEF, 1989). To know one's age is required for many things in life, such as going to school, work, getting married and getting a pension. It is also fundamental to enabling the provision of appropriate justice. The knowledge of age protects victims and offenders and enables the justice system to deal with them rightfully according to their age. It is known that between 30% and 50% of the 50 million live births each year are not recorded (Unisex, 2012). Dental age estimation is an estimation of a biological age as opposed to the chronological age of an individual.

Many methods of dental age assessment have been developed throughout the years. There are difficulties with some of these methods as, sometimes, there is no discrimination between male and female, and the pool of people investigated may be very small. There are also controversies between academic groups as to whether or not there is a difference between ethnic groups, but it is generally thought that any differences are merely biological (Liversidge and Marsden, 2010).

Dental age assessment of the living requires that dental radiographs are taken, and there are unresolved issues relating to the fact that this would mean irradiating an individual for no clinical benefit. However, there are those who believe that this is acceptable, as the risk related to radiation exposure is outweighed by the benefit to the individual and/or society as a whole. At present, dental age estimation is not often used.

Further reading material

- Adams, C., Carabott, R. and Evans, S. *Forensic Odontology – An Essential Guide* (2014, Wiley Blackwell)

- Pretty, I.A. 'Forensic dentistry: 1. Identification of human remains' *Dental Update*. 2007; 334(10): 621–2, 624–6, 629–30 passim

- Nanci, A. *Ten Cate's Oral Histology – Development, Structure and Function* (2007, 7th Edition, Mosby)

- Berkovitz, B.K.B., Holland, G.R. and Moxham, B.J. *Oral Anatomy, Histology and Embryology* (2009, 4th Edition, Mosby Elsevier), pp. 13–14

- AlQahtani, S.J. *Atlas of tooth development and eruption* (2009) www.dentistry. qml.ac.uk/atlas of tooth development and eruption/index.html

- INTERPOL (2009) www.interpol.int/INTERPOL-expertise/Forensics/DVI

- Pretty, I.A. and Sweet, D. 'A look at forensic dentistry – Part 1: The role of teeth in the determination of human identity' *British Dental Journal* 2001 Apr 14; 190(7): 359–66. Review

- *R v Rosemary Pauline West* (1996) LTL C0004000

- Bush, Mary A. 'Forensic Dentistry and Bitemark Analysis: Sound Science or Junk Science? A Guest Editorial' *JADA* 142(9), Sept 2011, 997–999

- MacDonald, D.G. 'Bite mark recognition and interpretation' *Journal of the Forensic Science Society* 1974; 14: 229–233

- www.BAFO.org.uk

- www.ABFO.org

- UNICEF (1989) 'Convention on the rights of the child', available from www. unicef.org/crc

- UNICEF (2012) 'Fact sheets: birth registration', available from www.unicef. org/newline/2003/03fsbirthregistration.htm

- Liversidge, H.M. & Marsden, P.H. 'Estimating age and the likelihood of having attained 18 years of age using mandibular third molars' *British Dental Journal* 2010; 209(8): E13

Chapter 17

Forensic toxicology

With Simon Elliott

Principles of forensic toxicology

17.1   The role of the forensic toxicologist lies in the detection, identification and measurement of drugs and poisons in human biological materials and its subsequent interpretation. This differs from that of the clinical toxicologist, who recognises poisoning from the symptoms and specialises in the care and maintenance of the poisoned patient. Both require knowledge of the physiological action of the drug or poison: the latter for the care of the patient, and the former to assist the forensic toxicologist and the court with the interpretation of the results.

The involvement of drugs or poisons may not always be immediately obvious to investigators and can often be regarded as an 'invisible weapon'. Even in instances where there is significant evidence to suggest that the ingestion of drugs has occurred, the exact drug (or, more usually, drugs) may not be known. Furthermore, even if a drug has been detected, the interpretation of its presence or amount can depend on many factors.

Legal aspects

17.2   The science of toxicology being used in court is most commonly in relation to road traffic offences. The current relevant United Kingdom legislation is contained in the Road Traffic Act 1988, as amended by the Road Traffic Act 1991.[1] This is dealt with in Chapter 10. Section 11(2) of the 1988 Act defines the prescribed limits as 35 micrograms of alcohol per 100 millilitres of breath, 80 milligrams of alcohol per 100 millilitres of blood, and 107 milligrams of alcohol per 100 millilitres of urine.[2]

The case law on this aspect of road traffic offending is gargantuan and complex, so cannot be sufficiently summarised here. Interested readers should examine the various legal texts on the subject.[3] Legislation also applies to other modes of transportation, such as aircraft and railways.

---

1   For Northern Ireland, the Road Traffic (Northern Ireland) Order 1995 and the Road Traffic Offenders (Northern Ireland) Order 1996.
2   Article 13(2) of the Road Traffic (Northern Ireland) Order 1995.
3   See, for example, *Wilkinson's Road Traffic Offences*, Sweet & Maxwell, Kevin McCormac; Peter Wallis (new edition due October 2015); *Stone's Justices' Manual* (published annually by Butterworths); Andrew Brown, *Wheatley's Road Traffic Law in Scotland* (Bloomsbury Professional, 2014); CPS website (www.cps.gov.uk/legal/p_to_r/road_traffic_offences).

17.3   In addition, the malevolent administering of drugs and poisons to others may result in offences relating to death and serious injury (outlined in Chapter 7), and there are also offences particular to drugs, poisons and noxious substances. For example, section 22 of the Offences against the Person Act 1861 prohibits the administering of chloroform, laudanum or any other stupefying or overpowering drug with the intent to commit any indictable offence and has a maximum sentence of life imprisonment. Sections 23–35 of the same Act relate to various offences prohibiting the administering of poison or noxious substance so as to endanger life or injure.[4]

17.4   Other medico-legal considerations of toxicology include:

- State of mind. Voluntarily and involuntary intoxication may lead to a person having available, at the most extreme level, the defence of insanity,[5] being unable to form specific intent, diminished responsibility (in chronic cases) and automatism. Further reading is suggested on these topics.[6]

- State of intoxication for other reasons:

  – Back calculations of alcohol levels and analysis of drug use will often be relevant in sudden death cases in both criminal and civil jurisdictions.

  – Similarly, such calculations and analysis may be relevant to both prosecution and defence in relation to the intoxication of complainant and defendant.

  – Whether a detainee was fit for detention or interview could, potentially, be ascertained by toxicology.

- Whether a sudden death is due to deliberate voluntary ingestion of drugs to induce suicide, or whether it is by misadventure, may depend on the quantity of drug/alcohol taken, where back calculations and post-mortem redistribution may be relevant.

- Medical reasons for behaviour which might be misinterpreted as evidence of drunkenness or drug use, such as head injury or disorders of carbohydrate metabolism, e.g. diabetes mellitus.

- Metabolism issues which might undermine back calculations or in relation to the post-driving drinking defence (that the alcohol level was above the prescribed limit because of alcohol consumed after the accused stopped driving: Road Traffic Offenders Act 1988, s 15(3)).

- Medical reasons for the 'reasonable excuse' defence for a failure to provide specimens of blood, urine or breath under section 7(6) of the Road Traffic Act 1988 (such as asthma, phobias or prostatic hypertrophy), but note that the courts impose strict limits on this (*R v Lennard* [1973] RTR 252).

---

4   'Drugging' in Scotland: see, for instance, Pamela R Ferguson and Claire McDiarmid, *Scots Criminal Law: A Critical Analysis* (2014, Edinburgh University Press) at 10.15–10.16. Section 11 of the Sexual Offences (Scotland) Act 2009 also prohibits administering a substance for sexual purposes.

5   Although see *R v Coley; R v McGhee; R v Harris* [2013] Crim LR 923, CA.

6   See, for example, Archbold, *Criminal Evidence Pleading and Practice*, chapter 17.

- Medical or other reasons for artefact levels of alcohol in breath or blood (e.g. syphoning of petrol, mouth alcohol from recent drinking, alcohol in throat sprays, lip salves etc usually eliminated within about 20 minutes); the significance of alcoholic atmosphere has been discounted (Mason 1972).

- Special reasons to avoid disqualification (such as drink lacing).

An overview

17.5   A 'drug' can be described as any substance, natural or synthetic, which has a physiological action on a living body. Drugs not made in the body can also be called xenobiotics and can be introduced into the body via different routes (e.g. oral ingestion, inhalation, injection).

If producing toxic effects at a particular dose, drugs can also act as poisons (as described below). Drug action usually occurs through interaction with particular molecules in the biological system, called receptors. Depending on the effect, mode and mechanism of action, drugs can be placed into different classes. Classification can also depend on the chemical structure and nature of the drug. For example, amitriptyline is part of a family of related compounds called tricyclic anti-depressants (based on structure and effect, respectively). Conversely, there can be many drugs with similar actions (e.g. anticonvulsants, used in the treatment of epilepsy or 'fits') but with very different structures (e.g. valproic acid and carbamazepine).

Pharmaceutical medicines are drugs used in the cure, prevention or treatment of disease. However, other drugs (including pharmaceutical medicines) are illicitly used, abused or misused, usually to produce a pleasant effect which endears them to the user. Use for a non-medical effect terms such substances as 'drugs of abuse'.

17.6   A 'metabolite' is the compound produced after the corresponding parent compound (e.g. the original drug ingested) has undergone a particular chemical change. Foreign and potentially toxic compounds introduced into the human body may not be easily excreted and may remain in the system for a long period of time, possibly with toxic effects. The process of biotransformation converts a foreign compound into a metabolite which is more readily excretable via the kidneys, hence reducing the potential for toxicity. In some cases, however, the metabolite itself may be toxic (e.g. acetaldehyde from ethanol) or may also be active in the body; this has also led some metabolites to be synthesised and used as drugs in their own right (e.g. desloratadine for hay fever). The metabolism of a compound principally occurs in the liver, usually as a multi-stage process, where the parent compound is converted to another compound which is converted again, etc. As such, a parent compound can have one or many metabolites, but there are usually only a few main metabolites. In casework, if a parent drug is present in biological fluid (e.g. urine or blood) but with little or no metabolite, this can suggest recent use prior to the sample being collected (including post-mortem samples).

Poison

17.7   The term 'poison', through popular usage, indicates a substance which, when ingested in small amounts, destroys life or impairs health. To the lay person, it suggests a limited range of substances that, by and large, have gained the reputation of being poisons through past use. Such popular or historical poisons include arsenic, cyanide and strychnine.

A better definition of a poison is a substance which, when taken by any route, has a deleterious action on the body. This definition sets no boundaries on the types of substance involved, the quantities ingested or the route of entry to the body. Far from limiting his or her field of expertise, it dictates that the toxicologist's ability as an analyst must be comprehensive, since practically all substances are poisons when taken into the body in sufficient amounts. There are, for example, many reports of water poisoning resulting from the excessive intake of water.

In practice, the type and range of poisons encountered are determined largely by the availability of the necessary materials. The poisons available in the United Kingdom are mostly illicit drugs, medicinal drugs, alcohol, volatile substances (e.g. butane), and household and garden chemicals. Exposure to gases (in particular, carbon monoxide) is also possible. Chemicals such as solvents have to be considered in an industrial environment; industrial pesticides and herbicides would be included in an agricultural area.

Poisoning can be seen, from the medico-legal viewpoint, as being of two main types – that affecting large sections of the community, and that involving individuals only. Industrial poisoning is an example of the former, whereas examples of the latter type include accidental, iatrogenic, suicidal or homicidal poisoning.

- A 'drug' is any substance, natural or synthetic, which has a physiological action on a living body.

- A 'metabolite' is the compound produced after the parent compound (the drug) has undergone chemical change.

- A 'poison' is a substance which, when taken by any route, has a deleterious action on the body.

Key concepts

Half-life

17.8   The half-life of a drug is the time that it takes for the blood concentration of a drug to halve. The half-life is very variable between drugs and also between individuals. Furthermore, particular disease states can affect the usual mechanisms of drug elimination (e.g. liver and renal disease).

Post-mortem redistribution

17.9   As the name implies, this phenomenon applies to samples recovered after death. The basic concept is that drugs diffuse or migrate from areas within the body that are at a high concentration to those at a low concentration. Invariably, the concentrations are higher in solid organs, the gastro-intestinal tract and the bladder, and lower in blood; and therefore redistribution usually results in elevated, even so-called 'fatal', blood levels.

The susceptibility of each drug to redistribution is highly variable: some drugs, such as fentanyl, can be dramatically elevated; whereas others, such as morphine, are less affected. Metabolites of drugs are also susceptible to redistribution. Although it is recognised that some drugs are more susceptible, the extent of redistribution is not constant, and therefore this knowledge cannot be used to back calculate or estimate the level at the point of death.

In an attempt to alleviate the effect of redistribution, sampling of blood from the peripheral vasculature is recommended, as these sites demonstrate the least extent of redistribution. This is most commonly from the femoral vein (situated in the groin).

Dependence/tolerance/withdrawal

17.10   Drug dependence is defined by the WHO International Classification of Disease 10 (ICD-10) as being the presence of three of more signs from:[7]

- a strong desire or sense of compulsion to take the substance;

- difficulties in controlling substance-taking behaviour in terms of its onset, termination, or levels of use;

- a physiological withdrawal state when substance use has ceased or been reduced, as evidenced by: the characteristic withdrawal syndrome for the substance; or use of the same (or a closely related) substance with the intention of relieving or avoiding withdrawal symptoms;

- evidence of tolerance, such that increased doses of the psychoactive substances are required in order to achieve effects originally produced by lower doses (clear examples of this are found in alcohol- and opiate-dependent individuals who may take daily doses sufficient to incapacitate or kill non-tolerant users);

- progressive neglect of alternative pleasures or interests because of psychoactive substance use, increased amount of time necessary to obtain or take the substance or to recover from its effects; and

- persisting with substance use despite clear evidence of overtly harmful consequences, such as harm to the liver through excessive drinking, depressive mood states consequent to periods of heavy substance use, or drug-related impairment of cognitive functioning; efforts should be made to determine that the user was actually, or could be expected to be, aware of the nature and extent of the harm.

In dependence, issues of tolerance and withdrawal are highlighted and these concepts are frequently encountered in post-mortem toxicology. In relation to tolerance, there is no post-mortem test that can be utilised to assess someone's

---

7   See www.who.int/substance_abuse/terminology/ICD10ClinicalDiagnosis.pdf.

tolerance; and, in cases where toxicity is considered, the diagnosis of it must be made on the basis of a combination of toxicological data, circumstantial evidence and in light of other post-mortem findings. Tolerance is also relatively rapidly lost; a classic example is the recently released prisoner, who uses a 'normal dose' but a loss of tolerance results in death.

Interactions

17.11 A common misconception is that drugs act in isolation. In reality, drugs interact with each other and their potential effects are often heightened when taken in combination. This is more straightforward to comprehend for drugs that act in the same manner (e.g. opioid drugs and other central nervous system depressants). However, enhanced interactions arise in the context of drugs that operate in opposing means. For example, the mixing of cocaine (or amphetamine) and heroin together, which is known as a 'speedball', is particularly toxic.

- The 'half-life' of a drug is the time that it takes for the blood concentration of a drug to halve.

- 'Post-mortem redistribution' is the effect of concentrations of drugs changing after death, due to movement of drugs from one site or structure to another.

- Dependence, tolerance and withdrawal are consequences of habitual drug (even prescribed) use.

- Drugs do not act in isolation.

Samples

17.12 In the case of the living, appropriate specimens are generally blood and urine. Hair and nail clippings can be used to determine chronic exposure. These specimens are utilised to detect past usage of drugs in order to prove compliance with prescribed medication or abstinence from drug abuse over a period of months.

Post-mortem samples can, in addition, include vitreous humour, bile, portions of liver, kidney, lung and brain, and the contents of stomach or intestine. The retention and use of these specimens is more controlled following the introduction of the Human Tissue Act 2004; but, in the main, samples related to either coronial or criminal investigation (retained under the Police and Criminal Evidence Act 1984) are excluded (certainly initially) from the auspices of the Act.

Blood and urine samples

17.13 Such samples should be clearly labelled as to the site of origin. Blood should be taken from the periphery of the body (e.g. femoral vein) using appropriate methods, usually by direct puncture with a needle and syringe so as to minimise the effect of post-mortem redistribution of drugs (see above).

Urine should be obtained preferably by direct puncture of the bladder to avoid contamination.

The blood and urine specimens should be divided into two clean containers. One set should be preserved with adequate (greater than 1%) sodium fluoride (for both blood and urine), and the other set should be free of preservatives (plain/unpreserved). The fluoride preservative is used to prevent the formation of ethanol should the specimens be contaminated with yeast or bacteria.

Other samples

17.14   Tissue samples collected in secure glass or plastic containers should be packaged in clean, sealed and properly labelled evidence bags; hair and nail samples for trace element analysis can also be packaged in folded paper in clean evidence bags for delivery to the laboratory.

Hair analysis

17.15   For drug analysis, about a pencil thickness of hair should be plucked (post-mortem) or cut (post-mortem or in life) from the vertex of the scalp, wrapped and secured into a bundle (e.g. in aluminium foil) with a clear indication of the 'root' end, and placed in an envelope prior to being placed in an evidence bag. Each centimetre of hair represents approximately one month's growth.

Brain, lung and liver

17.16   Due to the limited number of analytical procedures that can be used for brain, lung or liver, it is unusual for a large portion or a whole organ to be required for any of these tissues. Therefore, an appropriate portion for each that fits into a 20 ml glass universal can suffice. If multiple tissues are submitted, separate containers must be used. A portion of the right lobe of the liver can be taken, since it should be uncontaminated with bile and less affected by drug diffusion from the stomach. For lung tissue, a portion of the apex of the lung can be taken, since it should be less influenced by proximity to the liver (compared to the lower regions of the lung).

As the liver continually processes the metabolism of drugs, it generally provides a more historic view of drug use and cannot be used on its own for determining very recent ingestion (requires blood analysis). Better recovery of drugs from tissue (especially the liver) requires the use of proteinase enzymes (e.g. subtilisin) to break down the tissue prior to analysis. Much of the literature regarding liver concentrations is older and involves homogenisation (mashing) of the tissue, with resultant lower recovery of drugs. This makes comparison of results with existing data difficult and less appropriate.

The brain and lung are particularly required in cases of volatile substances (e.g. lighter fluid – butane and propane) as they provide the best opportunity to detect these volatile gases which can easily evaporate after collection. Due to the short action and volatile nature, such substances are very rarely detectable in blood after death.

In all cases, specimens should be kept cool and transported to the laboratory as quickly as possible. Frozen specimens are not usually required; freezing and thawing can cause drug stability issues or can crack containers, but freezing tissues or specimens may be of particular benefit in cases of solvent abuse.

Analysis of medication/tablets/substance

17.17   Unless there is any doubt as to the identity of medication/tablets found, direct analysis of these is not normally required, and the name of the medication can be recorded. However, items can be submitted to the laboratory if analysis is required (e.g. to identify possible 'fake' or counterfeit medication or unknown items).

Maggot analysis

17.18   A further 'seized item' that has been popularised by television forensic programmes is the potential analysis of maggots found on and in decomposing bodies. The concept involves the consumption of any drugs present in the deceased's body by the feeding maggots. Analysis is possible, to some extent, but interpretation can be difficult.

Information

17.19   For appropriate and complete chain of evidence, records must be kept of the handling of the specimens, from collection, delivery to the laboratory and any return to the police. Continuity of samples is essential, requiring signatures of all involved, as well as date, time and place.

The information required by the laboratory, for administrative and particularly for interpretative purposes, comprises:

- Details of the deceased or individual, including name, sex and date of birth.

- Relevant medical history, particularly with regard to prescribed medication or other drugs accessible (including that of family, if appropriate).

- Details of the names and dosage (if known or applicable) of the substances thought to be involved.

- Circumstances surrounding the death or incident, including date/time of occurrence if known.

- For deaths, a copy of the pathologist's preliminary report indicating the likely cause of death or any observations of the organs (e.g. kidney and liver features).

- Details of the type of specimens obtained and the specific site of anatomical collection if post-mortem.

For in-life specimens, exact date and time of collection should be stated.

- In-life specimens are typically blood and urine; at post-mortem examination, more varied specimens are obtained.

- Hair and nails can be analysed to identify evidence of chronic exposure.

- Solid organs, such as brain and lung, are useful in solvent identification.

- The specimens should be appropriately collected (especially post-mortem) and appropriately stored.

- Adequate information should be provided to the toxicologist.

Analysis of specimens

17.20   Following specimen selection and collection, analytical toxicology is used to detect, or exclude, drugs or poisons. The use of inappropriate techniques can result in the misidentification of a drug or may not be able to detect certain substances important to the case. Inaccurate analysis of a specimen will result in incorrect measurement of the concentrations present. Interpretation relies on the analytical results, and so problems or errors during analysis will have a significant impact on the meaning. Ultimately, interpretation is only as good as the analytical findings that it is based on, so it is imperative that appropriate detection (screening) and accurate measurement (quantitation) of drugs has been undertaken.

17.21   The analysis of a biological specimen for a compound has four steps: the substance must be isolated from the biological matrix; it must be detected; it must be identified; and, if appropriate, the quantity present must be measured. The first problem is isolating a substance that may or may not be present in very low amounts in the sample. An extraction procedure that recovers most of the substance, contaminated with as little co-extractable biological material as possible, is required. The analytical steps are designed to make the substance as insoluble as possible in the biological material and as amenable as possible to the extraction procedure. In the case of volatile solvents, such as alcohol and solvents, simply warming aliquots of material in a closed vial causes sufficient solvent to escape into the vapour above the sample for the analysis to be made (headspace analysis).

Most analysis is carried out for drug substances. This is the area where terminology causes greatest confusion for the non-scientist. The analytical toxicologist is primarily interested in that property of the drug that can be used in its isolation. As a result, drugs are classified as acids, neutrals, bases, amphoterics (which behave as acid or base) or water soluble (such as quaternary ammonium compounds).

17.22   Most medications prescribed today, as well as many drugs of abuse (e.g. amphetamines, cocaine, methadone), are bases, but drugs exhibiting other chemical properties should also be included in any analysis.

Whilst an analytical request may include a particular interest in, for example, analgesics, such a classification is based on the pharmacological action of the drug and not drug chemistry which would provide a wider coverage of analysis. Specifically, analysis for chemically basic, neutral and acidic drugs would include the extraction and detection of many narcotics, hypnotics, anticonvulsants, antidepressants, tranquillisers, etc. Similarly, sample extraction for the opioid, methadone (a chemically basic drug), would still extract the anti-depressant, amitriptyline (another chemically basic drug), but the detection and identification may be tailored to one or both drugs, allowing 'targeted' or 'non-targeted/general' drug screening.

The advantage of a targeted system is usually sensitivity (i.e. a lower concentration can be detected), but the analysis will only detect those drugs that it is 'targeting'. Whereas, although a non-targeted technique will detect a far greater range of drugs, it may only detect them at higher concentrations. This analytical method selection is particularly important in determining case strategy.

Drug recoveries are generally high and reproducible, and the procedure can be automated. However, problems can occur when using whole blood and, particularly, highly viscous or clotted post-mortem blood; otherwise, if incorrect volumes are used, this may reduce the likelihood of drug detection during screening or can result in inaccurate measured concentrations during quantification. In these instances, prior to analysis, the sample will need preparation or dilution.

17.23 This guide is by no means comprehensive. It outlines the initial steps necessary to produce an extract of the biological materials that can then be concentrated and used for further analysis. The extracts produced may be impure and contain co-extractable biological materials, such as lipids, from which the drug must be separated. Extraction processes may change one drug to another or may destroy it completely (e.g. if using the wrong pH buffer or inappropriate solvent). Alternatively, materials (artefacts) similar to drugs may be fabricated or observed, such as putrefactants (e.g. phenylethylamine and tryptamine), that can interfere with drug identification and measurement, especially if not separated by chromatographic analysis. Ultimately, it is the forensic toxicologist's job to be aware of this and to proceed accordingly, and the toxicologist acting for the defendant needs to ensure that the appropriate considerations have been made.

- The analysis of a biological specimen involves isolation, detection, identification and quantification.

- The nature of the drug to be tested affects the means by which it can be identified.

- In the majority of specimens, the process can be automated.

- Analysis for a drug may be hampered by artefacts including difficulties with extraction, alterations in the chemical structure and the presence of chemically similar drugs.

Techniques

17.24 The following section provides an overview of the different techniques involved in analysing a specimen.

Chromatography

17.25 The most common and appropriate technique in toxicology involves chromatography (meaning separation). Once extracted from the biological fluid, this is used to separate the component drugs and metabolites from each other and compounds in the matrix (i.e. present in the blood). Historically, paper or thin layer chromatography (TLC) was used, but nowadays it is general practice for separation to be achieved by gases (e.g. helium) or liquid (e.g. acetonitrile or methanol solvent) flowing through a separating tube (called a column).

Within the column are specific chemical groups bound either to the column itself (e.g. long, thin glass tube for gas chromatography, GC) or small beads (e.g. stainless steel tube for liquid chromatography, LC). When a certain temperature (for gas chromatography) or solvent (for liquid chromatography) condition is reached, the interactions keeping the drug/compound bound are broken or disrupted, and the drug/compound is released to flow along and out of the column (elution).

The carrier gas or liquid sweeps the sample extract through the column, where the packing material retards its progress. As a result, components of samples (e.g. drugs, metabolites, compounds and other extract components) are retarded to different degrees and are thereby separated; they emerge from the column at various times after injection (retention time).

As a component emerges from the column, it passes through a detector, which causes an electrical signal to be generated; this signal is amplified and displayed on a strip chart recorder. Examples of detection systems are nitrogen-phosphorus detection (for compounds containing either of these atoms), flame-ionisation detection (primarily used for volatile substances), and mass spectrometry.

The amount of component that passes through the detector determines the size of area of the peak, and this measurement of area can be calibrated to measure the quantity of drug in the extract.

Comprehensive tables of relative retention times for drugs sought under standard conditions have been compiled and are consulted for the initial identification of a drug. The initial separation method determines part of the name of the technique (e.g. GC or LC), and the detection method determines the hyphenated second part of the name (e.g. DAD or MS).

Gas chromatography

17.26   Gas chromatography is most commonly used in the laboratory for the detection and measurement of alcohol in blood samples. Other instruments with different columns and detectors are set to measure drugs, solvents, gases and pesticides. The technique is specific, in that it will separate a drug from its metabolites and measure each individually, but it is constrained by the availability and scope of reference tables of retention data.

High-performance liquid chromatography

17.27   The main advantage of this procedure over gas chromatography lies in its ability to separate chemically polar or thermolabile compounds and components that are not volatile. Sample preparation can be minimal and may involve no more than the precipitation of proteins. Also, the separated components can be collected for further analyses since the technique is non-destructive. Although, due to their chemical nature, the procedure is not amenable to some groups of drugs for which the use of gas chromatography is appropriate, the technique has replaced and improved many of the analyses formerly carried out by gas chromatography.

Mass spectrometry

17.28   The mass spectrometer can be used on its own or coupled to either a gas chromatograph or a high-pressure liquid chromatograph. The instrument functions by bombarding the unknown drugs with a stream of electrons that cause the drug to break down reproducibly into charged fragments. Separating and measuring the mass to charge ratio of these fragments results in a unique pattern for the drug. It can be used to identify the drug by comparison with a library of drug spectra. If no matches are found, a skilled spectroscopist can still identify the chemical formula of each fragment and slowly piece together possible structures for the unknown.

Furthermore, an increasingly used detection technique is accurate mass spectrometry based on time of flight (TOF) or Fourier transform methodology. Accurate mass spectrometry (also known as high-resolution MS, HRMS) can be coupled to GC or LC systems to introduce analytes to the ionisation source. The cost of equipment is often higher than traditional GC-MS or LC-MS systems but can provide sensitive and selective detection for a very wide range of compounds, with the additional ability to retrospectively re-interrogate data for potential compounds without re-analysis.

There are issues, however, if the empirical formula of two drugs is the same, as this results in identical accurate mass values. In this instance, retention time separation would be needed to distinguish between the two drugs, or utilisation of accurate mass fragmentation by introducing collision energy.

Ultraviolet spectrometry

17.29 Just as the eye can differentiate between coloured dyes in daylight, the ultraviolet spectrometer can record the 'colour' of the drugs in the ultraviolet region of the spectrum. The ultraviolet spectrometer sequentially shines different wavelengths of ultraviolet light through a solution of the drug, and measures and plots the amount of light absorbed.

This plot is an instrumental look at the 'colour' of the drug in the ultraviolet region and is a useful, non-destructive analytical aid. The overall 'shape' of the absorbance can be plotted across the range of wavelengths (e.g. 200 to 600 nm) and is called an ultraviolet spectrum. This can be compared against libraries of ultraviolet spectra for various compounds, to enable identification.

The presence and possible identity of a drug can be indicated when the crude extract is dissolved in acid, alkali or ethanol. However, the identification is not always absolute, since drugs of similar molecular structure can produce very similar (and, in some situations, identical) spectra. Metabolites of drugs can also have spectra identical to those of the parent drug, which in some circumstances can be an advantage, allowing the presumptive detection of metabolites related to a particular drug or drug class. Therefore, although ultraviolet spectrometers can be used as stand-alone instruments for detection and, sometimes, quantification of drugs (e.g. salicylate), it is common practice to couple ultraviolet detectors (particularly diode-array detectors) with high-performance liquid chromatographs to separate the components of an extract. This enables the use of a secondary method of identification (retention time), which can provide more confidence to the analyst – as does the coupling of chromatography with other detection systems (e.g. gas chromatography with mass spectrometry).

Immunoassays

17.30 Radio-immunoassays and enzyme-multiplied immunoassays are techniques that make use of the body's immune response to foreign proteins. Antibodies can be obtained from a host animal that has been injected with a foreign protein to which the drug of interest has been linked. The antibody will recognise and bind itself to the drug molecule in a solution, and this binding has been used as the basis of both techniques.

The techniques are sensitive, they require small sample volumes, and they are relatively rapid. Unfortunately, they are not totally specific, due to the structural similarity of drugs within the same class type. For example, an antibody raised to recognise morphine will cross-react, to a greater or lesser extent, with the other opiate drugs. An antibody raised to recognise diazepam will cross-react with other benzodiazepines. Also, an antibody raised to recognise amphetamine will cross-react with the putrefactant phenyl-2-ethylamine, which is structurally related to amphetamine, and will give a 'false positive' which is common in post-mortem casework. As a result, these assays, although useful and highly acceptable in the clinical laboratory, have to be treated with caution for evidential purposes. Without preliminary separations, they are best used in the laboratory as presumptive tests for the presence or absence of a group of drugs, with subsequent confirmation by a specific (e.g. chromatographic) method, as described above.

Alcohol

17.31   The main social significance of alcohol rests on its being a drug of dependence. Heavy drinking is strongly correlative with ill-health and death. Alcohol is a central nervous system depressant. Since it is the highest and the most recently evolved brain functions that are first affected by depressants, the immediate effect of a dose of alcohol is to inhibit those cerebral functions that are associated with orderly community behaviour and with finer critical judgements; an illusion of cerebral stimulation is thus established, with few physical ill-effects. Chronic alcoholism, however, almost inevitably leads to physical and social problems.

Physiology of alcohol

Alcohol absorption

17.32   Alcohol (ethanol) is absorbed from the stomach and, more importantly, from the small intestine. This is by a process of diffusion. The rate of absorption and its transfer to the blood stream is variable, dependent on a number of internal and external factors – for example, the stronger the alcoholic drink, the faster the rate of absorption. If the stomach empties unduly fast, as in post-bypass surgical operations, the rate of absorption is increased by, in effect, its earlier presence in the small intestine.

At the same time, alcohol retained in the stomach is degraded by the gastric enzyme alcohol dehydrogenase, and this accounts for the commonly observed 'sobering' effect of a full stomach.

As a result, between 90% and 98% of consumed alcohol is typically absorbed; and, once absorbed, the alcohol is dissolved in the body water and is distributed according to the water content of the tissues. Blood contains relatively more solid material than, say, the cerebrospinal fluid, and so will contains less alcohol per volume as a result.

Elimination of alcohol

17.33   The greater part of the absorbed alcohol is destroyed by the liver through the action of the hepatic alcohol dehydrogenase. This converts it into acetaldehyde, and it is this chemical that is, in part, responsible for the 'hangover'. Acetaldehyde is then converted via aldehyde dehydrogenase into acetate, which in turn is converted, through a number of steps, into water and carbon dioxide.

Between 2% and 10% of alcohol is excreted in the urine, sweat and breath.

The combined effect of destruction and elimination is to reduce the blood alcohol by an amount that is variously estimated but which can, for practical purposes, be estimated – based on a recent review of the literature – as being equivalent to 13.3 mg/ 100 ml blood per hour (±2.9 S.D.) for men and 15.1 mg/100 ml blood per hour (±2.02 S.D.) for women. This, however, can only be regarded as most likely figures; in practice, the metabolic rates for individuals can vary within relatively uncertain limits. From the lawyer's point of view, it is convenient to accept these as lying between 9 and 29 mg alcohol/100 ml blood/hour, with an average rate of 19 mg alcohol/100 ml blood/hour. Various factors affect the elimination rate. There is a genetic component relating to variations in the phenotype of the hepatic alcoholic dehydrogenase, but non-genetic factors (such as obesity and the extent of prior exposure to alcohol) may affect it.

Jones has provided a best practice range (Jones). He has suggested that elimination rates could be grouped into slow, moderate, rapid and ultra-rapid, and the groupings are highlighted in the table below:

	Expected rate (mg/100 ml/hour)	Individuals
Slow	8–12	Malnourished. Liver cirrhosis with portal hypertension.
Moderate	12–15	'Healthy individuals'.
Rapid	15–25	'Regular drinkers'. Individuals who consumed high levels of alcohol which activates alternative enzymes to eliminate alcohol.
Ultra-rapid	25–35	'Alcoholics' with chronic heavy drinking.

Auto-generation of alcohol

17.34   Mention should be made of the possibility of endogenous production of alcohol during life; the so-called 'auto-brewery syndrome'. Theoretically, bacteria which produce alcohol during putrefaction should be able to do the same thing in the bowel. The formed alcohol could then pass into the bloodstream. The liver would be able to deal effectively with the small amounts involved, and no researcher has ever claimed a natural production equivalent of more than about 3 mg/100 ml blood, with a more typical range being suggested of between 0 and 0.08 mg/100 ml (Logan BK, 2000).

- Between 90% and 98% of consumed alcohol is typically absorbed, and the rate of absorption is affected by a number of internal and external factors.

- The majority of the absorbed alcohol is destroyed by a liver enzyme.

- The elimination rate is typically between 9 and 29 mg alcohol/l00 ml blood/hour, with an average rate of 19 mg alcohol/100 ml blood/hour.

- Auto-generation of alcohol is suggested to be at levels of between 0 and 0.08 mg/100 ml.

The clinical effects of alcohol

17.35   The central nervous system-depressant effects of alcohol (broadly) correlate with blood alcohol concentration and, therefore, the amount consumed. Tolerance to alcohol through alcoholism/habitual intoxication will modify the relative effect, and a level that would kill a rare consumer of alcohol may barely be noticed by a hardened alcoholic. The effects are summarised simply in the table below, but it is important to appreciate that these are very generic and dependent on an individual's tolerance amongst other factors.

10–100 mg/100 ml	Loss of self-control, an increase in self-confidence, talkativeness and alterations in judgement.
100–200 mg/100 ml	Distinct loss of skill, slurring of speech and commencing loss of co-ordination.
200–300 mg/100 ml	Loss of equilibrium, decrease in pain sense, marked disturbances in vision.
300–400 mg/100 ml	Increasing dissociation, stupor and probably coma.
400+ mg/100 ml	Coma (with its attendant hazards, such as hypothermia) and possible death.

The 'symptoms' and effects of alcohol intoxication are more significant during the period when the blood alcohol level is rising, rather than at its peak or when it is falling. This in part accounts for the false feeling of sobriety the morning after.

The important concept of withdrawal is covered earlier in this chapter and in Chapter 18.

Long-standing alcohol misuse and natural disease

17.36   The consequences of alcoholism principally result in natural disease processes to the central nervous, cardiovascular and gastro-intestinal systems, although these are often associated with effects of neglect and malnutrition predisposing to infection, including tuberculosis.

Liver damage

17.37   The classical pathology relates to changes associated with the liver. In its early stages, this is associated with accumulation of fat within the liver cells. This is not specific to alcohol misuse, but in itself is suggestive. In due course, fibrosis or scarring commences, and regenerating nodules of liver tissue result in cirrhosis. As a result of cirrhosis, an increase in the portal venous pressure (the vasculature taking blood from the gastro-intestinal system to the liver) arises, and this results in the enlargement of the spleen and the formation of varices (most commonly at the gastro-oesophageal junction). Varices are blood vessels that have enlarged as a consequence of the portal hypertension. They are thin walled and tortuous and so are vulnerable to rupture, with resulting catastrophic bleeding.

Pancreatitis (inflammation of the pancreas)

17.38   This is a common occurrence and can be fatal if sufficiently severe (and acute). With chronicity, the pancreatic tissue is replaced by fibrous (scar) tissue, and chronic pancreatitis arises.

Gastritis

17.39   Gastritis is inflammation/damage to the mucosa (lining) of the stomach. Bleeding may be evident in the mucosa of the stomach lining – so-called 'alcoholic gastritis', which can give rise to massive gastro-intestinal haemorrhage.

Central nervous system effects

17.40   Alcohol has several metabolic effects on the central nervous system. Deficiency of thiamine (vitamin B1) due to malnutrition leads to Wernicke's encephalopathy (the mid part of the brain and mammillary bodies degenerate). Signs and symptoms include memory loss and unsteadiness.

   Alcohol misuse in itself is associated with cerebral atrophy as a result of loss of water from the brain tissue as well as damage to nerve cells. This is sometimes reversible. Central pontine myelinosis is a rare condition, most frequently associated with chronic alcohol misuse secondary to electrolyte imbalances, and is frequently fatal. It is the result of degeneration to the central structures in the brain stem.

The heart

17.41   The heart muscle is vulnerable to the effects of alcohol misuse, although there is some degree of protective effect against atherosclerosis (furring of the coronary arteries). The morphology of alcohol-related heart disease is of a cardiomyopathy (see also Chapter 6), with dilatation of the heart chambers and 'flabbiness' of the muscle. Alcohol intoxication and alcoholism are also associated with the development of arrhythmias, particularly prolongation of the QT interval (i.e. elongation of the length of time between the QRS complex and T wave on the electrocardiogram (ECG)).

Sudden death in alcoholics

17.42   There exists a group of alcoholics who seem to die suddenly without obvious cause. The individual is invariably a middle-aged male with low to moderate levels of alcohol in his system and fatty change to his liver. The mechanism associated with this death is unclear but is considered most likely due to arrhythmia. These deaths are classified as 'sudden unexpected death in alcohol misuse' (Templeton, 2009).

17.43   A further potentially fatal complication of ethanol use can be alcoholic ketoacidosis (AKA). Continued ethanol intake results in dehydration (through urination and vomiting), poor nutrition and reduced glucose. This causes the body to shift its fuel pathway, utilising fatty acids to produce an increase in ketone bodies such as acetone, acetoacetate and β-hydroxybutyrate (BHB). The presence of excess ketone bodies in the blood causes a reduction in the blood pH (pH <7 acidic). This is ketoacidosis and is independent of the ethanol concentration. Symptoms include nausea, vomiting, abdominal pains, loss of appetite, lethargy, weakness, unconsciousness and, sometimes, death. Studies in this area have shown that, although acetone may be detected in the biological fluid, the blood BHB concentration is a more defining indicator of a pathologically significant ketoacidosis (Iten, 2000 & Elliott, 2010). Specifically, concentrations greater than approximately 250 mg/litre in the blood are associated with cases of sudden death in known alcoholics with no obvious cause of death. Concentrations less than approximately 50 mg/litre in the blood are 'normal', and concentrations of approximately 50–250 mg/litre could be deemed to be elevated but not 'fatal'.

- Gastro-intestinal consequences of alcoholism are most commonly associated with liver changes relating to a spectrum of findings, from fatty change to cirrhosis. Varices, pancreatitis and gastritis may also be encountered.

- Neurological complications include the consequence of electrolyte and vitamin deficiency.

- Cardiac complications may relate to structural and arrhythmic disorders.

Measurement of alcohol levels

17.44   The amount of alcohol present in the tissue fluids at any time is determined by more than the simple measure of the quantity ingested. It depends on the method of dosing, the amount destroyed in the stomach before absorption, the rate of absorption, the available water for distribution (a reflection of body weight, stature and sex) and the capacity of the liver to metabolise the alcohol. All these variables are commonly operating in the context of normal social drinking where the intake, itself, is likely to be sporadic, both as to timing and as to quantity. Consequently, the chances of converting a supposed intake to prospective blood or breath values with scientific accuracy are remote. The literature on the subject is vast, and many tables, nomograms and the like have been produced in an effort to provide ready conversion figures, but none overcome the problems inherent in an individualised biological process.

Widmark's original hypothesis can be used to provide some estimate of the blood alcohol concentration based on quantity of alcohol consumed. The calculation is expressed as:

$$a = bwr/100$$

where

$a =$ the amount of alcohol ingested in grams,

$b =$ the blood alcohol concentration in mg/100 ml blood,

$w =$ the subject's weight in kilograms, and

$r =$ Widmark's factor, which is the ratio of the water content of the whole body to the water content of the blood.

However, this method does not consider the highly variable enzymatic destruction of alcohol in the stomach or the amount of ingested alcohol which remains unabsorbed. Further, the 'Widmark factor' is based on the 'average' individual. A number of modifications have been suggested.

The amount of alcohol circulating in the body (and thus affecting the brain) is expressed in the United Kingdom in terms of milligrams of alcohol per 100 millilitres of the fluid under examination. Traditionally, this has been blood, on the grounds that blood is in direct contact with the brain. In Europe, the level is typically measured in grams per litre. This has the effect that the number quoted in the United Kingdom will be 100 times 'higher' than quoted in Europe.

17.45 Since alcohol diffuses uniformly in the body water, it will be present in the urine which is formed in the kidneys. But, as urine contains very few solid materials, there will be more alcohol per 100 ml of urine than per 100 ml of blood and, in order to compare the two fluids, a ratio of 1.33:1 is usually accepted. This, however, assumes that the urine and blood are in equilibrium, and this cannot be so in practice, because urine is isolated and stored in the bladder. The nearest one can get to equivalence of blood and urine is to empty the bladder and test the smallest amount that can next be voided naturally.

Of greater importance, in relation to current practice, is the fact that breath also contains water which is derived from the alveolar air that has been in immediate contact with the blood in the capillaries; theoretically, a constant breath/blood ratio should be achieved, and this is accepted as approximately 1:2,300. While it is true that a breath sample contains an inconstant amount of tidal air which has not been in contact with the blood, this can be compensated for in the method of testing.

Test results should be given in terms of either blood, urine or breath alcohol and this is the practice that is accepted by the courts (*Lockhart v Deighan* 1985 SCCR 204).

- The amount of alcohol circulating in the body (and thus affecting the brain) is expressed in the United Kingdom in terms of milligrams of alcohol per 100 millilitres of the fluid under examination.

- Analysis associated with blood and breath can be correlated to each other, whereas urine and blood are not usually in equilibrium.

Particular problems of post-mortem blood alcohol analyses

17.46 The measurement of alcohol levels following post-mortem examination is more complex, due to the occurrence of a number of artefacts. There is fairly widespread evidence that some bacteria and yeasts can produce ethanol as part of their normal metabolism and that, prominent among these, are bacteria responsible for post-mortem putrefaction. Post-mortem enzymatic activity may also convert sugar to alcohol. There is, therefore, a potential for falsely raised blood alcohol values to be obtained using post-mortem specimens. To a lesser extent, the alcohol levels may also decline following microbial activity. Since post-mortem activity can be variable between sites, it is recommended that more than one specimen type is analysed.

Therefore, the use of at least 1% fluoride containers for specimen collection is recommended, as this disrupts/kills the bacteria and reduces this effect, but only after sample collection. As there are fewer micro-organisms in urine, this fluid is less affected, but a high glucose concentration (e.g. in diabetes mellitus) or a yeast infection in the urine can still result in ethanol production. Due to its sterile and self-contained nature, vitreous humour from the eye is the least affected and is preferable (if available) in cases where a microbial influence is a possibility or suspected.

In addition to specimen selection and collection, the actual analysis is obviously of utmost importance. The 'gold standard' analytical technique used to measure ethanol is gas chromatography flame ionisation detection, particularly with headspace sampling. This is a specific technique that can isolate the separate alcohols present. This is in contrast to some enzymatic methods commonly used for alcohol analysis by routine clinical laboratories in live patients. Enzymatic methods are less specific and can be affected by post-mortem specimens. Furthermore, as well as detecting the presence of other alcohols such as methanol and isopropanol, gas chromatography is also able to detect the products of ketoacidosis such as acetone.

- Samples obtained post-mortem may be subject to changes in the ethanol level due to production, and possibly destruction, by microbial action.
- Inappropriate preservation may facilitate alcohol generation after sampling.

Alcohol and transportation

17.47   There is significant evidence to support the role that alcohol consumption has in the causation of road traffic collisions. Pathophysiologically, the effects of relatively low levels of alcohol on increasing reaction time to 'events' are of great importance. There is increasing evidence of the role of other drugs in causing road traffic collisions.

Studies of pedestrians killed in road traffic accidents indicate a very similar pattern of alcohol intoxication to that shown by drivers (Elliott et al 2009). All persons killed in traffic accidents should be examined post-mortem for evidence of intoxication, and any positive result should be made available to the defence of a driver.

These are, however, subjective criteria. Objective measurements show that even low concentrations – of the order of 50 mg/100 ml – cause a lengthening of the reaction time in response to a complex situation and a decrease in visual function. If one adds to this the impulsive psychological effects, there is good reason to suppose that the most dangerous person on the roads with respect to alcoholism is the man who is only moderately intoxicated; while he is not able to react in an emergency in the normal way, he is, at the same time, unable to appreciate the deterioration in his performance.

Such subtle changes are not disclosed by normal clinical tests – probably only those with a blood level of more than 150 mg alcohol/100 ml are detected as being unfit to drive by this means. This is, perhaps, the main reason why virtually all countries with a drink/driving policy have adopted the imposition of statutory tissue limits – and the limits in the United Kingdom are higher than in most.

Other alcohols

17.48   The 'consumable' ethanol is not the only alcohol and certainly not the only one that is abused. Unusual preparations containing alcohol, such as cheap Eau de Cologne, are often used, while hand lotions and rubbing alcohols can be ingested; the alcohol involved is isopropyl alcohol, which is more toxic than ethanol. Two of particular importance are methanol (methyl alcohol) and ethylene glycol.

Ethylene glycol is the basic ingredient of many antifreezes and produces much the same effects as ethanol but is frequently associated with metabolic acidosis. There is severe involvement of the central nervous system, and death in coma is to be expected when more than 100 ml is drunk. Severe damage to the kidneys may persist in the event of survival from the immediate effects. Oxalate crystals are commonly seen under the microscope.

Methyl alcohol is absorbed in the same way as ethyl alcohol, but it is metabolised far more slowly by the liver into formic acid. As a result, a cumulative effect is added to its inherent toxicity. Methanol is used in industry as a solvent and is a constituent of some antifreezes, but it is more generally available as 'methylated spirits' or 'surgical spirit'. Industrial methylated spirits, consisting of ethanol with 5% methanol added, is widely used in medicine and relatively easily obtainable as a result. The ordinary household equivalent is known as mineralised methylated spirits, which is 9% methanol in ethanol with added disgustants and colouring matter.

A blood level of 80 mg methanol/100 ml is dangerous. Toxicity is related to severe acidosis combined with central nervous system depression. The eyes are specifically affected and, even with survival, visual impairment (often permanent) is encountered. Voluntary drinking of 'meths' is encountered (as a source of cheap palatable alcohol), but involuntary consumption is relatively frequent in association with 'fake vodka'.

- Other alcohols, such as ethylene glycol and methyl alcohol, may be abused, often with fatal consequences.

Drugs of abuse

Heroin and other opioids

17.49   Opioid drugs are a group of drugs whose pharmacological activity is related to the morphine molecule. Those that are 'naturally occurring' are sometimes termed 'opiate', whereas the term 'opioid' incorporates both the naturally occurring as well as drugs that have been synthetically 'created'. Opioid drugs include morphine, heroin, codeine, oxycodone, methadone, pethidine, fentanyl, dihydrocodeine and tramadol. However, this is only a small representation and the number of opioid drugs increases frequently.

The mechanism of action for opioid drugs is by binding to specific receptors in the brain and preventing 'excitatory' activity. These receptors are the *mu, delta* and *kappa* opioid receptors. The *mu* receptor is involved principally in analgesia, whereas the *delta* receptor (as well as analgesia) is also consequent on respiratory depression and dependence. The *kappa* receptor is involved in spinal analgesia.

Clinically, the main usage of opioid drugs is in analgesia, although they have other uses such as suppressing coughs and the treatment of diarrhoea and respiratory distress. The most important side-effects relate to cardio-respiratory depression due to central nervous system depression. This is the mechanism by which most deaths related to opioid drugs occur.

All the opioid drugs have the potential to be abused, and are frequently so, for the euphoric effects that overlap with analgesia. Dependence, tolerance and withdrawal effects from opioid drugs are encountered with habitual use. This extends to those utilising opiates medicinally as well as illicitly.

17.50   The individual toxicological aspects of the opioid drugs are too broad and complex for this textbook. However, several important areas can be covered:

- The tolerance of an individual will significantly alter the 'fatal' levels.

- Heroin (diacetylmorphine) is relatively rapidly metabolised into 6-MAM (6-mono-acetylmorphine) before being converted into morphine. It is highly unusual for heroin itself to be identified. The presence of 6-MAM (most frequently in urine) confirms the use of heroin.

- Opioid drugs will have a synergistic effect with each other and other central nervous system depressants (such as alcohol and benzodiazepines).

Autopsy examination, on a death associated with an opioid, is highly variable. A consistent but non-specific finding is of congestion (blood vessels packed with blood). In cases of illicit drug misuse, needle puncture marks and associated scarring, intravenous drug abuse-related infection (such as hepatitis and HIV) and blockage of the smaller pulmonary vasculature by insoluble contaminants may be encountered.

Heroin

17.51   The classical drug of abuse in this group is heroin. Heroin, or diacetylmorphine, is synthetically produced for the medicinal setting, but is invariably acquired for the illicit market from alteration to the 'gum' of the opium poppy or from 'homebaking' codeine. Street heroin has a variety of names, including smack, H, horse, brown, hammer and tar, and is mixed with a number of contaminants (or 'cutting agents') affecting its purity. In the main, they are added to reduce the quantity of heroin in a sold 'bag', but some contaminants have psychoactive effects of their own. Heroin can be injected intravenously, snorted, inhaled or smoked. 'Chasing the dragon' is a euphemism for inhalation of the heated vapours from heroin.

Methadone is a synthetic opioid used in the treatment of opioid addiction. It is, in itself, a powerful opioid and associated with a number of deaths. Its benefit is the ability to provide controlled clean dosage which can be reduced, thus allowing the potential of an individual becoming drug-free.

Naloxone is the classical opioid antagonist (a drug that competes for the opioid's binding sites). It is used in the treatment of opioid toxicity and is an opioid itself but is not active.

- Opioid drugs are pharmacological activity drugs related to the morphine molecule. They may be naturally occurring or synthetic.

- Heroin, or diacetylmorphine, is synthetically produced for the medicinal setting, but is invariably acquired for the illicit market from alteration to the 'gum' of the opium poppy or from 'homebaking' codeine.

- Methadone is a synthetic opioid used in the treatment of opioid addiction.

- Mortality is associated with central nervous system depression.

Cocaine and other stimulants

17.52 The stimulant drugs are a group of drugs that interfere with the dopaminergic system within the brain. The group includes such drugs as amphetamine (and other amphetamine analogues), cathinone (khat) and cocaine. The drugs essentially increase the concentrations of dopamine, a neurotransmitter, although the means by which the dopamine is increased are variable.

Amphetamine is a historical medical drug with some limited modern uses; but amphetamine, methamphetamine and other designer amphetamines are now more frequently abused. An increasing number of these drugs are available. Common drugs include:

- *Amphetamine*, whose street names includes speed, uppers and base.

- *Methamphetamine*, whose street names include meth, crank, crystal (meth), ice and speed.

- *MDMA (3,4-methylenedioxymethamphetamine)*, whose street names include ecstasy, E, XTC, rolls, and Adam.

- *MDA (3,4-methylenedioxyamphetamine)* is a metabolite of MDMA, but is also available in its own right, with similar street names.

- *PMA (4-methoxyamphetamine) and PMMA (4-methoxymethamphetamine)*, which may be sold as ecstasy.

- *MDE* or *MDEA (3,4-methylenedioxyethylamphetamine)*, whose street names include Eve.

As can be appreciated, the street names for a number of drugs overlap.

Cocaine is a drug derived from the leaves of the *Erythroxylum coca* plant. It is a widely abused drug and is available in several different forms, dependent on the planned means of administration. Cocaine hydrochloride is a powdered form used for intravenous injection and snorting. This form is soluble in water and is usually an off-white colour due to contaminants. The cocaine is not absorbed in this form if smoked. 'Crack' (or freebase) cocaine is used for smoking and is an off-white creamy 'rock' that has been 'cooked' from the powdered form. Similar to heroin, the purity of street cocaine is highly variable.

The mechanism of action of amphetamines is either by promoting the release of neurotransmitters, such as dopamine, serotonin and adrenaline, or by replacing them; whereas cocaine prevents the re-uptake of the neurotransmitters following their release and thus prolonging their action. Cocaine has an additional effect which involves preventing the movement of sodium ions into sensory neurons. Similar drugs to cocaine, such a lidocaine, use these principles medicinally as a local anaesthetic. This also accounts, in part, for the propensity of cocaine to cause arrhythmias, by blocking conduction within the heart combined with the localised elevation of the catecholamines (e.g. adrenaline), which results in areas of micro-infarction.

Stimulants are abused for their psychological effects, which include a heightened sense of euphoria, and an elevation of mood and energy. The length of action is highly drug dependent; for example, cocaine is relatively short, whereas some of the amphetamines have prolonged action. Other physiological effects include elevation of the heart rate and blood pressure and elevation of body temperature and, as the name suggests, they are 'stimulant' on the body. Dependence on stimulants arises but is more variable compared to opioid drugs and more related to the individual drug.

The major adverse reactions relate to cardiovascular complications and hyperthermia (high body temperature). Cocaine cardiotoxicity is heightened, in part, due to its effects on blocking cardiac conduction. Psychosis is more frequently associated with amphetamines and may arise many years after discontinuation of use. Long-standing cardiovascular complications following stimulant, principally cocaine, misuse is common. This includes an increased propensity to atherosclerosis, cardiomegaly (heart enlargement) and infarction.

Tolerance can occur with long-standing abuse, but this is more idiosyncratic and variable than with the opioids. Tolerance may also not be total, in that there may be discordance between the levels of tolerance regarding 'desired' and 'deleterious' effects. Abstinence symptoms include fatigue and depression.

- Stimulant drugs interfere with the dopaminergic system within the brain to bring about a heightened sense of euphoria.

- Cocaine is the most commonly abused drug in this family, but amphetamines and other allied compounds are also common.

- Mortality is associated with cardiovascular complications and hyperthermia.

Benzodiazepine and other anxiolytics

17.53   The anxiolytic drugs are a group of drugs that interfere with gamma-aminobutyric acid (GABA), an inhibitory neurotransmitter, within the brain. The group includes, most importantly, benzodiazepines, such as diazepam, as well as other drugs such as barbiturates. The benzodiazepines bind to GABA receptors, which prevents GABA from activating the neurons. The GABA receptors are frequently involved in behavioural matters.

Benzodiazepines are widely used as appropriate medical drugs. Their uses are widespread, including anti-depressants, anti-convulsants, muscle relaxants, and for the treatment of acute alcohol withdrawal, as well as the more expected sedative-hypnotic usage.

Barbiturates are not frequently prescribed currently. Abuse of barbiturates was more common in the past.

Benzodiazepines are commonly abused, and this may be orally or intravenously. Toxicity is most frequently related with cardio-respiratory depression, although there is interaction between benzodiazepines and other central nervous system depressants, such as alcohol and opioid drugs.

- Anxiolytics drugs interfere with gamma-aminobutyric acid (GABA), an inhibitory neurotransmitter, within the brain.

- Benzodiazepines are the most common drug in this family.

- Similar to opiate drugs, toxicity is most frequently related with cardio-respiratory depression.

Cannabis

17.54 Cannabis refers both to the drug (also known as marijuana) as well as to the plant that it is derived from. Cannabis is most frequently sourced from the *Cannabis sativa* plant, although other plants from the same family also contain the active ingredient. Common street names include weed, grass, pot and dope. Utilising cannabis results in a 'high', due to impairment of cerebral function. It also increases cardiac output.

Cannabis is commonly consumed orally or smoked. Smoking results in more absorption than oral consumption. The active ingredient is delta-9-tetrahydrocannibol (THC). It principally binds to receptors known as endocannabinoid receptors, but also binds to other neurological receptors, including the opioid receptors.

The pharmacological effects of cannabis last for around three hours, and THC is rapidly absorbed into the tissues, meaning that blood levels fall. Low levels of THC persist, due to a relatively long half-life, and thus can be found after a long period in users. Its major metabolite (carboxy-THC, also referred to as THC-carboxylic acid) can be identified many days to weeks after the cannabis is used. This is due to the metabolite's long half-life in the body, and this ensures that it is difficult to be certain when the cannabis was taken based on the presence of this metabolite. Passive smoking can lead to elevated levels.

Chronic usage is likely to increase the risk of schizophrenia, as well as tolerance.

Whether or not cannabis can cause death is controversial, and there does not seem to be any direct evidence that cannabis can cause death. If deaths do arise, it is likely to relate to cardiac effects in those with significant pre-existing heart disease.

- Cannabis is a commonly abused drug associated with a 'high', due to impaired cerebral function.

LSD and other hallucinogens

17.55 Hallucinogens are a group of drugs associated with producing alterations in perception affecting the senses. The drug most commonly associated with this is lysergic acid diethylamide (LSD), but a number of other chemicals are also members. LSD is a compound derived from a fungus that grows on grain. It is commonly taken in the form of drug-infused paper, although other consumables can be similarly infused. Its mechanism of action is associated with variable effects on the serotonin receptors. Effects typically commence approximately five minutes following consumption. Toxicity is rare but deaths may be encountered in a situational context (e.g. falls).

Phencyclidine (PCP) and ketamine are synthetic drugs that were developed as anaesthetics. PCP is no longer medically used. Both are now abused illicitly. PCP is commonly known as angel dust, whereas ketamine has a number of street names principally associated with the letter K. These drugs block NMDA receptors. Ketamine is used as a 'date-rape' drug, in part due to its amnesic effect. PCP is more toxic than LSD and, as well as situational-type deaths, toxicity associated with respiratory depression and hyperthermia is encountered. Ketamine is similar to LSD in terms of toxicity.

- Hallucinogens, such as LSD, PCP and ketamine, are associated with producing alterations in perception affecting the senses.

- Deaths can be associated with toxicity, but are often situational (e.g. a belief that an individual can fly).

Gamma-hydroxybutyrate (GHB)

17.56   GHB is a naturally occurring chemical within the body, that had previous medical uses, and is now most commonly encountered as a 'date-rape' drug, due to its lack of odour and taste. The effects are similar to alcohol, including the important effect of amnesia. Toxic effects are associated with central nervous system depression. Interpreting levels of GHB (post-mortem) is more complicated, as it is a naturally occurring chemical and it has a propensity to form post-mortem (Elliott, 2004). Post-mortem generation can result in significant concentrations (primarily in blood compared to urine), especially with advanced decomposition, that may approach those associated with so-called 'fatal levels' of GHB (Andresen-Streichert et al 2015).

- GHB is a naturally occurring chemical most commonly encountered as a 'date-rape' drug.

- Post-mortem generation can result in blood levels that may approach those associated with so-called 'fatal levels' of GHB.

Volatile substances

17.57   Volatile substances are substances that are readily evaporated at room temperature into a gas. Deliberate inhalation of these evaporated gases leads to intoxication, and this is most readily associated with solvents, such as toluene (paint-thinner), diesel, and a large variety of other chemicals encountered in the household, medicine and industry. Previously, such abuse was known as 'glue-sniffing', but the sniffing of glue is less common. Alcohol is a solvent and can theoretically be sniffed.

Due to their gaseous and commonly lipid soluble nature, they are readily absorbed into the body and into the brain. Toxicity is associated with rapid central nervous system depression, but fatalities are broader, including plastic bag asphyxias and inhalation of stomach contents.

At post-mortem examination, abrasion/chemical burns may be found around the peri-oral and nasal region. Flame burns may also be seen if the volatile substance was ignited. In these cases, one lung (or part of the lung) can be retained in a nylon bag to assist with the identification of the agent involved.

- Volatile substance abuse involves inhalation of evaporated gases.

- Appropriate specimens need to be retained to facilitate analysis.

Novel stimulants and legal highs

17.58 Tryptamines, piperazines and cathinones are sometimes referred to as 'designer drugs' or 'legal highs' – although, with many drugs being controlled under the UK Misuse of Drugs Act 1971, this terminology is not correct. However, with the type and number of compounds constantly evolving, it is difficult for national and international control to keep up. Over the last few decades, there have been various drug groups: phenethylamines (e.g. MDMA, PMA, 2C-I), tryptamines (e.g. DMT, AMT, 5-MeO-DALT), piperazines (e.g. BZP, TFMPP), cathinones (e.g. mephedrone, methylone, 4-MEC, MDPV), aminoindanes (e.g. MDAI, 5-IAI), synthetic cannabinoids (e.g. JWH-018, AM-2201, PB-22, 5F-AKB48), as well as many separate drug entities, such as desoxypipradrol, methoxetamine and methiopropamine (MPA) (Brandt et al 2014). The drugs are often in the form of powders, pellets and/or tablets, with many (particularly recently) available over the internet and sold as 'plant food', 'bath salts' or 'research chemicals'. Generally, all are stimulating, some with hallucinogenic properties. From an analytical point of view, they can be difficult to detect and/or identify, typically due to lack of an example of the pure certified drug to allow laboratory comparison.

- Novel stimulants are often known as 'legal highs', are stimulating, and are sometimes hallucinogenic.

- Due to the relative newness and the number of drugs of this type, identification and detection can be compromised.

Medicinal drugs

17.59 Nearly every medicinal drug may be involved in producing a toxic effect; two drugs are worthy of additional brief consideration.

Paracetamol

17.60 Paracetamol is a common 'over the counter' analgesic that is widely used by the general public. Overdose with Paracetamol is encountered. Unlike other drugs, the consequences of a Paracetamol overdose are typically delayed over a course of two to four days. This relates to Paracetamol overdosage overwhelming the enzyme responsible for its breakdown and causing significant destruction of the liver in a characteristic pattern known as centri-lobular necrosis. By this stage, levels of Paracetamol are invariably very low or even absent. Very occasionally, if the quantity of Paracetamol is very high, a rapid death may arise, although the mechanism is not entirely clear.

Insulin

17.61   Insulin is a naturally occurring hormone in the body produced by the pancreas. A reduction in levels of insulin (or a resistance of the insulin receptors in the body) results in diabetes mellitus. The mainstay therapy of sufferers with low production of insulin is the provision of exogenous insulin. Administration of insulin in excess results in hypoglycaemia (low blood glucose levels) which, if sufficiently prolonged, results in damage to the brain. The difference between exogenous insulin and endogenous insulin is C-peptide, which is produced on a one-to-one basis in life, but is not present in exogenous insulin. The finding of an elevated level of insulin, but a low or absent level of C-peptide, will thus suggest exogenous administration in an individual with hypoglycaemia. It is possible, with highly specialised work, to identify the 'brand' of insulin and comment on the likely concentrations of administration. In reality, the matter is far more complex and requires involvement of experts from a number of fields, as not all hypoglycaemic episodes relate to insulin administration.

- Paracetamol toxicity typically results in a delayed death due to liver failure.

- Insulin may be used as means to induce hypoglycaemia, but analysis will need input from a wide array of specialists, dependent on the nature of the case.

Interpretation of reports

17.62   Interpretation of the analytical results is often the most challenging aspect of toxicology, due to the various factors, problems and pitfalls that are involved in determining the significance of the presence, absence or concentration of a drug/ poison or metabolites. As such, there are numerous considerations that should be applied when providing interpretation. These include:

- Case information (it is necessary for the toxicologist to consider the circumstances of the death or incident and the individual's accessibility to drugs, usually through their medical/drug history, to put the results into context). For example, an individual may have a potentially fatal level of heroin in their system, but have received an in-life fatal shotgun wound to the head.

- Submitted specimens (where the nature and suitability of the specimens should be taken into consideration, especially if dealing with decomposed post-mortem samples).

- Analysis (the coverage and type of analysis should be considered, in addition to any problems that arose during analysis. The absence of a drug could indicate non-compliance with the prescription regimen).

- Tolerance (a very important factor affecting determination of fatal and non-fatal ranges for drug concentrations as well as effects on the individual. For example, a methadone concentration in a naïve user could be 'fatal', but just 'therapeutic' in a regular user).

- Drug stability and production (whereby a drug or substance may be lost or reduced in a specimen through breakdown, or a drug or substance may be produced in a specimen, usually as a result of microbial action – e.g. ethanol).

Where measured, the interpretation of any drug concentration found should be done in consultation with the clinical or pathological findings. The concentration of the drug may be checked initially against known therapeutic levels and, if available and as appropriate, concentrations that have been measured in cases of fatal and non-fatal poisonings (T. Launiainen and I. Ojanperä, 2014). A similar procedure must be adopted if a metabolite has been measured, since some metabolites are as pharmacologically active, or more so, than the parent drug. This approach will solve the majority of cases encountered and will generally explain the clinician's or the pathologist's findings when the known pharmacological effects have been considered. However, when interpreting post-mortem blood concentrations, the possible influence of redistribution (as mentioned previously) should be considered, depending on the drug(s) in question. For some drugs (e.g. tricyclic antidepressants), the concentration difference between blood samples collected from an anatomical site close to an organ can be extreme compared to blood obtained appropriately from a peripheral site away from such sources of the drug. Also, because of this, it is not appropriate to compare a measured post-mortem blood concentration to those obtained in-life (i.e. published 'therapeutic' and clinical concentration ranges); and, although often requested, these post-mortem changes mean that a calculation of dose ingested from a blood concentration is inaccurate, misleading and should not be attempted.

17.63 Many poisoning cases involving drugs also involve alcohol. Alcohol has a significant additive effect on some drugs, as it affects the same or related receptors in the brain and can depress the central nervous system. Specific examples include benzodiazepines, barbiturates, opiates (including heroin/morphine) and gamma-hydroxybutyrate (GHB).

A satisfactory explanation of death is not always possible in cases in which several drugs have been detected at low to therapeutic levels. However, careful review of the information available in the medical literature may reveal a recorded adverse reaction when two of the drugs have been used together.

Observed symptoms should be considered against those recorded.

Drug-drug interactions can be due to an exacerbation of effects at the molecular level or an effect on the metabolism of one or both drugs. Induction or reduction of a drug's metabolism (by another drug or environmental source, including certain foodstuffs) can cause an increase/decrease in the concentration or effect of that drug.

This can also occur due to the genetic profile of an individual, with 'slow' and 'fast' metabolisers in the population, and has resulted in the study area of pharmacogenomics. Metabolic aspects should be borne in mind when interpreting the concentrations of drugs or metabolites found in-life and post-mortem.

Further reading material

General textbooks

- Saukko, P. & Knight, B. *Knight's Forensic Pathology* (2004, 3rd Edition)

- Mason, J.K. & Purdue, B.N. *The Pathology of Trauma* (2000, 3rd Edition)

- Payne-James, J., Jones, R., Karch, S.B. & Manlove, J. *Simpson's Forensic Medicine* (2011, 13th Edition)

- Baselt, R.C. *Disposition of toxic drugs and chemicals in man* (2014, 10th Edition)

- Moffat, A.C., Osselton, M.D., Widdop, B. and Watts, J. *Clarke's analysis of drugs and poisons* (2011, 4th Edition)

Articles in update textbooks

- Huckenbeck, W. 'Neogenesis of Ethanol and Fusel Oils in Putrefying Blood' in Tsokos, M., editor. *Forensic Pathology Reviews*. Volume Four. Humana Press; 2006. 205–259

- Gill, J.R. 'Practical Toxicology for the Forensic Pathologist' in Tsokos, M., editor. *Forensic Pathology Reviews*. Volume Three. Humana Press; 2005. 243–269

- Hunsaker, D.M. & Hunsaker, J.C. 'Post-mortem Alcohol Interpretation' in Tsokos, M., editor. *Forensic Pathology Reviews*. Volume One. Humana Press; 2004. 307–338

Articles in journals

- Logan, B.K., Jones, A.W. 'Endogenous ethanol "auto-brewery syndrome" as a drunk-driving defence challenge' *Med Sci Law*. 2000;40(3):206–15

- Iten, P.X. and Meier, M. 'Beta-hydroxybutyric acid – an indicator for an alcoholic ketoacidosis as cause of death in deceased alcohol abusers' *J. Forensic Sci.* 2000, vol. 45 (3), pp. 624–632

- Elliott, S., Woolacott, H. and Braithwaite, R.A. 'The prevalence of drugs and alcohol found in road traffic fatalities: A comparative study of victims' *Science and Justice* 2009, vol 49, pp. 19–23

- Elliott, S.P., Smith C. and Cassidy, D. 'The post-mortem relationship between beta-hydroxybutyrate (BHB), acetone and ethanol in ketoacidosis' *Forensic Sci. Int.* 2010, vol. 198, pp. 53–57 + Corrigendum; *Forensic Sci. Int.* 2011, vol. 206, p. 217

- Elliott, S.P. 'Further evidence for the presence of GHB in postmortem biological fluid: implications for the interpretation of findings' *J Anal. Toxicol.* 2004, vol. 28(1), pp. 20–26

- Andresen-Streichert, H., Jensen, P., Kietzerow, J., Schrot, M., Wilke, N., Vettorazzi, E., Mueller, A. and Iwersen-Bergmann, S. 'Endogenous gamma-hydroxybutyric acid (GHB) concentrations in post-mortem specimens and further recommendation for interpretative cut-offs' *Int J Legal Med.* 2015, vol. 129(1), pp. 57–68

- Templeton, A.H., Carter, K.L.T., Sheron, N., Gallagher, P.J., Verril, C. 'Sudden Unexpected Death in Alcohol Misuse – An Unrecognized Public Health Issue?' *Int. J. Environ. Res. Public Health* 2009, 6, 3070–3081

- Mason, J.K., Blackmore, D.J. 'Experimental Inhalation of Ethanol Vapour' *Med Sci Law.* 1972 Jul;12(3):205–8

- Launiainen, T. and Ojanperä, I. 'Drug concentrations in post-mortem femoral blood compared with therapeutic concentrations in plasma' *Drug Test Anal.* 2014, vol. 6(4), pp. 308–316

- Brandt, S.D., King, L.A. and Evans-Brown, M. 'The new drug phenomenon' *Drug Test Anal.* 2014, vol. 6(7–8), pp. 587–597

Chapter 18

Care of detainees

With Ian Wall

Introduction

18.1   Individuals can be detained in police custody for a variety of reasons: arrested on suspicion of an alleged offence; as a place of safety; detained by immigration services; remanded or sentenced prisoners; or detained under terrorism legislation. For the purposes of this chapter, persons detained in police custody will be called 'detainees'.

Many detainees have physical or mental health problems, and these are often complicated by problems of alcohol or substance misuse. Furthermore, these vulnerabilities are sometimes complicated by violence.

The Istanbul Protocol[1] makes it clear that a person deprived of their liberty should have the right of access to a physician, including, if he or she so wishes, a physician of his or her own choice. The medical care that a detainee receives should be of the same standard as they would have received had they not been in custody.

Initial assessment in custody

18.2   For England and Wales, the Police and Criminal Evidence Act 1984 (PACE) Code of Practice C sets out the statutory framework for custodial care and the rights and entitlements of a detainee in police custody.[2] On arrival at a police station, the custody officer is responsible for the risk assessment of the detainee. In terms of health and injuries, the custody officer should:

- visually assess the condition of the detainee, including their general health and any injuries, recording and interpreting their behaviour in the context of health and risk issues;

1 Istanbul Protocol. (2004). Manual on the Effective Investigation and Documentation of Torture and Other Cruel, Inhuman or Degrading Treatment or Punishment. United Nations. New York and Geneva.
2 Code C Revised. Code of Practice for the detention, treatment and questioning of persons by police officers. October 2014. The equivalent legislation for Northern Ireland is the Police and Criminal Evidence (Northern Ireland) Order 1989, SI 1989/1341 ('the Northern Ireland Order'); separate codes are issued in Northern Ireland. The equivalent code is also Code C and carries the same title as its counterpart in England and Wales. The relevant legislation in Scotland is Part II of the Criminal Procedure (Scotland) Act 1995 and the Custody Manual of Guidance, formerly published under the auspices of the Association of Chief Police Officers in Scotland, now by Police Scotland.

- where appropriate, seek medical attention from a healthcare professional;

- determine if the person is fit to be detained and fit to be interviewed;

- record and act on behaviour or information that may suggest that a detainee is likely to harm themselves (risk of suicide and self-harm);

- establish a care plan for monitoring any risks to the detainee; and

- manage appropriate monitoring, observation and engagement.

18.3   It is important that appropriate medical attention is given as soon as practicable to any detainee, and PACE (namely, Code C and the Detention and Custody Authorised Professional Practice (APP) guidance produced by the College of Policing, with which the Code must be read) recommends that a healthcare assessment should take place for detainees who:

- appear to be suffering from physical illness;

- are injured;

- appear to be suffering from mental ill health (or disablement or difficulty that means that the detainee is likely to be mentally vulnerable or likely to require additional support);

- appear to have a drug or alcohol dependence or withdrawal likely to affect safety;

- appear to need medical attention; or

- request a medical examination.[3]

18.4   The custody officer is also responsible for managing the supervision and level of observation of each detainee, and this should be based upon the risk assessment and any recommendations that a health professional has made following a medical assessment. Recognised levels of observation are:[4]

- Level 1 – General observation. This would include a cell check at least every hour, where visits and observations, including the detainee's behaviour/ condition, are recorded in the custody record and where, if the detainee is awake, the officer should communicate with the detainee.

- Level 2 – Intermittent observations. This would include the detainee being visited and roused every 30 minutes in accordance with Annex H of PACE Code C, i.e. ensuring they are rousable and can respond to questions and commands. This type of checking would typically be used for a detainee who is under the influence of alcohol and/or drugs.

---

3   See note 8C, paragraph 9.5 and accompanying notes to paragraph 9 of Code C and the section on medical attention in the College of Policing's guidance, available at www.app.college.police.uk/ app-content/detention-and-custody-2/arrest-detention-transportation/ (accessed 17 June 2014).

4   See the College of Policing's guidance at www.app.college.police.uk/app-content/detention- and-custody-2/detainee-care/ at point 2.1.

- Level 3 – Constant observation. This would include constant observation, which may be by CCTV but with physical checks and visits carried out at least every 30 minutes. It would also mandate a review by a healthcare professional (HCP).

- Level 4 – Close proximity. This involves the detainee being physically observed at close proximity and communicated with at frequent and irregular intervals. This would normally be reserved for detainees at the highest risk of self-harm, in order to allow immediate physical intervention to take place if necessary, and is facilitated by an officer sat in the doorway of a cell or, in more modern custody suites, sat outside the cell but visible through a glass wall.

Some police forces may have slightly different levels of observation, e.g. Metropolitan Police Standard Operating Procedures.

18.5   Under current PACE legislation in England and Wales and in Northern Ireland, the relevant detention time is when the custody officer authorises the detainee's detention. An officer of at least the rank of inspector must undertake a first review at 6 hours, then every 9 hours up to 24 hours. An officer of at least the rank of superintendent must authorise any detention after 24 hours for a further 12 hours and, following this, further detention must be authorised by a magistrates' court. The maximum duration of detention is 96 hours, after which the detainee must be charged or released (sections 40–44 of PACE and articles 41–45 of the Northern Ireland Order). The PACE 'clock' stops if a detainee is transferred to hospital (section 41(6) of PACE and article 42(4) of the Northern Ireland Order). There are some differences in detention relating to Terrorism Act detainees that will be considered later. Scotland operates markedly shorter periods of detention: 12 hours, with a further 12-hour extension (sections 14–14B of the Criminal Procedure (Scotland) Act 1995).

Provision of healthcare in custody

18.6   Previously, in England, primary medical care and prison health care was the responsibility of the National Health Service (NHS); however, health care in police custody remained the responsibility of the police via the Home Office. The Audit Commission report, *The Doctor's Bill*,[5] led to the outsourcing of the health provision to private provider companies such that, by 2008, over half of the police forces in England and Wales used this type of service provision.[6] Now, most police forces use a mixed model of healthcare provided by forensic physicians (doctors who are sometimes known as 'forensic medical examiners', 'forensic medical officers' or 'police surgeons') and other healthcare professionals, e.g. nurses and paramedics. Similar mixed regimes exist in Northern Ireland and Scotland.

---

5   Audit Commission. (1998). The Doctor's Bill – the provision of forensic medical services to the police.

6   Payne-James, J.J., Anderson, W.R., Green, P.G. and Johnston, A. 'Provision of forensic medical services to police custody suites in England and Wales: Current practice' *J Forensic and Legal Medicine* (2009) 16 pp. 189–195.

Following these changes were reforms to the NHS, such that, from 1 April 2013, commissioning of health services was either the responsibility of GPs or, for more specialised services, NHS England. It has been decided that commissioning of forensic medical services, both for general forensic medicine and sexual offence medicine, will be the responsibility of NHS England from April 2015.

18.7   In many large metropolitan areas, such as London and Manchester, sexual offence services are provided by dedicated team of doctors who only undertake this type of work; whereas, in more rural areas, the service provision is inextricably linked such that both custody health care and sexual offence examinations are provided by forensic physicians and healthcare professionals, who have to be able to undertake both types of forensic health care.

The Faculty of Forensic and Legal Medicine (FFLM) has broadly supported the transfer of commissioning of forensic health care from the Home Office to the NHS, with the proviso that it does not lead to a reduction in funding or standards of health care provision. In doing this, the FFLM has developed a series of quality standards for forensic physicians and other healthcare professionals working in custody and in Sexual Assault Referral Centres (SARCs).

18.8   Concern has been expressed about the standards of training of doctors undertaking custodial healthcare.[7] The FFLM quality standards[8] give guidance on recruitment of doctors in terms of relevant necessary experience, initial training, workplace-based supervision, continuing professional development and service level standards. The FFLM has been actively trying to encourage commissioners to incorporate these standards into commissioning specifications. Similarly, the FFLM has issued guidance on the recruitment and training of other healthcare professionals.[9, 10]

Following the Government's response[11] to the Shipman Inquiry, regulatory changes have been introduced into the United Kingdom such that all doctors who have a licence to practise must periodically be assessed as fit to practise. From 3 December 2012, revalidation every five years became mandatory and, as a requirement for this, licensed doctors must produce evidence of an annual appraisal, at least 50 hours' Continuing Professional Development (CPD) per year, review of significant events and compliments and complaints, feedback from colleagues and patients, and some form of quality improvement activity, e.g. audit. There is a view amongst many that, despite these changes, revalidation will not prevent another 'Harold Shipman'. Revalidation for nurses is expected to be introduced by 2015.

7 Wall, I.F. 'Lack of training in custodial medicine in the UK – a cause for concern?' *J Forensic Legal Med.* (2008) doi:10.1016/j.jflm.2008.02.005.
8 Faculty of Forensic and Legal Medicine. Quality Standards in Forensic Medicine. http://fflm. ac.uk/upload/documents/1378397186.pdf (accessed 29 November 2013).
9 Faculty of Forensic and Legal Medicine. Quality Standards for Nurses and Paramedics in General Forensic Medicine (GFM). http://fflm.ac.uk/upload/documents/1382349188.pdf (accessed 11 July 2014).
10 Faculty of Forensic and Legal Medicine. Quality Standards for Nurses for Sexual Offence and Medicine (GFM). http://fflm.ac.uk/upload/documents/1395839844.pdf (accessed 11 July 2014).
11 HM Government. (2007). Learning from tragedy, keeping patients safe. Overview of the Government's action programme in response to the recommendations of the Shipman Inquiry.

Specific functions of healthcare professionals

18.9   The initial assessment will be by a forensic physician, nurse or paramedic. Some assessments – e.g. Mental Health Act assessments and currently some Road Traffic Act procedures – are required by law to be undertaken by a forensic physician. The assessment may be required to provide an opinion on one or more of the following:

- fitness to be detained in police custody, including the need for medication, referral to hospital etc.;

- fitness to be interviewed by the police;

- fitness to be charged;

- fitness to transfer, perhaps because a warrant has been issued elsewhere and a long journey may be necessary;

- the need for an appropriate adult;

- to accurately document injuries;

- to take forensic samples;

- to take a blood sample in a Road Traffic Act 1988 case;

- to assess whether there is a 'condition which might be due to a drug' under section 4 of the Road Traffic Act 1988;

- to undertake an intimate body search for drugs;

- to assess a person detained under section 136 of the Mental Health Act 1983;

- to assess and potentially treat injured police officers;

- to pronounce life extinct at a scene and advise whether there may be suspicious circumstances; and

- to examine and assess those detained under terrorism legislation.

Medical assessment of the detainee

18.10   Ideally, the person with the query should contact the doctor or healthcare professional. However, some police forces will have systems in place that have a single point of contact. Whilst this may be administratively easy for the police force, it often means that it is not possible for the call to go directly through to the clinician who can assess urgency of the call, when priority should normally be given to clinical cases, e.g. acute medical problems, suspicious deaths, drink/drive procedures.

On arrival at the police station, the clinician will require a briefing from the custody officer. This information should include:

- discussion on the reason called – physical, mental illness, medication, injury;

- details from custody record, including reason for arrest, review of the risk assessment form;

- other information from the custody officer and, where appropriate, arresting officer in relation to the circumstances of the arrest;

- whether any force was used, e.g. handcuffs, irritant sprays, batons, TASER, etc.;

- whether anything relevant was found in the detainee's property or when searched, e.g. medication, illicit drugs etc.;

- the likely length of detention and whether the detainee is likely to remain in custody overnight;

- whether the detainee is to be interviewed;

- whether any forensic samples are required;

- Police National Computer checks for, e.g., mental illness, violence, drugs; and

- any concerns about detainee's behaviour and his or her personal safety.

It sometimes may be necessary to obtain further information from the GP or local Mental Health Trust. In some areas, custody suites have separate computer systems where the clinician can access NHS records.

18.11   Clinicians should keep separate contemporaneous medical records of the consultation, which would normally be regarded as confidential medical records. Pro formas are commonly used, allowing easy identification of key issues. How this is done will depend on local arrangements but the same principles should apply. Sometimes the clinical record will be retained and stored by the clinician, sometimes the provider company will retain it and occasionally it may be entered directly into the NHS computer record. A short summary should be entered into the police custody record, giving sufficient information for the care and management of the detainee whilst in custody and after release. It is also good practice not only to give written advice to the custody officer but also to give the advice verbally at the charge room desk, where details of any conversation will normally be recorded.

The preferred location for any medical assessment is a well-equipped custody medical room. However, it may be necessary for the consultation to take place in the cell if a detainee is unable to walk to the medical room or is violent. In some cases, and for the safety of the forensic clinician, it may only be possible to make observations through the cell door hatch. Sometimes, a detainee will refuse to come to the medical room for an assessment. In this situation, it is recommended that the clinician goes to the cell and speaks with the detainee and clarifies issues of consent and that the detainee is actually declining an assessment.

18.12   The health and welfare of the detainee is paramount and any forensic issues are secondary. So what should a routine assessment entail? Firstly, the clinician needs to obtain informed consent to the assessment. Depending on the nature of the assessment, written consent may be necessary, e.g. for forensic sampling, intimate searches etc. It should be explained that the medical assessment is not mandatory and that there is no guarantee of confidentiality but that, normally, only relevant details for safe detention will need to be shared with the custody staff. The following information should then routinely be sought:

- history of the present problem, and whether any injury has been sustained;

- past medical history;

- past psychiatric history;

- medication, whether prescribed, over-the-counter or illicit; and, for each drug, the dose, how long prescribed and when last taken;

- past incidences of self-harm;

- relevant educational history (to assess for learning disabilities and difficulties);

- social history;

- specific enquiry about hearing, vision, asthma, diabetes, epilepsy, kidney and liver problems;

- allergies; and

- alcohol intake in the last 24 hours and weekly alcohol intake.

18.13   An examination should then be carried out which, as a minimum, should include:

- assessment of conscious level;

- pulse, blood pressure and temperature;

- examination of the eyes to assess pupil size and whether nystagmus (a flicking movement of the eyes when looking to the right or left and often associated with alcohol intoxication) is present;

- A brief assessment of mental state.

   A more detailed, systematic examination may be required, depending on the history elicited, which might include examination of the heart, lungs, chest, abdomen, a neurological examination and a more detailed assessment of mental state. Any injuries should be assessed and noted on body diagrams.

18.14   A management plan should then be formulated which should incorporate:

- fitness for detention and interview;

- the need or otherwise for an appropriate adult;

- medical advice to the detainee;

- medical advice to the custody staff (both verbally and in writing) and whether the detainee may need a medical review; and

- the need or otherwise for medication.

Common medical problems

18.15   Several medical problems are commonly encountered in custody; some are straightforward to manage, while others can be more difficult.

Cardiovascular disease

18.16   The commonest problems include a history of hypertension, heart disease (including angina) and previous history of myocardial infarction, deep vein thrombosis (often as a result of injecting into the deep veins in the groin) and arrhythmias. In these situations, a detailed history should be taken, along with an examination of the cardiovascular system. Medication should normally be continued, and detainees with angina should be allowed to keep their angina sprays with them in the cell, providing they have been checked for containing illicit substances and the detainee is not a self-harm risk. Caution should be exercised with a younger detainee who complains of chest pain, where cocaine misuse may cause heart disease prematurely. Anyone with chest pain that is not relieved following use of an angina spray or lasting more than 15 minutes should be transferred to hospital by 999 ambulance.

Asthma

18.17   This can usually be managed in the custody setting by continuing regular medication and inhalers. Again, detainees should normally be allowed to keep their asthma inhalers with them. If asthma is worsening, a clinical assessment will be required to assess the severity, which should include checking of pulse, blood pressure and temperature and listening to the chest and measuring peak flow rate. For severe exacerbations of asthma, consideration will need to be given to admitting the detainee to hospital.

Epilepsy

18.18   A history of seizures is common in the custodial setting, and a history should be taken of the type of seizure, frequency and date of the last one. An attempt should be made to ascertain if the detainee has true epilepsy or whether they suffer from withdrawal seizures, commonly due to alcohol or benzodiazepine withdrawal. Medication should normally be continued, along with treatment for withdrawal from alcohol and benzodiazepines. If a detainee with known epilepsy has a seizure, admission to hospital may not be required; but any detainee who has a first ever seizure or a second seizure whilst in custody should be admitted to hospital by 999 ambulance. Management of a seizure is by ensuring that the detainee cannot harm himself or herself, placing them in the recovery position and the administration of buccal midazolam (a benzodiazepine given orally).

Diabetes

18.19   For any diabetic detainee, it should be established whether they are controlled by diet, medication or insulin, and a baseline blood glucose measurement should be done. Most insulin-dependent diabetics carry their own blood glucose monitoring meters with them but, in any event, all healthcare professionals should have the means to measure blood glucose with a quantitative meter and also test blood or urine for ketones.

In assessing detainees, HCPs should determine the level of diabetic control, and assess other conditions associated with diabetes where complications (such as vascular disease, neuropathies, renal problems and visual impairments) are common. A general examination should be carried out and the blood glucose measured. Custody staff should be given a detailed management plan, which should include dietary requirements, medication/insulin requirements and the need for a medical review. Particular caution should be exercised with any detainee who is intoxicated or has a head injury.

The two main problems with insulin-dependent diabetics are hypoglycaemia and hyperglycaemia. The former is characterised by confusion, sweating, cold clammy skin and deteriorating level of response. Treatment is by giving the detainee something sweet to eat or some glucose gel; but, if the detainee is unresponsive, treatment is by giving intramuscular glucagon or intravenous glucose to raise the blood glucose. The detainee may require admission to hospital. Hyperglycaemia can result in diabetic ketoacidosis or non-ketotic hyperosmolar states, both of which can lead to coma. If the blood glucose is over 30 mmol/l, consideration should be given to immediately transferring the detainee to hospital. The same should apply to a detainee with a blood glucose over 25 mmol/l and evidence of impairment of consciousness or confusion.[12]

Managing the insulin-dependent diabetic can be a particular problem. Most diabetics have their insulin and eat afterwards but, in custody, some will have their insulin and then refuse food in order to deliberately precipitate hypoglycaemia. For this reason, it is advised that consideration should be given to preventing this by giving the detainee food before insulin. Many police forces have a policy that all insulin injections should be supervised by a healthcare professional. Some insulin-dependent diabetics are now maintained on 'insulin pumps', where a small amount of insulin is continuously infused under the skin. All of these patients should be assessed by a healthcare professional.

Injuries

18.20 Many detainees have sustained injuries prior to detention; it may be that these were sustained prior to the arrest or during the arrest. Consent should be established both for assessment of the injuries and the production of a witness statement if necessary. Fundamental to assessing any injury is taking an appropriate history and undertaking a physical examination. Relevant factors could include:

- How was the injury sustained and when?

- Was a weapon used?

- Has the injury been treated?

- Are there any relevant pre-existing illnesses?

- Is any regular medication being taken, e.g. anticoagulants?

- What clothing was the person wearing?

12 Faculty of Forensic and Legal Medicine. Management of Diabetes Mellitus in Custody. http://fflm.ac.uk/upload/documents/1334659904.pdf (accessed 11 July 2014).

It is essential that the injury is examined in good light, and sometimes it may be necessary to observe the area from a different direction to ensure that an injury is not missed. It is recommended that any injury be recorded on a body chart and consideration given to arranging for the injury to be photographed.

In terms of recording injuries, the size, shape, position and associated features (e.g. swelling, pain, bruising) should be noted, with reference to a fixed anatomical point (e.g. from the tip of the elbow etc.). Serious injuries, and in particular stab wounds, should be assessed at hospital.

18.21   A particular problem in custody is management of the detainee who has a head injury. (For further explanation of head injuries, see Chapter 9.) Again, a detailed history of the nature of the injury should be obtained, in particular noting whether there has been loss of consciousness and whether there has been any vomiting. A physical examination should take place, which should include pulse, blood pressure and a neurological assessment, including an assessment of conscious level using the Glasgow Coma Scale (GCS):[13]

Eye opening	
• Spontaneous	4
• To speech	3
• To painful stimuli	2
• None	1
Best motor response	
• Obeys commands	6
• Localises painful stimulus	5
• Withdraws (normal flexion)	4
• Flexes abnormally (spastic flexion)	3
• Extension	2
• No response	1
Best verbal response	
• Orientated	5
• Confused	4
• Says inappropriate words	3
• Makes incomprehensible sounds	2
• No verbal response	1
Maximum	15

A simpler means of assessment is to use the AVPU scale (an acronym of 'Awake', 'Voice', 'Pain' and 'Unresponsive'), where A = GCS of 15, V = GCS of 12, P = GCS of 8 and U = GCS of 3.

13 Jennett, B., Teasdale, G. 'Aspects of coma after severe head injury' *Lancet* (1977) 1:pp. 878–881.

18.22   The National Institute for Health and Care Excellence (NICE) has issued guidance on the management of head injuries, and this has been adapted by the Faculty of Forensic and Legal Medicine.[14] Following a head injury (defined as any trauma to the head, other than superficial injuries to the face), a detainee should be referred to hospital if any of the following are present:

- impaired consciousness (GCS <15/15) at any time since the injury;

- any focal neurological symptoms or signs (impairments of nerve, brain or spinal cord function, such as weakness in the limbs);

- any suspicion of a skull fracture or penetrating injury, e.g. cerebrospinal fluid leak, bleeding from the ear, or bruising over the mastoid process (the area behind the ear);

- pre- or post-traumatic amnesia;

- persistent headache since the injury;

- any vomiting since the injury;

- medical co-morbidity, such as anticoagulants;

- high-energy head injury, e.g. fall from a height of more than one metre or five stairs;

- current drug or alcohol intoxication;

- significant extracranial injuries;

- continuing uncertainty about the diagnosis after first assessment; and

- age greater than 65.

18.23   Custody staff should be advised to rouse and speak with the detainee, obtaining a comprehensible verbal response, every 30 minutes in accordance with Annex H of PACE Code C, and any detainee who:

- becomes unconscious;

- becomes increasingly sleepy or drowsy;

- complains of persistent or increasingly severe headache;

- complains of any visual disturbance such as double vision;

- vomits;

- has a fit; or

- exhibits behaviour that is of any concern;

should be immediately transferred to hospital by a 999 ambulance and specifically not in the back of a police van.

---

14 Faculty of Forensic and Legal Medicine. Head injury management. https://fflm.ac.uk/upload/documents/1195227243.pdf (accessed 11 July 2014).

When assessing the level of rousability, the '4Rs' provides a useful checklist:[15]

- *Rousability*: can they be woken? Go into the cell, call their name, shake gently.

- *Response to questions*: can they give appropriate answers to questions – 'what's your name?', 'where do you live?', 'where do you think you are?'?

- *Response to commands*: can they respond appropriately to commands – 'open your eyes!', 'lift one arm and then the other'?

- *Remember*: the possibility or presence of other illnesses, injury or mental condition. A person who is drowsy and smells of alcohol may have a head injury, but might also have diabetes, epilepsy, have had a stroke or be intoxicated from drugs etc.

Acute behavioural disturbance

18.24   Acute behavioural disturbance may occur secondary to substance misuse, physical or mental illness and can take a variety of forms, with the most extreme being the potentially life-threatening excited delirium, often related to cocaine ingestion, and characterised by symptoms of bizarre and/or aggressive behaviour, shouting, paranoia, panic, violence towards others, unexpected physical strength and hyperthermia.

Ideally, detainees with acute behavioural disturbance should not be taken to a police custody suite but directly to a hospital Emergency Department. However, if excited delirium is suspected in the custodial setting, the detainee should be taken immediately to hospital via 999 ambulance. The FFLM gives more detailed guidance on how this rare but serious condition should be managed.[16]

Pregnancy

18.25   The possibility of pregnancy should be borne in mind for all women of reproductive age who are detained in police custody. Substances misusers frequently have absent or infrequent periods, and pregnancy should always be excluded by means of history taking, examination and/or pregnancy testing.

Sudden cessation of opioids in an opioid-dependent pregnant addict can be life threatening for the foetus, and any drug- or alcohol-dependent pregnant detainee should be regarded as a high risk, with a low threshold for admission to hospital. Again, the FFLM gives detailed guidance on the management of the pregnant detainee.[17]

---

15 Police and Criminal Evidence Act 1984 (PACE) Code C Revised. Code of Practice for the detention, treatment and questioning of persons by police officers. Annex H Detained person: observation list. October 2013.

16 Faculty of Forensic and Legal Medicine. Acute behavioural disturbance: guidelines on management in police custody. http://fflm.ac.uk/upload/documents/1310745561.pdf (accessed 11 July 2014).

17 Faculty of Forensic and Legal Medicine. Management of the pregnant drug addict and/or Alcohol Dependent Patients in Custody. http://fflm.ac.uk/upload/documents/1369401315.pdf (accessed 11 July 2014).

Mental health

18.26   Mental health problems are common in the custodial setting. The custody officer should have undertaken a risk assessment, and it is hoped that this will have identified many detainees with mental health issues who should then be seen by a healthcare professional.

A mental state examination (essentially, a psychiatric 'physical examination') should be undertaken by the healthcare professional to assess whether there is, in fact, any evidence of mental illness. The mental state examination is a structured way of observing and describing a patient's current state of mind under the domains of appearance, behaviour, speech, thought, perception, obsessive/compulsive behaviours, mood and affect, cognitive function and risk behaviours, e.g. self-harm or harm to others. Many police forces use nurses either from a general nursing background or a mental health nursing background. It may be that a nurse will require the detainee to be assessed by a forensic physician and, in some cases, it may be necessary to obtain the opinion of a psychiatrist.

Assessment of the mental state is important medico-legally because some drugs or alcohol can lead to the development of a psychosis, which may have implications for the offence (for example, diminished responsibility, or inability to form intention) or fitness to interview.

Mental illness and substance misuse often occur together: this is known as 'co-morbidity' or dual diagnosis. Substance misuse may be the primary diagnosis, which then leads to a psychotic illness, e.g. amphetamine misuse; but, conversely, drug use can lead to a rapid worsening of a primary mental illness.

18.27   Deliberate self-harm is a particular problem in the custodial setting. Studies have estimated that, in 2005/06 in England and Wales, there were 465 very serious near-misses (defined as 'very likely' or 'fairly likely' that death would have occurred if action had not been taken) and, of these, 46% were attempted suicide/self-harm.[18] Drug dependency, mental illness or a previous history of self-harm have been identified as risk factors, and self-harm attempts are more likely to occur early during the period of detention. They are also higher in female detainees.

Intellectual disabilities

18.28   Learning disability is defined by World Health Organisation ICD-10[19] as 'a condition of arrested or incomplete development of the mind, which is especially characterised by impairment of skills manifested during the developmental period, skills which contribute to the overall level of intelligence, i.e. cognitive, language, motor and social abilities'. Estimates of learning disability in the prison population range from 1% to 10%, and it is known to be associated with significant psychiatric and physical co-morbidity. There is evidence that the identification of people with

---

18 Bucke, T. *et al.* 'Near Misses in Police Custody: a collaborative study with Forensic Medical Examiners in London' (2008). IPCC Research and Statistics Series: paper 10. p. 9.
19 World Health Organisation. (1992) The ICD-10 Classification of Mental and Behavioural Disorders: Clinical descriptions and diagnostic guidelines. Geneva, Switzerland: WHO.

learning disabilities is extremely poor, both by police custody staff and by custody healthcare staff (Criminal Justice Joint Inspection, 2014).[20]

It is important to identify detainees with intellectual disabilities, as they are more likely to be suggestible and acquiescent. Precautions must be put in place to safeguard their vulnerability by use of an appropriate adult. However, caution should be exercised in using a family member as an appropriate adult, given the potential for learning difficulties among close relatives. There are various screening tools for identifying persons with learning disability, but a structured question format is also helpful, asking questions such as 'were you told you had special educational needs at school?', 'did you need extra help or go to a special school?', 'did you have any tests by learning disability workers?' and 'what did they say?'.

Substance misuse

18.29   Substance misuse is a very common problem in the custodial setting, and all substance misuse detainees are vulnerable. It is important to take a comprehensive history, which should include details of past and present drug use as well as alcohol intake. For each drug that is being used, the following information should be ascertained:

- the type of drug;

- the duration of use;

- when it was last taken and route of administration; and

- the amount used per day.

A physical examination, as a minimum, should involve measuring vital signs (pulse, blood pressure and temperature) and looking for signs of intoxication or withdrawal. A mental state examination should be performed and risk of self-harm assessed. Consideration should be given to checking the blood glucose.

Generally, denial or minimisation of drug use is an issue for HCPs in the custodial setting. Some studies[21] have shown that substance misusers who are involved in opioid substitution programmes are generally honest when reporting details of drug use; however, one study[22] reported that details of alleged methadone intake could not be relied upon. This is important, from a patient safety perspective, where a detainee may have complex motivations for giving false information. It is also important from a medico-legal perspective, and so HCPs should be careful to record signs and symptoms which may indicate drug use contrary to patient reports.

There are various assessment scales for alcohol (Clinical Institute Withdrawal

20 Criminal Justice Joint Inspection. (2014) A joint inspection of the treatment of offenders with learning disabilities within the criminal justice system - phase 1 from arrest to sentence. Manchester, UK: HMI Probation.

21 Brown, J., Kranzler, H.R. and Del Boca, F.K. ,Self-reports by alcohol and drug abuse inpatients: factors affecting reliability and validity' *British Journal of Addiction* (1992) 87 pp. 1013–1024.

22 Stark, M.M., Norfolk, G.A., Rogers, D.J. and Payne-James, J.J. 'The validity of self-reported substance misuse amongst detainees in police custody' *J Clin Forensic Med* (2002) 9 pp. 25–26.

Assessment of Alcohol Scale, Revised – CIWA-Ar)[23] and opiate withdrawal (Clinical Opiate Withdrawal Scale – COWS), but these have not been validated in the custodial setting.

Prescribing in custody

18.30   Detainees may be prescribed medication whilst in custody from a variety of sources, e.g. by a forensic physician, other healthcare professional or by self-administration by the detainee, either kept in their own possession or supervised by a police officer.

The overriding principles of prescribing must be the clinical safety and well-being of the detainee and, again, the standard of clinical treatment is expected to be equivalent to that given to any person in the non-custodial setting. It is essential that an adequate clinical assessment of the detainee be undertaken prior to the prescription and administration of medication. Care must be taken to exclude the presence of intoxication by drugs and/or alcohol.

Sufficient medication should be prescribed to last until such time as the prescriber considers the detainee requires a further clinical assessment or is due to leave police custody. However, there are occasions when a full course of treatment should be prescribed and given to the detainee on release, e.g. a course of antibiotics after a penetrating dog bite.

Some nurses are authorised prescribers but, if this is not the case, and where multi-professional teams are providing care, the provision of medication can be accomplished by the use of Patient Group Directions in accordance with clinical policy. The FFLM has published detailed recommendations on prescribing medication in police custody.[24]

Fitness for interview

18.31   A person may be unfit for interview when:[25]

- conducting the interview could significantly harm his physical or mental state; or

- anything he says in the interview about his involvement or suspected involvement in the offence about which he is being interviewed *might* be considered unreliable in subsequent court proceedings because of his physical or mental state.

23 Sullivan, J.T., Sykora, K., Schneiderman, J., Naranjo, C.A. and Sellers, E.M. 'Assessment of alcohol withdrawal: The revised Clinical Institute Withdrawal Assessment for Alcohol scale (CIWA-Ar)' *British Journal of Addiction* (1989) 84: pp. 1353–1357.
24 Faculty of Forensic and Legal Medicine. Safe and Secure Administration of Medication in Police Custody. http://fflm.ac.uk/upload/documents/1391529726.pdf (accessed 11 July 2014).
25 Police and Criminal Evidence Act 1984 (PACE) Code C Revised. Code of Practice for the detention, treatment and questioning of persons by police officers. Annex G Fitness to be interviewed. October 2013.

It is important to be able to recognise individuals who are vulnerable to making false or misleading statements to the police and to ensure that appropriate safeguards are put in place where necessary. Failure to do so may result in any confession being ruled inadmissible because the detainee was unfit for interview.

Psychologists have classified false confessions into four different types: voluntary; accommodating-complaint; coerced-complaint; and coerced-internalised. Some of the reasons why a person may make a false confession include being allowed home after confessing, bringing an interview to an end, and avoiding being kept in police custody.

18.32   However, it is a fundamental principle of English law, enshrined in PACE, that confession evidence must not be adduced if it:

'... was or may have been obtained–

(a) by oppression ...; or

(b) in consequence of anything said or done which was likely, in the circumstances existing at the time, to render unreliable any confession which might be made by him in consequence thereof.'[26]

Similarly, PACE also states that the court may refuse to allow confession evidence if it appears that:

'... having regard to all the circumstances, including the circumstances in which the evidence was obtained, the admission of the evidence would have such an adverse effect on the fairness of the proceedings that the court ought not to admit it.'[27]

In assessing the detainee, the HCP should therefore advise on:

●   the need for an appropriate adult (concept of mental vulnerability);

●   whether reassessment of the person's fitness for interview is required at a later date;

●   whether a (further) specialist opinion may be required; and

●   the risks of unreliability, and attempt to quantify those risks.

In advising on these points, the HCP will need to:

●   consider whether the person's condition is likely to improve, or require or be amenable to treatment;

●   if so, indicate how long it may take for such improvement to take effect; and

●   ensure that any advice or recommendations are made in writing and form part of the custody record.

---

26 Section 76 of the Police and Criminal Evidence Act 1984.
27 Section 78 of the Police and Criminal Evidence Act 1984. Articles 74 and 76 of the Northern Ireland Order contain the equivalent terms for Northern Ireland. In Scotland, the matter is regulated by common law rules: see, inter alia, *Chalmers v HM Advocate* [1954] JC 66.

Assessing fitness for interview

18.33   Norfolk[28] advises on a suitable scheme for assessing fitness for interview using the mnemonic 'PHIT':

- **P**ersonality;

- **H**ealth – physical and mental;

- **I**nterview; and

- **T**otality of the circumstances.

Personality

18.34   Personality factors can include suggestibility, compliance and acquiescence:

- **Suggestibility** is the manner in which leading questions can produce distorted responses from suspects because they are phrased in such a way as to suggest the expected response and correlates with anxiety, lack of assertiveness, poor self-esteem and low intelligence.

- **Compliance** refers to the tendency of people to obey the instructions of others when they do not really want to, who may be over-eager to please, unable to resist pressure and particularly associated with feelings of guilt.

- **Acquiescence** is the manner by which people answer questions in the affirmative, irrespective of content, and is more highly correlated with low intelligence than suggestibility or compliance.

Although experienced forensic psychologists best assess these psychological vulnerabilities, the examining doctor needs to have a working knowledge of how the traits correlate with other characteristics of the individual. Broadly speaking, acquiescence depends more on lack of intelligence and poor educational background than temperament or personality variables; compliance is predominantly a personality measure; and suggestibility falls somewhere in between.

Health

18.35   This will include an assessment of both physical and mental health problems. Detainees who have a psychotic illness may be unable to distinguish fact from fantasy. Those with a learning disability are often able to disguise their disability, but they may have difficulty understanding legal rights, find it hard to communicate effectively and are at increased likelihood of suggestibility and acquiescence. Physical illnesses can affect general coping strategies.

Intoxication may affect memory and cause confusion and can distort an individual's perception of the strength of the case against him or her. Withdrawal from both

---

28 Norfolk, G.A. 'Fit to be interviewed by the police – an aid to assessment' *Medicine, Science and the Law* (2001) 41 pp. 5–12.

alcohol and opiates can increase suggestibility. There is some research evidence to suggest that those suffering from opiate withdrawal have higher levels of interrogative suggestibility. Thus, whilst the majority of confessions made by those withdrawing from illicit drugs are reliable, as a general rule it is reasonable to advise that those suffering from mild withdrawal are likely to be fit to be interviewed, whereas the physical and mental distress occasioned by severe withdrawal may render a person unfit for interview, and the withdrawal should therefore be treated with substitute medication before a person is interviewed.

Interview

18.36   Interview characteristics include when the detainee is going to be interviewed, for how long, and the seriousness of the alleged offence.

Totality

18.37   Totality of the circumstances can include whether the detainee has had access to legal advice, whether advice on legal rights has been given, and whether they are understood, whether adequate rest periods have been given, and whether there are significant social distractions (for example, a female detainee may have anxieties about childcare arrangements).

18.38   In terms of the assessment, the following should be obtained:

- background information;
- general medical history;
- psychiatric history;
- specific enquiry about drugs and alcohol;
- educational background, to assess for learning disability; and
- when the detained has last eaten and slept, and enquiry about social distractions.

The examination should include:

- general appearance;
- pulse rate, blood pressure and temperature;
- eye examination, to look for pupil size and nystagmus;
- signs of intoxication/withdrawal; and
- mental state examination.

At the end of this examination, the healthcare professional should be able to conclude whether the detainee is fit for interview, or if any treatment is needed and whether a reassessment is necessary. There will also be cases where it may not be possible to make a detainee fit for interview; for instance, if the person has dementia, they may never be fit for interview. In the event that a detainee is unfit to be interviewed, the police may consider that they have sufficient evidence to charge without interview, in which case the detainee will be bailed or kept in custody and taken to court. Alternatively, it may be possible to bail the detainee to return another day if, for example, an appropriate adult were not available.

Appropriate adults

18.39   Appropriate adults (AA) are required, to protect the rights and welfare of children and vulnerable adults when they are detained or interviewed by the police. They can be a parent, another family member, a social or care worker or a volunteer. They must be over 18 but must not be a police officer or employed by the police.

An AA must be called for any juvenile (see below) or vulnerable adult in police custody. There is no precise definition of mental vulnerability, but the Code of Practice (at C1.4) states that:

'If an officer has any suspicion, or is told in good faith, that a person of any age may be mentally disordered or otherwise mentally vulnerable, in the absence of clear evidence to dispel that suspicion, the person shall be treated as such for the purposes of this Code.'

Section 1(2) of the Mental Health Act 1983 defines a mental disorder as '... any disorder or disability of the mind'.[29]

Thus, in theory, any person with a history of mental illness could merit having an AA. In addition, a detainee does not have to have a recognised mental illness or learning disability to be classed as mentally vulnerable, and the assessment of vulnerability should also take account of the detainee's current situation and behaviour, in deciding whether he or she is vulnerable. Ultimately, it is the custody officer and not the healthcare professional who should make the decision.

18.40   In England and Wales,[30] the issue was to an extent clarified in *R v Aspinall*,[31] where a defendant who suffered from schizophrenia was arrested near a cache of drugs and his diagnosis was confirmed by a doctor who felt that he was fit to interview, which was subsequently carried out without an AA present or legal advice. The judge allowed the interview into evidence because Aspinall's apparent ability to deal with the interview obviated the need for an appropriate adult. The Court of Appeal overturned the conviction, holding that it was wrong to admit the interview, as the judge had given too much weight to Aspinall's apparent lucidity and not considered the purpose of the safeguard of an appropriate adult, including the latter's role in considering the question of legal advice being obtained. As a result of this, healthcare professionals would be advised to recommend that any detainee who has a past history of schizophrenia or a psychotic illness should have an AA.

29 Reproduced in article 3 of the Mental Health (Northern Ireland) Order 1986. In Scots law, the term is defined as 'any mental illness, personality disorder or learning disability, however caused or manifested' (section 328 of the Mental Health (Care and Treatment) (Scotland) Act 2003).
30 For Scotland, the legal framework and additional guidance can be found in the Scottish Executive's 'Guidance on Appropriate Adult Services in Scotland', available at www.scotland. gov.uk/Resource/Doc/1099/0053903.pdf.
31 *R v Aspinall (Paul James)* (1999) MHLR 12.

In England and Wales, the age requirement for an AA has also recently been changed: previously, PACE referred to 'juveniles' rather than children and young people. Juveniles are defined as aged 10 to 16, and therefore young people aged 17 are excluded but are still regarded as a 'child' within the meaning of the Children Act 1989. Following the deaths of two young people, Joe Lawton and Edward Thornber, aged 17, following periods of detention in custody, the Court of Appeal, in an application for judicial review, held that anyone under the age of 18 should be treated within the meaning of PACE as a 'juvenile' for the purposes of requiring an AA.[32]

If in doubt, an AA should be called, to safeguard the interests of the detainee and justice.

Terrorism Act detainees

18.41   The power to detain persons suspected of terrorism offences is under section 41 of the Terrorism Act 2000 and not PACE. Unlike PACE, the detention clock commences at the time of arrest and does not stop if the person is detained or transferred to hospital. The maximum period of detention is 14 days.

Because of the longer period of detention, and also because risks of ill-treatment are greater and allegations of ill-treatment more frequent, it is recommended that detainees have a medical examination on detention and before release and be offered a daily medical assessment by a forensic physician.[33]

A detailed assessment of fitness to detain and interview should be made on detention and, similarly, a complete body surface examination for injuries on detention and prior to release should be made. The detainee's weight should be measured on detention, in view of the possibility of a hunger strike.

Intimate searches

18.42   An intimate search is a search that consists of a physical examination of a body orifice other than the mouth – this could therefore include the nose, ear, rectum and vagina. In England and Wales, the rules governing intimate body searches are covered by section 55 of PACE, as amended by the Criminal Justice Act 1988 and the Drugs Act 2005. The same rules apply in Northern Ireland: see article 56 of the Northern Ireland Order. In Scotland, in contrast to the rest of the United Kingdom, the police must obtain a judicial warrant (from a sheriff) for intimate searches.[34]

---

32 *R (HC (A Child)) v Secretary of State for the Home Department & another* [2013] EWHC 982 (Admin). The legislation for Northern Ireland had already been amended to include 17-year-olds: see article 38(14) of the Northern Ireland Order. The Scottish practice is for the appropriate adult system only to apply to those aged 18 or over. Section 15 of the Criminal Procedure (Scotland) Act 1995 permits access of a parent or guardian to a child in detention.

33 Faculty of Forensic and Legal Medicine. Medical Care of Persons Detained Under the Terrorism Act 2000. http://fflm.ac.uk/upload/documents/1297872551.pdf (accessed 11 July 2014).

34 See, for instance, *Young v Procurator Fiscal, Selkirk* [2012] HCJAC 104. As with searches, BMA and FFLM consider that such searches should be carried out by a doctor only when the individual has given consent. If consent is not given, the doctor should refuse to participate and have no further involvement in the search – see British Medical Association and Faculty of Forensic and Legal Medicine (2010). Recommendations for healthcare professionals asked to perform intimate body searches. http://fflm.ac.uk/upload/documents/1281533595.pdf (accessed 11 July 2014).

In England and Wales and in Northern Ireland, under current PACE legislation, intimate searches can be carried out if an officer of the rank of inspector or above has grounds for believing that the detainee has concealed on him anything that might cause injury or be of use whilst in detention, or has class A drugs concealed with the intent to supply before arrest.

18.43 The detainee must give consent under PACE to a police inspector, but it is essential that the healthcare professional also obtains written informed consent and explains in detail the possible options and consequences, which could include:[35]

- a refusal may imply guilt;

- refusal may lead, in some circumstances, to the police officer carrying out the search rather than a healthcare professional;

- the risks involved if the search is carried out; or

- the health risks of refusing the search, e.g. if a package of drugs concealed begins to leak and became absorbed, resulting in a sudden overdose.

Intimate searches for drugs must always be performed by a healthcare professional (unless an officer of at least the rank of inspector considers that this is not practicable) and in medical premises. Alternative options allowed under PACE include an X-ray or ultrasound examination, but again medical consent will be required (section 55A of PACE, article 56A of the Northern Ireland Order).

Further reading material

- Brown, J., Kranzler, H.R. and Del Boca, F.K. ,Self-reports by alcohol and drug abuse inpatients: factors affecting reliability and validity' *British Journal of Addiction* (1992) 87 pp. 1013–1024

- Bucke, T. *et al.* 'Near Misses in Police Custody: a collaborative study with Forensic Medical Examiners in London' (2008). IPCC Research and Statistics Series: paper 10. p. 9

- Jennett, B., Teasdale, G. 'Aspects of coma after severe head injury' *Lancet* (1977) 1:pp. 878–881

- Norfolk, G.A. 'Fit to be interviewed by the police – an aid to assessment' *Medicine, Science and the Law* (2001) 41 pp. 5–12

- Payne-James, J.J., Anderson, W.R., Green, P.G. and Johnston, A. 'Provision of forensic medical services to police custody suites in England and Wales: Current practice' *J Forensic and Legal Medicine* (2009) 16 pp. 189–195

- Stark, M.M., Norfolk, G.A., Rogers, D.J. and Payne-James, J.J. 'The validity of self-reported substance misuse amongst detainees in police custody' *J Clin Forensic Med* (2002) 9 pp. 25–26

---

35 Ibid.

- Sullivan, J.T., Sykora, K., Schneiderman, J., Naranjo, C.A. and Sellers, E.M. 'Assessment of alcohol withdrawal: The revised Clinical Institute Withdrawal Assessment for Alcohol scale (CIWA-Ar)' *British Journal of Addiction* (1989) 84: pp. 1353–1357

- Wall, I.F. 'Lack of training in custodial medicine in the UK – a cause for concern?' *J Forensic Legal Med.* (2008) doi:10.1016/j.jflm.2008.02.005

Chapter 19

Deaths in state settings

With Kate O'Raghallaigh

Introduction

19.1   The aim of this chapter is to give a broad overview of deaths that occur in the United Kingdom in custodial or state settings. It is intended to assist medical and legal practitioners alike in understanding the types of deaths which give rise to state investigations, either in the form of internal and/or administrative inquiries, as well as inquest proceedings before a coroner, and the role that is played by medical evidence within those contexts. The first part, therefore, sets out the investigative responses provided by state agencies in respect of such deaths, including how investigations are used in, and bear upon, inquest proceedings. The inquest procedure itself and its Scottish and Northern Irish equivalents are considered separately in Chapter 5. The second part then considers the pathology of the various forms of death that may occur in custodial settings.

The legal viewpoint

Statistical overview

19.2   Between 2000 and 2013 (the last available year of statistics), there were 7,630 recorded deaths in state custody in England and Wales.[1] The custodial settings in which those deaths occurred were:

- prisons;[2]

- police custody;

- hospital in-patients detained under the Mental Health Act 1983;

---

1   Report of Independent Advisory Panel on Deaths in Custody 'Statistical analysis of all recorded deaths of individuals detained in state custody between 1 January 2000 and 31 December 2013' (February 2015), page 5. Equivalent collated statistics are not available for Northern Ireland or Scotland, although both jurisdictions do publish regular statistics on deaths in prison together with causes of death when established. See www.sps.gov.uk/Corporate/Information/PrisonerDeaths.aspx and www.niprisonerombudsman.com/index.php/publications/.
2   This category includes men and women of 18 years and over in prison, and young people between the ages of 15 and 17 detained in young offender institutions.

- approved premises;[3]

- secure training centres (STCs) and secure children's homes (SCHs);[4] and

- immigration removal centres.

Of those deaths, 60% were patients detained under the Mental Health Act; and 33% were within prison settings.[5] Death by natural causes is the largest proportion of deaths in state custody, for instance, accounting for 63% of deaths in 2013.[6] Between 2000 and 2010, there were 1,812 self-inflicted deaths in state custody, some 24% of total deaths.[7] The most common method of self-inflicted death was hanging (accounting for 69% of self-inflicted deaths in 2013 alone). Other less common methods included jumping/falling and overdose/poisoning.

Types of state settings

19.3   Listed below are the most typical state settings in which deaths occur, as those deaths feature in coronial and civil proceedings and, to a lesser extent, criminal proceedings and public inquiries:

- deaths involving police contact;

- deaths in prison;

- deaths in psychiatric units; and

- deaths in hospitals.

Medical evidence regularly features in all of these litigation contexts and, in many cases, such as cases of police restraint, will be at the forefront of the litigation.

Investigations into deaths in state settings

19.4   There are a number of investigative responses which are triggered by a death in a state setting. The main judicial form of investigation is that of the coroner's inquest or, for Scotland, the fatal accident inquiry (FAI), which are discussed in more detail in Chapter 5. The common feature of both systems is the need to record a cause of death. However, where a death has occurred in prison or during police detention, both the coroner's task and the task of a sheriff conducting an FAI will often involve

---

3   Accommodation which is approved (by the Secretary of State under section 13 of the Offender Management Act 2007) to house adults subject to bail in criminal proceedings and/or those released on licence following release from prison. This accommodation is managed by the Probation Service or voluntary organisations.
4   STCs are privately run, education-focused centres for offenders up to the age of 17. SCHs are run by social services to provide a structured but secure home setting for young people aged 10 to 17 who meet the conditions specified in section 25 of the Children Act 1989, namely that the child is being looked after by a local authority and either: (a) is likely to abscond and suffer significant harm; or (b) if kept in any other accommodation is likely to injure himself or others.
5   See the Independent Advisory Panel's February 2015 report at p 6.
6   Ibid at p 28.
7   Ibid at p 21.

an investigation of the wider circumstances surrounding the death, including an analysis of whether and, if so, how future similar deaths could be prevented.

19.5   In England and Wales, there are also a number of investigative bodies which play an important role in dealing with deaths in state settings, for example:

- the Independent Police Complaints Commission (IPCC) is responsible for investigating all deaths involving police contact;[8] and

- the Prisons and Probation Ombudsman (PPO) is responsible for investigating all deaths which occur in prisons, probation hostels and immigration detention centres.[9]

Both the IPCC and the PPO (and their counterparts) play a crucial role in inquest proceedings and, in most cases, will disclose their investigative findings to the coroner during the inquest process. In many cases, the investigations of the IPCC and PPO will form the main basis of the coroner's investigation.

19.6   At present, there is no independent body comparable to the IPCC or the PPO which automatically investigates deaths in a mental health setting (e.g. deaths of voluntarily or involuntarily admitted psychiatric patients).[10] Such deaths, however, may be investigated prior to any inquest, through internal NHS investigations or independent investigations commissioned by the NHS.[11]

As well as the coroner and independent investigatory bodies such as the IPCC and the PPO, a Government Minister has the power to establish a public inquiry into a death which has 'caused, or [is] capable of causing, public concern' or where there is 'public concern' as to a death which has occurred.[12]

In respect of the relatively small number of deaths which occur in a state setting which involve a third party, for example where an individual is killed in prison or in a mental health setting,[13] the police play the primary role in investigating the circumstances of the death.

---

8   The equivalent bodies for Northern Ireland and Scotland are the Police Ombudsman and the Police Investigations and Review Commissioner respectively.
9   For Northern Ireland, the Northern Ireland Prisoner Ombudsman; for Scotland, although the Scottish Public Services Ombudsman may receive complaints relating to the Scottish Prison Service, it has no specific statutory duty in relation to the investigation of deaths, as, in any case, all deaths in prison will result in a fatal accident inquiry. A further reason for the absence of specific investigative bodies in Scotland is that the Lord Advocate has general responsibility for the investigation of sudden, suspicious, accidental and unexplained deaths in Scotland.
10 Neither domestic law nor European human rights law requires an independent investigation prior to an inquest: *R (on the application of Antoniou) v Central and North West London NHS Foundation Trust and Others* [2013] EWHC 3055 (Admin).
11 Department of Health: Independent Investigation of Adverse Events in Mental Health Services (2005); National Patient Safety Agency: Independent Investigation of Serious Patient Safety Incidents in Mental Health Services (2008).
12 Section 1(1) of the Inquiries Act 2005. The power is one that applies to Ministers in all three UK jurisdictions (section 1(2)).
13 Between 2000 and 2013, there were 25 deaths caused by others (including homicide) in custodial settings in England and Wales: Independent Advisory Panel, 2015 report, at p 14.

Deaths in custody

19.7   When an individual dies in custody, the state is obliged to conduct an independent investigation into the death.[14] This obligation arises from Article 2 of the European Convention on Human Rights, which places an obligation upon the state to respect and protect the right to life.[15] In the case of deaths in custody in England and Wales and in Northern Ireland, the investigative obligation is almost invariably discharged by the holding of an inquest before a coroner; in Scotland, it is discharged by the holding of a fatal accident inquiry (FAI) before a sheriff. In England and Wales and in Northern Ireland, such inquests are commonly referred to as 'Article 2' inquests (see further Chapter 5).

In an Article 2 inquest involving a person who has committed suicide in custody, the coroner will often collate written and live evidence from medical practitioners who treated the deceased and who can comment on his or her medical records. In some cases, the coroner will instruct an independent physician to comment upon the care given to the deceased, including whether or not the care that he or she received played a role in the death. Similar, though broader, powers apply to FAIs before sheriffs.

Deaths in hospitals

19.8   A death which occurs in a hospital in England and Wales or in Northern Ireland will not be investigated at an inquest unless it appears to the coroner that the death was violent, unnatural or unknown. In such circumstances, the coroner is under a duty to investigate the death, and may hold a post-mortem (as described in Chapter 5) as well as an inquest hearing.[16]

Although the scope for hospital deaths to be investigated by way of an inquest is narrower than custody deaths (which require a coroner to hold an inquest),[17] there are a number of areas of hospital deaths which may give rise to issues of state responsibility, and which will attract the jurisdiction of the coroner and/or the holding of an independent investigation. These include deaths in psychiatric hospitals/wards of those detained under the Mental Health Act 1983, certain deaths (e.g. suicides) of voluntarily admitted psychiatric patients, deaths involving allegations of staff abuse and/or neglect in hospitals, and any death which gives rise to concerns of a systemic failure.

---

14 *R (on the application of Middleton) v West Somerset Coroner and Another* [2004] 2 AC 182; *R (on the application of Amin) v Secretary of State for the Home Department* [2004] 1 AC 653.

15 Article 2 ECHR has been incorporated into UK law by the Human Rights Act 1998.

16 Similar considerations apply in Scotland: a fatal accident inquiry will be triggered where it appears to the Lord Advocate that an inquiry should be held into the circumstances of the death on the ground that it was sudden, suspicious or unexplained, or has occurred in circumstances such as to give rise to serious public concern: see section 1(1)(b) of the Fatal Accidents and Sudden Deaths Inquiry (Scotland) Act 1976.

17 Section 1(2)(c) of the Coroners and Justice Act 2009.

Deaths in psychiatric hospitals

19.9   The death of a patient who is detained in a psychiatric hospital or ward/unit pursuant to the provisions of the Mental Health Act 1983 will be investigated by a coroner at an inquest.[18] In addition, the death of a patient who is voluntarily admitted for psychiatric treatment may be investigated at an inquest, because such a patient is considered as being under the state's control.[19]

Neither category of death is required to be investigated by an independent body prior to an inquest (and there is, at present, no independent investigatory body comparable to the IPCC or the PPO).[20] However, the Department of Health has issued guidance recommending three forms of investigation where such deaths occur: an initial NHS management review, an internal NHS Mental Health Trust investigation, and an independent investigation.[21]

Deaths involving police contact

Categories of death

19.10   Deaths involving police contact in England and Wales are investigated by the Independent Police Complaints Commission (IPCC), an executive non-departmental public body established by the Police Reform Act 2002.[22]

Police forces in England and Wales have a duty to refer to the IPCC all deaths involving police contact, including those that occur in or following custody and where the police contact may have contributed to the death.[23] The IPCC annually compiles statistics on such deaths in its report 'Deaths during or following police contact' (also known as the 'annual death report').

19.11   There are a variety of circumstances in which a death typically involves police contact. Those which feature in the IPCC's annual death report fall into the following categories:

- deaths in police custody;

- fatal police shootings;

---

18 Ibid.
19 *Rabone v Pennine Care NHS Foundation Trust* [2012] UKSC 2. In both circumstances, in Scotland the investigation obligation will be met by the holding of a fatal accident inquiry.
20 See footnote 11 above.
21 See footnote 12 above.
22 The equivalent legislation creating the Police Ombudsman for Northern Ireland is the Police (Northern Ireland) Act 1998. The Scottish Police Investigations and Review Commissioner was first established by the Police, Public Order and Criminal Justice (Scotland) Act 2006, now amended by the Police and Fire Reform (Scotland) Act 2012.
23 Paragraphs 4(1)(a), 13(1)(a), 14C(1) of Schedule 3 to the Police Reform Act 2002, as amended by Serious Organised Crime and Police Act 2005, Schedule 12. For statutory definition of 'death or serious injury', see section 12 of the Police Reform Act 2002. In Northern Ireland, the equivalent duties are set out in section 55(3) of the Police (Northern Ireland) Act 1998. In Scotland, the equivalent duties are set out in sections 41B and 41D of the Police, Public Order and Criminal Justice (Scotland) Act 2006.

- road traffic incidents;

- apparent suicides following police custody; and

- other deaths following police contact.

Each of these categories is defined by the IPCC with reference to a number of published criteria. For example, a death will be categorised by the IPCC as an 'apparent suicide following police custody' where it occurs either within 48 hours of release from police custody, or after 48 hours from release but where the period spent in custody may be relevant to the death.[24]

19.12   In considering deaths commonly described or understood as 'deaths in police custody', it should be noted that the concept of 'deaths in police custody' extends beyond deaths which occur in a cell in a police station. The following types of death all fall within the purview of 'deaths in custody', as considered by the Home Office,[25] and similarly within the definitions of 'deaths in or following police custody' which are investigated by the IPCC:[26]

- death while, or shortly after, being detained by the police for a 'stop and search';

- death while being transferred to or from hospital (or some other premises) from the police station;

- death while in the care of the police, having been detained under the Mental Health Act 1983;

- where the death is of a child or young person detained for their own protection;

- where the person is in police custody, having been arrested by officers from a police force in Scotland exercising their powers of detention under section 137(2) of the Criminal Justice and Public Order Act 1994;

- where the person is in police custody, having been arrested under section 3(5) of the Asylum and Immigration Appeals Act 1993;

- where the person is in police custody, having been served a notice advising them of their detention under powers contained in the Immigration Act 1971;

- where the person is a convicted or remanded prisoner held in police cells on behalf of the Prison Service under the Imprisonment (Temporary Provisions) Act 1980; and

- following police detention, where there is a link between the detention and the death.

24 IPCC 'Deaths during or following police contact report – Guidance', p 5.
25 Home Officer Circular 31/2002.
26 IPCC 'Deaths during or following police contact report – Guidance', p 4. More generally, a person is in 'police detention' if: he has been taken to a police station following arrest for an offence, or after an arrest under section 41 of the Terrorism Act 2000; he is arrested following voluntary attendance at a police station and is detained there or elsewhere by a constable; or he is in lawful custody under paragraph 22, 34(1) or 35(3) of Schedule 4 to the Police Reform Act 2002: section 118 of the Police and Criminal Evidence Act 1984.

Investigating the death: the IPCC

19.13   Once a referral is made to the IPCC about a death involving police contact, the IPCC must determine whether the death should be investigated. If it decides that the matter should be investigated, it must determine the mode of investigation, having regard to the seriousness of the case and the public interest.[27]

There are four kinds of investigation which the IPCC can carry out:

(1)   local investigation;

(2)   supervised investigation;

(3)   managed investigation; or

(4)   independent investigation.

An independent investigation is the highest level of investigation that the IPCC is empowered to conduct. Such investigations are carried out by the IPCC itself, as opposed to local, supervised and managed investigations, which are conducted by appointed members of the police force.

An independent investigation is often used for the most serious incidents and/ or those with significant public interest, e.g. those that cause a high level of public concern, have the greatest potential to impact on communities, or have serious implications for the reputation of the police. This is the mode of investigation most frequently used for deaths involving police contact.[28]

The purpose of an IPCC independent investigation into a death involving police contact is to establish the relevant facts of the death, the sequence of events and their consequences. The investigation is ultimately directed at determining how and to what extent, if any, the person who has died or been seriously injured had contact with the police, and the degree to which this caused or contributed to the death.

During an independent investigation, investigators will attend the scene of the death and will make efforts to obtain evidence. The investigation may involve appealing for witnesses, taking witness statements, interviewing police officers or members of police staff, analysing CCTV footage and obtaining other documents and records.

In many cases, the IPCC investigator will liaise with the coroner, the Crown Prosecution Service (CPS) and/or other agencies, such as the Health and Safety Executive.

Special case – deaths in the police station

Treatment in the police station

19.14   The detention and treatment of suspects in police custody is governed by the Police and Criminal Evidence Act 1984 (commonly known as 'PACE'), specifically

---

27 Paragraphs 5, 14, 14D and 15 of Schedule 3 to the Police Reform Act 2002.
28 There were 54 independent investigations in 2013/14. A further three were supervised by the IPCC. The remaining 70 cases were either the subject of local investigations or referred back to the relevant police force by the IPCC. Source: 'Deaths during or following police contact: Statistics for England and Wales 2013/14' at www.ipcc.gov.uk/sites/default/files/Documents/ research_stats/Deaths_Report_1314.pdf.

PACE Code C.[29] Code C sets out police officers' obligations towards suspects in police custody, including the compilation of records and access to medical care, and further provides for minimum standards of the conditions of detention.

Once a detainee is 'booked in' to the police station, a custody record must be opened for that person. The custody record is intended to document various information about the suspect and the details of their detention in the police station, including (but not limited to) the reasons for the person's detention, the duration of detention, the need for medical treatment, whether the detainee receives medical treatment, and the result of any observations of the detainee; the provision of medical assessment and treatment is considered at length in Chapter 18.

The use of force

19.15 Police officers are entitled to use force when lawfully exercising their powers of arrest, search and seizure (section 117 of PACE). The police employ a number of techniques for using force, which typically include the following:

- handcuffs;
- CS spray;
- physical restraint;
- batons; and
- tear gas.

There are a variety of situations where detainees may be subject to physical restraint while they are in custody in the police station. For example, a detainee may refuse to comply with a search, and therefore be restrained so as to allow him or herself to be searched. If officers, when dealing with a detainee, feel that the detainee is physically threatening, the detainee may be physically restrained, including having handcuffs placed on him or her.

Handcuffs may be used when police think that a detainee poses a risk of escape or violence. When applying handcuffs, the police are obliged to consider the detainee's physical condition, including whether the use of handcuffs may pose a risk of injury or a risk to the detainee's health: The Association of Chief Police Officers (ACPO) has issued 'Guidance on the use of Handcuffs' (2012).

19.16 A particular area of concern in recent years has been the area of restraint-related deaths. Typically referred to as 'restraint deaths', such deaths involve detainees who have been physically restrained by police officers (or staff involved in the removal of immigration detainees) and who have died as a result of positional asphyxia. The Independent Advisory Panel's report of February 2015 records 65 such deaths between 2000 and 2013 across all custody settings. The majority of

---

29 'Code C Revised Code of Practice for the Detention, Treatment and Questioning of Persons by Police Officers', revised by the Home Office in 2013.

these deaths (48) occurred in respect of patients detained under the Mental Health Act 1983, followed by deaths in police custody (13).[30]

Deaths in prison

Prisons and Probation Ombudsman

19.17   The Prison and Probation Ombudsman (PPO) is appointed by the Secretary of State for Justice in order to investigate complaints from prisoners, immigration detainees and residents of 'approved premises'.[31] A significant function of the PPO's investigative remit is to consider all deaths that occur among prisoners in those settings. The PPO's investigative remit also includes deaths of inmates that occur while the inmate is being transferred to and from custody, or while they are at court or in hospital. Where an inmate has been released from custody, the PPO has a discretion to investigate cases which raise issues about the care provided by the relevant custodial setting.

The aims of the PPO's investigations are to:[32]

'●   establish the circumstances and events surrounding the death, especially regarding the management of the individual by the relevant authority or authorities within remit, but including relevant outside factors;

●   examine whether any change in operational methods, policy, practice or management arrangements would help prevent a recurrence;

●   in conjunction with the NHS where appropriate, examine relevant health issues and assess clinical care;

●   provide explanations and insight for bereaved relatives; and

●   assist the Coroner's inquest [to] fulfil the investigative obligation arising under Article 2 of the European Convention on Human Rights ("the right to life"), by ensuring as far as possible that the full facts are brought to light and any relevant failing is exposed, any commendable action or practice is identified, and any lessons from the death are learned.'

In respect of prisons, the PPO commences its investigation upon notification of the death. The PPO will appoint a lead investigator, who will attend the prison to collate relevant medical and prison records and interview staff at the prison, including (where necessary) prison healthcare staff. The investigator will also speak to the deceased's family members and the prison governor.

The remit of the investigation will include all relevant matters for which the particular authority was responsible, for example:

●   the healthcare arrangements within a prison;

●   the arrangements in place for monitoring self-harm;

---

30 Different definitions are used, which may account for the statistical disparity: for mental health cases, the broader definition of any death in which restraint was used in the previous seven days is applied; for police cases, restraint has to be mentioned in the post-mortem for it to be counted as restraint-related death. See the February 2015 report at p 13.

31 As stated at footnote 9 above, the equivalents for Northern Ireland and Scotland are the Prisoner Ombudsman for Northern Ireland and the Scottish Public Services Ombudsman.

32 Prisons and Probation Ombudsman 'Terms of Reference September 2013', at www.ppo.gov.uk/docs/Terms_of_Reference_September_2013_(updated_to_inc._STC_comps).pdf.

- the particular location of a prisoner within a prison; or

- the facilities for prisoners to store their own medication.

The investigation also includes services commissioned by the Ministry of Justice from outside the public sector, such as prisons that are contracted out to private companies. The local Primary Care Trust ('PCT') will also carry out a clinical review of the health care provided to the person before their death, which will be considered by the PPO investigator and may be appended to the final PPO investigation report.

The pathological viewpoint

19.18   Deaths in custody are defined as those deaths that occur when an individual dies during custody of the police or other legal authority, such as a prison or secure unit. In the former situation, deaths may occur during contact with the police, such as during an altercation in a crowd or a 'riot' situation. These may be accidental, natural or as a result of trauma. Deaths may also occur during arrest, transportation to a police station and within the police station. Cases where there has been police involvement and then a subsequent death may also fall into the category investigated by the authorities – for example, in the domestic violence situation, where prior contact with the authorities has occurred.

Deaths in prison include not only natural causes but also hanging and traumatic causes of death, including assault as well as deaths associated with alcohol or drugs. A small number of deaths also take place in secure units, where an individual may have been sectioned or otherwise detained. Deaths may also take place if an individual has either escaped or discharged themselves. Internationally, there are significant numbers of both torture and death in custody in many countries. Torture is covered in more detail later in this chapter.

Deaths in state settings include those as listed at **19.11** above.

'Asphyxial' deaths including traumatic asphyxia

19.19   In this situation, the restrained individual is held in the face down (prone) position. Being held prone, especially with the weight of another person on the victim's back, hinders respiration, affecting breathing as well as affecting the movement of the diaphragm. The sufferer is likely to struggle in order to breathe. In addition, there will be an increase in the catecholamines (adrenaline-like substances) and electrolyte changes, which sensitise the heart to fatal cardiac arrhythmia. There may also be a build-up of the breakdown products of muscle damage in the blood. Additional tools which may have been used include sprays and Tasers (see **19.21** and **19.22** below).

These deaths occur predominantly in law enforcement and in psychiatric practice. The deceased may be struggling or resisting arrest, at times violently. Other findings may include marks caused by weapons, such as batons or rubber bullets. Head injuries or injuries elsewhere may also occur during falling/pushing and contact with the ground or other surface such as a wall. Other blunt trauma may be as a result of blows by fist, elbow or knee. Both head injuries and blunt abdominal trauma may be difficult to diagnose from the clinical aspect, particularly in a background of intoxication from alcohol or drugs. Presentation may also be delayed.

Some individuals may have taken cocaine or other stimulants, which may lead to the acute behavioural disturbance of excited delirium (see **19.20** below). This causes difficulty in restraint. There is additional controversy with the issue of the sickle cell trait and sickle cell anaemia. Red blood cells in the blood become 'sickled' (like a scythe, instead of round), with reduction in their ability to transport oxygen. This is found in families from Africa, the Caribbean and some Mediterranean countries. The sickle cell trait is more common than sickle cell anaemia. It is still debated whether or not this makes an individual more susceptible to death during restraint.

These cases are often contentious and the pathology may be difficult. Typically, there may be congestion, with petechial haemorrhages of the upper thorax and neck, although in some cases there may be nothing externally.

- The prone position, in particular with additional weight, hinders respiration.

- Cardiac arrhythmias commonly occur.

- Observation should be made for other injuries, in particular head injury, as well as other injuries including those which may be caused by a weapon.

- Toxicology may show the presence of stimulant or other drugs/alcohol.

Excited delirium

19.20   Excited delirium occurs as a result of stimulant abuse and is at the extreme end of acute behavioural disturbance (see Chapter 17). Stimulants are a group of drugs which include amphetamines, cocaine and derivatives thereof. The syndrome was first recognised in the 1980s in cocaine users, where the victims became confused and violent. In addition, hyperthermia (increase in body temperature) also occurs. These deaths have been controversial, because the individuals often died whilst being restrained or in custody. Aside from cocaine and other stimulant drugs (usually methamphetamine), an underlying psychiatric disorder and other drugs may also be present. Death often occurs when a struggle or situation has ceased or reduced and the individual is relatively inactive. The precise mechanism of death in excited delirium is not fully understood, but is likely to relate to the consequences of alterations in potassium and catecholamine concentrations, and it may be simply part of the spectrum of stimulant drug toxicity. It is thought that restraint, positional asphyxia and various sprays or Tasers do not contribute to death in these circumstances directly, but they may well be part of the physiological stress that increases vulnerability.

Other injuries

Use of a Taser

19.21   The Taser is a hand-held electrical device which fires electrical charges. This is either by barbs, which come into contact with the body but remain in contact with the device, or by direct contact with the device.

These devices are used to immobilise an individual rather than cause serious injury or death. The results of the electrical discharge cause painful neuromuscular stimulation. Pathological findings include small areas of burn where the barbs have contacted the skin. In addition, other injuries may occur as a result of falling because of secondary muscular contractions.

Fatalities have been reported following the use of Tasers, although these are infrequent. The precise role in these deaths is not clear on current evidence, and these individuals are also typically under the influence of drugs, in particular amphetamine derivatives or cocaine. The use of Tasers continues to be controversial, particularly in terms of whether or not it is capable of inducing cardiac arrhythmias.

Sprays

19.22 A variety of spraying agents have been used. These include CS spray and sprays containing the synthetic equivalent of capsicum. This is an active ingredient of pepper.

Effects of these sprays are mainly confined to the head and neck, with conjunctival reddening, lacrimation and other ocular problems. They also may cause various respiratory and oral symptoms, including burning, coughing and broncho-spasm. Symptoms usually resolve within an hour or so.

Underlying natural diseases may be exacerbated, particularly heart diseases such as hypertension and angina.

Skin effects include burning, erythema and irritation.

Torture

19.23 Article 1 of the 1984 United Nations Convention Against Torture (UNCAT)[33] defines torture as:

> 'any act by which severe pain or suffering, whether physical or mental, is intentionally inflicted on a person for such purposes as obtaining from him or a third person information or a confession, punishing him for an act he or a third person has committed or is suspected of having committed, or intimidating or coercing him or a third person, or for any reason based on discrimination of any kind, when such pain or suffering is inflicted by or at the instigation of or with the consent or acquiescence of a public official or other person acting in an official capacity.'

Both the perpetrators and forms of torture employed vary enormously across the world. Medical findings are similarly varied. Some forms of torture may leave little in the way of physical evidence – for example, 'water boarding', known and admitted to be used by US military and intelligence personnel at Guantanamo Bay. Here, an individual is 'choked' by pouring water over the face of an immobilised captive.

19.24 Other forms of torture include:

---

33 The full title is the Convention against Torture and Other Cruel, Inhuman or Degrading Treatment or Punishment. 156 States are parties to the Convention.

- Blunt trauma. This may be similar to that seen in woundings/deaths in the general population. There may be the outline of a baton or club identifiable. These typically have a linear or circular type of bruising. Bruising may also occur most commonly on the back, but also elsewhere to the body including the soles of the feet ('bastinado', 'falanga' or 'falaka') and genitalia. Scarring in survivors may be seen.

- Burns may take place by a variety of methods, including cigarettes and other direct burns, as well as contact with hot liquids.

- Sharp force injuries may be seen, with knives as well as other objects such as a bayonet.

- Suffocation, including partial suffocation, may occur with items such as a plastic bag.

- Electrical torture may or may not leave injuries (see Chapter 13). If injuries are identifiable, they may include burns to the genitalia.

- Shooting causing non-fatal injury, such as to the knee caps.

- There are a number of 'enhanced interrogation techniques' which leave little or no physical trace. Examples include: nudity; food, drink and sleep deprivation; hooding; and subjection to noise and stress positions.

  A stress position, also known as a submission position, places the human body in such a way that places strain on a particular muscle set. For example, a subject may be forced to stand on the balls of his feet, then squat so that his thighs are parallel to the ground. This creates an intense amount of pressure on the legs, leading first to pain and then muscle failure. Other, more extreme examples include reverse hanging (arms behind back and then body suspended by arms, which can dislocate the shoulders or cause long-term brachial plexus injury).

Signs and symptoms of torture:

- Blunt trauma caused by a weapon such as a baton or club.

- Burns, including by cigarettes, hot liquids or implements.

- Sharp force injuries.

- Suffocation, including partial suffocation.

- Electrical torture may involve the genitals.

- Shooting, involving sites such as the knee caps.

- Subtle signs, such as dehydration or tendon damage.

Arm locks/neck holds

19.25 These have been the subject of considerable investigation over recent decades. Their use has been markedly reduced, as these methods of restraint have been prohibited due to the number of deaths. See also Chapter 11.

The carotid sleeper

19.26 This produces compression of the carotid arteries and the jugular veins which travel up both sides of the neck. It produces transient cerebral ischaemia (that is, a lack of blood/oxygen getting to the brain). Death in these circumstances may occur as a direct result of prolonged cerebral ischaemia or, potentially, due to a reflex cardiac arrest caused by pressure on the carotid arteries. The carotid sinus is a small nodule structure which is situated within the internal carotid, just above where the common carotid artery bifurcates. If this is stimulated, it may produce cardiac arrhythmia/arrest in a similar mechanism to that which can occur during manual strangulation.

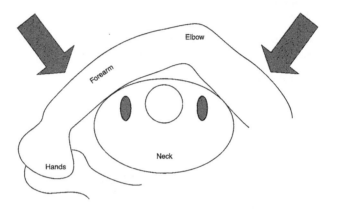

Figure 19.1 Carotid sleeper – direction of force on neck aimed at compressing the carotid arteries.

Choke hold or bar arm

19.27 This is where a forearm applies pressure to the front of the neck through the crook of the elbow. The pressure is directly onto the larynx/trachea, producing airway obstruction. Fracture of the thyroid cartilage and other neck structures may occur infrequently. There is also occlusion of the upper airways due to obstruction by the tongue.

Underlying natural disease is likely to make an individual more susceptible to the effects of either of these neck holds. This includes atherosclerosis as well as underlying heart disease rendering an individual more vulnerable to the effects of a cardiac arrhythmia.

Toxicology should be undertaken in all these cases.

- The use of these methods of restraint has fallen due to the risk of injury/death.
- Findings are variable, ranging from minimal to pronounced asphyxial changes.
- Pressure on blood vessels or neck structures may occur, with cardiac arrest and/or occlusion of the airways.

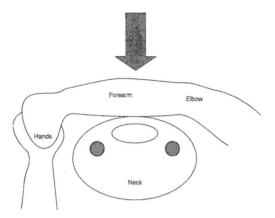

Figure 19.2 Choke hold – force applied across the front of the neck compressing the airway.

Deaths in custody due to other causes

Alcohol

19.28   Acute alcohol poisoning may cause death, particularly in those detained after arrest by the police. Some jurisdictions have introduced so-called 'drunk' cells. The topic of acute alcohol intoxication is covered in Chapter 17. Increasing knowledge amongst law enforcement officers has led to individuals being placed in the semi-prone conditions, with frequent observations. In this situation, differentiating from an occult head injury with increasing intracranial haematoma may be difficult. Alcohol-intoxicated individuals are also more likely to vomit and aspirate, causing choking. However, caution must be exercised when attributing the cause of death to this mechanism, as it is not infrequently found at post-mortem examination where death has been due to other causes. Alcohol can contribute to falls whilst intoxicated, and differentiation from assault should be undertaken. The clinical aspects are covered in Chapter 17.

Drugs

19.29   Drugs are available not only in the general population but also in the prison population. The issue of excited delirium has been covered above. Physical injury may also be caused whilst under the influence of other 'excitement-producing' drugs. Overdose of such drugs as heroin/morphine, as well as other substances, may occur in the institutional setting. Such cases may be accidental or suicidal.

Suicide

19.30   Suicide in prison most commonly occurs as a result of hanging. The method of suspension varies and includes items such as clothing, towels or bedding. In contrast to suicidal hangings in the general population, there is a wide spectrum of more unusual suspension points, such as windows, beds, door handles and hooks. In the situation of very low-level hanging, the so-called 'asphyxial' features may be prominent, together with a more horizontal ligature mark. It is well-recognised that death in hanging occurs extremely rapidly and, even in situations where there is frequent observation of an individual, it can be notoriously difficult to intervene. Assessment of the scene may be important in these cases, particularly in low-level hangings. As with all custody deaths, the subsequent inquests into these cases may be prolonged and problematic.

Deaths from natural causes

19.31   This may be from a variety of conditions, including ischaemic heart disease, cerebrovascular disease and epilepsy, as well as a variety of malignant conditions. These cases can also prove contentious as, despite death being due to natural causes, issues such as lack of care, management of the condition and drug therapy may play a prominent role.

- Alcohol intoxication can cause death, either as a result of toxic levels of alcohol or by inhaling vomit.

- Accidental or suicidal overdose of drugs is relatively common in the custody/prison environment.

- Alcohol and drugs can mask signs of injury, in particular a head injury.

- Suicide includes a variety of methods, including hanging; 'asphyxial' features are usually absent.

- In a death from natural causes, lack of care and/or management may be important.

Further reading material

General textbooks

- Karch, S.B. *Karch's Pathology of Drug Abuse* (2002, 3rd Edition, CRC Press)

- Saukko, P. & Knight, B. *Knight's Forensic Pathology* (2004, 3rd Edition)

- Di Maio, T.G., Di Maio, V.J.M. *Excited delirium syndrome* (2006, CRC Press)

Articles in update textbooks

- Gill, J.R. 'The Medicolegal Evaluation of Excited Delirium' in Tsokos, M., editor. *Forensic Pathology Reviews*. Volume Five. Humana Press; 2008. 91–111

- Woodford, N.W.F. 'Injuries and Death resulting from Restraint' in Rutty, G.N., editor. *Essentials of Autopsy Practice, Current Methods and Trends*. London: Springer; 2006. 171–188

Articles in journals

- Chan, T.C., Vilke, G.M., Clausen, J., Clark, R.F., Schmidt, P., Snowden, T., Neuman, T. 'The effect of oleoresin capsicum "pepper" spray inhalation on respiratory function'. *J Forensic Sci.* 2002 Mar; 47(2): 299–304

- Ho, J.D., Miner, J.R., Lakireddy, D.R., Bultman, L.L., Heegaard, W.G. 'Cardiovascular and physiologic effects of conducted electrical weapon discharge in resisting adults' *Acad Emerg Med.* 2006; 13: 589–95

- Michaelewicz, B.A., Chan, T.C., Vilke, G.M., Levy, S.S., Neuman, T.S., Kolkhorst, F.W. 'Ventilatory and metabolic demands during aggressive physical restraint in healthy adults' *J Forensic Sci.* 2007; 52: 171–5

- O'Halloran, R.L., Frank, J.G. 'Asphyxial death during prone restraint revisited: a report of 21 cases' *Am J Forensic Med Pathol.* 2002; 21: 39–52

- Reay, D.T., Howard, J.D., Flinger, C.L., Ward, R.J. 'Effects of positional restraint on oxygen saturation and heart rate following exercise' *Am J Forensic Med Pathol.* 1988; 9:16–8

- Vilke, G.M., Sloane, C.M., Bouton, K.D., Kolkhorst, F.W., Levine, S.D., Neuman, T.S., Castillo, E.M., Chan, T.C. 'Physiological effects of a conducted weapon on human subjects' *Ann Emerg Med.* 2007; 50: 569–75

Chapter 20

Criminal justice in the United Kingdom

Introduction: the United Kingdom's criminal justice systems

20.1   There is no single criminal justice system for the United Kingdom but three separate criminal justice systems, which cover the country's three different legal jurisdictions of England and Wales, Northern Ireland and Scotland.

The reasons for the existence of three jurisdictions are historical and constitutional. Scotland has always retained a wholly separate criminal justice system from the rest of the United Kingdom. Traditionally, Northern Ireland has followed the criminal law and procedure of England and Wales, although differences have appeared in recent years, particularly since the development of devolved institutions created by the Belfast (Good Friday) Agreement. England and Wales still form a single jurisdiction but, with the creation of the devolved institutions for Wales in 1998, some limited efforts have been made to recognise Wales' changed constitutional position.

20.2   The purpose of this chapter is not to explore the reasons for these differences, but to set out the main practical differences and similarities between the three criminal justice systems in a way intended to assist the expert who may become involved in these systems either at the investigation, trial or appeal stage. The chapter necessarily focuses on procedural differences and similarities between the three jurisdictions, rather than differences and similarities between the substantive criminal law of the jurisdictions. It is not intended to be comprehensive, but to set out the basic principles that apply; for example, the labyrinthine exceptions that apply in terrorism cases in all three jurisdictions are not dealt with here.

20.3   Two short observations may, however, be made on the substantive criminal law. First, in respect of certain offences where there is a clear public interest in homogeneity throughout the United Kingdom, Parliament has endeavoured, so far as is possible, to create the same offence throughout the United Kingdom. This is most frequently seen in areas where there is a clear cross-border element: tax, customs and excise, road traffic and immigration offences are all obvious examples. Second, notwithstanding the amount of criminal law which is now based on statute enacted by Parliament, there remain differences in the substantive criminal law, a difference most clearly seen in respect of time-honoured offences such as homicide and rape, where the criminal law of Scotland differs from that of the other jurisdictions. Generally, however, the same type of conduct is criminalised both north and south of the border, and, more often than not, the differences which exist are different means of reaching the same outcome.

As far as criminal procedure is concerned, it should be stated at the outset that, whatever differences they may have, all three jurisdictions have two defining characteristics in common: they are adversarial in nature; and they are accusatorial in form.

20.4   Criminal proceedings in the United Kingdom are adversarial in nature because, in common with most other types of legal proceedings in the United Kingdom, there are only two parties – the defence and the prosecution – and it is the task of the court (the judge or the jury) to determine the guilt of the defendant. It must do so on the evidence presented to it by the parties, rather than engage in an open-ended inquiry into the case. This type of adversarial procedure is a characteristic of the common law. It is commonly contrasted with more inquisitorial systems, which distinguish the criminal justice systems of civil law countries such as France and the Benelux countries, where investigating magistrates, judges and juries all have a much freer role in conducting inquiries into the case before them and where third parties, such as victims, have the right to participate in the proceedings, rather than simply to give evidence.

20.5   Criminal proceedings in the United Kingdom are accusatorial in form, because it is the prosecution which brings the case against the accused and the prosecution which must prove its case against him or her. This is referred to in all three jurisdictions as the 'burden of proof'. In all three jurisdictions, the prosecution must prove its case beyond reasonable doubt, commonly referred to as the 'criminal standard of proof'. The accusatorial nature of the proceedings has a further dimension: it is for the prosecution, not the court or any third party, to decide what charges to bring and, subject to rules relating to the admissibility of evidence, what evidence to lead in order to prove those charges.

With these preliminary remarks in mind, it is convenient for present purposes to continue by considering the four stages of criminal proceedings: investigation, prosecution, trial and appeal. A final section considers how the work of experts is funded.

Investigation

20.6   The investigation of most crime in the United Kingdom is carried out by 'territorial' police forces, i.e. police forces responsible for policing a particular area of the United Kingdom. There are currently 43 police forces covering England and Wales and a single police force each covering Scotland and Northern Ireland. In addition to these territorial police forces, there are specialist, non-geographic forces. The largest such forces are the British Transport Police and the Ministry of Defence Police.[1] With the coming into force of the Crime and Courts Act 2013, there is now a National Crime Agency (NCA), which has investigative powers with a focus on serious and organised crime.

20.7   In addition to the police and NCA, officials in other specialist bodies have been given the power to investigate offences that may occur in their field of work.

---

1   Others include the Central Motorway Policing Group (a group comprised of officers from three Midlands police forces responsible for motorways in that area), the Civil Nuclear Constabulary (responsible for civilian nuclear power stations) and the Port of Dover Police.

These include: the Department of Business Innovation and Skills (the investigation of offences under the Companies Act 2006); HM Prison Service, and its Scottish and Northern Irish counterparts (initial investigation of offences committed in prisons); HM Revenue and Customs (customs and tax offences); the Serious Fraud Office (complex fraud and corruption offences); and the UK Border Force (immigration offences).

20.8   A great deal of the development in the criminal law of the United Kingdom in the last 30 years has been in the regulation and codification, through Acts of Parliament, of the powers of the police and these other bodies to investigate crime and gather and retain evidence. The main Acts to have done so are: for England and Wales, the Police and Criminal Evidence Act 1984 ('PACE', upon which the equivalent legislation for Northern Ireland, the Police and Criminal Evidence (Northern Ireland) Order 1989, is modelled) and, for Scotland, the Criminal Procedure (Scotland) Act 1995.

20.9   Although PACE, the 1989 Northern Ireland Order and the Criminal Procedure (Scotland) Act 1995 are by no means comprehensive codes on criminal evidence and procedure for their respective jurisdictions, they do cover matters such as: the powers of police officers to stop and search individuals (although they do not create a general right of search); procedures for obtaining and executing warrants for entry and search of premises and seizure of material found; powers of arrest and detention (including time limits for detention); the questioning and proper treatment of suspects, and their right of access to legal advice when detained; and the taking and retention of fingerprints, DNA and other samples.

20.10   Perhaps the most significant feature of PACE and the 1989 Northern Ireland Order is that they direct the Home Secretary and Northern Ireland Secretary to issue Codes of Practice to the police on the exercise of their powers on search and arrest, on the detention, treatment, questioning and identification of persons by police officers, on the search of premises, and on the seizure of property.[2] There are currently eight codes (entitled Codes A to H) for each of England and Wales[3] and for Northern Ireland.[4] Although the codes themselves are not law, their significance lies, first, in the detailed provisions set out within them and, second, in the fact that any evidence obtained by a significant and substantial breach of them is likely to result in that evidence being excluded at trial.[5] There is no such equivalent direction to issue codes under the Criminal Procedure (Scotland) Act 1995.

20.11   Another Act of some significance for the investigation of crime is the Regulation of Investigatory Powers Act 2000 ('RIPA') and its Scottish equivalent, the Regulation of Investigatory Powers (Scotland) Act 2000. RIPA makes provision for broadly four types of investigatory powers: directed surveillance (covert surveillance involving observing an individual in public); covert human intelligence sources (agents); intrusive surveillance (observing an individual in private or surveillance

2   Section 66 of PACE; article 65 of the Northern Ireland Order.
3   See www.gov.uk/government/collections/police-and-criminal-evidence-act-1984-pace-current-versions.
4   See www.dojni.gov.uk/index/public-consultations/current-consultations/consultation-on-revisions-to-pace-codes.htm.
5   *R v Absolam* (1988) 88 Cr App R 332, CA; *R v Walsh* (1990) 91 Cr App R 161.

which is carried out by means of a surveillance device); and interception of communications via a public telecommunication system.[6] Senior officers may authorise the first three; only the Home Secretary or other Ministers can issue a warrant for the fourth. There is still prohibition on the admission of intercepted communication as evidence in criminal proceedings in the United Kingdom, save for disclosure to a judge in exceptional circumstances where the judge is satisfied that disclosure is essential in the interests of justice.[7]

20.12   In all three jurisdictions, criminal proceedings against an individual will invariably begin when he or she is charged or summonsed. Charge will normally follow arrest in serious cases. For other, less serious offences (such as minor road traffic offences), a person may be summonsed and prosecuted without ever being arrested. A person cannot be arrested in any of the three jurisdictions without reasonable grounds for suspecting that he or she has committed an offence.[8] In England and Wales and in Northern Ireland, when a person has been arrested, he or she must be charged as soon as it becomes apparent that there is sufficient evidence to do so.[9] By contrast, in Scotland, there are no such statutory rules as to when a person must be charged. In all three jurisdictions, there are very strict time limits as to how long a person can be detained before charge (although they differ as to length), with the added requirement that, when charged, the person must be released on bail or brought before a court by the end of the next court day.[10]

Prosecution

The independence of the prosecution

20.13   A common feature of the prosecution of offences in all three jurisdictions is that the prosecuting authorities alone retain the prerogative of deciding whether to prosecute that individual. This prerogative follows from the fact that, in all three jurisdictions, the prosecuting authorities are independent from both the police and the executive; they are under a duty to prosecute fairly and impartially, and so they must form their own view as to the strength of the prosecution case, the manner in which the prosecution should be conducted and the propriety of prosecution.

---

6   Each is defined in section 26 of the Act; the relevant powers of authorisation are set out respectively in sections 28, 29, 32 and 5 of the Act. The corresponding provisions in the Scottish Act are sections 1, 6, 7 and 10. The interception of communications in Scotland is regulated by the same provisions of the UK Act, save that the authorisation for interception is to be taken by the Scottish Ministers. The UK Act also makes provision for the disclosure, subject to authorisation, of other forms of communications data (e.g. details of telephone traffic) to investigatory bodies: sections 21–25.
7   Sections 17 and 18(7), (8) of RIPA.
8   Section 24 of PACE; article 26 of the 1989 Northern Ireland Order; sections 14 and 21 of the Criminal Procedure (Scotland) Act 1995. Clause 1 of the Criminal Justice (Scotland) Bill will, if enacted, create new powers for police constables to arrest, without a warrant, a person suspected of having committed or committing an offence. If the offence is not punishable by imprisonment, in addition to reasonable grounds for suspicion, the arrest will have to pass an 'interests of justice' test: clause 1(2), as currently drafted.
9   Section 37(10) of PACE; article 38(1) of the 1989 Northern Ireland Order.
10 Section 46 of PACE; article 47 of the Northern Ireland Order; and, when enacted, clause 18 of the Criminal Justice (Scotland) Bill.

The prosecuting authorities

20.14   In England and Wales, the Crown Prosecution Service (CPS) conducts the vast majority of prosecutions, although other bodies may conduct specialist prosecutions, subject to the discretion of the CPS to take over such prosecutions.[11] The head of the CPS is the Director of Public Prosecutions, who falls under the superintendence of the Attorney-General for England and Wales but is operationally independent. When it prosecutes offences, the CPS will be represented in court either by salaried prosecutors of the CPS or by outside counsel.

20.15   The system in Northern Ireland is largely similar, save that the Director of Public Prosecutions for Northern Ireland is head of the Public Prosecution Service (PPS). One significant difference from England and Wales (although a point in common with the position of the Lord Advocate and Procurators Fiscal in Scotland) is that the Director of Public Prosecutions for Northern Ireland can require the police to investigate an incident which appears to involve an offence and to send to him or her any information concerning the incident, to consider whether a prosecution should be brought.[12] The PPS employs in-house prosecutors to conduct magistrates' court prosecutions, and it instructs outside counsel to conduct Crown Court prosecutions.

20.16   In Scotland, responsibility for prosecutions lies with the Lord Advocate, the ministerial head of Scotland's prosecution service, the Crown Office and Procurator Fiscal Service (COPFS). Who actually conducts the prosecution, in practice, depends on the court in which it takes place. Prosecutions in Scotland take place in one of three courts: in justice of peace courts ('JP courts', comprising benches of lay or stipendiary magistrates); in the sheriff court (either before a sheriff sitting alone or with a jury); or, for the most serious offences, in the High Court of Justiciary (before a judge of that court sitting with a jury).

20.17   In JP courts and sheriff courts, the prosecutor is the procurator fiscal or one of his or her deputies. There is one procurator fiscal for each of Scotland's six sheriffdoms. The procurators fiscal fall under the authority of the Lord Advocate, although all potential matters for prosecution are first referred to the local procurator fiscal by the police or other investigative agencies, and only thereafter in serious cases to the Lord Advocate.[13] Similarly, it is the local procurator fiscal who directs

---

11 Section 6(2) of the Prosecution of Offences Act 1985. These may include prosecutions initiated by bodies as diverse as the Civil Aviation Authority, the Food Standards Agency, the Health and Safety Executive and the Service Prosecuting Authority (the prosecuting authority for the Armed Forces). Full lists of such prosecutions and prosecuting authorities can be found in the DPP's Guidance on 'Relations with other prosecuting agencies', available at www.cps.gov.uk/legal/p_to_r/prosecuting_agencies_relations_with_other_agencies/.

   There remains a right for an individual to prosecute privately, although this is subject to the CPS's discretion to take over (and to discontinue) such prosecutions.

12 A power now contained in section 35 of the Justice (Northern Ireland) Act 2002.

13 A distinctive feature of prosecutions in Scotland is that there is no tradition of specialist prosecutions by bodies such as the Health and Safety Executive or the Food Standards Agency, as there is in England and Wales and in Northern Ireland; instead, all agencies which have the power to investigate potential offences in their field of expertise report cases to the local procurator fiscal for his or her decision on prosecution. There are over 50 such 'specialist reporting agencies'.

the police and other agencies in their investigations. In the High Court of Justiciary, prosecutions are conducted in the name of the Lord Advocate by advocate deputes. These may either be senior advocates of the Scottish bar appointed to that role by the Lord Advocate for a specified period of time to prosecute serious or complex cases or, in less complex cases, may be seconded from the COPFS.

Ethical obligations on the prosecution: when and how to prosecute

20.18   In all three jurisdictions, prosecutors must apply a double test in deciding whether to prosecute a case. These tests are set on in respective codes for prosecutors in each jurisdiction.[14] In England and Wales and in Northern Ireland, the prosecutor must first ask whether the evidence which can be adduced in court is sufficient to provide a reasonable prospect of conviction (the 'evidential test'). In Scotland, the prosecutor must be satisfied that there is sufficient admissible evidence to justify commencing proceedings. In all three jurisdictions, this requires the prosecutor to give consideration to matters such as the credibility and reliability of the evidence. Prosecutors are then required, by their respective codes, to consider whether prosecution is in the public interest (the 'public interest test'). All three codes set out lists of non-exhaustive factors which are to be considered in determining this question, including matters such as the nature and gravity of the offence, the effect on the victim, the personal characteristics of the accused, and the time since the offence.

20.19   These codes are supplemented by further guidance covering now virtually all aspects of prosecution work, including relations with other authorities in the criminal justice system (the police, forensic experts etc.), the duty of disclosure of evidence to the defence (see further below), how to deal with victims and witnesses, the prosecution of certain offences that may raise complex or sensitive issues, and when to accept guilty pleas. It is impossible to summarise all of the guidance covering the three jurisdictions, but it may be said that, in all three jurisdictions, such guidance has three underlying purposes. The first is to emphasis the prosecution's duty, as outlined above, to prosecute fairly, impartially and independently. The second purpose is to ensure that prosecutors are aware of and respect not only the rights of the defence, but also – and this is of growing importance in all three criminal justice systems – the rights of victims and witnesses, particularly those who may be vulnerable on account of age, gender, race, mental health etc. The third purpose is to ensure transparency and accountability in prosecution. This has developed from within the prosecution agencies themselves but also because the courts have become slightly more willing to review prosecutorial decisions on administrative law principles and human rights grounds.[15]

---

14 The Code for Prosecutors in Northern Ireland, the Prosecution Code in Scotland and the Code for Crown Prosecutors in England and Wales, each available from the PPS, COPFS and CPS websites.

15 See, for instance, the finding of the House of Lords in *R (Purdy) v DPP* [2009] UKHL 45 that the DPP should be required to promulgate a policy as to when he would exercise his discretion to prosecute assisted suicide, the absence of such a policy being incompatible with the right of Ms Purdy (a terminally ill woman wishing her husband's assistance to travel to Switzerland, where assisted suicide was unlawful) to respect for private and family life under Article 8 of the European Convention on Human Rights.

Disclosure

20.20   It is something of a structural flaw in the adversarial system (and not one limited to the United Kingdom jurisdictions) that those responsible for prosecuting a defendant possess virtually all relevant evidence in the case, but are simultaneously responsible for deciding what evidence is disclosed to the defendant and the court, and do so with no independent oversight or review.[16] As a result of high-profile miscarriages of justice, where key exculpatory evidence was not disclosed to the defence, and to implement European human rights rulings which found fault with the disclosure regime as it then applied, from the mid-1990s onwards, clearer and stricter rules have been put in place in all three jurisdictions to set out the prosecution's obligation as to what evidence must be disclosed. The precise wording varies between the jurisdictions but the common, general principle is that the prosecution must disclose any evidence which might be reasonably considered capable of undermining the case for the prosecution against the accused or assisting the case for the accused.[17] This applies equally to expert as to other evidence: for instance, any evidence undermining a prosecution expert and his or her methodology must be disclosed. It is also a continuing duty on the prosecution rather than one which applies only at the start of the case when the evidence is normally served on the defence; hence, if such material comes to light later, in the course of the trial, it must be disclosed to the defence.[18]

20.21   Accordingly, experts must consider which elements of their work on a case might meet the disclosure test. Guidance has been produced by the CPS and the COPFS to help expert witnesses to meet their disclosure obligations, and expert witnesses would be well advised to read both before commencing any work.[19] The guidance is extensive, but has been summarised using the mnemonic 'retain, record, reveal' (the Scottish guidance adds 'review'). Thus, experts should retain all materials they receive (until instructed otherwise), they should make records of all work carried out, and they should reveal everything that they have recorded. The Scottish guidance adds that the expert should review his or her conclusions if any new information comes to light, both before and after a trial and appeal – an approach that experts in the other jurisdictions must surely also follow in order to comply with the continuing duty to disclose.

20.22   Experts should also consider what material, in the broader sense of the word, might meet the disclosure test of undermining the case for the prosecution or assisting the case for the accused. This might include:

16 Contrast civil law systems, where an independent investigating magistrate with judicial status oversees the investigation and, in some cases, the prosecution of a case, and has full access to all documents in the possession of the police and prosecution.

17 Set out for England and Wales and Northern Ireland in section 3 of the Criminal Procedure and Investigations Act 1996. The Scottish disclosure regime is set out in section 121 of the Criminal Justice and Licensing (Scotland) Act 2010 and uses the formulation 'materially weaken or undermine the evidence that is likely to be led by the prosecutor in the proceedings against the accused' or would 'materially strengthen' the accused's case.

18 See section 7A of the 1996 Act and, for Scotland, section 123 of the 2010 Act.

19 Available at www.copfs.gov.uk/images/Documents/Prosecution_Policy_Guidance/Guidelines_ and_Policy/Guidance%20booklet%20for%20expert%20witnesses.PDF and www.cps.gov.uk/ legal/d_to_g/disclosure_manual/annex_k_disclosure_manual/#a05.

(i) any reports or research papers which undermine the scientific propositions put forward;

(ii) any symptoms or signs which might point away from the conclusion reached;

(iii) any results of any tests which contradict or might tend to undermine the prosecution case or might lead to a new line of enquiry; and

(iv) any history given to the expert which might undermine the account given to the police (and the full history that the expert has been given should be set out in the expert's report).

Trial

Ensuring a fair trial

20.23   The objective of any criminal trial is not only to convict the guilty and acquit the innocent, but also to ensure that the trial is fair to both the defence and the prosecution and, more broadly, to ensure that the justice system is not brought into disrepute by improper conduct. It would be impossible to set out all of the means by which the three jurisdictions endeavour to achieve these ends, particularly when they include matters as diverse as the extent of the reporting restrictions on pending and current trials (designed to ensure that potential and later serving jurors are not prejudiced by media coverage), the rules on the admissibility of evidence, and the means designed to achieve 'equality of arms' between the defence and the prosecution. It suffices to say that, in all three jurisdictions, the courts have wide common law and statutory powers to protect both the right to a fair trial and the proper administration of justice.

20.24   Arguably, the most important of these powers is the inherent power of the court to stay (stop) the proceedings indefinitely if a prosecution amounts to an abuse of the process of the court. In England and Wales and in Northern Ireland, this has been defined as 'something so unfair and wrong that the court should not allow a prosecutor to proceed with what is in all other respects a regular proceeding'.[20] Examples of situations which may constitute an abuse of process include serious misconduct by investigators, breach of prior assurances of non-prosecution, inordinate delay in prosecution, and adverse publicity before or during the trial. In Scotland, the court has the power to stop the trial on grounds of 'oppression' (and most of the above examples would be dealt with under this head). Abuse of process, while also available, is reserved for cases where the court considers that its procedures are being used for an improper purpose.[21]

20.25   It should be added that, in all three jurisdictions, staying the proceeding is a remedy of last resort. The court will normally consider whether other, less severe remedies can be used to ensure that the trial is fair, such as not admitting tainted evidence or, in cases where there has been adverse publicity, giving directions to the jury that they must disregard anything that they might have heard or read about the case outside the courtroom.

20 *Hui Chi-Ming v R* [1992] 1 AC 34, PC.
21 See *Jones and Doyle v HM Advocate* [2009] HCJAC 86 per Lord Reed at para 35.

Pre-trial procedure and mode of trial

20.26   Before a case can come to trial, a series of procedural steps must take place. These vary greatly between the jurisdictions, and it would be impossible to set out in full all of the pre-trial procedures that take place in each jurisdiction. However, it may be said that, whatever the jurisdiction and whatever the eventual form that the trial will take, the common purpose of the UK's pre-trial procedures is to ensure that: (i) a person who is arrested and charged and who remains in custody appears in court as soon as possible, so that consideration can be given to whether he or she can be released on bail until trial; (ii) where the accused intends to plead guilty, such a plea can be taken as early as possible and sentence passed; (iii) if the accused intends to contest the charge, the case is properly prepared before it comes to trial and, where possible, legal matters such as applications to admit or exclude evidence can be considered in advance of trial; and (iv) the mode of trial is properly identified.

20.27   The last of these is the most significant. All three jurisdictions make provision for different modes of trial, depending on the seriousness of the offence. Generally, less serious offences will be tried before a judge sitting alone or before a bench of lay magistrates assisted by a legally qualified adviser or clerk (referred to in all three jurisdictions as a 'summary trial'). More serious offences (usually the type which will require expert evidence) will be tried before a judge and jury, with the jury to determine whether the defendant is guilty or not and the judge to preside at the trial and decide on matters of law as they arise. This is trial 'on indictment' (it is also referred to as 'solemn procedure' in Scotland). The manner for determining whether an accused will be tried summarily or on indictment in each jurisdiction is described in the following paragraphs.

20.28   In England and Wales, summary trials take place in the magistrates' court (either before a bench of lay magistrates or a district judge), and trials on indictment take place in the Crown Court before a judge and jury. There are three categories of offences: offences which are summary only; offences which are triable only on indictment; and offences which are triable either way. Summary offences are offences which have been created by statute where the statute provides a maximum penalty for the offence after summary conviction and does not make provision for trial on indictment. This now covers a vast number of minor offences: common ones include minor road traffic offences, minor public order offences, and minor licensing or regulatory offences (such as failure to pay the TV licence). Offences triable only on indictment include all common law offences (such as murder and manslaughter) and other serious offences (such as rape and other serious sexual offences) which are contained in statute and where the relevant statute specifies that the offence is triable on indictment only. Offences which are triable either way include slightly less serious statutory offences, such as theft, assault occasioning actual bodily harm, and possession of drugs.[22] Such offences may be tried in the magistrates' court if both the magistrates and the defendant agree.[23]

---

22 An offence is triable either way if the statute creating it so specifies or it is contained in Schedule 1 to the Magistrates' Courts Act 1980.

23 For the magistrates, the principal concern will usually be whether their sentencing powers (six months' imprisonment for one offence, and 12 months' imprisonment for two or more offences) are sufficient to deal with the case.

20.29   Northern Ireland follows a different practice. It does not allow for trial before a bench of lay magistrates – such trials in that jurisdiction always place before a district judge – and there are broadly five modes of trial. First, certain offences are summary only. These are generally the same as 'summary only' offences in England and Wales. Second, certain offences are 'hybrid' offences, which can be tried summarily or on indictment, and it will be for the prosecution to decide on the mode of trial. Third, certain indictable offences may be tried summarily if the accused consents.[24] Fourth, certain summary offences may be tried on indictment if the accused is liable to a sentence of more than six months and he or she asserts the right to be tried by jury.[25] Fifth, offences triable only on indictment are tried in the Crown Court. However, such 'indictable only' offences are first subject to committal proceedings before a district judge sitting in the magistrates' court. This procedure – now abolished entirely in England and Wales – requires the magistrates' court to conduct a preliminary investigation or inquiry[26] into the case against the accused, and to decide whether there is sufficient evidence for the accused to be 'committed' for trial on indictment; if it decides that there is, the accused is sent for trial in the Crown Court; if it decides that there is not, the accused is discharged.[27]

20.30   Scotland follows a different practice again. The basic distinction is between summary and solemn procedure, with the latter covering all jury trials, whether those jury trials take place in the sheriff court or the High Court. All common law offences may be tried on indictment by a jury and, of these, murder and rape[28] must be tried on indictment in the High Court. For statutory offences, as in the rest of the UK, these are divided into those triable only on indictment, those triable either on indictment or summarily, and those triable only summarily. Thereafter, it is for the prosecution to decide on mode of trial (e.g. summary or solemn for offences triable either way) and the appropriate court (e.g. in solemn procedure cases, whether to prosecute in the sheriff court before a sheriff and jury, or in the High Court). It will do so principally on the basis of whether the maximum sentencing powers of the various courts suffice for the seriousness of the offence.[29] There is, therefore, no right for the accused in Scotland to elect trial by jury.

The procedure at trial

20.31   With the exception of Northern Ireland, witnesses are not normally permitted to sit in court and listen to proceedings until they have given evidence. Owing, perhaps, to other demands on their time, after they have given evidence,

---

24 Article 45 of the Magistrates' Courts (Northern Ireland) Order 1981.
25 Article 29 of the same Order.
26 Investigation involves witnesses giving oral evidence; inquiry involves their written statements simply being presented to the court.
27 See articles 30–37 of the Magistrates' Courts (Northern Ireland) Order 1981. It is the intention of the Northern Ireland Executive to abolish committal proceedings although, at the time of writing, legislation to that effect has not been enacted.
28 Rape is a common law offence in Scotland but a statutory offence in the rest of the UK.
29 Sixty days' imprisonment in the JP courts, 12 months' imprisonment in the sheriff court in summary procedure, five years' imprisonment in the sheriff court in solemn procedure, and life imprisonment in the High Court.

experts do not generally remain in court to hear the rest of the evidence, even though they are entitled and encouraged to do so. For the expert who does not participate in the trial process from beginning to end, the following passages provide a brief sketch of the trial process and its various stages in the three jurisdictions. Since it is rare for experts to give evidence in summary trials, the focus is on jury trials in each of the three jurisdictions.

Where there is no trial

20.32   The first feature of UK criminal trials to note is that it is rare for a criminal investigation to end in a full trial, with a verdict being returned by a jury. Obviously, not all criminal investigations result in prosecution and, when a prosecution is brought, many cases will end with a guilty plea being entered by the defendant, either in advance of trial or during the trial itself. Trials may 'collapse' because of difficulties in the prosecution's case or because of legal rulings by the trial judge on matters such as the admissibility of evidence.

Unfortunately, even when both sides wish a trial to proceed, adjournments are all too common in each of the three jurisdictions. This can be as a result of a lack of resources or the difficulties in co-ordinating participants as diverse as the police, legal representatives, courtroom availability, the trial judge and witnesses. It is to minimise this problem that experts are asked to provide details of their availability and dates to avoid.

Trials: jury swearing

20.33   When a trial is ready to proceed and all preliminary legal and administrative matters have been dealt with, in jury trials, the trial proper will begin with the jury being sworn. Generally, in jury trials in all three jurisdictions, at this point the trial judge will normally make a few brief words of introduction.[30]

Prosecution case

20.34   Thereafter, in both summary and jury trials, the trial always begins with the prosecution case. In England and Wales and in Northern Ireland, this starts with an opening speech by counsel for the prosecution, in which he or she will set out the charges against the defendant, summarise the evidence that the prosecution intends to call to prove its case and, in a jury trial, briefly outline the relevant law. At the conclusion of the speech, the prosecution will proceed to call its evidence. In Scotland, there is no opening speech, and the case simply begins with the prosecution calling its evidence.

20.35   There are no set rules in any of the jurisdictions as to the order in which prosecution witnesses will be called: it is normally for the prosecution to decide how to present its case in a way most likely to assist the jury in understanding the case.

---

30 Usually confined to administrative matters, such as court hours, introducing the various participants to the jury, and advising them not to discuss the case and to report anything untoward.

Thus, for instance, in a murder trial the case might begin with the evidence of any eyewitnesses to the killing, continue with the evidence of the police and experts who attended the scene, and conclude with any police interviews that the defendant might have given after his arrest. This obviously makes it difficult to predict, in advance, the days on which experts will be called to give their evidence and explains why, when they attend court, they may be kept waiting before finally being called.

Giving evidence – examination-in-chief

20.36   When an expert gives evidence for the prosecution, their evidence will begin with their being called into court, directed to the witness box and asked to swear or affirm the traditional oath/declaration. Their 'examination-in-chief' will then begin. This will involve being asked questions by counsel for the prosecution. These questions will begin with standard questions as to their full name, and professional qualifications and experience, with the aim of demonstrating that they are qualified to give expert evidence. The questions will then move to the substance of that expert evidence itself. It is normal practice for the expert witness to have any notes or reports that he or she has made with them while giving evidence. The jury do not see a copy of the expert's report (although there are moves towards doing so in Scotland), and so the aim throughout examination-in-chief is not only for the expert to give his evidence in as full and impartial a manner as possible, but also to give it in a way which is readily understandable to the non-expert jury. For that reason, it is often necessary for advocates to ask experts to clarify their evidence (for instance, to explain or define terms of art in layman's terms).

Giving evidence – cross-examination

20.37   Once examination-in-chief has been completed, the advocate for each defendant will have an opportunity to cross-examine the witness. The nature and duration of cross-examination will vary, depending on the significance of the expert witness's evidence to the particular defendant. The purpose of cross-examination is to test the prosecution case and to put the defendant's case to the witness, so that he or she may have an opportunity to comment on it. It may involve exploring the evidence, its limits and caveats, eliciting evidence from the witness which assists the defendant's case, or testing the expert's methodology and the reasons for his or her conclusions. Once cross-examination is completed, counsel for the prosecution has an opportunity to re-examine the witness, though re-examination must be limited to matters that have arisen in the course of cross-examination. Again, when answering questions in cross-examination, it is vital for an expert witness to ensure that they are impartial, and do not see themselves as part of the prosecution team, or acting on behalf of the complainant or the police.

20.38   When the expert gives evidence for the defence, the order is reversed: he or she is subject to examination-in-chief by the advocate for the defendant. He is then cross-examined by the advocate for any co-defendants, and then cross-examined by the advocate for the prosecution. The importance of impartiality remains.

   Lastly, for both prosecution and defence witnesses, the trial judge may ask questions, although it is not uncommon for the judge to interpose with questions during both examination-in-chief and cross-examination. It is rare, but the jury may also put questions which they wish to have answered; they are not, however, invited to ask questions. When there are no further questions, the witness is released, usually with an instruction not to talk about the case with anyone due to give evidence.

Giving evidence – points of law

20.39   A final point of procedure relating to the giving of evidence may be noted. In a jury trial, all points of law (i.e. all matters of legal argument between the parties) are determined by the trial judge. The normal practice is for the jury to be asked to leave the courtroom while the judge hears and decides on these points of law. It is common for such points of law to arise while a witness is giving evidence. If this occurs, counsel for either the prosecution or the defence will simply draw this to the attention of the trial judge, who will invite the jury to retire. Normally, the trial judge will also invite the witness to leave the courtroom. It is understandable for the expert witness – having been temporarily sent out of court – to speculate on what point of law has arisen and whether it has any merit, and perhaps even to feel responsible for it having arisen. Such concerns are unnecessary: if any matter has arisen of which the witness should be aware, the trial judge will simply explain this after the witness has been recalled to court and before the jury return to hear the rest of their evidence. The expert witness should ensure that they do not refer to evidence of which the jury may not be aware, such as the bad character of the defendant or complainant, without checking first with the party for whom they are called, or the judge in the absence of the jury.

20.40   Once all of the prosecution evidence has been given, the prosecution formally closes its case. All three jurisdictions make provision for the defence, at the close of the prosecution case, to submit to the court that there is no case to answer because, even taking the prosecution case at its highest, there is not sufficient evidence for a jury to convict. The trial judge will hear submissions on the matter and, in jury trials, will do so in the absence of the jury. If he or she upholds the submission, the defendant is acquitted. If he or she rejects the submission, the trial continues.

Defence case

20.41   The defence will then present its case. The first witness for the defence is normally the defendant, if they intend to give evidence, followed by any other witnesses, including expert witnesses. However, expert witnesses occasionally give evidence 'back to back' in order to assist the jury, which means that the prosecution calls its witness in a particular specialism and, immediately afterwards, the defence calls its expert witness in that specialism, so that the jury can hear both experts in the same time period and assess them together.

Speeches

20.42   When the defence case or cases have been concluded, all three jurisdictions allow the prosecution and defence to make closing speeches.[31] There will always be a

---

31 In summary trials, the defence will always have the right to a closing speech, but the prosecution only has the right to a closing speech if the defendant is represented or the defence has called evidence from anyone other than the defendant.

closing speech by both sides in a jury trial: the rule is always that the prosecution goes first, followed by the defence. Closing speeches are the opportunity for prosecution and defence advocates not to give evidence, but to summarise and comment on the evidence that the court has heard. Expert evidence will almost always attract comment from both sides, as they seek to draw the jury's attention to its strengths or weaknesses and the conclusions that the jury may draw from it.

Summing up/charge to the jury

20.43   In summary trials, after hearing the closing speeches the lay bench or judge will consider and then announce their verdict. By contrast, in jury trials, the speeches are followed by the trial judge's summing up (known as 'charge to the jury' in Scotland). In all three jurisdictions, this will involve the judge giving legal directions to the jury on matters such as the burden and standard of proof, the elements of the offences that the jury must find present before they can convict, and directions on the law of evidence as it applies to the case.

20.44   In all three jurisdictions, where expert evidence has been called, the trial judge will be expected to give the jury directions on how to approach that evidence (particularly when conflicting evidence might have been given by different experts). There are now also specific directions that the appellate courts have said should be given in respect of certain forms of expert evidence, particularly those which purport to identify the defendant or link him to a crime scene, such as DNA evidence and statistical evidence.[32]

20.45   The greatest difference between the jurisdictions is that, in England and Wales and in Northern Ireland, the trial judge will be expected to summarise the evidence for the jury and, where appropriate, to comment upon it. In Scotland, the trial judge does not summarise the evidence and will only refer to it where, in the course of his legal directions to the jury, it is necessary to do so. Any comment on the evidence is deprecated and may give grounds for a successful appeal.

Jury retirement

20.46   When the trial judge has finished his or her summing up/charge to the jury, the jury will retire to consider their verdict. The jury's deliberations give rise to four of the most marked differences between Scots criminal law and the practice in the rest of the United Kingdom:

- Scottish juries have 15 members rather than 12.
- While juries in England and Wales and in Northern Ireland have only two verdicts open to them (guilty and not guilty), uniquely Scottish juries have three: guilty, not guilty and not proven. The origin and meaning of the 'not

---

32 A full discussion of the courts' approach to such forms of evidence, and the directions which have to be given to the jury, can be found, for instance, in chapter 14 of Archbold: Criminal Pleading, Evidence and Practice 2015.

proven' verdict are still the subject of debate,[33] but there is no practical difference between a verdict of not guilty and a verdict of not proven; each is a verdict of acquittal.

- A Scottish jury has the right to return a guilty verdict, but to delete those elements of charge which they find have not been proven to their satisfaction, provided that what remains still constitutes a crime by Scots law. The significance of doing so lies in the severity of the offence for which the accused is then convicted, and may therefore affect what sentence is passed.

- Majority verdicts. In England and Wales and in Northern Ireland, juries must return a verdict which is unanimous or, after a certain period of deliberation, a majority verdict. The majority is normally 10 votes to 2, with appropriate adjustments where, through sickness or other compelling reason, the number of jurors falls below 12. In the event that no such majority is attained, the jury is deemed to have been unable to reach a verdict and will be discharged ('a hung jury'). The accused may then be retried at a later date. In Scotland, there have to be at least eight votes for a verdict of guilty; anything less than eight votes for guilty results in a verdict of acquittal.[34] The result is that a verdict is always returned; thus, there is no possibility in Scotland of a hung jury and a retrial taking place.

Sentencing

20.47   In the event of a guilty verdict, the issue for the court is then what sentence should be passed. In contrast to other common law jurisdictions, in the three United Kingdom jurisdictions the prosecution has no right to ask for a particular sentence and, if a defendant has been convicted after trial, the prosecution's role in sentencing is confined to assisting the court with its powers, placing details of the defendant's previous convictions before the court, and asking for additional orders such as forfeiture of drugs etc. More recently, prosecutors have been prepared to make submissions on the length of sentence, as they are expected to outline where the offence might fall within a particular sentencing guideline.[35] The defence always has the right to draw to the court's attention any mitigating factors in the case: in all three jurisdictions, this is known as a 'plea in mitigation'. Thereafter, the judge has the option of passing sentence there and then, or adjourning so that pre-sentence reports can be prepared.

20.48   Sentencing has become a much more complex practice in recent years. There are two reasons for this. First, judges are required to have regard to a great deal

---

33 For one overview, see the House of Commons Library briefing note of 15 May 2009, 'The "not proven" verdict in Scotland' at www.parliament.uk/briefing-papers/sn02710.pdf.

34 The current proposal before the Scottish Parliament in the Criminal Justice (Scotland) Bill is to require 10 votes for a guilty verdict, with appropriate reductions when the number of jurors falls below 15: clause 70 of the draft Bill.

35 In England and Wales, the Sentencing Council replaced the Sentencing Guidelines Council – see http://sentencingcouncil.judiciary.gov.uk/sentencing-guidelines.htm.

   In Scotland, the Scottish Sentencing Council will begin its work in October 2015.

   In Northern Ireland, the Judicial Studies Board has published guidelines: www.jsbni.com/Publications/sentencing-guidelines/Pages/default.aspx.

of guidance – both statutory and non-statutory – as to the appropriate sentence to pass for certain offences, and as to what aggravating and mitigating factors to consider. Second, Parliament has created a range of sentences that may be imposed instead of, or in addition to, a sentence of imprisonment. These vary between the jurisdictions, but will include fines, community orders (mainly supervision by probation services and/or an unpaid work requirement) and extended sentences for dangerous offenders. These may also be accompanied by a wide range of ancillary orders, such as criminal behaviour orders, anti-social behaviour orders, compensation and forfeiture orders, and drug rehabilitation and alcohol treatment requirements. The Proceeds of Crime Act 2002 also provides for the making of confiscation orders in separate, subsequent proceedings to divest individuals of property obtained through criminal conduct.

Appeal

20.49   Appeal procedures will vary, depending on the nature of the appeal pursued and the court that has convicted the defendant (the route of appeal).

In all three jurisdictions, the defendant may appeal against conviction, sentence or both. Appeals against conviction turn on the questions as to whether the conviction is unsafe or, in Scotland, whether there has been a miscarriage of justice. Appeals against sentence are more straightforward, and normally only involve the appeal court hearing submissions that the sentence imposed by the trial/sentencing court was manifestly excessive or, in Scottish cases, simply excessive.

20.50   The procedure, the route of appeal, varies considerably between England and Wales and Northern Ireland, on the one hand, and Scotland on the other. Those different routes are briefly set out below, before turning to a common route of appeal – that of an appeal following a reference from the relevant Criminal Cases Review Commission for each jurisdiction. Lastly, there is now, in all three jurisdictions, the limited possibility for the prosecution to bring appeals, which is considered in the final section below.

England and Wales

From the magistrates' court

20.51   In England and Wales, when the defendant is convicted in the magistrates' court, there are three routes of appeal. First, there is a right of appeal against both conviction and sentence to the Crown Court. This will involve a re-hearing of the case before a Crown Court judge and a lay bench. Second, if the appeal is on a point of law, the defendant can apply for a case to be 'stated' (an 'appeal by way of case stated'), in which case the magistrates' court will prepare a short summary of the case, its conclusions, the point of law which arose in the trial, and how it dealt with it. Such an appeal is then heard by the High Court (composed of either one or two judges). Finally, if the defendant alleges an irregularity in proceedings (for example, a lack of impartiality on the part of the bench), he or she can seek judicial review of the magistrates' decision in the High Court.

From the Crown Court

20.52   When the defendant is convicted in the Crown Court, the only route of appeal against conviction and/or sentence is to the Court of Appeal Criminal Division. Initially, the appeal will be considered on the papers (that is, without a hearing) by a single judge of that court. The single judge can give leave to appeal, in which case the appeal will be heard by the full court of either three or, in particularly important cases, five judges. If, on the other hand, the single judge refuses leave to appeal, there will be no further public funding provided for legal representation but the appellant can renew his application for leave to appeal to the full court, which can either refuse leave to appeal or grant leave to appeal and proceed to hear the appeal. If an appeal is allowed and the conviction quashed, the Court of Appeal will decide whether to order a retrial.

20.53   If the Court of Appeal does not give leave to appeal against conviction, there is no possibility of appealing to the Supreme Court of the United Kingdom. If the court gives leave to appeal against conviction but goes on to dismiss the appeal, there is the possibility of an appeal to the Supreme Court of the United Kingdom, provided that: (i) the Court of Appeal certifies that the case raises an issue of general public importance; and (ii) either the Court of Appeal gives leave to appeal to the Supreme Court, or the Supreme Court itself gives leave to appeal. It is almost unheard of for the Court of Appeal to certify questions and give leave to appeal to the Supreme Court; the more common course is for the Court of Appeal to certify questions but leave to it the Supreme Court itself to decide whether it wants to give leave to appeal. The Supreme Court gives leave to appeal in very few of the cases that come before it, and criminal cases are no different; if anything, fewer criminal cases are heard by the Supreme Court than other areas of law, such as human rights law or other public law matters.

Northern Ireland

20.54   For Northern Ireland, there are two principal differences. First, when a defendant is convicted after a summary trial in a magistrates' court by a district judge, appeals against conviction and sentence are not heard by the Crown Court, but by the county court before a county court judge sitting alone. Second, when the appeal is by way of case stated, the appeal is heard by the Court of Appeal in Northern Ireland. Decisions by the Cowurt of Appeal in Northern Ireland may, in turn, be appealed to the Supreme Court, with the same need for certification that the question is of general public importance as in England and Wales.

Scotland

20.55   The appeal procedure is slightly simpler in Scotland, because appeals in both summary and solemn proceedings are heard by the High Court of Justiciary sitting as a court of criminal appeal ('the Appeal Court'). In summary proceedings, appeals against conviction are by way of case stated, although, in contrast to the rest of the UK, such appeals are not confined to points of law but include appeals against conviction.[36] By contrast, appeals against conviction in solemn proceedings, and all appeals against sentence, are made simply by lodging a note of appeal.[37]

20.56 In appeals from both summary and solemn proceedings, leave to appeal is required from a single judge of the High Court (also known as 'the first sift'). As in the rest of the United Kingdom, if leave to appeal is given, the appeal proceeds before a bench of three or, occasionally, five or even seven judges; if leave is refused, there is the possibility of review by a bench of three judges ('the second sift').[38]

20.57 A distinctive feature of Scottish appeals is that, when an appeal is lodged, the trial judge will be asked by the Appeal Court to produce a report on the case (or a sentencing report in summary cases, where appeal is against sentence only) in which he gives his opinion on the case generally and on the grounds of appeal. The report is disclosed to the convicted person and to the prosecution, and then forms part of the papers that the Appeal Court will consider before deciding the appeal.[39]

20.58 In contrast to the rest of the United Kingdom, there is no right of appeal to the Supreme Court in criminal cases. This has always been the position in Scots law. One very recent exception is that the Supreme Court is able to hear appeals on human rights grounds, most commonly that the trial and conviction were contrary to the right to a fair trial enshrined in Article 6 of the ECHR.[40]

The Criminal Cases Review Commissions

20.59 Traditionally, when there had already been an appeal in a case, the only possibility for a fresh appeal was a decision by the relevant cabinet minister (the Home Secretary or the Scottish or Northern Ireland Secretary) to refer the case back to the relevant appeal court. In the wake of several high-profile miscarriages of justice in the late 1980s and early 1990s, Parliament decided to remove that executive power of referral and to enact two Criminal Cases Review Commissions: one for Scotland (the Scottish Criminal Cases Review Commission), and the other for England and Wales and Northern Ireland (simply the Criminal Cases Review Commission). The commissions have the task of investigating potential miscarriages of justice and, where appropriate, referring cases back to the relevant appeal court.

---

36 Section 176 of the 1995 Act. In summary proceedings, there is also the possibility of an appeal by way of a bill of suspension, suspension being a process whereby illegal or improper decisions of an inferior court can be reviewed and set aside by the High Court. See *Renton & Brown's Criminal Procedure*, chapter 33. There is no exhaustive list of grounds for bringing a bill of suspension, but they are generally confined to matters relating to fundamental defects in the proceedings; other grounds of appeal must be by way of case stated (see *Renton & Brown* at 33-07).

37 Section 110 of the 1995 Act.

38 Section 107(4) of the 1995 Act.

39 Section 113 of the 1995 Act.

40 See, for instance, *Cadder v HM Advocate* [2010] UKSC 43 at para 11, and further references therein.

20.60   The commissions have wide powers of investigation, including examining material which has not been disclosed to the defence on grounds of public interest, to receive evidence and to examine witnesses. A decision not to refer a case back to the relevant appeal court can be challenged by way of judicial review, although the test is a high one and it will be rare for such a challenge to be successful. Where the relevant commission decides to refer the case to the relevant appeal court, the appeal then skips the leave application and takes the course of any normal appeal with leave.[41]

Prosecution appeals

20.61   The various prosecuting authorities in the three jurisdictions have acquired the right to bring appeals in certain, limited circumstances.

In all three jurisdictions, the prosecution in a summary trial may appeal by way of case stated (in the same way that the defendant can). In England and Wales, in a trial on indictment, the prosecution has the right of appeal to the Court of Appeal against a 'terminating ruling' – that is, any ruling which has the effect of stopping the case.[42] In Scotland, the Lord Advocate may appeal against a decision of the trial judge either to direct the jury to acquit the accused or to direct the amendment of the indictment following a submission of no case to answer or insufficient evidence.[43]

20.62   All three jurisdictions also provide for the prosecution to appeal against 'unduly lenient' sentences which have been passed after trial on indictment: in England and Wales and in Northern Ireland, this power is limited to some, but not all, indictable offences. There is no such restriction in Scotland, with the possibility of appeal applying to all indictable offences.[44]

Moreover, all three jurisdictions also now make provision for the prosecution to seek the retrial of an accused who has already been acquitted on indictment. In England and Wales and Northern Ireland, this will be if new and compelling evidence emerges; in Scotland, this retrial can be secured where an acquittal had been tainted by an attempt to pervert the course of justice, the accused has admitted his guilt, or there is new evidence substantially strengthening the case against the accused. In

---

41 Sections 9(2) (England and Wales) and 10(2) (Northern Ireland) of the Criminal Appeal Act 1995; section 194B of the Criminal Procedure (Scotland) Act 1995.

42 Sections 57–61 of the Criminal Justice Act 2003. A similar right of appeal in respect of evidentiary rulings, under sections 62 and 63 of the Act, has not yet been brought into force.

43 Sections 97, 97A and 107A–107F of the Criminal Procedure (Scotland) Act 1995. A right of appeal in respect of evidential rulings has entered into force in Scots law: under section 107B of the Criminal Procedure (Scotland) Act 1995, the prosecution may appeal against a decision of the trial judge on the admissibility of evidence. This requires the leave of the trial judge.

 There is also the possibility of the prosecution seeking review of irregularities in the preliminary stages of a case by way of a bill of advocation. This is the prosecution's equivalent of a bill of suspension (see footnote 36 above), but is available to the prosecution in both summary and solemn proceedings: see *Renton & Brown* at 33-19.

44 Sections 35 and 36 of the Criminal Justice Act 1988; section 108 of the Criminal Procedure (Scotland) Act 1995. In Scotland, the Lord Advocate may also appeal against certain other, non-custodial sentences on the grounds that the particular sentence was 'inappropriate' in the case.

all jurisdictions, the retrial requires leave from the court (the Court of Appeal or the High Court of Justiciary).[45]

20.63   Finally, in trials on indictment, all three jurisdictions allow the prosecution to refer, to the relevant appeal court, a point of law that has arisen at trial for its opinion (a procedure known as an Attorney-General's Reference or a Lord Advocate's Reference).[46] This is not an appeal: such references can be made in cases where the accused has been acquitted, although the reference procedure has no effect on the acquittal, and will generally only be done where a point of general importance arose at trial.[47]

Expert evidence in appeal proceedings

20.64   It is by no means uncommon for fresh evidence from experts to be considered in the course of an appeal: indeed, it may be the very fact of this fresh evidence which has led to the appeal in the first place. Each jurisdiction has detailed rules on when the relevant appeal court will consider fresh evidence. Clearly, it would not be in the interests of justice if a conviction could stand, even if fresh evidence showed that it was likely to be unsafe. At the same time, the courts are entitled to be sceptical as to the weight to be attached to certain forms of fresh evidence, such as witnesses recanting the evidence that they gave at trial. The appeal courts are therefore directed by statute to consider matters such as whether it would be in the interests of justice to receive the evidence, and whether there is a reasonable explanation for the failure to adduce that evidence at trial.[48] If anything, these statutory rules apply more strictly to expert evidence, since there will rarely be a reasonable explanation for failure to call expert evidence at trial, as experts will be 'interchangeable' in a way that factual witness will not be.[49] Nonetheless, fresh expert evidence is often admitted, typically when that evidence casts doubt on the methodology or conclusions of the experts who gave evidence for the prosecution at trial, and thus doubt on the safety of the conviction.[50]

Funding

20.65   Many, if not all, experts are highly qualified professionals, and the question inevitably arises as to how their services will be paid for. This depends on who seeks their services.

In the early stages of a police investigation, experts' costs will be met by the police. The decision to instruct outside experts – for example, to assist in the recovery of

---

45 Part 10 of the Criminal Justice Act 2003; Double Jeopardy (Scotland) Act 2011.
46 Section 36 of the Criminal Justice Act 1972; section 123 of the Criminal Procedure (Scotland) Act 1995.
47 In Scotland, the reference can also be made in cases where the accused has been convicted: 1995 Act, Sch 6, para 91.
48 See section 25 of the Criminal Appeal (Northern Ireland) Act 1980, section 23 of the Criminal Appeal Act 1968 and section 106(3) of the Criminal Procedure (Scotland) Act 1995.
49 See, for instance, *R v Jones (Steven Martin)* [1997] 1 Cr App R 86.
50 See, for instance, the conviction quashed in *R v T (footwear mark evidence)* [2011] 1 Cr App R 9, in part because of the Court of Appeal's dissatisfaction with the statistical formulae used in calculating the likelihood of a particular shoe matching a mark.

evidence from a crime scene – will be taken by the senior investigating officer in consultation with the crime scene manager. This is because the crime scene manager will often have the scientific expertise necessary to determine what kind of expertise is likely to be of most assistance to the investigation, whereas the senior investigating officer will have ultimate responsibility of weighing the budgetary implications of seeking that expert expertise against its potential evidential yield.

20.66 If a police investigation results in someone being prosecuted, and an expert witness is required to attend court and give evidence for the prosecution, the costs will be met by the relevant prosecuting agency (i.e. CPS, PPS or COPFS).[51] Generally, travel and accommodation allowances are paid on a standard scale. Hourly rates are paid for preparation, and a daily fee is paid for attendance at court. These rates and fees will vary according to the type of expertise, with consultant medical practitioners such as psychiatrists and pathologists commanding the highest rates. The approximate rates are published on the CPS and BMA websites.

20.67 When experts are instructed by the defence, funding will depend on whether the defendant is paying privately for his defence costs or is legally aided.[52] Clearly, if a defendant is paying privately, then he or she is at liberty to instruct experts at a rate to be privately agreed. When a defendant is legally aided, it is possible, in serious cases, for the legal aid to extend to obtaining expert reports. This is, however, strictly controlled. Therefore, before instructing an expert, the defendant's legal representatives will normally have to seek prior approval/sanction from the relevant legal aid authority[53] by setting out, on the appropriate application form, the reasons why an expert's report is thought necessary for the proper conduct of the defence. This will often need to be supported by advice to that effect from counsel. The application will usually need to be supported by quotes from several experts. If authorisation is granted, in each of the three jurisdictions, the rates which can be paid to experts from the legal aid budget are set by subordinate legislation. Again, the hourly rates will vary depending on the level of expertise, but are considered too low by many in the medical profession for example, and the defence's ability to instruct experts on an equal footing to the prosecution has, arguably, been curtailed.[54] There is an appeals procedure which, in rare cases, can result in funding above the published rates.

51 See **20.14–20.16** above.
52 The granting of legal aid is generally subject to a two-stage test: an 'interests of justice' test, and a 'means' test. The interests of justice test will depend on factors such as the nature of the offence and the risk of a custodial sentence, but will usually be met in cases serious enough to require expert evidence. The means test is applied to determine whether the defendant's income (or lack thereof) means that they: (a) should be granted legal aid entirely; (b) should be granted legal aid but also asked to make a contribution to their defence costs; or (c) will not be granted legal aid at all and will be expected to pay privately from their own funds. The formulae applied are complex and vary between the jurisdictions and, indeed, between the various types of criminal proceedings within each jurisdiction. As a general guide, however, in England and Wales, for a Crown Court case, a defendant will not be granted legal aid if their household disposable income is above £37,500. If their disposable income is less than £37,500, a full means test will determine how much they need to contribute towards their defence costs.
53 The Legal Aid Agency (for England and Wales), the Legal Services Agency Northern Ireland (from 1 April 2015) or the Scottish Legal Aid Board.
54 Ranging, for instance, from £25 per hour for a photographer to £136 per hour for neurosurgeons: see Schedule 5 to the Criminal Legal Aid (Remuneration) Regulations 2013, SI 2013/435.

20.68   When the expert is instructed in the course of an appeal against conviction, slightly different considerations apply in England and Wales and in Northern Ireland. Legal aid is available to instruct an expert. However, once the appeal is lodged, legal aid is administered through the Court of Appeal Criminal Division/Court of Appeal in Northern Ireland by way of a 'representation order', granted in the first place by the registrar of the court. Thus, where a legally aided appellant wishes to call expert evidence during the appeal, counsel must submit an advice on evidence to the registrar, setting out the expert to be called and the nature of their evidence, so that the registrar can decide whether to extend the representation order to cover the costs of the expert. Where the order is not extended by the registrar, it is possible to ask the court itself to do so after the appeal hearing, but it is by no means certain that it will do so.[55]

Further reading material

England and Wales
- *Archbold* (released every year)
- *Blackstone's Criminal Practice* (released every year)
- Sprack, J. *A Practical Approach to Criminal Procedure* (2012, 14th Edition)
- Criminal Procedure Rules: www.justice.gov.uk/courts/procedure-rules/criminal/rulesmenu

Northern Ireland
- Dickson, B., *Law in Northern Ireland* (2013, 2nd Edition)

Scotland
- Brown, A.N., *Criminal Evidence and Procedure* (2010, 3rd Edition)
- Shiels, R. (et al) *Criminal Procedure (Scotland) Act 1995* (2014, 13th Edition)
- Gordon, G.H. and Renton, R.W. *Criminal Procedure According to the Law of Scotland* (1996, 6th Edition with updates; 2-volume looseleaf)

---

55 *R v Bowman* [2006] EWCA Crim 1077.

Chapter 21

Role and duties of the expert

21.1   The principles applying to experts are broadly similar in the criminal and the civil courts and in all three jurisdictions of the United Kingdom. It would be impossible to outline here the differences in procedure in relation to expert evidence in the civil and criminal courts, particularly as, within those two delineations, there are myriad different rules which apply, for instance, to specialist courts or tribunals. Therefore, this chapter outlines the principles upon which experts are instructed, how their evidence is adduced, and the duties incumbent upon them. It concentrates on the regime in England and Wales and in Northern Ireland. It also seeks to provide tips for the expert witness in best presenting their evidence in court. The bibliography alerts readers to the relevant texts for further study in relation to the different regimes and jurisdictions.

In both civil and criminal courts, there are three main issues upon which a court decides if an expert's evidence can be adduced: the admissibility test; whether the expert and the report are objective; and whether the party seeking to adduce the evidence has complied with the appropriate procedure. Thereafter, it will be for the tribunal of fact, whether that be a lay or judicial tribunal, to consider the weight of the evidence.

Admissibility

Background and history

21.2   Witnesses may, with a number of exceptions, only give evidence of facts that they personally perceived and not opinions or inferences drawn from those facts. Over time, however, one important exception emerged: opinion evidence from experts. In 1782, Lord Mansfield CJ said:

> 'On certain matters, such as those of science or art, upon which the court itself cannot form an opinion, special study, skill or experience being required for the purpose, "expert" witnesses may give evidence of their opinion.'[1]

21.3   In *R v Turner*,[2] a singularly important ruling which established the common law test for admitting expert evidence, the court said:

---

1 *Folkes v Chadd* 3 Doug KB 157.
2 [1975] QB 834, 841. See also, for Scotland, *Gage v HM Advocate* [2012] SCCR 161: expert evidence is admissible only if it is necessary for the proper resolution of the dispute and only if the tribunal of fact would be unable to reach a sound conclusion without it, a test subsequently approved in the civil case of *Kennedy v Cordia Services* [2014] CSIH 76. Even where the evidence may be necessary, it must also meet a certain quality or standard to be admitted: it must be based on a recognised and developed academic discipline; it must be based on tested theories; it must follow a developed methology; and it must produce a result capable of being assessed and given more or less weight in light of all the evidence before the finder of fact (*Thomas Ross Young v HM Advocate* [2013] HCJAC 145 at para 54).

'An expert's opinion is admissible to furnish the court with … information which is likely to be outside the experience and knowledge of a judge or jury. If on the proven facts a judge or jury can form their own conclusions without help, then the opinion of an expert is unnecessary.'

The three factors relevant to the *Turner* test were conveniently set out an Australian case, *Bonython*,[3] which has become the test upon which courts in many jurisdictions rely to determine whether evidence should be, prima facie, admitted.

21.4   The *Bonython* three-stage test is as follows:

(1)   whether the subject matter of the opinion is such that a person without instruction or experience in the area of knowledge or human experience would be able to form a sound judgement on the matter without the assistance of a witness possessing special knowledge or experience in the area;

(2)   whether the subject matter of the opinion forms part of a body of knowledge or experience which is sufficiently organised or recognised to be accepted as a reliable body of knowledge or experience, a special acquaintance with which by the witness would render his opinion of assistance to the court; and

(3)   whether the witness has acquired by study or experience sufficient knowledge of the subject to render his opinion of value in resolving the issues before the court.

Scope

21.5   The topics on which expert evidence has been adduced in accordance with this principle is a large and ever-expanding field, embracing subjects as diverse as: battered woman syndrome, voice identification,[4] sudden infant death syndrome, handwriting,[5] gang culture, drug use and drug values, obscenity and indecent photographs. It is clear that the list is not closed: as Steyn LJ said in *R v Clarke* [1995] 2 Cr App R 425, at p 430:

'It would be entirely wrong to deny the law of evidence the advantages to be gained from new techniques and … advances in science and in recent times expert evidence has been received as to ear prints, facial mapping, voice identification and video reconstruction, and in relation to all manner of technological advances, in particular concerning the use (and misuse) of information technology.'

Qualifications

21.6   The case of *Silverlock* (above) established that it is for the judge to determine whether the expert is sufficiently expert in the given subject. However, it is not necessary for that expertise to be derived from formal qualifications. Moreover,

3   (1984) 38 SASR 45, 46 to 47 (Supreme Court of South Australia).
4   *R v Robb* (1991) 93 Cr App R 161.
5   *R v Silverlock* [1894] 2 QB 766.

if the expert does have the necessary competence, a judge may not prevent him from acting as an expert *per se*. Nonetheless, the judge can exercise his or her discretion to exclude the evidence in the trial in certain circumstances – for example, in view of doubts on objectivity or integrity, failure to disclose important information, or failure to consider important information. The courts retain the power to exclude evidence, if it may impact on the fairness of the proceedings, or even to stay the proceedings in extreme cases.

21.7   The Court of Appeal and the Law Commission for England and Wales have been troubled by expert evidence and its admissibility for some time. In response to these concerns, the Criminal Procedure Rules Committee has made a new addition into the Criminal Procedure Rule on expert evidence, dealing specifically with admissibility. It merits careful reading, as it summarises succinctly the principles which govern the admissibility of expert evidence in the criminal courts and the justice system more generally:

'CPD 33A: EXPERT EVIDENCE

33A.1 Expert opinion evidence is admissible in criminal proceedings at common law if, in summary, (i) it is relevant to a matter in issue in the proceedings; (ii) it is needed to provide the court with information likely to be outside the court's own knowledge and experience; and (iii) the witness is competent to give that opinion.

33A.2 Legislation relevant to the introduction and admissibility of such evidence includes section 30 of the Criminal Justice Act 1988, which provides that an expert report shall be admissible as evidence in criminal proceedings whether or not the person making it gives oral evidence, but that if he or she does not give oral evidence then the report is admissible only with the leave of the court; and Part 33 of the Criminal Procedure Rules, which in exercise of the powers conferred by section 81 of the Police and Criminal Evidence Act 1984 and section 20 of the Criminal Procedure and Investigations Act 1996 requires the service of expert evidence in advance of trial in the terms required by those rules.

33A.3 In the Law Commission report entitled "Expert Evidence in Criminal Proceedings in England and Wales", report number 325, published in March, 2011, the Commission recommended a statutory test for the admissibility of expert evidence. However, in its response the government declined to legislate. The common law, therefore, remains the source of the criteria by reference to which the court must assess the admissibility and weight of such evidence; and rule 33.4 of the Criminal Procedure Rules lists those matters with which an expert's report must deal, so that the court can conduct an adequate such assessment.

33A.4 In its judgment in *R v Dlugosz and Others* [2013] EWCA Crim 2, the Court of Appeal observed (at paragraph 11): "It is essential to recall the principle which is applicable, namely in determining the issue of admissibility, the court must be satisfied that there is a sufficiently reliable scientific basis for the evidence to be admitted. If there is then the court leaves the opposing views to be tested before the jury." Nothing at common law precludes assessment by the court of the reliability of an expert opinion by reference to substantially similar factors to those the Law Commission recommended as conditions of admissibility, and courts are encouraged actively to enquire into such factors.

33A.5 Therefore factors which the court may take into account in determining the reliability of expert opinion, and especially of expert scientific opinion, include:

(a) the extent and quality of the data on which the expert's opinion is based, and the validity of the methods by which they were obtained;

(b) if the expert's opinion relies on an inference from any findings, whether the opinion properly explains how safe or unsafe the inference is (whether by reference to statistical significance or in other appropriate terms);

(c) if the expert's opinion relies on the results of the use of any method (for instance, a test, measurement or survey), whether the opinion takes proper account of matters, such as the degree of precision or margin of uncertainty, affecting the accuracy or reliability of those results;

(d) the extent to which any material upon which the expert's opinion is based has been reviewed by others with relevant expertise (for instance, in peer-reviewed publications), and the views of those others on that material;

(e) the extent to which the expert's opinion is based on material falling outside the expert's own field of expertise;

(f) the completeness of the information which was available to the expert, and whether the expert took account of all relevant information in arriving at the opinion (including information as to the context of any facts to which the opinion relates);

(g) if there is a range of expert opinion on the matter in question, where in the range the expert's own opinion lies and whether the expert's preference has been properly explained; and

(h) whether the expert's methods followed established practice in the field and, if they did not, whether the reason for the divergence has been properly explained.

33A.6 In addition, in considering reliability, and especially the reliability of expert scientific opinion, the court should be astute to identify potential flaws in such opinion which detract from its reliability, such as:

(a) being based on a hypothesis which has not been subjected to sufficient scrutiny (including, where appropriate, experimental or other testing), or which has failed to stand up to scrutiny;

(b) being based on an unjustifiable assumption;

(c) being based on flawed data;

(d) relying on an examination, technique, method or process which was not properly carried out or applied, or was not appropriate for use in the particular case; or

(e) relying on an inference or conclusion which has not been properly reached.'

Objectivity

21.8   Although there is a requirement to be impartial, surprisingly, perceived partiality does not necessarily make the expert's evidence inadmissible. Perceived partiality may lead to an application to exclude the evidence but, in any event, will affect the weight of the evidence in the eyes of the tribunal.[6] The expert should always explicitly disclose any actual or apparent interest in the outcome of the proceedings.

Most importantly, the expert has an overriding duty to the court and not to the party calling them. That is enshrined in both the Civil and the Criminal Procedure Rules.

Rule 33.2(1) of the Criminal Procedure Rules 2014 states:

'An expert must help the court to achieve the overriding objective by giving objective, unbiased opinion on matters within his expertise.'

Rule 35.3 of the Civil Procedure Rules and rule 25.3 of the Family Procedure Rules are identically drafted:

'(1) It is the duty of experts to help the court on matters within their expertise.

(2) This duty overrides any obligation to the person from whom experts have received instructions or by whom they are paid.'

Tips for experts:

- Our courts are generally adversarial, and, while having conferences with advocates or solicitors who instructed the expert, it is easy to be unwittingly dragged into partisanship (see *R v Ward* (1993) 96 Cr App R 1). In particular, it can be difficult for an expert, who has been part of the investigative team (for example, seeking to find DNA matches) to then step back from that role and become non-partisan. Frequently, being called by the prosecution does not make, for example, a forensic medical examiner a prosecution witness, and they should be scrupulous in ensuring that they do not feel part of the 'prosecution team'.

- Other dangers include ideology and finance: the high fees that experts in civil cases can command may, even subconsciously, lead an expert down a partisan path. Similarly, an expert may feel strongly that a particular theory or methodology is flawed or that a pattern of symptoms or signs is conclusive. However, they should temper their strong views by outlining the other arguments against their contentions. Experts have been criticised for testimony in which they became partisan. In extreme cases, experts have been reported to their professional body by the courts.

Procedure

21.9 Again, procedures are too diverse in the different jurisdictions and different courts to be set out here; this chapter focuses on the underlying principles. It would be wise for the medical practitioner to be aware of the different approaches, and of the burdens and standards of proof, in the relevant court in which they propose to give evidence. Chapter 20 gives an overview of the criminal justice system in the three jurisdictions of England and Wales, Scotland, and Northern Ireland. Chapter 5 deals with procedures in the coroners' court. For more detailed analysis of civil and criminal procedure, see the bibliography at the end of the chapter.

6 *Toth v Jarman (Note)* [2006] 4 All ER 1276.

The relevant sections of the Criminal Procedure Rules (Part 33), the Civil Procedure Rules (Part 35) or the Family Procedure Rules (Part 25) are a helpful starting point for any practitioner, legal or medical.

21.10　The courts will expect a report to be written and then served in advance of the trial or hearing. Experts are often expected to have joint conferences with expert witnesses for other parties, and to provide a document outlining areas of agreement and disagreement. Depending on the court and the particular case, the report will either be read as evidence, and the other party will provide written questions to be answered in a further report; or, alternatively, the expert will answer oral questions during live testimony (and the report will provide the foundation for questions to the expert), but the report will not form the evidence itself.

It is usual, in the family courts, for one joint expert to be instructed by all the parties, and for the experts to have a joint conference to 'iron out' issues. That conference will often be chaired by one of the lawyers and recorded. Joint expert reports are sometimes ordered in civil cases. However, in the criminal courts, one joint expert is a rare occurrence and, although the courts are keen to encourage the experts to have joint conferences, the funding for such consultations is often not forthcoming from the Legal Aid Agency.

21.11　Funding can be an issue, if the case is publicly funded. The Civil Legal Aid (Remuneration) Regulations 2013 and the Criminal Legal Aid (Remuneration) Regulations 2013 have introduced new maximum rates for certain types of expert. Extraordinarily, at the time of writing, the funding for experts based in London is far less than for those based outside London. Solicitors can apply for funding to be granted outside those rates in exceptional circumstances. 'Exceptional circumstances' are defined, in the guidance from the Legal Aid Agency, as where:

> 'the expert's evidence is key to the client's case and either–

> (a)　the complexity of the material is such that an expert with a high level of seniority is required; or

> (b)　the material is of such a specialised and unusual nature that only very few experts are available to provide the necessary evidence.'

The solicitor may need assistance from the expert in explaining why the case falls within those exceptional circumstances.

Content of expert reports

21.12　The Criminal Procedure Rules, the Family Procedure Rules and the Civil Procedure Rules and their annexes set out some requirements of expert reports.

Expert reports should normally contain:

- the expert's qualifications, accreditations and experience and any limitations thereof;

- a statement that the witness had complied with the duty to the court to provide independent assistance by way of objective unbiased opinion in relation to matters within his or her expertise and an acknowledgment that the witness would inform all parties and, where appropriate, the court in the event of any change of opinion on the material issues;

- reference to all documents and material considered;

- the data relied upon or, if it is too voluminous to set out in the report, how access to it can be obtained;

- a statement setting out the instructions received and the questions asked of the expert (NB see 'Privilege' at **21.18** below);

- tests undertaken, methodology used and by whom, and research relied upon (in medical cases, this might include clinical examination techniques, assistants in autopsies, or trainees taking histories from patients. This section should include sufficient detail for another expert to consider whether the methodology was flawed);

- full explanation of reasoning for conclusions;

- if there is a range of opinion on the topic, the expert should highlight that fact, summarise the range, indicate any material which might point to a contrary opinion, and give reasons for their own opinion on the point;

- any material facts or matters which detracted from the witness's opinion and any points which should be made against it;

- if any issue falls outside their expertise, or their conclusions are based on inadequate evidence, that should be made clear; and

- the report, or a document accompanying it, should set out any relevant disclosure and provide copies of, or access to, any research or extracts from relevant literature relied upon.

Sources of information

21.13   The expert may, to an extent, rely on what he or she has been told by others. Such evidence is admissible as being relevant to the process leading to the formulation of his opinion but, if no direct evidence as to the truth of those facts is called, or if the quality of the evidence of those facts is poor, the value of the opinion may suffer correspondingly. Experts should enquire as to the information that they are given before placing undue reliance on it in formulating their view.

If experts rely not on evidence of observation or information supplied by a third party, but on assumptions made for the purpose of the preparation of their report, they should say so in the body of that report, and not await questioning as to the source of the information at a later stage.

21.14   Expert witnesses may make references to their own research, the work of others, articles in respected publications, research papers and even unpublished research. In the case of *R v Abadom*,[7] evidence was permitted to be adduced of

7   [1983] 1 WLR 126, (1983) 76 Cr App R 48.

unpublished statistics of the Home Office Central Research Establishment, it being noted by the Court of Appeal that part of the value of expert witnesses lies in their knowledge of such unpublished material; there can be no reason for not permitting experts to rely on such material, provided that they refer to it in their evidence so that the value of their conclusions can be tested by reference to it. Wherever reliance is placed on such material, experts should specify the source material in the body of their report and should provide copies of extracts.

Duties

21.15   Particular duties of an expert are set out in the Family Procedure Rules Practice Direction 25B (Duties of an expert, the expert's report and arrangements for an expert to attend court).

The Practice Direction and the Protocol for the Instruction of Experts to give Evidence in Civil Claims (which is annexed to Part 35 of the CPR) similarly set out some ground rules as to the duties of an expert in the civil courts. The equivalent provision for the criminal courts is set out in Rule 33.2 of the Criminal Procedure Rules.

The court in *National Justice Compania Naviera SA v Prudential Assurance Co Ltd (The 'Ikarian Reefer')* [1993] 2 Lloyd's Rep 68 summarised the duties of an expert:

> '1. Expert evidence presented to the court should be, and should be seen to be, the independent product of the expert uninfluenced as to form or content by the exigencies of litigation (*Whitehouse v Jordan* [1981] 1 WLR 246, HL, at 256, per Lord Wilberforce).

> 2. An expert witness should provide independent assistance to the court by way of objective unbiased opinion in relation to matters within their expertise (see *Pollivitte Ltd v Commercial Union Assurance Company Plc* [1987] 1 Lloyd's Rep 379 at 386, per Garland J; and *Re J* [1990] FCR 193, per Cazalet J). An expert witness in the High Court should never assume the role of an advocate.

> 3. An expert witness should state the facts or assumption on which their opinion is based. They should not omit to consider material facts which could detract from their concluded opinion (*Re J*, above).

> 4. An expert witness should make it clear when a particular question or issue falls outside their expertise.

> 5. If an expert's opinion is not properly researched because they consider that insufficient data are available then this must be stated with an indication that the opinion is no more than a provisional one (*Re J*, above). In cases where an expert witness who has prepared a report could not assert that the report contained the truth, the whole truth and nothing but the truth without some qualification, that qualification should be stated in the report (*Derby & Co Ltd v Weldon (No 9)*, The Times, November 9, 1990, CA, per Staughton LJ).

> 6. If, after exchange of reports, an expert witness changes their view on the material having read the other side's expert report or for any other reason, such change of view should be communicated (through legal representatives) to the other side without delay and, when appropriate, to the court.

7. Where expert evidence refers to photographs, plans, calculations, analyses, measurements, survey reports or other similar documents, these must be provided to the opposite party at the same time as the exchange of reports.'

That list was reiterated by the Court of Appeal Criminal Division in *R v Harris and others* [2006] 1 Cr App R 5.

Those duties are echoed in the Criminal Procedure Rules, the Family Procedure Rules and the Civil Procedure Rules.

Disclosure

21.16   In all criminal jurisdictions, the prosecution (but not the defence) has a duty to disclose any material which might undermine the prosecution case or support the defence case. However, the prosecution does not provide *all* material to the defence, and there will remain an amount of material generated in the investigation which is 'unused', i.e. material not provided to the other side. The prosecution must be able to assess whether it falls within the criteria above. In order to ensure that the prosecution is able to comply with its duties in relation to expert evidence, any such material (data, research, or findings against the expert) ought to be contained in the expert's report, so as to ensure that the other party is immediately aware of it. The expert should ensure that any material which may fall within this category is provided to the prosecution and referred to in their report. Examples may include scans, photographs, body maps, medical notes or other records, research papers and copies of judgments where the expert has been criticised.

21.17   In the infamous case of Judith Ward (*R v Ward* (1993) 96 Cr App R 1, CA), the court criticised the behaviour of the prosecution experts. It indicated that:

- it is the duty of an expert instructed by the prosecution to act in the cause of justice;

- if the expert has carried out or is aware of a test which casts doubt on his opinion, there is a duty to disclose that to the defence;

- the expert should not wait for a request;

- the disclosure duty includes documentation, reports of experiments and references, and extends to anything which might arguably assist the defence; and

- the duty is positive: the prosecution should enquire of forensic scientists whether there is disclosable material rather than rely on the expert to volunteer, or the defence to request.

The duty is, therefore, wider in scope than the obligations imposed by rule 33.4 of the Criminal Procedure Rules.

Civil, family and other court systems have different rules, but the expert should follow the above guide in all cases, to ensure that they do not inadvertently fail to disclose important material to the other side.

Privilege

21.18   Legal professional privilege is the confidentiality agreement between a client and his or her legal advisers. It extends, unless waived, to instructions to an expert. Only the client, and not the solicitor or third party, can waive privilege. Once waived, it allows access by another party to previously confidential discussions between client and solicitor.

In civil courts, CPR 35.10(4) abrogates privilege, and the expert is required, in the report, to indicate all the material instructions and the fact that those instructions are not said to be privileged. Once the report is served, privilege is deemed to be waived in relation to the instructions in the report.

The position in the criminal courts is slightly different. There is no similar provision, and so privilege remains in relation to instructions to an expert. Experts should be cautious before asking junior staff in solicitors' offices for specific instructions on the index offence. Those instructions may have been withheld deliberately because, in theory, they could be disclosable to the prosecution if provided to the expert. The prosecution, however, is under a duty to disclose anything which may assist the defence case or may undermine the prosecution case (see Chapter 20).

The ultimate issue

21.19   An expert is permitted to give his opinion on what has been called 'the ultimate issue' – that is, the main issue for the tribunal of fact (i.e. the jury or judge) to determine, such as the identity of the offender, or whether the offender had the requisite mental state. Even if there is no contrary evidence, the judge should make it clear to the jury that they are not bound by the expert's opinion, and that the issue is for them to decide.[8]

However, although the law is relatively well settled on this point, an expert may wish to check carefully with the party calling them if they should avoid such areas. It might be helpful, if an expert does propose to trespass into this area, they should bracket the relevant paragraph in their report, to highlight the fact to the parties so that they may indicate if they wish the expert not to deal with this in the trial, or so that the court may exclude that evidence from the trial or hearing. In any event, the expert should ensure that they make it clear that they are expressing an opinion (which the court can reject).

Hints and tips for experts writing reports:

- Avoid dealing with statistics unless you are a trained statistician or have had specific training from a statistician. Set out that expertise or training in your qualifications.

- Try and keep the report as structured as possible.

- Ensure that it is written for a non-expert reader, and that it sets out clearly the conclusions, and the evidence on which the conclusions are based.

---

8   *R v Stockwell* (1993) 97 Cr App R 260.

- Experts should avoid opining as to the views of other experts in the field, unless there is statistical evidence available. If the expert wishes to indicate that the statement is well recognised, it is safer to refer to academic texts rather than make statements about the opinion of the majority in a field.

- Ask someone to read it before you send it, to check it for clarity.

- It is often helpful to create a template for yourself for use in every case.

- Have a folder of references ready to provide to the solicitor.

Party's duty to disclose expert's report

21.20 If one party instructs an expert in a civil case, they are not entitled to rely on the report or to call the expert to give evidence orally unless they have complied with the disclosure rules or unless the court gives permission: CPR 35.13. Until a report is disclosed, it remains privileged.

Duty to disclose – civil

21.21 In the civil courts, a party is normally under no duty to serve a report if he chooses not to rely on it.[9] However, in family proceedings in particular, the rule is that all parties are under a duty of full and frank disclosure.

Duty to disclose – criminal

21.22 In the criminal courts, there is a different approach. The position of the defendant is similar to that in civil matters – that is, they are under a duty to disclose if, and only if, they intend to rely on the report. However, the prosecution has an overriding duty of disclosure – that is, it must disclose anything which might assist the defence case or undermine the prosecution case (see the Criminal Procedure and Investigations Act 1996, discussed in Chapter 20). This would include an expert's report adverse to the prosecution case.

Case management

21.23 In cases that turn on medical evidence, justice depends on proper preparation and control of the evidence from the outset of the investigation; only by properly marshalling the evidence before it is presented will it be possible adequately to direct the jury so as to enable them to reach a logically justifiable conclusion.[10] The pre-trial process is of particular importance: without robust pre-trial management, the real medical issues cannot be identified and, absent such identification, a judge is

---

9   *Carlson v Townsend* [2001] EWCA Civ 511, [2001] 1 WLR 2415.
10 *R v Henderson; R v Butler; R v Oyediran (Practice Note)* [2010] 2 Cr App R 24, CA, per Moses LJ.

unlikely to be able to prevent experts from wandering into unnecessary, complicated and confusing detail. Accordingly, a judge who is to hear a case of this type should deal with all pre-trial hearings, save for those in which no issue of substance arises. By the time a trial starts, the court said, the essential medical issues which the jury have to resolve, and the expert evidence identifying the source on which the evidence is based, should all be clear.

However, the *dicta* of the Court of Appeal in *Henderson* assume that resources (both time and funding) are available to the parties and criminal courts which are, in fact, rarely available.

The court went on to give specific directions in relation to shaken baby cases, arguably of broader relevance and assistance to medical experts generally:

- where there is a realistic possibility of an unknown cause of death (in a 'shaken baby' case), the jury should be reminded of that, and they should be instructed that unless the evidence leads them to exclude any realistic possibility of an unknown cause they cannot convict; where it is relevant to do so, they should be reminded that today's scientific orthodoxy may become tomorrow's outdated learning; and, in cases where developing medical science is relevant, they should be instructed that special caution is needed where expert evidence is fundamental to the prosecution;

- the jury must be directed as to how they should approach conflicting evidence; to suggest, in cases where expert evidence is fundamental, that they should approach the evidence in the same way as they do in any other criminal case, is inadequate; rather, they must be directed as to the pointers to reliable evidence and the basis for distinguishing that which may be relied upon and that which should be rejected; where relevant, they should be asked to consider whether an expert has assumed the role of an advocate, whether he has stepped outside his area of expertise, whether he was able to point to a recognised, peer-reviewed, source for his opinion and whether his clinical experience is up-to-date and equal to that of others whose opinions he seeks to contradict.

Tips for experts giving oral evidence

21.24   An expert should always stay within their expertise, and should not succumb to counsel's invitations to stray.

Experts should not rely on the pronouncements from the Court of Appeal or other courts for support for their propositions or theories. Judges are not scientists or doctors. Controversy in a particular area must be resolved by the practitioners and not the judges: *Henderson* at para 6.

Experts have a duty to disclose any judgments or rulings made in which they are criticised, or any relevant findings against them by professional bodies.

The most fantastically eminent, qualified and experienced doctors have been known to forget the presentational aspects of being an expert witness. For this reason, experts are advised to bear in mind the following:

- Turn up in plenty of time; it may be necessary to have a conference at court with counsel.

- Before giving evidence, discuss with the party you represent any visual aids that might be useful – they will need to be agreed and prepared for court.

- Bring all your papers and any books or references you refer to.

- Refresh your memory about anything that you have written and published in the past. If the lawyer has done some research, they may quote your words back at you!

- Wear a suit.

- Speak slowly and clearly, as the court needs to write down what you say.

- Keep each answer as short as possible, while expressing any qualifications you want to make to the opinion.

- Explain medical terminology as you go along.

- Avoid giving anecdotal evidence, except as illustrations; try and stick to propositions based on the body of learning that you represent.

- If you are relying on your own experience to form your opinion, as opposed to a body of published evidence, you should make this explicit in your answers and underline that it is a subjective opinion.

- Politely decline to answer questions outside your expertise.

- Avoid becoming a specialist for one side or another (e.g. for prosecution in criminal cases, or for parents in family cases). This will become a stick with which you will be beaten by lawyers, and make you an expert that parties will seek to avoid in joint instruction cases. You may end up being criticised by the judge and, in extremis, reported to your professional body.

Tips for lawyers

Obtaining expert testimony

21.25

- Always try to find the most specialised expert – look up the expertise on a legal search engine.

- Be clear: what are the issues and your questions?

- Always have a conference – the best expert witnesses do not always write the clearest reports.

- Ask your expert 'what would you cross-examine yourself on?' and 'what would you cross-examine the prosecution expert on?'.

- Ask your expert about the other side's expert.

- Ensure that questions and issues have been answered.

- If your expert, or the other side's expert, relies on any literature to support their findings, ensure that they provide you with those extracts.

In order to challenge an expert

21.26

- Obtain and read the medical notes/expert's notes – put them in chronological order. If they are too technical to understand, get funding for an expert to translate the notes for you.

- Preparation – read, research, check articles.

- Put expert's name into a legal search engine in order to find discredited facial mapping experts etc.

- Ask own expert for areas to challenge and ammunition.

- Consider scientific method – measurability, verifiability, reproducibility.

- Bear in mind purpose: are you seeking to discredit/undermine, or to rely on an alternative version that they cannot rule out?

- Keep to the issue, bit by bit.

- Keep your common sense.

- Don't forget unknown causes.

- Don't rely, or allow the other party to rely, on the courts to resolve a medical issue: that's for medical science.

- Ask in advance for any data or references on which the expert relies to support their expressed opinions. If none are forthcoming, it may provide ammunition to argue for the expert evidence to be excluded, or limited, or for comment.

Further reading material

Scotland

- The Law Society of Scotland Code of Practice: expert witnesses engaged by solicitor (www.expertwitnessscotland.info/codepract.htm)

Northern Ireland

- Dickson, B., *Law in Northern Ireland* (2013, 2nd Edition)

Criminal procedure

- *Archbold* (released every year), in particular chapters 10 and 11

- *Blackstone's Criminal Practice* (released every year)

- Sprack, J. *A Practical Approach to Criminal Procedure*, (2012, 14th Edition)

- Criminal Procedure Rules: www.justice.gov.uk/courts/procedure-rules/criminal/rulesmenu

Civil procedure

- High Court: Civil Procedure: *The White Book* (released every year)
- County Court: The Civil Court Practice: *The Green Book* (released every year)
- Civil Procedure Rules: www.justice.gov.uk/courts/procedure-rules/civil/rules

Coroners' courts
(see also Chapter 5)

- Thomas, Straw, Machover, Friedman *Inquests: a practitioner's guide*
- *Jervis on Coroners*

Family courts

- *Family Court Practice* (released every year)
- Family Procedure Rules: www.justice.gov.uk/courts/procedure-rules/family

Appendix A

A guide to medical terminology

Prepositional prefixes

Prefix	Meaning	Example
A- or An-	Without	Anoxia = without oxygen
Ante-	Before	Ante-mortem = before death
Anti-	Against	Antiseptic = prevents sepsis
Circum-	Around	Circumoral = around the mouth
Contra-	Against, opposite	Contralateral = on the other side
De-	Away from	Dehydrate = remove water
Dia-	Through	Dialyse = to pass through a membrane
Dys-	Abnormal	Dysfunction = abnormal function
En- or Endo-	Within	Endotracheal = within the trachea
Epi-	Outside	Epidermis = outermost part of the skin
Extra- or Exo-	Outside	Extradural = outside the coverings of the brain Exogenous = produced from outside
Hetero-	Different	Heterotopic = in the wrong place
Homo-	Similar	Homozygous = similar genes combined
Hyper-	Excessive	Hypertrophy = overgrowth
Hypo-	Too little	Hypotension = low blood pressure
Infra-	Below	Infraorbital = below the eye
Inter-	Between	Intercostal = between the ribs
Intra-	Within	Intrahepatic = within the liver
Juxta-	Beside	Juxtaposition = closeness together
Para-	Close to, around	Paravertebral = near the spine
Per-	Through	Percutaneous = through the skin
Poly-	Many	Polymorphic = many-shaped
Post-	After	Post-traumatic = after injury
Pre-	In front of	Prepatellar = in front of the knee cap
Proto-	First	Prototype = the original of the form
Retro-	Behind	Retrosternal = behind the sternum

Prefix	Meaning	Example
Sub-	Beneath	Subcutaneous = beneath the skin
Supra-	Above	Supralabial = above the lip
Syn-	Together	Syndactyly = web fingers
Trans-	Through, across	Transplacental = across the placenta

Some suffixes

Suffix	Meaning	Example
-aemia	In or of the blood	Anaemia = no (or less than normal) blood
-algia	Pain	Neuralgia = pain in a nerve
-ectomy	Removal	Prostatectomy = removal of the prostate
-genic	Producing	Pathogenic = causing disease
-itis	Inflammation of	Laryngitis = inflammation of the larynx
-logy	Study of	Pathology = study of disease
-megaly	Enlargement of	Splenomegaly = enlargement of the spleen
-oma	Tumour	Adenoma = a tumour of glands
-osis	Abnormal process other than inflammation	Fibrosis = proliferation of fibrous tissue (scarring)
-pathy	Abnormal structure	Myopathy = abnormal muscle
-plasia	Growth	Hyperplasia = excessive growth
-stomy	Making a hole	Tracheostomy = artificial opening in trachea

Anatomic prefixes

Prefix	Relating to	Example
Aden(o)-	Glands	Adenitis = inflammation of glands
Angio-	Blood vessels	Angiospasm = spasm of the arteries
Arthr(o)-	Joints	Arthralgia = pain in the joints
Cardio-	Heart	Cardiomyopathy = abnormality of the heart muscle
Cerebro-	Brain	Cerebrospinal fluid = fluid surrounding the brain and spinal cord
Chol(o)- or (e)-	Bile	Cholecystitis = inflammation of the gall bladder
Chondro-	Cartilage	Chondroma = a tumour of cartilage
Colo-	Large bowel	Colostomy = making an opening in the colon

Prefix	Relating to	Example
Costo-	Ribs	Costochondral = of the rib cartilages
Encephal(o)-	Brain	Encephalitis = inflammation of the brain
Enter(o)-	Intestines	Enteritis = inflammation of the intestine
Gastr(o)-	Stomach	Gastroenterostomy = making a connecting hole between stomach and intestine
Haem(o)-	Blood	Haemothorax = blood in the thoracic cavity
Hepat(o)-	Liver	Hepatomegaly = enlargement of the liver
My(o)-	Muscle	Myesthenia = wasting of the muscle
Nephr(o)-	Kidney	Nephrosis = an abnormal process in the kidney
Neur(o)-	Nerve	Neurotoxic = poisonous to nerves
Pneumo-	Lung (or simply air)	Pneumoconiosis = an abnormality of the lung associated with dust Pneumothorax = free air in the thoracic cavity
Oste(o)-	Bone	Osteology = the study of bones

Note: American medical writing does not usually use diphthongs. Hence, anaemia becomes anemia; tumour becomes tumor; and oesophagus becomes esophagus.

Appendix B

Table of multiple, and fractions of, units

With the advent of the internet and phone applets, conversion of units is now much more straightforward, and this should be the preferred method. One area that still causes confusion is the use of decimal multiples and fractions of units. The following table provides a guide:

10^{12}	tera	T		10^{-1}	deci	d
10^9	giga	G		10^{-2}	centi	c
10^6	mega	M		10^{-3}	milli	m
10^3	kilo	k		10^{-6}	micro	μ
10^2	hecto	h		10^{-9}	nano	n
10	deca	da		10^{-12}	pico	P
				10^{-15}	femto	f
				10^{-18}	atto	a

Appendix C

Medical and dental qualifications in the United Kingdom

Primary medical qualifications

MB (or BM), BCh (or BS or ChB)	Bachelor of Medicine and Surgery Graduating degree awarded by UK universities with medical schools
MD	Doctor of Medicine Graduating degree awarded by many overseas universities with medical schools

All qualifying degrees refer both to medicine and to surgery, but not every doctor practises major surgery. Many doctors are also qualified BA (or, subsequently, MA), BMedSci or BSc; these are intermediate university degrees taken before clinical training.

Historic medical qualifications

LMSSA	Licentiate in Medicine and Surgery of the Society of Apothecaries
LRCS, LRCP	Licentiate of the Royal College of Surgeons of England and of the Royal College of Physicians of London
LRCP, LRCS (Edin. or Irel.)	Licentiate of the Royal Colleges of Physicians and Surgeons of Edinburgh or in Ireland
LRCPS	Licentiate of the Royal College of Physicians and Surgeons of Glasgow

This was an alternative means to obtain medical registration without a formal university degree. This is no longer a valid mechanism, but some practitioners will still have this qualification.

Postgraduate medical degrees

MD	Doctor of Medicine Obtained by thesis; this may be a primary medical qualification overseas
MS (or MChorChM)	Master of Surgery Sometimes taken by thesis, sometimes by general examination
PhD	Doctor of Philosophy Obtained by thesis after a period of approved scientific research
MSc	Master of Science Obtainable in many scientific subjects related to medicine

Such degrees indicate research in depth of a particular subject. They imply that there is some specific field in which the holder is an authority. Other special masterships are offered – e.g. in radiology.

Membership of the Royal Colleges and Faculties

Possession of these higher qualifications is certain evidence of specialisation. They are obtained by means of a examination; only rarely is 'membership' conferred by virtue of published work or reputation. The Colleges of Physicians in London, Edinburgh and Glasgow (Physicians and Surgeons) at one time conferred individual memberships; examinations are now on a United Kingdom basis. In general, members are elected to be fellows of individual colleges after a delineated period; some colleges, however, confer fellowship by examination.

FRCA	Fellow of the Royal College of Anaesthetists
FRCOphth	Fellow of the Royal College of Ophthalmologists
FRCR	Fellow of the Royal College of Radiologists
FRCS	Fellow of the Royal College of Surgeons
FRCPath	Fellow of the Royal College of Pathologists
MRCGP	Member of the Royal College of General Practitioners
MRCOG	Member of the Royal College of Obstetricians and Gynaecologists
MRCPsych	Member of the Royal College of Psychiatrists
MRCP	Member of the Royal College of Physicians
MFOM	Member of the Faculty of Occupational Medicine (RCP, Lond.)
MFPHM	Member of the Faculty of Public Health Medicine (RCP, UK)
MFFLM	Member of the Faculty of Forensic and Legal Medicine

These qualifications form the basis on which certificates of completion of training are awarded, which indicate that the person has undergone the training needed before he or she can engage in independent medical practice in the specialty. In addition to the specialities indicated by the names of the colleges and faculties, certificates of training can be acquired in paediatrics and clinical oncology.

Postgraduate medical diplomas

The universities and the Royal Colleges issue diplomas on the basis of examination. The role of the diploma, in indicating the narrower field of interest and expertise of the holder, has been very much reduced by the growth of increasingly specialised Royal Colleges; in many cases, however, they are the sole indication of a particular proficiency, while others may be looked upon as 'stepping stones' to membership. The following list is certainly not exhaustive. Some will have been taken over as diplomas of the Royal Colleges and are not mentioned below.

DAvMed	Diploma in Aviation Medicine
DipBact	Diploma in Bacteriology
DCH	Diploma in Child Health
DForM	Diploma in Forensic Medicine
DIH	Diploma in Industrial Health
DLO	Diploma in Laryngology and Otology
DMJ	Diploma in Medical Jurisprudence
BAO	Bachelor of the Art of Obstetrics (given in Ireland)
DPhysMed	Diploma in Physical Medicine
DipSocMed	Diploma in Social Medicine
DTM & H	Diploma in Tropical Medicine and Hygiene
DTPH	Diploma in Tropical Public Health

Dental qualifications

Primary dental qualifications

LDS	Licentiate in Dental Surgery of the Royal Colleges
BDS	Bachelor of Dental Surgery Graduating degree awarded by most universities with dental schools

Some postgraduate dental degrees

MDS or MChD	Master of Dental Surgery Generally only available in universities that do not offer a DDS
MDentSc	Master in Dental Science
MCDH	Master of Community Dental Health
DDS	Doctor of Dental Surgery
DDSc	Doctor of Dental Science

Some postgraduate dental diplomas

DCDH	Diploma in Child Dental Health
DDH	Diploma in Dental Health
DDO or DDOrth	Diploma in Dental Orthopaedics
DDPH	Diploma in Dental Public Health
DOrth	Diploma in Orthodontics
DRD	Diploma in Restorative Dentistry

Dental pathologists may also qualify as members or fellows of the Royal College of Pathologists. Many dentists are also medically qualified and may proceed to higher medical qualifications; these may be specialised – e.g. FRCS in faciomaxillary surgery.

Index

[all references are to paragraph number]

A

Abdominal cavity
anatomical divisions and susceptibility, and, 1.9

Abrasions
children and young persons, and, 14.26
brush, 7.14
crush, 7.15
generally, 7.12
parchmented, 7.16
'simple', 7.13

Abuse of process
criminal justice system, and, 20.24

Acute behavioural disturbance
treatment of detainees, and, 18.24

Acute renal failure
urinary system, and, 1.56

Admissibility of evidence
criminal justice system, and, 20.23
expert evidence, and
background, 21.2–21.3
Criminal Procedure Rule, 21.7
objectivity, 21.8
qualifications, 21.6–21.7
scope, 21.5

Adipocere
changes associated with increasing post-mortem interval, and, 4.22

Adrenal gland
endocrine system, and, 1.69

Aircraft
injuries, 10.11

Alcohol
absorption, 17.32
artefact levels, 17.4
auto-generation, 17.34
blood-alcohol thresholds, 17.2
clinical effects, 17.35
elimination, 17.33
introduction, 17.31
long-standing misuse, 17.36–17.43
measurement of levels, 17.44–17.45

Alcohol – *contd*
misuse
central nervous system effects, 17.40
gastritis, 17.39
heart, 17.41
introduction, 17.36
liver damage, 17.37
pancreatitis, 17.38
sudden death, 17.42–17.43
other, 17.48
physiology, 17.32–17.34
problems of post-mortem blood alcohol analyses, 17.46
transportation, and, 17.47

Alimentary canal
gastro-intestinal system, and, 1.49

Alzheimer's disease
head injuries, and, 9.43

Anaesthesiophilia
asphyxiation, and, 11.47

Anal injury
sexual assault, and, 15.23

Anatomy
cellular structures, 1.12–1.16
coagulation, 1.25–1.27
confusion, 1.5
divisions and susceptibility, 1.6–1.11
endocrine system, 1.65–1.70
gastro-intestinal system, 1.48–1.51
haematological system, 1.28–1.34
musculoskeletal, 1.71–1.78
nervous system, 1.40–1.47
planes, 1.3
propensity to injury, and, 1.12
relationships, 1.4
reproductive system, 1.62–1.64
respiratory system, 1.35–1.39
skin, 1.79
urinary system, 1.52–1.61

Animal injuries
death, and, 4.25

Autoerotic deaths
asphyxiation, and, 11.47
Autonomic nervous system
generally, 1.46
Autopsy
ballistics, and, 8.21–8.22
consented examination, 3.1
exhumations, 3.33–3.35
fire, and , 13.18
firearms, and, 8.21–8.22
introduction, 3.1
medico-legal examination
circumstances, 3.7
external, 3.9–3.10
histology, 3.17–3.19
history, 3.7
identification of body, 3.6
initial, 3.8
internal, 3.11–3.15
introduction, 3.2
persons present, 3.5
photographic recording, 3.28
prior to, 3.4
radiology, 3.27
report, 3.20–3.21
sample retention, 3.16
scene examination, 3.28
standards, 3.22–3.23
timing, 3.3
toxicology, 3.16
'routine' examination, 3.25–3.26
second autopsy, 3.29–3.32
terminology, 3.1

B

Ballistics
accidental discharge, 8.20
air weapons, 8.17
autopsy examinations, 8.21–8.22
categories, 8.1
certificates for possession, 8.3
clothing, 8.21
CT scanning, 8.21
determining shot distance, 8.9
discharge
accidental, 8.20
determination of manner, 8.18–8.20
homicidal, 8.20
introduction, 8.5
suicidal, 8.19
entry wounds, 8.21
examinations
suspect, of, 8.23
victim, of, 8.21–8.22
'firearm', 8.1
fluoroscopy, 8.22
homicidal discharge, 8.20

Ballistics – *contd*
introduction, 8.1–8.4
offences, 8.4
radiography, 8.21
residues
suspect, on, 8.23
victim, on, 8.21–8.22
rifled barrels, 8.5
rifled weapons
ammunition, 8.12
generally, 8.11
introduction, 8.5
morbidity, 8.16
wounds, 8.13–8.15
shotguns
after discharge, 8.8
cartridge, 8.7
determining shot distance, 8.9
generally, 8.6
introduction, 8.5
unlawful shortening, 8.10
smooth bore, 8.5
statutory background, 8.1–8.4
suicidal discharge, 8.19
trajectory, 8.22
types, 8.5–8.20
unlawful shortening, 8.10
Bar arm
custodial deaths, and, 19.27
Benzodiazepine
toxicology, and, 17.53
Bite mark analysis
generally, 16.17–16.18
introduction, 16.15
typical appearances, 16.16
Black eyes
head injuries, and, 9.4
wounding injuries, and, 7.55–7.59
Bladder
urinary system, and, 1.58–1.60
Bleeding diatheses
coagulation, and, 1.26
Bleeding within skull cavity
chronic subdural, 9.14–9.15
contusional brain injury, 9.20–9.21
epidural, 9.10–9.11
extradural, 9.10–9.11
intracerebral haemorrhage, 9.19
introduction, 9.9
subarachnoid haemorrhage, 9.16
subdural, 9.12–9.13
traumatic subarachnoid haemorrhage,
9.17–9.18
types, 9.9
Blood
cellular structures, 1.15
Blood flow disorders
head injuries, and, 9.37–9.38

403

Doughty Street Chambers

Doughty Street Chambers is now amongst the largest, most prestigious and wide-ranging civil liberties practices in the world, providing specialist advice, advocacy and training in the UK and around the world. The barristers from Doughty Street Chambers deploy their expertise across a range of practice areas, frequently compiling multi-disciplinary teams to deal with the increasingly complex and multi-faceted legal problems their individual, corporate, and other clients face. Those practice areas include crime and criminal appeals, international crime (including war crimes), fraud and financial services regulation, extradition, prisoners' rights, actions against the police, immigration, media law, professional regulation, clinical negligence, social welfare and housing, and more.

The Criminal Team is the largest practice group in Doughty Street Chambers. Its members defend the most serious and complex criminal trials, appeals and extradition cases to come before the Magistrates' Courts and up to the Supreme Court and European Court of Human Rights. We also handle appeals from overseas to the Judicial Committee of the Privy Council. The Team are involved in high-profile trials of defendants charged with terrorism, political crime, homicide and other non-fatal violence, regulatory and financial crime, human trafficking, and serious sexual offences. Doughty Street Chambers also houses a specialist Appeals Unit which is widely regarded as home to several of the best appellate lawyers in the United Kingdom.

Doughty Street Chambers is particularly renowned for its public law expertise. The teams specialising in Inquests, Inquiries and Actions Against the Police have been ranked as the number one barristers' set for police claimant work by the Chambers and Partners 2015 Directory for over a decade and have an unrivalled reputation in this specialist field. Doughty Street Chambers has extensive experience of acting in inquests and inquiries, and related judicial review proceedings and civil claims and has been responsible for landmark cases in this area. It is also ranked in this field.

More information about Doughty Street Chambers and its barristers can be found at www.doughtystreet.co.uk or by e-mailing crime@doughtystreet.co.uk.